GIACOMO PUCCINI AND HIS WORLD

GIACOMO PUCCINI
AND HIS WORLD

EDITED BY
ARMAN SCHWARTZ AND EMANUELE SENICI

PRINCETON UNIVERSITY PRESS
PRINCETON AND OXFORD

Published by Princeton University Press, 41 William Street,
Princeton, New Jersey 08540
In the United Kingdom: Princeton University Press,
6 Oxford Street, Woodstock, Oxfordshire OX20 1TW
press.princeton.edu

For permissions/credits, see page viii

Library of Congress Control Number: 2016933980

Cloth ISBN: 978-0-691-17285-9
Paper ISBN: 978-0-691-17286-6

British Library Cataloging-in-Publication Data is available

This publication has been produced by the Bard College Publications Office:
Mary Smith, Director
Irene Zedlacher, Project Director
Karen Walker Spencer, Designer
Emily Hart, Cover Design
Text edited by Paul De Angelis and Erin Clermont
Music typeset by Don Giller

This publication has been underwritten in part by grants from Roger and Helen Alcaly
and Furthermore, a program of the J. M. Kaplan Fund

Printed on acid-free paper. ∞

Printed in the United States of America.

1 3 5 7 9 10 8 6 4 2

Contents

Acknowledgments

Above all, we would like to thank the many authors and translators whose contributions are featured in this volume. It has been a pleasure to work with all of them, and their efforts have left us not just hopeful, but tremendously excited, about the future of Puccini scholarship. Our work would not have been possible—or, indeed, half as enjoyable—without the extraordinary support of the Bard Music Festival team. We are especially grateful to Christopher Gibbs, for the invitation to serve as scholars-in-residence and for many stimulating transatlantic conversations about all manner of topics relating to both the volume and the festival; to our editor Paul De Angelis for his peerlessly generous and insightful work on the book; to Irene Zedlacher, the festival's executive director, for her kindness and enthusiastic assistance with manifold practical matters; and to Leon Botstein, for his visionary stewardship of the festival itself. We would also like to thank the entire production office, especially Erin Clermont for her meticulous copyediting, Karen Spencer for her graphic design, and Don Giller for his work setting the musical examples.

Gabriella Biagi Ravenni, president of the Centro Studi Giacomo Puccini in Lucca, kindly put her unrivalled knowledge of Puccini at our disposal. Virgilio Bernardoni gave us generous permission to use Steven Huebner's English translation of the staging manual for Madama Butterfly, originally commissioned by the Edizione Nazionale delle Opere di Giacomo Puccini, over which he presides. Annalisa Bini (Accademia Nazionale di Santa Cecilia, Rome) and Maria Pia Ferraris (Archivio Storico Ricordi, Milan) offered welcome assistance with images. Longtime Puccinians Arthur Groos, Roger Parker, and David Rosen guided us by advice and example.

A final note of thanks to Vincenzo Borghetti and Heather Wiebe for their love and support throughout the project.

Whisky per tutti!

Arman Schwartz, London, UK
Emanuele Senici, Rome, Italy

Permissions

These copyright holders have graciously granted permission to reprint or reproduce the following photographs:

Archivio Storico Ricordi, Milan:
Giacomo Puccini on the Brooklyn Bridge, Figure 1 (p. 89); Bigtree Mariposa Grove, Figures 2 and 3 (p. 90); prop card for *La fanciulla del West*, Figure 4 (p. 92); various Ricordi Archive stills from David Belasco's 1905 production of *The Girl of the Golden West*, Figures 5, 6, 7, 8, 11, 12, 13, and 14 (pgs. 92, 93, 94, 95, 102, 103, 104, and 105 respectively); Metropolitan Opera still from a scene in Act 3 of *La fanciulla del West*, Figure 9 (p. 96); Vittorina Peruzzi as Minnie, Figure 10 (p. 97); all the above in "*Laggiù nel Soledad*: Indexing and Archiving the Operatic West," by Ellen Lockhart.
The stage set sketches for *Il tabarro*, Figures 1 and 2 (pp. 136 and 137), in "Puccini's Things: Materials and Media in *Il trittico*," by Alessandra Campana and Christopher Morris.
The stage set sketches for *Madama Butterfly* used as Figures 3, 4, 5, and 6 (pp. 295, 296, 298, and 299 respectively) in Michele Girardi's introduction to "Albert Carré's Staging Manual for *Madama Butterfly* (1906)."

The Metropolitan Opera Archives, New York:
Lucrezia Bori as Magda, Figure 1 (p. 118); Beniamino Gigli and others from Act 2 of *La rondine*, Figure 2 (p. 120); set design by Joseph Urban, Figure 3 (p.127), in "The Swallow and the Lark: *La rondine* and Viennese Operetta," by Micaela Baranello.
Enrico Caruso as Dick Johnson, Figure 3 (p. 235) in "Puccini on His Interpreters," by Emanuele Senici.

Accademia Nazionale di Santa Cecilia, Rome:
Puccini and his wife with Leopoldo Mugnone, Figure 8 (p. 253) in "Puccini on His Interpreters," by Emanuele Senici.

Michele Girardi:
Bridge in the Japanese garden in Boulogne-Billancourt, Figure 2 (p. 294) in Girardi's introduction to "Albert Carré's Staging Manual for *Madama Butterfly* (1906)."

Also, Theodore Presser Company has graciously granted permission to reproduce measures 171–76 from Act 2 of *I Shardana* by Ennio Porrino. Courtesy of Casa Musicale Sonzogno, Theodore Presser Company, authorized representative. All rights reserved. Used with permission. Example 1 (p. 174) in "Puccini, Fascism, and the Case of *Turandot*," by Ben Earle.

The authors and publisher have made every effort to trace holders of copyright. They much regret if any inadvertent omissions have been made.

Introduction:
Puccini, His World, and Ours

EMANUELE SENICI

Marco Malvaldi is a writer of detective novels that have met with wide-spread success in Italy over the last decade. In 2015 he published *Buchi nella sabbia* (Holes in the Sand), set in his hometown of Pisa, Tuscany, in September 1900. The plot revolves around a performance of Giacomo Puccini's recently premiered *Tosca* in the presence of King Victor Emmanuel III, who had just succeeded his father Umberto I to the throne of Italy following Umberto's assassination by an anarchist. In the book, the political aspects of the opera—especially the assassination of the opera's male protagonist Mario Cavaradossi—are considered rather too topical by the authorities in the light of these recent events, to the point of making the choice of *Tosca* to celebrate the King's visit to Pisa a highly questionable one. At the same time, a group of local anarchists, which includes the tenor singing Cavaradossi, sees the performance as the perfect opportunity to stage a demonstration against the King. In Act 3 the tenor is shot for real, however, and most of the book is devoted to the search for the assassin by various parties, including the police and a left-leaning journalist who had been asked by his newspaper to report on the event. Malvaldi, who turned to musicologists for information on *Tosca* and the world of opera in Italy at the turn of the twentieth century, is unusually accurate on these aspects; at the same time, he has invented a plot not only with evident parallels to that of the opera, but with obvious political connotations for present-day readers in Italy, where the alleged connections between the political parties and recent high-profile investigations by police and the judiciary have been fiercely debated.[1]

I begin with this very recent novel because it can function as an unfamiliar yet useful starting point for introducing at least some of the circumstances, assumptions, and expectations that shape the discourse on Puccini in the early twenty-first century. First among them is the immense success of Puccini's operas over the course of the twentieth century, which is related to their significant presence in cultural spheres where opera does not normally feature (such as the detective novel) but has tended to make us focus more on continuities than differences when discussing them. At the same time, the diminishing hold that opera in general has on present-day collective consciousness in the so-called West should not go unmentioned, since it has an impact on the position of even the most famous among Puccini's works within this consciousness, and therefore on the kinds of assumptions that can be made about them at different cultural levels. No less relevant is the Italian national context in which Puccini's operas were first conceived and to which they are thought to belong "genetically" for a historically informed interpretation of at least some of their most significant features. Conversely, their popularity reached almost immediately a truly transnational dimension, and therefore they have interacted ever since with several different cultures, of which they have been part for about a century—most prominently the culture defined by the English language, to which the present volume is, of course, primarily addressed. Finally, we need to take into account the interaction between what we tend to consider the more fixed components of an operatic work, the libretto and the score, and the more fluid and unstable ones, the staging and the musical interpretation, for a rounded understanding of the varied and sometimes even opposite meanings that Puccini's operas can have, and have had, for different audiences attending different productions in different performative contexts. The contributions collected here address some of these issues more directly than others, at the same time broadening the scope of their investigation to include other equally important themes. One of the overarching aims guiding the editors' preparation of this volume has been to present a plurality of historical, critical, and methodological standpoints, in the belief that a wide spectrum of approaches best serves the equally wide spectrum of concerns and issues that Puccini brought to the lyric stage about a century ago.

A related aim of this book has been to address all of Puccini's regularly performed operas, from *Manon Lescaut* to *Turandot*, albeit in differing levels of detail. Some works are devoted individual essays, even two in the case of *Madama Butterfly*: Arthur Groos discusses its dramatization of the tension between East and West, and Michele Girardi introduces a translation of portions of the staging manual prepared on the occasion of the 1906 Parisian premiere. In her essay on *La fanciulla del West*, Ellen Lockhart ponders a wealth of visual documents, recently emerged from the archives, that relate to its genesis and first production. Micaela

Figure 1. Puccini, drawing by Lina Rosso, 1918.

Baranello considers Puccini's most ambiguous work, *La rondine*, from the point of view of Viennese operetta. Finally, *Il trittico* is probed by Alessandra Campana and Christopher Morris, who explore the representational and aesthetic goals of its three component parts: *Il tabarro*, *Suor Angelica*, and *Gianni Schicchi*. More concentrated attention on these works has not come about entirely by chance: *Madama Butterfly* and *Fanciulla* have emerged in recent years as especially fertile ground for musicological and critical debate (*Fanciulla* being performed more frequently than ever before), since they evidently bring to the fore aspects that appear particularly relevant to us; *Il trittico* seems poised to do the same in the near future; and *La rondine* was sorely in need of a balanced and historically grounded assessment of its contradictory genre discourse.

Other operas are discussed as a group from a specific critical perspective, such as *Manon Lescaut*, *La bohème*, and *Tosca* in Arman Schwartz's essay on the tension between idealism and realism in the early works—in which *Edgar* also has a supporting role. These same works receive indirect but no less illuminating light from Schwartz's and Walter Frisch's presentations of a few important Italian and German contributions to the debate on *verismo* and realism on the lyric stage that raged throughout the 1890s. Alexandra Wilson's introduction to excerpts from critic Fausto Torrefranca's anti-Puccinian 1912 pamphlet, *Giacomo Puccini and International Opera*, highlights a set of recurring themes in the early reception of the operas up to and including *Madama Butterfly*. Puccini's last work, *Turandot*, has pride of place in Ben Earle's investigation of the complex and ambiguous relationship between Puccini and fascism, examined mostly from the viewpoint of the opera's critical (mis)fortunes in 1920s and 1930s Italy. Finally, Leon Botstein's wide-ranging essay on Puccini and his contemporaries, and my own contribution on the composer's discourse on the interpreters of his operas address the whole of his artistic output from specific viewpoints, highlighting connections between apparently distant works, times, places, and people.

In keeping with the practice of previous volumes in the Bard Festival series, the present one purposefully refrains from delving into the history of Puccini's works, reputation, and image after the composer's death in 1924 and the posthumous premiere of *Turandot* two years later—with the necessary exception of Ben Earle's discussion of critical pronouncements on this opera in the later 1920s and 1930s in connection with fascism. In any case, to address properly a topic such as "Puccini after Puccini" would require a separate book—one that would fill an evident gap in scholarship. At the same time, all the contributions cannot but have been influenced by more recent performances and stagings, experienced either live or through audiovisual media. To name just the most obvious case, the exceptional popularity of "Nessun dorma" from *Turandot* following its use by television as the theme song for broadcasts of the matches of the 1990 Soccer World Cup in Italy must have had an impact—conscious or, more likely, unconscious—on both stagings and critical interpretations of this individual piece as well as the whole opera, although it is difficult to understand the precise workings and consequences of such impact.

The fact that, generally speaking, the present and the recent past are not explicitly discussed in the following essays does not imply an active attempt to sidestep them; on the contrary, the approaches adopted here and the concerns exhibited by the various authors are inevitably but by no means unconsciously rooted in our early twenty-first-century sensibility, and therefore are a fruit of the century that separates us from Puccini. In the following pages I will present a brief overview of some of these approaches and concerns, trying to suggest ways in which they might inflect our views of the whole of Puccini's oeuvre, or at least of other works beside those already discussed in each specific essay.

Modernism

A crucial theme addressed in several essays and touched upon by a few others is that of Puccini's modernism, or, in a wider sense, his works' relationship with modernity. In the twentieth century, art music, like all other artistic expressions, was dominated by what could be called the imperative of originality, the obligation to "Make It New!" to cite Ezra Pound's famous injunction from the 1920s. Pound's slogan is usually taken to refer to modernism proper, the aesthetic movement that, by most accounts, emerged at the end of the nineteenth century and flourished especially in the first half of the twentieth, and of which the avant-garde, pushing at the boundaries of what is generally accepted as the norm, is considered the quintessential expression.

As many have argued, however, modernism is just the most explicit manifestation of an orientation typical of high-cultural production during the last two centuries, that is to say, the era generally known as modernity proper, as opposed to early modernity, the period encompassing the sixteenth, seventeenth, and eighteenth centuries. To summarize in doubtlessly simplistic terms a complex and multilayered discourse: in the context of the increasing levels of repetition—often *mechanical* repetition—that came to characterize most aspects of modern life, art took it upon itself to offer something different from this life, something, in fact, whose distance from it was measured precisely in terms of difference—not only its difference from everyday life, but also its difference from itself, its difference within. In art, change, novelty, originality were the yardstick by which new contributions were measured. Modernism took this aesthetic imperative to a point where, at least ostensibly, public success mattered less than innovation and uniqueness; indeed, for the avant-garde success became highly suspect (at least in public discourse), since it could be taken as a sign that an artist had not been sufficiently innovative, had not "made it new" enough. Thus far I have used the past tense, but as I hope readers realize, much of what I have said still holds largely true for several present-day artistic expressions, including art music.

Puccini composed his operas between the 1880s and the 1920s, and therefore found himself working right at the time when modernism was coming to dominate the aesthetic and cultural field. As a consequence, these operas were—and have largely continued to be—measured according to a modernist aesthetic outlook, either explicitly or implicitly. Not surprisingly, they have been mostly found wanting: their enormous success alone would guarantee them a negative assessment. Therefore, although Puccini's career belongs more to the twentieth century than to the nineteenth, his presence in histories of twentieth-century music has usually been marginal: his works were not considered "modern" enough to be discussed next to those by Debussy, Schoenberg, Berg, Stravinsky, or even Richard Strauss, to name only opera composers working in the initial decades of the century. I have put "modern" in quotes because I should have written "modernist"; however, in the twentieth century modernism was generally considered *the* artistic orientation of modernity, the only one truly modern, and "modern" was used when "modernist" should have been said instead. Clearly, if a work was not modernist, then it could not be truly modern.

In the last few decades, however, considerable effort has gone into conceptually separating modernism and modernity in art and culture, and exploring other ways in which various artifacts from the last two centuries might be considered modern, in the sense of responding creatively to the conditions of modern life without necessarily being modernist. This changed intellectual environment has been significantly beneficial to the critical and scholarly reputation of Puccini's operas, and its influence is evident in many of the essays that follow. Before, the only way for critics and scholars to "rescue" Puccini was to emphasize the innovative, advanced, original, in a word *modernist* aspects of his art, usually looking closely at the scores for evidence—Puccini, apparently, could only be a modernist composer, not a modernist musical dramatist. This activity has yielded interesting results, since Puccini was indeed interested in making it "fairly new," if not exactly in hardcore modernist terms. The final assessment, however, could only be that he was an imaginative but rather cautious follower of other, more "advanced" composers, guardedly incorporating their novelties into an essentially conservative musical fabric.[2] If we broaden the scope of our inquiry to an investigation of the ways in which Puccini responds to the conditions of modernity, specifically not only to its aesthetic and cultural aspects but also to its intellectual, social, political, and ideological dimensions, then the composer's works emerge as particularly rich and multifaceted sites of a broad-ranging exploration of ideas, actions, emotions, and fantasies characteristic of the late nineteenth and early twentieth century—but also largely of our time, since modernity, albeit in its supposedly late guise, is still stubbornly with us.

Several contributors to the present volume share an interest in investigating precisely the relationship between Puccini's works and modernity, especially in its late nineteenth- and early twentieth-century manifestations. Arman Schwartz, for example, connects Puccini's dramaturgical concerns in the operas composed during the 1890s with the realist theater of Henrik Ibsen, illuminating the ways in which these operas stage modern existential anxieties prominently explored by Ibsen for the newly disenchanted, post-idealist culture of the fin de siècle. The extent to which this culture was *post*-idealist is explicitly tested by Schwartz's contribution to this book's "Documents" section, in which three texts by Italian critics published between 1892 and 1901 lament in different but complementary ways some of the more explicitly realist traits of contemporary Italian opera and do so precisely in terms of disenchantment. German critic Hans Merian's 1893 discussion of Ruggero Leoncavallo's *Pagliacci*, on the other hand, overtly equates realism with modernity, promoting it as the aesthetic orientation best suited to the contemporary world; and though this stance would seemingly place him at odds with his Italian colleagues, his text nonetheless reveals a strong idealist vein—for example, in its concluding equation of truth and beauty.

In light of Schwartz's interpretation of Puccini's early operas, and keeping in mind that one of the features that the critic praised in *Pagliacci* is the commedia dell'arte play-within-a-play, as Walter Frisch reminds us in his introduction to Merian's text, it might be interesting to contrast

Leoncavallo's recourse to an explicitly meta-theatrical device to address representational concerns with Puccini's choice to probe the nature of lyric theater without resorting to play-within-a-play moments, but from within the fabric of his operas, as Schwartz explains in his essay. What seems ultimately at stake both in the critical debate of the 1890s and in Leoncavallo's and Puccini's different dramaturgical choices is in fact the function of opera—but also of art as a whole—in a disenchanted world. Should it counter such disenchantment? Or rather stage it? And if so, how? In Schwartz's reading, Puccini's answers to such questions in his early works, especially *La bohème*, emerge as startingly original, more so than we had previously thought.

Both Ellen Lockhart and Alessandra Campana and Christopher Morris explore the relationship between some of Puccini's later works and modernity from the viewpoint of their representation of time and memory. In each of these essays this broad theme is approached in terms of these works' engagement with typically modern media, photography and cinema, even if the nature of such engagement is rather different. In the case of *La fanciulla del West*, the wealth of photographic evidence related to its genesis and initial production serves as an entry point into a dramaturgy that seems to favor the individual moment—the snapshot, as it were—over longer-span connections. Conversely, by means of specific kinds and uses of repetition, the music of *Il trittico* promotes the kind of representational aesthetics most thoroughly explored by cinema, as exemplified in different but comparable ways by Jean Vigo's *L'Atalante* (1934) and by Bernard Herrmann's soundtracks for post-classical Hollywood movies. The relationship between time and space, narratives and objects, that emerges in both cases distances these operas not only from previous works by Puccini, but also from the traditional dramatic aesthetics of nineteenth-century opera. What Lockhart sees as *Fanciulla*'s foregrounding of surface phenomena, and ultimately its gesturing toward an epistemology of contingency, singularity, and chance, strongly resonates with *Trittico*'s allegiance to the everyday and to the materiality of theatrical and musical objects—stage props as well as musical ideas—discussed by Campana and Morris. Their interpretation is inspired by the critical orientation known as "thing theory," which investigates the role of objects that no longer function according to the uses for which they were originally devised, and thus become "things" whose specific materiality emerges as particularly worthy of attention. For Campana and Morris, both *Trittico*'s stage props and its musical objects—such as recurring motives—stubbornly refuse to acquire narrative and dramatic meaning, stubbornly refuse to be "useful" in the ways common not only in nineteenth-century opera but also in Puccini's previous works. Hence they turn into "things," in the process "shedding their patrimony of memory" and "forgoing their work of nostalgia."

The everyday is also a recurrent theme in Schwartz's interpretation of the early operas, especially *La bohème*, whose music, in the words of an early critic, "willingly attaches itself to concrete, palpable reality, to the outward and to appearances, to its exterior and insignificant signs." According to Schwartz, this attitude is best embodied by one particular character, Mimì, "who represents [. . .] a commitment to shared experience and the poetics of the everyday," in contrast with the deluded idealism of Rodolfo, who refuses to come to terms with the reality surrounding him. In light of this suggestion, it seems worth noting that in Lockhart's and Campana and Morris's essays dramaturgical, aesthetic, and even cultural agency is assigned to the operas themselves: *they* exhibit a commitment to the poetics of the everyday, whereas in *La bohème* it is a character, Mimì, who does so.

In the context of a broad discussion of Puccini and modernity, I wonder whether this difference might not be read in terms of different levels of agency on the part of the individual in the modern world. In *Bohème* the possibility of different kinds of engagement with modern reality and different attitudes toward human interaction is still open: Rodolfo might be a skeptical idealist, while Mimì can be a realist instead. *Fanciulla* and *Trittico*, however, are more pessimistic: they stage a world in which characters, like objects, also become things. Individuals here no longer have access to a spectrum of positions and attitudes, but are trapped instead within a dramatic world in which the choice between realism and idealism is no longer possible—a world made of material things rather than useful objects. If it were so, the "reconfiguration of what theater and music can do" on the part of *Trittico*, which Campana and Morris deem "progressive and courageous," emerges as the manifestation of a loss of faith in the possibility of individual agency and autonomy.

This set of aesthetic and cultural concerns raised by the essays discussed thus far might have something valuable to say about *Turandot*. Ben Earle challenges some recent interpretations of this opera that look at its characters and plot in overtly fascist terms as he delves into its reception in the 1920s and 1930s by Italian critics of different aesthetic persuasions and political leanings (that is, as far as this was possible in 1920s and especially 1930s Italy). The picture that emerges is quite unexpected and far from unified, with the kind of fascism evoked by present-day scholars nowhere in evidence. In Earle's account, matters of style are certainly brought up by early critics, but evidence seems to come mostly from characters and plot, just as in more recent readings. But what happens to *Turandot* if we look at it from the point of view of the insights about *Fanciulla* and *Trittico* offered by Lockhart, Campana, and Morris? Despite what many have heard as a regressive attitude, especially in the supposedly old-style lyricism pervading the music of Liù and in part that of Calaf, Puccini's last opera might emerge as the next step in the composer's exploration of a thoroughly modern dramaturgy.

Although it seems unwarranted to mention the everyday as a prominent element in *Turandot*, I believe it is justified to evoke concepts such as surface, materiality, and repetition in connection with the ways in which the music constructs the drama.[3] Furthermore, there is a sense in which this opera is, like *Fanciulla*, a succession of individual moments; but these photographs are no longer snapshots, instead bringing to mind carefully composed and grandly conceived images. And does the following description of cinema by Campana and Morris not strike a chord with anybody familiar with *Turandot*?: "Cinema's machinic mediation of existence promises . . . to bypass the subjective and its conventional apparatus of representation by foregrounding the role of material, objective means; yet it promises that this mediation, unlike its conventional-subjective counterpart, will not compromise but only accentuate immediacy of experience." This particular kind of mediation-induced immediacy might be linked to the way in which *Turandot*, just like *Trittico*, forgoes the work of nostalgia. In so doing *Turandot* reconfigures time as a kind of eternal, and eternally repeatable, present, although this present evokes not the everyday as it does in *Trittico,* but a potentially infinite series of relatively unrelated freeze frames.

Furthermore, if, as I have suggested summarizing Lockhart, Campana, and Morris, *Fanciulla* and *Trittico* stage a world in which characters, like objects, also become "things," and especially if *Trittico* constitutes the manifestation of a radical loss of faith in the possibility of individual agency and autonomy on the part of the modern subject, then in *Turandot* it is the whole opera that becomes a "thing": no longer an object whose function is universally understood, but an item for display, a museum piece that demands reflection on the reasons for its existence. *Turandot*, then, would no longer represent "the end of the great tradition," to cite the subtitle of a famous book about the opera, standing instead *after* the end of the great tradition, and being, in a sense, *about* this very end.[4] This stance, incidentally, seems to consign the question of individual agency and autonomy to the dustbin of history—not least the history of Puccini's own career. We might want to call this stance fascist; or we might invoke commodification; or we might ponder the unprecedented pessimism it reveals, about life, and specifically life in the modern world, no less than about opera as Puccini used to conceive of it, up to and including *Trittico*.

Gender

Gender has been a conspicuous feature of the discourse on Puccini from the beginning, as amply demonstrated here by the excerpts from Fausto Torrefranca's 1912 pamphlet, in which gender binaries permeate the discussion not only of the operas' characters, but also of the composer's personality and even some of his music's features—albeit in rather vague terms. More than this, Torrefranca casts the very genre of opera as "female," in opposition to the supposed maleness of instrumental music. As Alexandra Wilson highlights in her introduction to Torrefranca's work as well as in her monograph on Puccini's Italian reception, such opinions were far from isolated during the composer's lifetime. Indeed, they colored many critical reactions to his works, if not often with the venomous hostility—and rhetorical sharpness—displayed by Torrefranca.[5] We should not be surprised, then, to find instances of such coloring in the texts discussed by Ben Earle in his chapter on Puccini and fascism, where it tends to acquire more specifically political tones.

At the same time, Arman Schwartz's investigation of idealism and realism in the early operas aligns the former with male characters such as Des Grieux in *Manon Lescaut* and Rodolfo in *La bohème*, and the latter with female ones, especially Mimì. In this sense, Schwartz's perspective affords us a viewpoint from which Puccini's "Big Three" operas, usually grouped together not least in their treatment of their female protagonists, emerge as profoundly different. In his words, "Tosca and Cio-Cio-san function, perhaps too easily, as the objects of our voyeuristic gaze, and they are not counterposed with figures who, like Mimì, offer a compelling alternative to their delusions." Whereas with Des Grieux and Rodolfo Puccini offers us "the discomforting spectacle of male, skeptical hysteria," I would add that the "self-theatricalizing fantasies" of the protagonists of *Tosca* and *Madama Butterfly* are less discomforting in the sense intended by Schwartz precisely because they are women. In the world in which these operas were created and first seen and heard, being a woman was taken to mean being inclined to hysteria, and it meant being the object of voyeuristic gaze far more commonly than men—something that remains true in our own world, although in different ways and to different extents.

If we consider this position in light of Arthur Groos's essay on *Madama Butterfly*, however, its perspective is expanded in perhaps unexpected ways that might help us further to differentiate among the "Big Three" using a gender-based viewpoint. Addressing the opera's representation of the encounter between the American naval officer Pinkerton and the young Japanese woman Cio-Cio-san in the context of the Orientalism dominating Western discourse on the East, Groos highlights the different contributions of its team of authors, Puccini and librettists Luigi Illica and Giuseppe Giacosa. According to him, Illica, who was in charge of the scenario, conceived a drama that "demanded limitations on Butterfly's character as Japanese and victim," while Giacosa, who wrote the poetry for the main solos and duets, prepared musical highpoints that "required tragic stature and therefore something approaching Western interiority." In the end, the three authors "turned this contradiction to their advantage, creating a complexity of character unmatched in fin-de-siècle Italian opera." Groos illustrates various instances of such complexity, ending with "a death scene with two distinct episodes and two suicide attempts." The first, conceived by Illica and more complicit with standard Orientalist discourse, presents Cio-Cio-san as a victim both of Pinkerton's deception and of her country's patriarchal and religious code; the second, however, "draws attention to the modicum of tragic freedom a heroine trapped between East and West has been allowed in choosing death: the freedom to assert her maternal love even while sacrificing herself for a future denied to her—her son's assimilation into a Western race and culture."

In light of these considerations, Cio-Cio-san's self-theatricalizing fantasies seem rather different from Tosca's. For example, Butterfly would have been just another Tosca if she had died the death that Illica had devised for her, completely annihilated by both Pinkerton and the ghost of her father, by both West and East—in a sense, a complete victim of her self-theatricalization. However, Tosca dies without having understood the world in which she moves—indeed, dies *because* she has been unable to understand it—whereas Cio-Cio-san's final suicide arrives at the end of a process that has seen her move from complete skepticism to a modicum of realism. This might even be one of the reasons why early critics heard echoes of Mimì in her music.

Comparing this process to Tosca's trajectory lies beyond the scope of this text, but it is worth considering the different kind of company these two characters keep. Cio-Cio-san enters surrounded by women, and her servant-cum-friend Suzuki never leaves her side; Tosca, on the other hand, is not only the sole female character in the whole opera, but seems to have in her life no one but her lover Cavaradossi; and whereas Suzuki might present, if not a compelling alternative to Cio-Cio-san's delusions, then an occasional reminder that, in the context of the opera, delusion is not the only possibility open to a Japanese woman (not least in her attention to the everyday), Cavaradossi has no alternative to offer when it comes to delusions.

Tosca and Cavaradossi are erotically invested in each other, but have no other common ground; in fact, he repeatedly dismisses her precisely because she is too trustworthy, too emotional, too pious, too good—in short, because she is a woman, according to late nineteenth-century stereotypes of femininity. Moreover, when in Act 3 she tells him that she has done something that might be construed as masculine, i.e. killing Scarpia, he launches into a paean to her hands, "O dolci mani mansuete e pure" (O sweet hands, meek and pure), in a fetishizing move that, in belittling her gesture and objectifying her body, speaks volumes about his conception of their relationship and of Tosca herself. But there is more: with "O dolci mani" Cavaradossi begins a sonnet—an extremely rare poetic form in Italian opera, and therefore a marked choice on the part of the librettists. Tosca interrupts him after the first two quatrains, but Cavaradossi, undeterred, has a second go at his poem, "Amaro sol per te m'era il morire" (Death was bitter to me only because of you), this time managing to bring it to completion (with Tosca's support) in an unusually regular musical setting: the two quatrains are almost strophic, a rare occurrence in Puccini.[6] Is Cavaradossi self-consciously singing a sonnet? Or is he singing in the form of one without "knowing" that this is what he is doing? As there are no signs pointing unequivocally to diegetic music or stage song, I suppose we must opt for the latter option, though I suggest that a degree of ambiguity is crucial to the dramatic and psychological effect of this scene: whether consciously or not, at a moment of maximum dramatic and psychological tension all Cavaradossi thinks about is making poetry, and he will not give up until he has satisfied this urge. In a sense, then, Cavaradossi is no less prone than Tosca to self-theatricalizing fantasies: she might be an opera diva, but he, as a painter—and evidently possessor of a rich poetic vein—is equally apt at conjuring up imaginary worlds and imaginary persons, as he openly declares in his Act 1 aria, "Recondita armonia."

The other prominent male characters in *Tosca* and *Madama Butterfly*, Scarpia and Pinkerton, are realists, but of a merely pragmatic, transactional sort, as Schwartz says. But *Madama Butterfly* features another important man, one who is neither an idealist nor a pragmatic realist: Sharpless, the American consul in Nagasaki, the first to grant Cio-Cio-san depth of interiority (when he describes her voice before she arrives, as Groos points out), and the only one who has the full measure of her predicament. Together with Suzuki, he functions as a mediating presence for audiences: theirs are the eyes through which we see Cio-Cio-san and comprehend her intolerable position. Here might lie a reason why audiences have generally found *Tosca* thrilling but not particularly moving, whereas the opposite is true of *Madama Butterfly*. Tosca is trapped between an idealist just like her, Cavaradossi, and a crudely pragmatic realist, Scarpia; Cio-Cio-san, on the contrary, might start out in fully idealist fashion and in the thralls of another vulgarly pragmatic realist, Pinkerton. Thanks in part to Suzuki and Sharpless, however, she attains a tragic dimension by her decision to commit suicide and the manner in which she does so.

Transnationalism

I believe it is fair to say that the works of no other previous composer had the kind of wide and rapid international dissemination enjoyed by Puccini, not least thanks to the crucial impact of the gramophone on the consumption of music in Western and West-influenced lands in the early twentieth century. What is more, the significant improvement in the conditions and times of travel by train and ship meant that Puccini himself could travel almost incessantly all over Italy and the rest of Europe, and make two journeys to the United States, mainly in order to supervise important productions of his works, including the premieres of his final completed works—*La fanciulla del West* at the Metropolitan Opera (1910), *La rondine* at the Monte Carlo Opera (1917), and *Il trittico*, again at the Metropolitan (1918). As a consequence of these circumstances, Puccini wrote as much for the whole of the operatic world as he did for a specific national setting—certainly more than any of his predecessors, Italian or otherwise. This orientation should be placed in the context of an almost century-long practice on the part of Italian composers to search for the literary sources of their works among non-Italian texts: not a single opera by Puccini is based on an Italian play, short story, novel, or poem, with the partial exceptions of Carlo Gozzi's commedia dell'arte play *Turandotte* (but via an Italian translation of Friedrich Schiller's adaptation) and the few lines from Dante's *Divine Comedy* that inspired *Gianni Schicchi*. Moreover, and partly as a consequence, only *Tosca* and *Gianni Schicchi* are clearly set in Italy—the action of *Suor Angelica* takes place "in a monastery in the late seventeenth century," with no further specification.

It will come as no surprise, then, that all the contributions in the present volume touch upon a transnational theme, dimension, or perspective, however tangentially. To name just one feature of this kind for each essay: Schwartz brings the plays of Norwegian playwright Ibsen to bear on his interpretation of Puccini's early operas; Groos discusses the double perspective on Japan, American and Italian, in *Madama Butterfly*; the photographs of and for *Fanciulla* discussed by Lockhart crossed the Atlantic in both directions; Campana and Morris bring up a French film and a Hollywood composer; Earle contrasts Puccini's cosmopolitan outlook and fascism's "organic" nationalism; Botstein compares and contrasts *Butterfly*, *Fanciulla*, and *Suor Angelica* with three almost exactly contemporary works by German and Czech composers: Janáček's *Jenůfa*, Strauss's *Der Rosenkavalier*, and Hindemith's *Sancta Susanna*, respectively; the documents on *verismo* chosen by Schwartz lament the foreign influences on the Italian national tradition; Frisch's commentary on Merian's text highlights the meanings of Italian operatic realism for German culture; Girardi points out that *Madama Butterfly* reached its final form in Paris on the occasion of a production sung in French; and I call attention to the international and indeed intercontinental star status of many singers and conductors who performed Puccini's works during his lifetime.

The two essays that most explicitly address the transnational components of Puccinian discourse are those on Fausto Torrefranca's *Giacomo Puccini and International Opera* and on *La rondine*. As Alexandra Wilson explains in her introduction, Torrefranca strongly objected to the composer turning to non-Italian operatic and musical traditions and works in search of inspiration and stimuli for his art. Micaela Baranello explores instead the international nexus of people, texts, genres, and ideas that contributed to the genesis and initial reception of *La rondine*, with Austria, France, and Italy acting as the main settings of complex operatic, cultural, and political negotiations made even more difficult by the world war that was raging at the time. The perspectives afforded by these two contributions point to a larger scenario worth outlining here.

Nationalism was among the most powerful political, social, cultural, ideological and emotional factors in the world in which Puccini lived and worked, shaping individual and collective identity to a degree unthinkable only half a century before the composer's birth in 1858, or after his death in 1924. All art, including opera, was called upon not simply to express but to bolster the supposedly specific features of an individual nation. This task was made particularly difficult for Puccini by the transnational dimension in which he operated. During this same era, opera was considered the Italian art form *par excellence*, with Puccini the most famous Italian opera composer as well as the most famous living Italian artist— indeed, his only rival might have been tenor Enrico Caruso. What is more, Italy, only recently established as a nation-state, was particularly nervous about its position on the international stage, eager to play a major role and at the same time conscious of its socio-economical limitations compared to France, Great Britain, Germany, or the United States. Witness, for example, Torrefranca blaming Puccini above all others for "our national art" not having had "as much as a single word to say to the world that was truly its own, nothing that was truly characteristic or deeply expressive of its unique historical moment." Such criticism placed Puccini under intense pressure to make his operas into the ultimate manifestation of Italian art for both Italy and the rest of the world. This stress is evident in much of the rhetoric characterizing the Puccinian discourse that can be found not only in the Torrefranca and *Rondine* essays, but also in Ben Earle's text on fascism.

This complex scenario has potentially important consequences for interpretation, be it critical or performative—ones that, to my mind, are not always properly acknowledged. One contribution to the Puccinian discourse that does keep them in sharp focus is David Rosen's on the impact that a more international outlook might have had on the changes in the representation of religion in Puccini's operas. The works up to and including *Madama Butterfly*, all premiered in Italy, seem to reflect "some prevalent and well-documented currents in Italian culture: a male liberal anti-clericalism countered by a female orientation towards religion, especially towards a Marian devotion," whereas the later operas' "more positive, or at least less hostile, attitude toward religion" might be related, on the one hand, to the "changing, more relaxed church-state relationships in Italy after the turn of the century," and on the other, to the fact that these operas were initially performed in foreign theaters (which does not mean written with these theaters in mind from the beginning).[7] Similarly, a decade ago I analyzed the discourse of nostalgia in *La fanciulla del West* from a double perspective, American and Italian, highlighting how its meaning might change in light of the socioeconomic and cultural differences between the two countries, especially as they concern migration at the turn of the twentieth century.[8]

Here I would like to mention one further case that brings together a transnational perspective and a gender-oriented one. The emphasis on Cio-Cio-san's motherhood in *Madama Butterfly* is not to be found in the opera's literary sources, and is therefore due to Illica, Giacosa, and Puccini, especially when it comes to the protagonist's final aria, "Tu, tu, piccolo Iddio," as explained by Arthur Groos, who ponders the dramaturgical consequences of this choice. Behind a drama and its characters there are always people, however, not only its authors but also its intended spectators, and in general a society, a culture, a worldview; taking them into consideration helps shed light on authorial decisions that might otherwise seem less than clear. In this specific case, why the emphasis on Cio-Cio-san's motherhood and her overwhelming emotional investment in her son? Why that final aria? Because, in short, Cio-Cio-san is an Italian single mother as well as a Japanese one, and displays feelings and concerns that belonged in very particular ways to the Italian discourse on single motherhood at the turn of the twentieth century.

As cultural historians have recently argued, "the Italian mother," that well-known and still enduring stereotype, was invented in the nineteenth century and is closely linked to the Italian discourse of the nation at the time of the movement toward unification, the Risorgimento.[9] After the proclamation of the kingdom of Italy in 1861 and the annexation of Rome in 1870, attention turned to the construction of a "modern," "strong," "healthy" society (to mention the most frequently recurring adjectives in the rhetoric of the time) that could support the fledgling nation's international aspirations—colonial conquest not least among them. The Italian peninsula had long been a site of systematic infant abandonment, more so than any other European country; during the nineteenth century, and especially after unification, this came to be regarded as a shockingly shameful practice, one that compromised the child's future psychological, emotional, and physical development and even survival—death ratios were much higher for children placed in orphanages—and consequently robbed the nation of many of its children.[10] Therefore, a medical, social, political, and cultural discourse emerged that was aimed at convincing single mothers to keep their babies—a discourse for "the moral promotion and support of motherhood," as an administrative document related to the Rome city orphanage and dated 1897 proclaims.[11] In the early twentieth century "the Italian mother" had reached her full maturity, and was constantly debated in the national discourse; what is more, the "moral promotion of motherhood" was a prominent component of this discourse, especially geared at single mothers.

Cio-Cio-san's agreement to give up her son at the end of *Madama Butterfly*, and at the same time her desperate farewell to her *piccolo Iddio* (little god) before killing herself, acquire depth of perspective and meaning in the context of this specifically Italian discourse of the mother, and signally the single mother, a discourse that was still relatively new in Italy and to which Puccini's opera doubtlessly contributed—as would *Suor Angelica*. When *Madama Butterfly* started to be produced abroad, however, it encountered different national contexts in which this discourse was not as intense or relevant as it was in Italy. I would suggest that, in such contexts, the end of the opera might have had a partially different emotional impact in comparison to Italy, perhaps adding to the already common stereotype of Italian excessive sentimentality and visceral emotionality—bolstered primarily, it should be noted, by opera. At the same time, seeing *Madama Butterfly* outside Italy might have contributed to the construction of the stereotypical "Italian mother," even if Cio-Cio-san is ostensibly Japanese.

Performance

A final theme that connects a few of the contributions to the present volume pertains to the interaction between the different components of the operatic work in performance. Two essays, Ellen Lockhart's and Michele Girardi's, pay attention to the visual aspect, concentrating respectively on photographs that either inspired or document the initial staging of *La fanciulla del West* and the staging manual based on the first French production of *Madama Butterfly*, which took place at the Opéra-Comique in 1906, with which Puccini was closely involved, and for which he prepared the final version of the opera. It is interesting to compare the composer's high opinion of this staging, as revealed in Girardi's text, and his reiterated, almost obsessive complaints about the protagonist, Marguerite Carré, wife of the Opéra-Comique's impresario and director of the production Albert Carré, that can be read in many letters to various recipients, some of which are translated in my contribution on Puccini's interpreters. On the one hand Puccini considered the soprano "never [. . .] sincere, and [. . .] never convincing," and thought that her interpretation was "wholly made of mannerisms instead of being the living, true exposition of a most pain-

Figure 2. Giacomo Puccini in the late 1910s.

ful drama"; on the other, he found the staging so convincing and gained such valuable insights as he watched it take shape during the prolonged rehearsal period that he ended up using this production as the occasion for settling on a final version of the opera. How, in the space of a few months, could he go from writing that "they are cutting the opera too much. Madame Carré will do fairly well, but she wants too many cuts, because she surely feels that the effort is too much for her strength" to considering that such cuts were exactly those needed? And yet, he evidently did. I call attention to this question not in search of an answer, but rather as a way to invite reflection on the several different angles from which we may consider the matter of performance when it comes to Puccini, as well as the vast amount of potentially contradictory evidence that we have at our disposal in the early twenty-first century.

Consider staging, for example. Puccini's works have been the preserve of what are generally if misleadingly called "traditional" approaches longer than those by other canonical opera composers such as Handel, Mozart, Wagner, Verdi, and Strauss. As Ellen Lockhart put it in a 2011 essay, Puccini's "repertory is held to require considerable *loyalty* in staging: it offers a visual medium that adheres to scenic indications and eschews directorial intervention."[12] However, Puccini's operas have begun to emerge as a notable opportunity for more "critical" productions that explore onstage the resonances that these works may have acquired since their first appearances. An early and reportedly compelling example of this stance was Jonathan Miller's *Tosca* at the 1986 Maggio Musicale, Florence, set in late 1943 or early 1944 at the time of the Nazi occupation of Rome.[13] A more recent, much lauded, and more radical instance than Miller's *Tosca* is Stefan Herheim's *La bohème* (Norwegian National Opera, 2012), which has received a certain amount of musicological attention as well.[14] The parallels between, on the one hand, the traditional view of Puccini as the reluctant, cautious modernist and the "traditional" approach to staging his operas, and, on the other, recent attempts to reassess the composer's relationship with modernism and modernity and the equally recent "critical" turn in staging his works are striking. In both fields, a long-standing focus on continuities is being replaced, or at least complemented, by more sustained attention to discontinuity and difference.

If we move from staging to vocal performance, however, the situation changes considerably. The recent digital revolution has made widely available an exceptional number of recordings dating from the entire history of recorded sound, whose initial decades overlap with Puccini's life. We can therefore hear many of the singers who created prominent roles in his operas: for example, searching on YouTube for the name of Cesira Ferrani, the first Manon Lescaut and first Mimì in *La bohème*, brings up excerpts from both operas recorded ca. 1902–1903, only a decade after the premiere of *Manon Lescaut* (1893) and even less after that of *La bohème* (1896). Listening to these as well as to the hundreds of others by the singers I discuss in my essay in this volume immediately shatters any illusion of continuity between then and now. Vocal technique, tempo, dynamics, rhythm, textual delivery—almost everything fails to conform to what over the last few decades has been commonly considered an acceptable Puccinian style of singing.

Yet more surprises are in store for us if we now turn to the repertory of these singers. As Girardi has pointed out, several of them were as well versed in Straussian roles as they were in Puccinian ones. To mention just one example, Salomea Krusceniski, who sang Cio-Cio-san at the premiere of the second version of *Madama Butterfly* (Brescia, 1904) to the composer's complete satisfaction, would take on the title role of *Salome* under Toscanini at La Scala two years later, and then would be the first Italian Elektra in 1909.[15] By our standards Cio-Cio-san and Salome are rather different but not absolutely incompatible roles—American soprano Catherine Malfitano sang both successfully in the 1990s. Seeing the title roles of *Butterfly* and *Elektra* mentioned in a singer's biography within a five-year span, however, has a decidedly defamiliarizing effect; and if a present-day casting director suggested hiring a currently successful Cio-Cio-san as Elektra, he would very likely be the object of scorn. I certainly have no intention to issue calls for authenticity, for a return to a "truly Puccinian" style of singing, or for some kind of "historically informed" casting.[16] It seems more interesting to consider instead the impact that different media histories might have had on our ideas on staging and singing Puccini.

Though both sound and audiovisual recording came of age during the initial decade of the twentieth century, their interactions with opera over the following decades took diverging paths. The initial meeting between sound recording and opera generated a *coup de foudre* that developed into a long, happy, and mutually satisfactory relationship, one that survived and indeed thrived upon technological innovations such as electrical recording, magnetic tape, the long-playing record, stereo, digital recording, and the Internet. The same cannot be said of opera and audiovisual recording: only with the advent of television in the second half of the century did a merely friendly acquaintance blossom into a serious engagement, the two partners eventually settling down together thanks to digital technology as recently as a couple of decades ago.[17] This means that when it comes to Puccini, and thanks mostly to the Internet, we have at our disposal a rich history of sound that goes all the way back to the composer's lifetime, while our collective visual memory goes back only a few decades.

Might this be one of the reasons why the discourse of staging Puccini tends to be more polarized nowadays than that of singing Puccini? After all, if we want difference in singing, we can easily find it, whereas difference in staging is significantly harder to come by—we might even have to attend a live performance to find it. Historiographically speaking, this situation means that we have plenty of compelling aural evidence to turn to in search of historically grounded stimuli for interpretation, whether we are interested in staying as chronologically close to the composer as possible or in exploring the Puccini of subsequent times—evidence that is only slowly being taken into serious consideration by musicologists.[18] The same cannot be said for visual evidence, since sketches or photographs of scenes and costumes and descriptions in reviews and other texts cannot even remotely compete with audiovisual recordings as testament of what happened onstage: the case of the Carré staging manual for *Butterfly* is an isolated one, and has attracted the attention of scholars precisely for this reason.

Modernity

At this point we have circled back to the theme of Puccini and modern technology, although from a different perspective than those adopted by Lockhart, and Campana and Morris in their essays. This trajectory seems to confirm that the matter of modernity is no less crucial today than it was during the composer's lifetime or after—not surprisingly, since we still conceive of our world as modern. Discussing Puccini and modernity, then, is in a sense a "historically informed" critical and historiographical pratice. As we have seen, and as the essays that follow make clear, the terms of this discussion have changed considerably over time, not least in the effort to separate conceptually modernity from modernism. And yet, there is no denying that these loaded words have dominated the discourse on Puccini since its inception. A final point I would like to make, then, is an invitation to keep the rich potential of these words for covert value judgment in sharp focus, since they have been used frequently to dismiss or belittle Puccini's works—an attitude that the authors and editors of the present volume have worked hard to counter.

Who is not "modern" these days? There seems to be no more common way of promoting artists from the past than claiming that they are modern, or more modern than we really thought, thus implying continuity between them and us, and therefore their continued—and hitherto only partially realized—relevance to us. As I have intimated above, however, continuity between then and now is, in a sense, the last thing Puccini needs, since this sense of continuity, crucially bolstered by the unchallenged dominance of many of his operas in the repertory, has substantially contributed to the remarkable resilience of the discourse on Puccini, which has been by and large a discourse of the "nearly but not quite," of the "almost." In other words, even alert uses of the rhetoric of modernity have often implied covert or casual value judgments. In modern times such judgments have tended to rely on notions of progress, of advance, of development—in a word, of difference. Puccini's works have often suffered from this rhetoric of difference, not least because of the sense of sameness that their unbroken and relatively prominent cultural presence has generated. And yet, one of our aims in this book is to inject a modicum of difference in, or at least to add new perspectives to, our ideas of Puccini and his operas, and therefore, in a sense, to make Puccini "modern," or at least more modern than before.

I can offer no simple way out of this tangle of contradictions—nor do I think that such a way exists. The uneasy and often baffling tension in the Puccinian discourse between continuity and discontinuity, sameness and difference, past and present, is just a particularly explicit and evident instance of the similar yet deeper tension that lies at the core of the image of itself cultivated by the modern world, in Puccini's time no less than in ours, even if in rather different terms. If *Giacomo Puccini and His World* succeeds in alerting its readers to the deep resonances, multiple facets, and momentous implications of the discourse of modernity, it will have gone some considerable way toward justifying its existence.

NOTES

1. *Tosca* has been featured in other contexts in the past, perhaps most memorably in Carmine Gallone's film *E avanti a lui tremava tutta Roma!* (1946). Set in Rome during the Nazi occupation of 1943–44, it tells the story of Ada and Marco, two lovers who belong to the anti-fascist resistance and who also play Tosca and Mario in a performance of the opera, during which an attempt by the Nazis to arrest Marco is thwarted. I would also like to mention Paola Capriolo's novel *Vissi d'amore* (1992, translated in English as *Floria Tosca*, 1997), an unsettling retelling of the opera from the point of view of the villain, Baron Scarpia.

2. Among recent music-analytical contributions that have attempted either to steer clear of modernist discourse or, conversely, to problematize it are James Hepokoski, "Structure, Implication, and the End of *Suor Angelica*," *Studi pucciniani* 3 (2004): 241–64; and "'Un bel dì? Vedremo!': Anatomy of a Delusion," in *Madama Butterfly: L'orientalismo di fine secolo, l'approccio pucciniano, la ricezione*, ed. Arthur Groos and Virgilio Bernardoni (Florence, IT: Leo S. Olschki, 2008), 219–46; Andrew Davis, "*Il Trittico*," "*Turandot*," and *Puccini's Late Style* (Bloomington: Indiana University Press, 2010); Nicholas Baragwanath, *The Italian Traditions and Puccini: Compositional Theory and Practice in Nineteenth-Century Opera* (Bloomington: Indiana University Press, 2011); and Marco Targa, *Puccini e la Giovane Scuola: Drammaturgia dell'opera italiana di fine Ottocento* (Bologna: Albisani, 2013).

3. For repetition and mechanicity in *Turandot*, see Arman Schwartz, "Mechanism and Tradition in Puccini's *Turandot*," *Opera Quarterly* 25 (2010): 28–50. For a wide-ranging discussion of Puccini and modernity, see Schwartz, *Puccini's Soundscapes: Realism and Modernity in Italian Opera* (Florence, IT: Leo S. Olschki, 2016).

4. See William Ashbrook and Harold Powers, *Puccini's Turandot: The End of the Great Tradition* (Princeton: Princeton University Press, 1991).

5. See Alexandra Wilson, *The Puccini Problem: Opera, Nationalism, and Modernity* (Cambridge: Cambridge University Press, 2007), esp. chaps. 4, 5, and 7.

6. The main melodic idea of "Amaro sol per te m'era il morire" comes from Act 4 of *Edgar* (1889), which had been cut in its entirety in later versions of the opera. The fact that this music had been conceived much earlier than the rest of *Tosca* might contribute to its "set-piece" effect, although Puccini made significant alterations to it. See Julian Budden, *Puccini: His Life and Works* (New York: Oxford University Press, 2002), 84–85.

7. David Rosen, "'Pigri ed obesi Dei': Religion in the Operas of Puccini," in Groos and Bernardoni, *Madama Butterfly*, 257–98, quotes at 289, 297–98.

8. See Emanuele Senici, *Landscape and Gender in Italian Opera: The Alpine Virgin from Bellini to Puccini* (Cambridge: Cambridge University Press, 2005), 256–60.

9. See Marina d'Amelia, *La mamma* (Bologna: Il Mulino, 2005), esp. chap. 1.

10. See David I. Kertzer, *Sacrificed for Honor: Italian Infant Abandonment and the Politics of Reproductive Control* (Boston: Beacon Press, 1993).

11. Cited in Gianna Pomata, "Madri illegittime tra Ottocento e Novecento: Storie cliniche e storie di vita," *Quaderni storici* 15 (1980): 497–542, quote at 517.

12. Ellen Lockhart, "Photo-Opera: *La fanciulla del West* and the Staging Souvenir," *Cambridge Opera Journal* 23 (2011): 145–66, quote at 148 (italics in original). For a rich visual repertory of Puccini stagings through the twentieth century, see the exhibition catalogue *La scena di Puccini*, ed. Vittorio Fagone and Vittoria Crespi Morbio (Lucca: Fondazione Ragghianti, 2003).

13. For two brief assessments of this landmark production, see Michele Girardi, *Puccini: His International Art*, trans. Laura Basini (Chicago: University of Chicago Press, 2000), 192–94; and Kate Bassett, *In Two Minds: A Biography of Jonathan Miller* (London: Oberon, 2012), 256–59.

14. See "Stefan Herheim's *La bohème* on DVD: A Review Portfolio," *Opera Quarterly* 29 (2013): 146–74, which includes an introduction by Arman Schwartz and reviews by Mark Schachtsiek, Roger Parker and Flora Willson, Schwartz, and Alexandra Wilson.

15. See Girardi, *Puccini*, 267.

16. It might be really interesting to hear a prominent Cio-Cio-san tackling Elektra just for once: What would a conductor sensitive to singers' needs do? How loud would those *echt*-Straussian orchestral blasts turn out, exactly? Carolyn Abbate and Roger Parker make a similar point in their "The Eternal Feminine," *Opera* 65/8 (August 2014): 943–51, quote at 950.

17. This is true for audiovisual versions of operas in their entirety (or near entirety), be they opera films, television studio productions, or "live" relays from theaters. If we widen our scope to include audiovisual objects inspired by, or based upon, an opera, then the pickings are richer. For the emblematic case of *Madama Butterfly*, probably the most popular among Puccini's operas in this sense, see W. Anthony Sheppard, "Cinematic Realism, Reflexivity, and the American 'Madame Butterfly' Narratives," *Cambridge Opera Journal* 17 (2005): 59–93.

18. For an interpretation of the duet closing Act 1 of *Madama Butterfly* that takes sound recording into prominent account, see Roger Parker, "The Act 1 Love Duet: Some Models (Interpretative and Otherwise)," in Groos and Bernardoni, *Madama Butterfly*, 247–56, esp. 255–56. The recording Parker discusses dates from 1939 (with Toti Dal Monte and Beniamino Gigli, Oliviero De Fabritiis conducting) and its sources are duly footnoted. He gives no sources, though, for the production he mentions, Graham Vick's for English National Opera, first seen in 1984 and repeatedly revived (evidently he saw it live, since no video has ever been released). In light of my considerations about the differences between the history of sound and that of staging, this lack is a telling detail.

PART I

Essays

Realism and Skepticism
in Puccini's Early Operas

ARMAN SCHWARTZ

The final act of Amilcare Ponchielli and Arrigo Boito's 1876 opera *La Gioconda* takes place in "the entry hall of a dilapidated palace" on Venice's Giudecca island. It is a lonely, indeterminate space, designed to contrast maximally with the glamorous, public, and—to any tourist or collector of lithographs—familiar Venetian tableaux that had dominated the previous three acts. As the curtain opens, Gioconda, a beautiful singer, is struggling to reconcile herself to an awful bargain she has made: she will offer her body to the malicious spy Barnaba if he frees Enzo, the object of her own unrequited love. After securing safe passage out of the city for Enzo and his lover, Laura, Gioconda attempts to flee, only to be cornered by her nemesis. There is no way out, and the singer consents to Barnaba's proposal, asking only for a moment to pretty herself first. Then, unexpectedly, Gioconda pulls out a small dagger and stabs herself in the heart. She "falls to the ground as if struck by lightning," and the opera concludes with what must count as one of the strangest stage directions in the history of Italian opera: "Bending over the corpse of Gioconda and screaming into her ear with furious voice," Barnaba informs her that he has killed her mother.

The unforgettable image of a man screaming into a dead woman's ear has no precedent in the literary source for *La Gioconda*, Victor Hugo's 1835 play *Angelo, tyran de Padoue*, nor does it feature in Saverio Mercadante and Gaetano Rossi's *Il giuramento* (1837), an earlier opera inspired by Hugo's text. Yet however murky its origins, Ponchielli and Boito's conceit would soon take on a life of its own. Scenes in which men confront deaf or silent women appear prominently in both Giacomo Puccini's *Manon Lescaut* (1893) and his *La bohème* (1896), and there are clear parallels between the conclusion of *La Gioconda* and the second act of *Tosca* (1900). (Indeed, if Puccini's diva had stabbed herself instead of Scarpia, the two scenes would be hard to tell apart.) This chapter proposes that the final act of *La Gioconda* constitutes something like the primal scene of Puccini's oeuvre; it is a scene he would revisit throughout his career, recasting its climactic confrontation in increasingly sublimated forms. By tracking these recurrences, we may gain a new understanding of Puccini's early operas. More specifically, we may be prompted to reconsider the composer's relationship with the *verismo* movement, and with the aesthetic and philosophical anxieties it provoked. Taking my cue from recent scholarship on the dramaturgy of "skepticism" in realist spoken theater, I suggest that Puccini uses isolated, desperate characters—figures who, like Barnaba, struggle to establish meaningful connections with those around them—in order to engage with larger questions about the situation of opera in a silent, newly disenchanted world.

From *La Gioconda* to *Manon Lescaut*

Although it remained enormously popular in Italy for generations after its premiere, *La Gioconda* might not seem to have had, from the perspective of current historiography, much of an afterlife at all. Ponchielli is often depicted as a conservative stalwart, purveying Meyerbeerian "effects without causes" well after the genre of grand opera had faded from fashion.[1] Nonetheless, *La Gioconda* exhibits a decidedly nontraditional anxiety about its own medial conditions. Diegetic performances, those hallowed vehicles for operatic self-reflection, abound in *La Gioconda*, and a relentless thematization of the human mouth—from the heroine's Leonardine name to the menacing statue of a *bocca di leone* that looms over the first act set and the speaking trumpets that the sailors place on their lips at the start of Act 2—helps call attention to the physicality of vocal production.[2] Hearing, too, takes on extraordinary importance: one of the main characters is blind, and many others spend whole scenes in masks. Barnaba may be the only spy in *La Gioconda*, but his profession is an apt metaphor for all the inhabitants of Ponchielli's world.

The opera's pervasive concern with performance, hearing, and spectatorship coalesces in its final scene. Crucially, Gioconda begins by describing herself as an operatic diva:

T'arresta. Raffrena il selvaggio delirio!   Halt. Restrain your savage joy!
Vo' farmi più gaia, più fulgida ancor.   I want to make myself even more
                                     gay and bright.

Per te voglio ornare la bionda	For you I want to adorn my
mia testa	blonde head
di porpora e d'or!	with purple and gold!
Con tutti gli orpelli sacrati	I'm already covered with all the
alla scena	tinsel of the
dei pazzi teatri coperta già son.	stages of frivolous theaters.
Ascolta di questa sapiente sirena	Listen to the sweet song
la dolce canzon.	of this skillful siren.

Ponchielli's music here amplifies Boito's imagery. Gioconda sings a series of flashy, but stock coloratura gestures—laughing ornaments, staccato broken triads—that sound nothing like the weightier music given to her elsewhere in the opera. Julian Budden has despaired that Gioconda's "descent [. . .] to the coquettish language of Violetta in Act 1 of *La traviata* verges on the bathetic."[3] Yet her lapse into an earlier and more self-consciously performative mode of operatic expression, at precisely the moment in which she presents herself as an opera singer, must be Ponchielli's point. Barnaba, too, is transported to the operatic past. Listening to Gioconda's "dolce canzon" he repeats the old formulas of Romantic desire—"Ebbrezza! Delirio!"—as mechanically as did any *primo ottocento* hero.[4]

Both the musical style and the distinctive poetic meter change the instant Barnaba realizes that he has been deceived:

Ah! ferma! irrision! ... ebben ...	Ah! stop! derision! . . . well then . . .
or tu ...	now you . . .
m'odi ... e muori dannata:	hear me . . . and die damned:
(curvandosi sul cadavere di	*(bending over Gioconda's corpse and*
Gioconda e gridandogli all'	*screaming with a furious voice in*
orecchio con voce furibonda)	*her ear)*
Ier tua madre m'ha offeso! Io l'ho	Yesterday your mother offended
affogata!	me! I drowned her!
Non ode più!!	She hears no more!!

Ponchielli sets these faltering lines to a series of chromatically ascending octave drops that sound like a desperate attempt to reassert authority, but also suggest a voice on the verge of breaking. Similarly, Barnaba's words are both emphatic and inscrutable. Is it Gioconda, or her mother, that no longer hears him? Should "m'odi" be translated as "you hear me" or (as some English language translators render the phrase) "you hate me"?[5] It is as if Gioconda's deafness has infected the audience; we, as much as the protagonist, are unable to fathom the message that Barnaba so violently intones.

Indeed, the final moments of La Gioconda are full of strange transfers and reversals. Just as previously Barnaba had been a passive spectator, now he struggles to make himself heard. By a similar logic, Gioconda ceases to perform for Barnaba and is instead recast, however unwillingly, as his silent audience. Barnaba's final speech to Gioconda's corpse might thus be described as replaying the earlier deception scene, but with its conventionalized gender roles reversed. Yet this reversal also unchains a string of paradoxes: a performer who speaks sincerely, an audience that cannot hear. If the final scene of La Gioconda asks to be read as an allegory of theatrical performance, it is a cautionary tale: truth and meaningful connection are precluded from its rigid roles. Perhaps this is why Barnarba, after emitting a final unpitched and incoherent "Ah!!!," rushes off into the darkened alleyways of Venice. They resemble the mess of hallways that wind behind the stage of any theater: a maze to get lost in, but also a place to hide from the footlights' deadly glare.

With this cluster of concerns in mind, let us turn from the fourth act of La Gioconda to the fourth act of Manon Lescaut. Puccini studied composition with Ponchielli during his final two years at the Milan Conservatory (1882–83) and La Gioconda was a formative influence on the young composer. From it, Puccini learned the technique of recycling short melodic fragments to create grand orchestral perorations at the end of acts, and he drew on La Gioconda for more local models as well. "Suicidio!," Gioconda's famous final aria, seems clearly to have inspired "Sola, perduta, abbandonata," Manon's last, and equally despairing, solo utterance.

Puccini also seems to have adapted from La Gioconda an altogether more eccentric set of dramaturgical ideas. Like his teacher's opera, Manon Lescaut follows three busy, crowded acts with a shorter final act that focuses exclusively on the main characters and seems designed to frustrate expectations for spectacle. (Here the scene is a flat and barren desert "on the borders of New Orleans.") What is more, and perhaps not unrelated to these final scenic voids, both La Gioconda and Manon Lescaut feature heroines who seem to lack coherent selves. In Budden's assessment of the former work, "Gioconda herself is less a personality than a succession of moods and attitudes—wilting and forlorn in Act One, the avenging tigress in Act Two, an almost 'veristic' victim in her great aria in Act Four."[6] Similarly, Alessandra Campana describes how Manon "adapts to the changing background, mirroring and fulfilling the expectations prepared by each setting."[7] Campana perceives a connection between the large-scale dramaturgy of *Manon Lescaut* and the peculiar character of the heroine who inhabits it. If the first three acts of Puccini's opera position Manon as the willing object of the audience's gaze (sutured through the obsessive onstage looking of Manon's lover, Des Grieux), the last act implies that, outside of this spectacular structure, there is nothing. Tellingly, and thinking back again to *La Gioconda*, Campana invokes the figure of a spy to make her argument. In Acts 1 through 3, we look at Manon as if through a keyhole; in Act 4, we hear footsteps, and realize that we, too, are being seen. "No longer hidden behind the look of onstage spectators, those in the theatre are abruptly deprived of that illusion of mastery over the scene that they had been surreptitiously and repeatedly granted thus far," Campana writes, and her words could easily be applied to the final moments of Ponchielli's opera.[8] So could her final judgment: "Act Four reveals how the operatic machinery is necessarily founded on voyeurism."[9]

Like many critics since the work's premiere, Campana treats the last act of *Manon Lescaut* as a single, undifferentiated span of time. It may be possible, though, to pinpoint the moment when the "operatic machinery" first goes awry. Near the beginning of the act, Des Grieux attempts to communicate with his unconscious lover:

Manon, senti, amor mio!	Manon, listen, my love!
Non mi rispondi, amore?	You don't answer, love?
Vedi, son io che piango,	Look, it is I who weep,
io che imploro, io che carezzo	I who implore you, I who caress
e bacio	and kiss
i tuoi capelli d'oro!	your golden hair!
Ah, Manon! Manon, rispondi a me!	Ah, Manon! Manon, answer me!
Tace! Maledizione! [. . .]	She is silent! Curses! [. . .]
Rispondimi, amor mio!	Answer me, my love!
Tace! Manon, non mi rispondi?	She is silent! Manon, won't you answer me?

As in *La Gioconda*, but even more explicitly, a character who has spent the opera gazing at the object of his attraction now yearns, however belatedly, to be acknowledged as within *her* presence. Barnaba screamed desperately into Gioconda's ear; Des Grieux appeals to a whole variety of sensory stimuli, to vision, touch, and hearing. Like Barnaba, he is driven mad by the silence of his partner. Twice Des Grieux exclaims the fatal verb *Tace!*; and his emphatically repeated *io* suggests that existence itself is at stake in this appeal to recognition.

The conclusion of *La Gioconda* enacted a reversal of roles, as a (male) spectator assumed the position previously occupied by a (female) performer. A similar point might be made here. Puccini sets Des Grieux's opening lines to a grandly expanded version of a melody that had only been sung once previously in the opera, near the end of Act 2. At the climax of that act, Des Grieux recoils from his unfaithful lover:

Fango nel fango io sono	Mud in mud I am
e turpe eroe da bisca	and depraved hero of the gambling den,
m'insozzo, mi vendo.	I defile myself, sell myself.
L'onta più vile m'avvicina a te!	The vilest disgrace brings me nearer to you!
Nell'oscuro futuro, di',	In the murky future, tell me,
che farai di me?	what will you do with me?

To this, Manon responds simply:

Un'altra volta ancora, deh, mi perdona!	Once again, pray forgive me!
Sarò fedele e buona, lo giuro!	I will be faithful and good, I swear it!

Strangely, though, it is her melody, not his, that Puccini turns to in Act 4. From a psychological perspective, the allusion makes little sense: Des Grieux hardly needs to remind Manon of his own fidelity at this point in the drama (he has followed her to America, after all), nor of her previous promises. Another way of interpreting the melodic connection might proceed from the observation that, in their original context in Act 2, Manon's statements were far from obviously sincere. It is not so much that Des Grieux is lying in the desert but rather that, by adopting Manon's role, he has found himself in a situation in which the truth of his utterances can no longer be taken as self-evident. Des Grieux's vocal line soon fragments into stuttered phrases (themselves based on another of Manon's motives), and then Manon repeats his main tune, but less in sympathy than as an uncomprehending echo: "Is it you that weeps? Is it you that implores?" ("Sei tu che piangi? Sei tu che implori?"), she sings. His bid for self-assertion has gone unheeded.

From Shakespeare to Puccini, via Ibsen

In a famous essay on *King Lear*, Stanley Cavell poses a question that strikes me as getting to the heart of the scenarios enacted in the final moments of *Manon Lescaut* and *La Gioconda*. "How is acknowledgement expressed," he asks, "that is, how do we put ourselves in another's presence?" His answer:

> By revealing ourselves, by allowing ourselves to be seen. When we do not, when we keep ourselves in the dark, the consequence is that we convert the other into a character and make the world a stage for him. [. . .] The conditions of theater literalize the conditions we exact for existence outside—hiddenness, silence, isolation—hence make that existence plain. Theater does not expect us simply to stop theatricalizing; it knows that we can theatricalize its conditions as we theatricalize any others. But in giving us a place within which our hiddenness and silence and separation are accounted for, it gives us a chance to stop.[10]

Des Grieux and Barnaba spend most of their respective plots behaving as if "in the dark," treating the objects of their fantasy not as independent beings, as presences to be acknowledged, but rather (merely) characters onstage. When they struggle to overcome this state of separation, though, they fail, resembling in their failure actors in another silent hall. Des Grieux and Barnaba make themselves exposed, feminized, hysterical; they seem unable to believe or to confirm or to establish the grounds for human connection that would allow them to accept that the world outside their self-theatricalizing performances is really there. Cavell names this condition, both a philosophical and a psychological condition, skepticism. "The skeptic does not gleefully and mindlessly forgo the worlds we share, or thought we shared," he writes. "He forgoes the world for just the reason that the world is important, that it is the scene and stage of connection with the present: he finds that it vanishes exactly with the effort to *make* it present."[11]

Skepticism is a problem as old as modern subjectivity itself, and it is far from clear why its concerns would erupt suddenly on the Italian operatic stage, a terrain that has not figured prominently in the history of thought.[12] To begin to sketch an answer to this problem, it may be instructive to consider Toril Moi's study *Henrik Ibsen and the Birth of*

Modernism, which explores how the existential anxieties diagnosed by Cavell in dialogue with Descartes and Shakespeare emerged and were reconfigured in the specific context of late nineteenth-century realist theater. Any Puccini scholar will feel a shudder of recognition at Moi's opening gambit: "In Anglophone academic circles the bare mention of Ibsen's name tend[s] to elicit responses marked by boredom, disdain, or condescension," she writes. "I cannot count the number of times that otherwise well-read people have told me that they have never read and never bothered to see any plays by Ibsen, or that they haven't read any since they were students."[13] Tellingly, this "disdain" has a historiographical counterpart (as it does in Puccini's case) in a confusion about Ibsen's chronological position: "On the one hand, Ibsen represents the unquestioned beginning of modernism in the theater; on the other, there is a widespread feeling that however important he was for the development of modernism, Ibsen himself was not a modernist." No one, of course, would refer to Puccini as the "unquestioned beginning of modernism" in opera, but the sense of a figure poised uncomfortably between the end of the nineteenth century and the beginning of the twentieth is otherwise quite similar. And certainly the outrage that the composer's works produced in his own lifetime now seems impossible to understand.

Moi's project is not (along the lines of many recent musicological approaches to late Romanticism) to unearth some technical device or theoretical concept that might place Ibsen in the company of Antonin Artaud and Samuel Beckett. Instead, she searches for a context in which Ibsen's dramas *could once have seemed* provocative. That context lies, however unglamorously, in the institutionalized legacy of German idealist aesthetics: less Friedrich Hölderlin's triumphant 1796 proclamation that "truth and goodness are only siblings in beauty" than the "debased, diluted, vulgarized, and simplified" forms of this notion that pervaded discourse on culture during the later nineteenth century, especially in the geographic and cultural periphery of Europe.[14] (Had Moi's history been concerned with the Mediterranean instead of Scandinavia, it might well have given the philosophy of Puccini's contemporary Benedetto Croce a starring role.) Idealism's concerns now seem so quaint that it is easy to forget both their ubiquity and how actively early modernists struggled against them, whether by asking—as decadent aestheticists like Oscar Wilde and Joris-Karl Huysmans asked—if there was anything moral about beauty, or by denying, like Emile Zola and another naturalists, that there was anything beautiful or redemptive about truth.[15] Ibsen, for Moi, charts a path between idealism and its naturalist negation; his mature (and most radical) plays, beginning with *A Doll's House* (1879), turn to the everyday, "not as something that has to be overcome, exaggerated, or idealized" but as a potential source of meaning in itself.[16] Ibsen's modernism works, that is to say, not by rejecting aesthetic idealism but rather by dramatizing and thinking through its "real world" effects. What would an attempt to transcend the immediate world feel like in practice? How could an idealist find his way back to all he has disavowed: the physical, the commonplace, the ordinary lives of women?

Nineteenth-century opera, in the forms taken by both its Verdian and its Wagnerian quintessence, was an especially emphatic mode of idealist theater. Its plots (all of them) were predicated on what Moi calls "the sublimated and sublime idealist notion of love, which is usually represented as a man worshipping an ideal woman, or as a woman sacrificing her life for the love of a man."[17] Its favored dramatists—Hugo, Friedrich Schiller—were heroes of idealism in its earlier, ecstatic flush. It faltered, more ineptly than any earlier or later operatic style has ever faltered, on the non-idealizing shoals of comedy. More fundamentally, operatic music seemed to all observers an inherently idealizing medium: it transfigured words, enclosing adulterers and assassins within a magic circle protected from the everyday. (That is what so disturbed nineteenth-century critics of *La traviata*: a fallen woman could not but sound beautiful and, hence, could not but sound good. Perhaps, although I get ahead of myself, that is why post-idealist operas like *La Gioconda* and especially *Manon Lescaut* contain so many references to Verdi's problematic work.) Seen in this broad perspective, fin-de-siècle opera might be described as struggling— more desperately than prose theater ever had to struggle—against the generic and medial conditions of its art. Richard Strauss followed Wilde and Huysmans's path—and his late works have long disturbed critics precisely because they seem cloven into gorgeous sound and vile politics. Adrian Daub has catalogued the diverse narrative and musical strategies through which other German composers resisted Wagner's equation of aesthetic and sexual transcendence.[18] In Italy, meanwhile, *veristi* like Ruggero Leoncavallo and Pietro Mascagni were clearly naturalists, drawing on Zola and his local imitators not just in their plots, but in their struggle to write a music so natural that it seemed free from subjective expression.[19]

It is tempting to conflate Puccini's project with that of his Italian contemporaries. As I have argued elsewhere, his early operas all contain radically static and impersonal depictions of worlds unfolding as if outside of human perception: the desert in *Manon Lescaut*, the snowy

Barrière d'Enfer at the opening of the third act of *La bohème*, the "depiction of the dawn" with its ethnologically correct folksongs and endlessly clanging bells in the last act of *Tosca*.[20] These "soundscape scenes" enraged early critics precisely through their refusal to subjectivize (or, better yet, idealize) landscape and might be considered the *ne plus ultra* of *verismo* style. At the same time, Puccini's most sensitive critics have also heard a note of difference in his works. In a famous essay from 1898, Camille Bellaigue suggested that in *La bohème* "the reality [the music] searches for, at least that which for the most part it finds, is not often the reality that is hidden, intimate, and, one might say, ideal, that makes for the depths or the life of the soul." Instead, Puccini seemed to have produced a "music from which music is almost absent," sound that "willingly attaches itself to concrete, palpable reality, to the outward and to appearances, to its exterior and insignificant signs."[21] Although Bellaigue's words draw heavily on idealist tropes, they also subvert them, stopping just short of condemnation. The music of *La bohème* seems "palpable" and "insignificant" but not ugly or inhuman, almost but not quite unmusical. What is more, Bellaigue claimed he could hear something else in *La bohème*: "The sign or memory, enfeebled but still affecting, of something great, almost sacred."[22] Poised between a new musical poetics of the ordinary and an ambivalent sympathy for the "enfeebled but still affecting" ideal, Bellaigue's Puccini may begin to sound like Moi's Ibsen.

From Vienna to New Orleans, via Flanders

It is no accident, then, that Puccini's harshest and most befuddled listeners were also committed—indeed entrenched—idealists. As Ben Earle wryly notes apropos Fausto Torrefranca's notorious *Giacomo Puccini e l'opera internazionale*:

> A philosopher-critic who had persuaded himself—in explicitly Schopenhauerian style (complete with reference to the "veil of Maya")—that "pure," instrumental music was superior to any that found its *raison d'être* in a mimetic or intensificatory relationship to drama and gesture, and who further (again following Schopenhauer) had attached to instrumental music a quasi-religious character as spiritual self-knowledge, was never going to find much of value in Puccini.[23]

A similar bias, albeit with a more psychoanalytic than Schopenhauerian understanding of the "veils" that separate us from reality, informs the other perennial *bête noire* of Puccini scholarship, Mosco Carner's 1959 "critical biography" of the composer. Carner's text has long confounded readers with its combination of penetrating musical analysis and embarrassingly literal Freudian interpretations. But he did not conceive his case history as separate from his larger project, and it may deserve a closer look.

For Carner, the "true significance"—elsewhere, the "latent, and, indeed ultimate significance"—of Puccini's art lay in "a neurotic fixation which may be defined as an unresolved bondage to the mother-image."[24] By "failing to sever his early bondage to the Mother" (henceforth capitalized, and a clear case of "man worshipping an ideal woman" if there ever was one), Puccini subjected himself to an intolerable pressure, from which he fled in both life and art.[25] On the one hand, Puccini's "fixation to the past—his reliving of an early stage of the child-mother relation— demand[ed] the choice of an 'unworthy' woman standing far below the exalted Mother; for this [gave] her the passport, not to his love, of which he [was] incapable on account of his unconscious bondage, but to his acceptance of her as a sexual partner."[26] On the other,

> each of [Puccini's] heroines shows a serious flaw in her character and stands at the bottom of that height on which Puccini had enthroned the Mother. It is, precisely, because of their degraded position that he was able to fall in love with his heroines, display such extraordinary empathy with them and achieve so complete an identification with their personalities. For them he wrote his most inspired, poetic and poignant music, music in which his creative potency—I employ this noun advisedly—is felt to be at its full strength.[27]

Although Puccini's taste for ordinary women may have exasperated a certain type of psychoanalyst, it seems to have produced quite positive results: acceptance, sexual pleasure, empathy, identification, even love.

This is a truth to which Carner seems unwilling to reconcile himself, and it leads him to uncomfortable extremes. "As though wishing to compensate [his heroines] for their moral and social unworthiness, [Puccini] invests them with the most endearing traits," Carner writes.

And for all that they are morally tainted, there is, even with such lights-o'-love as Manon, Mimì and Musetta, not the faintest suggestion of lubricity or lasciviousness in them; nor are any of his heroines, with the exception of Turandot, afflicted with such pathological traits as are the female protagonists in certain operas of Strauss, Schreker and Berg.[28]

If Puccini's women could not have been perfect, then at least they could have been monsters; anything seems preferable to a realistic acceptance of an imperfect world.

As it happens, Puccini did once write the opera that Carner seems to have wanted. *Edgar* (1889), his first full-length effort, is set in the typically Romantic terrain of medieval Flanders, and it depicts in typically idealist fashion a hero torn between the love of a self-sacrificing woman and the temptations of an evil Gypsy. (Fidelia and Tigrana are, unsubtly, their names.) *Edgar* was, of course, Puccini's one unmitigated failure, and it represents a path he would never take again. Years later, when confronted with rumors of a grandiose opera based on the life of Marie Antoinette, the composer is reputed to have exclaimed: "Those historical tragedies and historical dramas! Those heroes, those great memorable figures! That sort of thing is not for me. I'm not a composer of great things, myself; I feel little things and don't like to set anything other than little things. I like Manon because she was a nice girl with a big heart and nothing more."[29]

Yet Puccini's attempt to construct an opposition between grand, idealist opera and the modesty of his own efforts is somewhat disingenuous. After all, Des Grieux often expresses sentiments that would not have been out of place in the mouth of poor, tormented Edgar. In Act 1, besotted with the woman he has just met, the Chevalier declares:

Donna non vidi mai simile a	Never have I seen a woman like
questa! [. . .]	this! [. . .]
Come queste parole profumate	How these fragrant words
mi vagan nello spirito	linger in my spirit
e ascose fibre vanno a carezzare.	and caress hidden chords.

One act later, after having spent some time with his ideal woman, he cries out (in a passage already quoted above), "Mud in mud I am [. . .] / I have defiled myself, sold myself. / The vilest disgrace brings me nearer to you!" The difference between *Edgar* and *Manon Lescaut*, that is to say, entails less a rejection of idealist rhetoric than a shift in its dramatic function. For whether enraptured or disgusted, Des Grieux's speeches—conventional enough on their own terms—now come across as equally deluded. His tragedy resides in his inability to accept that Manon is no operatic archetype but merely what Puccini later claimed she was, "a nice girl with a big heart and nothing more."

If we consider Des Grieux as an idealist—as a relic, you might say, of an earlier scale of operatic value—then the critical stakes of *Manon Lescaut* come more sharply into focus. On the one hand, it presents us with an unprecedentedly ordinary heroine. On the other, it anticipates our recalcitrant frustration, channeling it through a character driven mad by his desire to believe that the world must offer something more. But crucially, before he cracks, Des Grieux expresses exactly the sort of sentiments a traditionally minded audience member would have wanted. Indeed, the ecstatic early reviews of *Manon Lescaut* are full of idealist rhetoric; as a critic for the *Gazzetta musicale di Milano* exclaimed, "A quiver of infinite, intimate emotion ran through my veins."[30] Written after the failure of *Edgar*, and submitted to an audience famously anxious about the future of its most important art form, *Manon Lescaut* allegorizes its own historical position, configuring skepticism—a failure, at root, to accept the everyday on its own terms—as the symptom (pleasurable, like all true symptoms) of realist opera.

From Sickness unto Death

Puccini's next opera would explore similar themes, if even more explicitly. Indeed, *La bohème* might be described as the key document in his emerging aesthetic. Not coincidentally, it is set in 1830s Paris—the heyday and the capital of Romantic idealism, whose tenets guide the lives of the first characters we see onstage. ("Oh, beautiful age of deceits and utopias," is how the painter Marcello will characterize his epoch in Act 2, "One believes, hopes, and all seems beautiful."[31]) After the briefest of orchestral flourishes, the poet Rodolfo is revealed to be hard at work on a historical tragedy; Marcello is busy painting a canvas full of "heroes and memorable figures."[32] They behave, in this scene, like textbook idealists: creating grandiose art that denies—or, more generously, aims to transcend—their immediate reality of starving bodies and cheap, cold rooms. How fitting, then, that when Rodolfo throws his tragedy into the hearth, the resulting fire music sounds quite a bit like Wagner.

Having thus alerted us to the perils of aesthetic idealism—its refusal of the surrounding world, its tendency to descend into self-important melodrama—Puccini introduces a character who represents its opposite: a commitment to shared experience and the poetics of the everyday. The philosophical stakes of the confrontation between Rodolfo and Mimì are presented clearly in the paired arias through which they first introduce themselves to each other. Rodolfo, the romantic egoist, identifies himself not by his name, which he never furnishes, but rather through his exalted profession: "Who am I? Who am I?—I am a poet" ("Chi son? Chi son!—Sono un poeta"). His realist partner, in contrast, imagines a more modest relationship between her sense of self and the needs of the community. Although her name may be Lucia, "They call me Mimì, / I don't know why" ("Mi chiamano Mimì / il perché non so"). Rodolfo, as we have seen, defines poetry as necessarily apart from the world around him. Mimì counters this by offering, in the simplest possible language, an image of art as part of quotidian routine:

A tela o a seta	On canvas or silk,
ricamo in casa e fuori.	I embroider at home or outside.
Son tranquilla e lieta	I'm calm and happy
ed è mio svago	and my pastime
far gigli e rose.	is making lilies and roses.

Unlike Rodolfo, she is painfully aware that art has no power to restore the world to itself, or to transform it:

Così gentil è il profumo d'un fior!	A flower's perfume is so delicate!
Ma i fior ch'io faccio, aihmè [. . .]	But the flowers that I make, alas [. . .]
non hanno odore!	they have no odor!

There are telling musical differences between Rodolfo and Mimì's solos. His is written in what would come to be Puccini's "heroic tenor" style: like Cavaradossi's "E lucevan le stelle" in *Tosca* and Calaf's "Nessun dorma" in *Turandot*, "Che gelida manina" begins with a simple, declamatory section, slowly building to a grandiose climax, doubled in octaves by the full orchestra, as the character's emotions leave the prosaic world behind. (It should be noted, though, that Cavaradossi and Calaf, unlike Rodolfo in his song of himself, are actually concerned with matters of life and death.) In contrast, "Mi chiamano Mimì," set a full tritone apart from Rodolfo's opening key of A-flat major, is a more restrained, and more tonally grounded rondo. Yes, Mimì is allowed a *fortissimo* outpouring of her own at the words "Il primo bacio dell'aprile è mio!," but what seems important is that she immediately retreats from this, concluding her aria, at the words "Altro di me non le saprei narrare," with the plainest unmetered recitative. Her aria ends, in other words, where Rodolfo's began. It sounds like a corrective, an attempt to reverse the poet's flight of fancy and bring it back to earth.

"I am your neighbor," read Mimì's final lines, "who comes at the wrong hour to bother you" ("Sono la sua vicina, / che la vien fuori d'ora a importunare"). This strikingly un-operatic concern with propriety is telling. Indeed, perhaps the greatest contrast between Rodolfo and Mimì obtains in the way these characters address each other. Mimì constantly interrupts herself, asking if she is being understood, worrying that she may have gone on too long. Rodolfo seems oblivious, if not hostile, to the needs of his interlocutor. His aria begins when he takes Mimì by the hand, but if this is meant as an affectionate gesture, it soon overstays its welcome. Some twenty measures later, we encounter the stage direction "Mimì would like to take her hand back." Rodolfo dismisses this with a somewhat imperious "Aspetti signorina," and when, after another fifteen measures, the poet finally does stop to ask if his partner might perhaps want to hear more about him, the libretto instructs "Mimì remains silent. Rodolfo lets go of Mimì's hand, as she draws back, finding a chair on which she places herself, as if dropping overcome by emotion." This is not the behavior of a newly enraptured lover, but rather the gesture of a woman resigned to be the mute audience for an interminable performance.

The gulf of silence that separates Rodolfo from Mimì—a gulf in which Rodolfo alternately figures as actor and spectator, but never as equal partner—will grow wider, and more tragic, as the opera progresses. Instead of talking to his lover, Rodolfo generates ever more paranoid fantasies to explain her utterly ordinary behavior. As Mimì complains to Marcello in Act 3:

Un passo, un detto, un vezzo,	A footstep, a word, a compliment,
un fior lo mettono in sospetto [. . .]	a flower, all arouse his suspicion [. . .]
Talor la notte fingo di dormire	Sometimes at night I pretend to sleep
e in me lo sento fiso,	and feel him staring at my face,
spiarmi i sogni in viso.	spying on my dreams.

Rodolfo's mad, unjustified suspicion of Mimì constitutes *La bohème*'s most significant departure from its literary source. As Carner indelicately puts it, "In Puccini's gentle hands Murger's little gold-digger becomes all sweetness and innocence."[33] It is possible, of course, to attribute this whitewashing of Mimì's character to Puccini's inveterate sentimentality, or to his issues with the mother-image. Alternately, it might be claimed that Puccini's decision to depict his heroine as "a nice girl with a big heart and nothing more" was made to place Rodolfo's attitude to Mimì (like Des Grieux's to Manon) in especially stark relief, to make his paranoia the central problem of the opera. The image of a man spying on a sleeping woman—a woman so close that he could have escaped from his nightmare by merely touching her; a woman who, in his jealous fury, he fails to realize is not even actually asleep—encapsulates Rodolfo's behavior throughout *La bohème*, and it sets the stage for the awful final scene. Mimì dies, silently; Rodolfo, distracted by the light coming in through the window, does not notice.

Such is the fate of all idealists. In Moi's account of Ibsen's aesthetic psychology, the poet's or philosopher's attempt to transcend the everyday inevitably leads to a condition of isolation and radical skepticism, "a loss of faith in language [. . .], which is now experienced as incapable of conveying reliable knowledge about others, as well as of expressing [one's] own feelings and thoughts."[34] The skeptic, in turn, consoles himself by turning the world into his audience.

> Then I will be in your presence, but you will not be in mine.
> [. . .] I will be the star of my performance, and you will be
> in the dark for me; if you are in pain, I will not perceive it.
> (In the theater, we do not expect Othello or Desdemona to
> acknowledge our pain: our task is to acknowledge theirs.)[35]

La bohème, like *Manon Lescaut* and *La Gioconda* before it, concludes with a version of this scene: "As Rodolfo rushes over to Musetta he notices the strange attitude of Marcello and Schaunard, who, filled with dismay, look at him with profound pity." "What does that coming and going mean," he cries, "That looking at me like this?"[36] Rodolfo has finally found the rapt and sympathetic audience he always wanted, and he realizes too late what Des Grieux and Barnaba had also realized, that the true cost of his self-theatricalization is exile from the surrounding world.

From Denial to Acceptance

The conclusion of *La bohème*, like the conclusions of Puccini's other "Big Three" operas, *Tosca* and *Madama Butterfly*, is often described casually as "sadistic." One thing this claim can mean is that these scenes rely for their effects on a situation in which there is a disproportionate gulf between the audience's understanding of the events onstage and the characters' own self-awareness. Rodolfo does not know that Mimì has died; Tosca does not realize that Cavaradossi's "fake" execution—unfolding before her very eyes!—is real; Cio-Cio-san spends the whole of *Madama Butterfly* believing that her marriage to Pinkerton is something other than a sham. Tosca and Butterfly's self-theatricalizing fantasies prove even more destructive than Rodolfo's did, and yet there is nothing pleasurable about our knowledge of their folly: it would seem to engender feelings of helplessness more obviously than those of power.

Alternately, it might be claimed that the intolerable distance Puccini creates between his audience and his protagonists allows us to experience, affectively, the distance that a character like Rodolfo himself feels from those around him. We, as much as Marcello and Schaunard, "look at him with profound pity," and Rodolfo's isolation is thus doubled, as he is cast out both from the fictional world and from our own. Significantly, both *Tosca* and *Madama Butterfly* conclude with similar scenes of helpless looking. After the famous suicide that ends the former work, "Sciarrone and some soldiers, who have come up in confusion, run to the parapet and look down. Spoletta remains terrified, aghast." And, after the famous suicide that ends the latter, "Pinkerton and Sharpless rush into the room, running to Butterfly, who with a weak gesture points to the child and dies. Pinkerton kneels, as Sharpless picks up the child and kisses him, sobbing." It is a curious feature of Puccini's heroines that they always kill themselves in the presence of other people.

The two possible attitudes toward Puccini's denouements that I am trying to describe—voyeuristic pleasure and a shared experience of separation—are, for Cavell, the central options given any spectator in the theater. "Why do I do nothing when faced with tragic events?" he asks.

> If I do nothing because I am distracted by the pleasures of witnessing this folly, or out of my knowledge of the proprieties of the place I am in, or because I think there will be some more appropriate time in which to act, or because I feel helpless to un-do events of such proportion, then I

continue my sponsorship of evil in the world, its sway waiting upon these forms of inaction. I exit running. But if I do
nothing because there is nothing to do, where that means
that I have given over the time and space in which action is
mine and consequently that I am in awe before the fact that
I cannot do and suffer what it is another's to do and suffer,
then I confirm the final fact of our separateness. And that is
the unity of our condition.[37]

Puccini's operas restate this dilemma with almost unbearable intensity.
At the same time, it seems worth noting that, after his experiments with
Des Grieux and Rodolfo, Puccini never again used male characters to
stage his philosophical concerns. The discomforting spectacle of male,
skeptical hysteria—the lesson that Puccini learned from *La Gioconda* and
expanded to such unforeseeable dimensions—largely vanishes after *La
bohème*. Tosca and Cio-Cio-san function, perhaps too easily, as the objects
of our voyeuristic gaze, and they are not counterposed with figures who,
like Mimì, offer a compelling alternative to their delusions. Scarpia and
Pinkerton are realists, of a sort, but their pragmatism is merely transactional. There was to be no *Doll's House*, no *King Lear*.

NOTES

1. The phrase *Wirkung ohne Ursache* (effects without causes) derives, of course, from Richard Wagner's polemics against Meyerbeer. See *Opera and Drama*, trans. W. Ashton Ellis (Lincoln: University of Nebraska Press, 1995), 95.

2. For a more extended discussion of the thematics of vocal production in *La Gioconda*, see the chapter "Boito's Materials" in my *Puccini's Soundscapes: Realism and Modernity in Italian Opera* (Florence, IT: Leo S. Olschki, 2016).

3. Julian Budden, "Gioconda, La," *The New Grove Dictionary of Opera*, Grove/Oxford Music Online (Oxford University Press), http://www.oxfordmusiconline.com/subscriber/article/grove/music/O004514.

4. There may also be a significantly more esoteric Verdian reference at work here. The form of Boito's stanzas throughout the *scena ultima* (three eleven-syllable lines followed by one five-syllable line) recalls the famous "Sapphic stanza." Boito had written a similarly structured poem before, the *ode saffica* "All'arte italiana" (1863), whose description of the altar of Italian art "*bruttato come un muro / Di lupanare*" (sullied like a brothel's wall) famously enraged Verdi, and led to a nearly twenty-year rift between the two men. If, as Budden suggests, Ponchielli responded to Boito's verses with a calculated imitation of *La traviata* (itself, of course, a work about a prostitute), the allusion to Boito's earlier ode seems far from accidental.

5. Due to a rare ambiguity in Italian, the phrase can be understood as a conjugation of either the verb *udire* (to hear) or *odiare* (to hate). Given the centrality of hearing to *La Gioconda*'s final scene, *udire* would seem to be the more obvious option.

6. Budden, "Gioconda, La."

7. Alessandra Campana, *Opera and Modern Spectatorship in Late Nineteenth-Century Italy* (Cambridge: Cambridge University Press, 2015), 154.

8. Ibid., 169.

9. Ibid., 170.

10. Stanley Cavell, "The Avoidance of Love: A Reading of *King Lear*," in *Must We Mean What We Say?*, rev. ed. (Cambridge: Cambridge University Press, 2002), 333–34.

11. Ibid., 323. Original emphasis.

12. For one important, albeit very different, attempt to place the history of opera in dialogue with the history of modern subjectivity, see Gary Tomlinson, *Metaphysical Song: An Essay on Opera* (Princeton: Princeton University Press, 1999).

13. Toril Moi, *Henrik Ibsen and the Birth of Modernism: Art, Theater, Philosophy* (Oxford: Oxford University Press, 2006), 1.

14. Ibid., 72 and 70.

15. Ibid., 67.

16. Ibid., 89.

17. Ibid., 215.

18. See Adrian Daub, *Tristan's Shadow: Sexuality and the Total Work of Art after Wagner* (Chicago: University of Chicago Press, 2013).

19. For an interpretation of *verismo* in these terms, see my "Rough Music: *Tosca* and *Verismo* Reconsidered," *19th-Century Music* 31/3 (2009): 228–44.

20. See Schwartz, *Puccini's Soundscapes*.

21. Quoted in Arthur Groos and Roger Parker, *Giacomo Puccini: La bohème* (Cambridge: Cambridge University Press, 1986), 137.

22. Quoted in ibid.

23. Ben Earle, *Luigi Dallapiccola and Musical Modernism in Fascist Italy* (Cambridge: Cambridge University Press, 2013), 42.

24. Mosco Carner, *Puccini: A Critical Biography* (New York: Knopf, 1959), 255 and 256.

25. Ibid., 256.

26. Ibid., 257.

27. Ibid., 258.

28. Ibid.

29. The composer Ildebrando Pizzetti quoted these lines at the start of an important essay on Puccini, attributing them to an interview with an unspecified journalist "some years ago." Although Puccini's remarks, and especially the phrase "cose piccole," have entered the critical literature as one of the best descriptions of his aesthetic, the possibility that they were invented by Pizzetti himself should not be discounted. See Ildebrando Pizzetti, *Musicisti contemporanei: Saggi critici* (Milan: Treves, 1914), 51.

30. Quoted in Alexandra Wilson, "Defining Italianness: The Opera that Made Puccini," *Opera Quarterly* 24/1–2 (2008): 87.

31. "O bella età d'inganni e d'utopie! / si crede, spera, e tutto bello appare." Marcello's lines, with their somewhat ambiguous use of the word *età*, have also been interpreted as referring to youth more generically. However, *La bohème* as a whole seems clearly to conflate the eternal delusions of young love with those of the specific social and philosophical world it depicts. See Michele Girardi, *Puccini: His International Art*, trans. Laura Basini (Chicago: University of Chicago Press, 2000), 127.

32. From here through the end of the next paragraph, I hew closely to my interpretation of this scene, first presented in the context of my review of the DVD of Stefan Herheim's 2012 production of *La bohème* in "The Eye of a Poet," *Opera Quarterly* 29/2 (2013): 163–64. Herheim's extraordinary staging, for the Norwegian National Opera, seems invested in many of the same issues that interest me in Puccini's opera.

33. Carner, *Puccini*, 317.

34. Moi, *Ibsen*, 212.

35. Ibid., 213.

36. "Che vuol dire quell'andare e venire [. . .] / quel guardarmi così . . . ?"

37. Cavell, "The Avoidance of Love," 339.

Madama Butterfly Between East and West

ARTHUR GROOS

Puccini discovered John Luther Long's and David Belasco's one-act play *Madame Butterfly* on 21 June 1900 at the Duke of York's Theatre in London, where he was helping prepare the first *Tosca* at Covent Garden.[1] Although he later said that the effect was like pouring gasoline on an open fire,[2] work on a libretto could not begin immediately because Belasco's demands for rights to the play stalled negotiations for nearly a year.[3] But well before an agreement was reached, Puccini and librettist Luigi Illica began pursuing other options based on Long's original story, "Madame Butterfly" (1898). As early as 20 November 1900, Puccini wrote to his publisher Giulio Ricordi, noting that he was thinking of using Long's story to expand the focus of the opera to two acts, one set in North America and one in Japan:

> Ah! If only I had Butterfly here with me to work on! I think that instead of one act one could make two very long acts out of it, the first in North America and the second in Japan. Illica could certainly find what is needed in the story.[4]

This letter reveals two things about the opera's genesis. The first is that Puccini had not read Long's story, which is set entirely in Japan; a translation described as "so-so" was not available until early March 1901.[5] The second is that he originally conceived the opera in terms of contrasting American and Japanese locations, emphasizing an underlying dramatic conflict between West and East. Given the importance of local color for Puccini's compositional technique, the attraction of this opposition lay at least partly in terms of contrasting musical ambiences.

At the same time, however, this organizing principle—suggested by neither the story nor the play—relates the inception of opera to the widespread fin-de-siècle discourse of Orientalism, whose tendency to divide the world between the West and an Eastern Other reflects part of a larger process by which European colonial powers defined and imagined distant portions of the globe.[6] Orientalizing thought operates both as a binary opposition and as a means of hierarchical subordination, positing not only difference but also inequality between West and East, "white" and "yellow" or "black" races, "civilized" and "primitive" societies, male and female, etc. Moreover, the relationship of the European subject to the Oriental Other is complex, involving both attraction and aversion to difference, fuelled in representations of male-female relationships by fantasies of desire as well as by fears of racial miscegenation and degeneration. Orientalism's binarisms also appear in colonizing agendas that proceed with the "westernization" of other cultures for the purpose of "civilizing" them, only to discover that "inferior" cultures or races are incapable of internalizing and mastering the demands of "civilization," thus confirming the original need for colonization.

Of course, few orientalizing works that have retained their popular appeal are as reductive or blatant as this summary might suggest. Although the colonialist discourse that dominated much of the European conception of Japan at the fin de siècle may seem to have little in common with *Madama Butterfly*, it is important to note that, immediately after the original plan to structure the opera in terms of a West-East binary opposition, Puccini's discussions with Illica reveal a fascination with processes of degeneration caused by the intermingling and partial assimilation of different cultures and races. Directing his librettist's attention to Belasco's still unavailable "comedy,"[7] he emphasized the potential of Yamadori's "debauched" westernization for their representation of East-West relations:

> But I maintain that it's necessary to have a copy of the comedy, where there are things that will go very well, for example the Japanese lord who tempts Cio-Cio-san has changed into a debauched American millionaire. This change is entirely to the advantage of the so-called European element that we need.[8]

To be sure, the finished opera does not have the prominent West-East act structure originally proposed by Puccini, and the Italian perspective of its librettists and composer distances them from the American representatives of the West almost as much as from the Japanese East. But Illica, not having the material for an independent act set in North America, achieved his goal in a less obvious way: he drafted a first-act "prologue" set in Japan, extrapolating Pinkerton's rental of the house on Nagasaki's

Higashi Hill and his "temporary" marriage to Cio-Cio-san from sections 2 and 3 of Long's story, and created a contrasting sequence of scenes, introducing the Americans, then the Japanese in a series of entrances before ending the act with a duet for the American hero and Japanese heroine. Shortly thereafter, he sketched a second act with similarly contrasting scenes, the middle one located at the American Consulate in the section of Nagasaki set aside for European residents, drawing attention to its potential for staging Butterfly's inability to deal with Western culture:

> And I should mention something that seems extremely good about the second act, namely, that the Consul lives in a European villa in the area called the "European concession." Thus the three scenes of the second part will acquire greater variety: 1) *Butterfly's cottage*— 2) *The Consul's villa*— 3) *Butterfly's cottage*. Note that one can take advantage of the villa furnished in European style for some little details to embarrass Butterfly, etc., etc.[9]

We will return to the "little details to embarrass Butterfly"—not limited to the subsequently deleted Consulate scene, they pervade the heroine's interactions with the West, revealing her difficulty in assimilating Western culture.

This form of the libretto continued to dominate the team's attention well into the composition of the opera, until Puccini suddenly decided to delete the Consulate scene, notifying Illica on 16 November 1902 that "the opera ought to be in two acts: your Act 1 and the other Belasco's drama with all its particulars."[10] In reducing the opera to a version approximating the one we know today, Puccini nonetheless retained the contrast between Western and Eastern cultures in Illica's "prologue," leaving the second part, based on the play, to begin with the heroine's struggle to assert her identity as "Mrs. B. F. Pinkerton," a failure made clear even without the "details to embarrass Butterfly" from the Consulate scene. The following interpretation will suggest how *Madama Butterfly*'s orientalizing "comedy" of Cio-Cio-san's failed acculturation coexists with conventional expectations for a "tragic" heroine in Italian opera.[11]

I

Although the introductory stage direction emphasizes a Japanese setting,[12] the musical action opens with a typically Western musical form, a fugato, sometimes thought of as an introduction to the busy, diminutive world of the Japanese.[13] Inasmuch as this introduction is soon enriched by an orientalizing motive variously associated with the movable Japanese house and Nagasaki (rehearsal numbers 7 + 2 mm. and 18 + 5 mm.), the fugato pattern also seems a reminder of the underlying Western stance of the score and the fact that the busy activity anticipates what Sharpless calls Pinkerton's "pseudo sposalizio" (pseudo-wedding).[14] The Japanese setting—the house, servants, Goro, and ultimately the wedding party—are there at his behest, helping orchestrate the latest "cosmopolitan" adventure the "Yankee vagabond" defines in his opening aria.

From the outset, Pinkerton's responses to his surroundings are divided between his repugnance toward the Japanese in general and his animal attraction to Butterfly in particular. His response to the servants, deleted after the La Scala premiere (1904), disparagingly reduces them to physiognomic uniformity as *musi* (mugs), while the new in-laws at the wedding feast seem so alien that he mockingly orders appropriate refreshments:

Qua i tre musi. Servite	Call the three mugs. Serve
ragni e mosche candite.	spiders and candied flies.
Nidi al giulebbe e quale	Julep nests and whatever
è licor più indigesto	is the most indigestible liqueur
e più nauseabonda leccornìa	and most nauseating delicacy
della Nipponerìa.[15]	of Nipponry.

Even in the revised and more restrained Paris version of 1906 (the basis for most productions today), Pinkerton considers the Japanese a primitive, even animal race, referring to Butterfly's family as her "tribe" and their ostracism as "gracchiar di ranocchi" (the croaking of frogs).[16]

Pinkerton's fascination with Butterfly within this general racial prejudice emerges as a particular corollary of his colonialist credo in the aria "Dovunque al mondo" and the immediately ensuing "Amore o grillo." The first part, a jaunty Allegro sostenuto con spirito, is framed by a nationalizing citation of "The Star-Spangled Banner" set for a combination of winds and brass reminiscent of a military band. Although not officially recognized as the national anthem until 1931, it was played as an "unofficial" one by military bands on ceremonial occasions from the 1890s on. In this particular instance, it accompanies a transposition of American gunboat diplomacy into the private sphere, presenting a "Yankee vagabond's" credo of reckless adventurism, its rocking 3/4 meter and melody in G-flat major—identified in sketches as a "Boston waltz"[17]—underpinning his pursuit of pleasure throughout the world. Sharing his thoughts "frankly" in informal conversation, Pinkerton even interrupts the reprise of the opening phrase to ask Sharpless his choice of drink, then begins again, following the thrill-seeking metaphor of the sea voyage to its stormy conclusion:

Dovunque al mondo il yankee vagabondo
   si gode e traffica
   sprezzando i rischi.
	Throughout the world the Yankee vagabond
	   enjoys himself and trades,
	   scorning the risks.

Affonda l'àncora alla ventura
   finché una raffica ...
(Pinkerton s'interrompe per
   offrire da bere a Sharpless)
Milk-Punch, o Wiskey? (riprende)
... scompigli nave, ormeggi,
   alberatura.
	He drops anchor randomly
	   until a squall . . .
	(*Pinkerton interrupts himself to offer
	   Sharpless a drink*)
	Milk-punch, or whiskey? (*resumes*)
	 . . . upsets ship, mooring, masts.

and finally reveals a motivation that is disturbingly global ("every region," etc.) for a wedding day:

La vita ei non appaga *se non fa suo tesor* *i fiori d'ogni plaga,* *d'ogni bella gli amor.*	Life isn't satisfying if he doesn't make his treasure the flowers of every region, the love of every beauty.

Ignoring the Consul's objections, Pinkerton continues with another reprise of the initial melodic phrase, placing his faith in a talent to succeed "in every place" before switching disjunctively from the third to first person, clarifying the relationship between the vagabond's search for pleasure and his own behavior in Japan with a shift to jaunty patter about his own desires, unabashedly displacing his deception of Butterfly to the "Japanese custom" of temporary marriage:

Così mi sposo all'uso	So I'm marrying in the Japanese
giapponese	custom
per novecento	for nine hundred
novantanove	ninety-nine
anni. Salvo a prosciogliermi ogni	years, free to release myself every
mese.[18]	month.

Only now do his discussion with Goro about the mobility of the house as well as the comment to Sharpless about the elasticity of Japanese houses and contracts become clear: the house is also a metonymy for its future mistress, the escape clause from the rent an escape from a temporary marriage that is also terminable by the month. When Sharpless again objects, Pinkerton takes refuge in patriotism, forcing the discussion to a close by appropriating the "Star-Spangled Banner" for a toast: "America forever!"

When Sharpless inquires about the precise nature of Pinkerton's involvement with Butterfly, the lieutenant refuses to specify whether his fancy is "love or whim" or whether he considers her a "woman or trinket," shifting responsibility instead to the character traits that have ensnared him. Composed as a delicate Allegretto moderato in B-flat, the piece begins with an accompaniment that shadows the hero's melody, leaving it without any sense of emotional depth:

Amore o grillo – [donna o	Love or whim—[woman or
gingillo]	trinket,]
dir non saprei. – Certo colei	I couldn't say. Certainly she
m'ha colle ingenue – arti invescato.[19]	has ensnared me with her
	ingenuous wiles.

The ensuing description of the heroine as delicate as "blown glass" and resembling a "figure from a screen" are conventional figures of Orientalism, reflecting the fact that the Western image of Japan and the Japanese was largely derived from imported artifacts—prints, bronzes, ceramics, fans, screens, and lacquerware.[20] With the image of the butterfly Pinkerton's description begins to reveal the obsessive and potentially destructive nature of his desire:

Ma dal suo lucido – fondo di	But from her bright lacquer
lacca	background
come con subito – moto si	how, with a sudden movement,
stacca,	she detaches herself;

qual farfalletta – svolazza
   e posa
	like a little butterfly she flutters and
	   lands

con tal grazietta – silenzïosa	with such silent gracefulness
che di rincorrerla – furor m'assale	that a frenzy to chase her assails me,
se pure infrangerne – dovessi l'ale.	even if I should break her wings.

It proceeds from a static accompaniment to the extended flight of an ani-mate being, expressed by a rising and falling melodic line with contrary pizzicato motion in the bass, in which the sudden intrusion of verbs of motion and then violence, to increased dynamic emphasis, indicate the hero's obsessive pursuit of his quarry (Example 1). The conflation of the proper name Butterfly and the insect order Lepidoptera, which enables the hero to think of the heroine in terms less than human, will have ram-ifications throughout the opera.

Sharpless again opposes this reckless hedonism, citing his impres-sion of the heroine's visit to the Consulate two days before. Countering Pinkerton's insect simile with a warning not to break her wings, he draws attention to Butterfly's voice, a fetishizing gesture in any opera, and one that pointedly ignores visual signifiers (and racial otherness) in favor of a vocal one (and interiority):

Ier l'altro, il Consolato *sen' venne a visitar!*	The day before yesterday she came to visit the Consulate!

Io non la vidi, ma l'udii
   parlar.
	I didn't see her, but I heard her
	   speak.

Di sua voce il mistero *l'anima mi colpì.*	The mystery of her voice struck my soul.
Certo quando è sincero *l'amor parla così.*	Surely when it's sincere love speaks this way.

Pinkerton's "Amore o grillo" and Sharpless's response delineate for the first time a discursive space in which conflicting assessments of the hero-ine compete, viewing her as either Japanese and alien or almost Western. For Pinkerton, the visible character-Butterfly is ethnically and racially Other, allowing him to equate her conceptually with an insect and affec-tively with an object. For Sharpless, the audible voice-Butterfly bespeaks the interiority of a loving and trusting heart, which deeply moves him while also exuding a mystery. The conflict fades, unresolved, into the boozy prenuptial conversation.

Example 1. *Madama Butterfly*, Act 1, "Che di rincorrerla furor m'assale."

II

The opening of Act 1 presents a particularized "American" ambience and the agenda of Pinkerton's sexual adventurism, gesturing toward a traditional double aria while preparing for the entrance of the heroine. In contrast, the ensuing action devoted to the Japanese is both more distended and more variegated. There are, in fact, three different entrances of Japanese characters: Butterfly and her friends; the Imperial Commissioner, registry official, and relatives; and finally the Bonze. Since Butterfly's entrance will be complex and ambiguous, as the argument between Pinkerton and Sharpless suggests, it may be helpful to discuss the latter two before returning to Cio-Cio-san.

These other entrances introduce representatives of the Japanese sociopolitical and religious order, respectively, the former bringing comic confusion to the action, the latter overt hostility. The arrival of the Imperial Commissioner to strains of "Kimigayo," the Japanese national anthem (rehearsal number 59 + 1 measure) also brings a chorus of Butterfly's relatives, who comment excitedly and at comic length on the arranged marriage and the couple's future prospects, and have to be brought to order, first by Goro and then by the heroine. Immediately after the wedding, as Pinkerton attempts to take advantage of Yakusidé's dipsomania by plying him with drink, the "strange cries" of the Bonze from offstage, obsessively repeating "Cio-Cio-san" to the rumble of the low tamtam, interrupt the beginnings of a happy drinking song, "O Kami! O Kami!," progressively isolating the heroine from her friends and relatives (rehearsal number 100 + 2 mm.). His interrogation of her visit to the American Consulate culminates in an imprecation, followed by a group ostracism, its alien hostility emphasized by the exclamation "Hou!"—notated like *Sprechstimme* by rhythm and relative pitch without note heads—and by the group's fetishizing of her name to an orchestral *fortissimo* punctuated by the "oriental" battery of the low tamtam, bass drum, and cymbals. This ritualized ostracism returns nine times, diminishing only as the group fades offstage into the distance. In spite of the facade of westernization suggested by the national anthem, bureaucratic officials, and Goro's clothes, the Japanese here seem collectively closer to the primitive "tribe" that Pinkerton immediately accuses them of being.

The "Japanese" entrance for Butterfly and her girlfriends, however, contrasts sharply with this male-directed hostility, presenting a pervasive atmosphere of sexual allure. The importance of this entrance required a greater variety of musical material and a more extended scene than

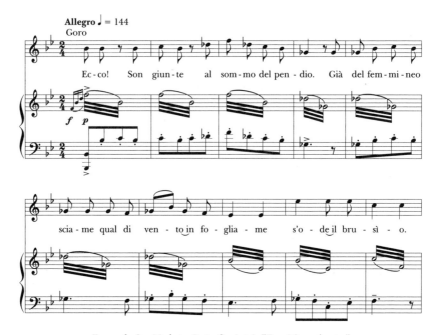

Example 2a. *Madama Butterfly*, Act 1, "Ecco! Son giunte."

for Puccini's earlier heroines such as Mimì or Tosca, who also enter the action as offstage voices.[21] Cio-Cio-san enters to three distinct types of music, first introducing her as a Japanese woman, then as an effusive young bride, and finally as a particular individual.

This multiple entrance also forms an increasing audiovisual concentration on the heroine that proceeds from Goro's announcement of an approaching group of women, to the sound of her voice heard in dialogue with her friends, and finally to her arrival in the foreground as the center of attention. The sequence begins with a mordant contrast to the Western male focus of the preceding scene. As Pinkerton closes the conversation with Sharpless with a toast to a future "vere nozze" (real wedding) with "una vera sposa americana" (a real American wife), the music shifts abruptly as Goro excitedly announces the arrival of a "feminine swarm" to the melody of "Echigo jishi," one of the most famous pieces of the koto repertory (Example 2a).[22] It is played by staccato violas, cellos, and bassoons in unison, gesturing toward the plucked strings of the koto and the Kabuki accompaniment of shamisen and flute that Puccini had heard when he saw Japanese actress Sadayacco perform the piece in Milan in late April 1902.[23]

Example 2b. *Madama Butterfly*, Act 1, "Siam giunte."

Sharpless has already individualized Butterfly in terms of her voice, and the second part of her entrance accordingly focuses on her offstage song as a living and breathing part of the ambience she celebrates. The ravishing melody that accompanies this evocation of landscape and love, "Spira sul mare," will return at the conclusion of the Act 1 duet, subsuming the lovers' differences in the enveloping starry night (rehearsal nos. 39–41 and 134–36), and it continues as the heroine and her friends become visible upstage. Finally, as they arrive downstage and Butterfly cadences with her friends to an evocation of the "richiamo d'amor" (call of love), winds, bells, and harp introduce the heroine herself with a third melody (Example 2b). Often thought to have been provided to Puccini by a French source in 1902,[24] it was recently identified as the Chinese melody "Shiba mo," apparently taken from a Chinese music box produced for export that also contains the motive of the father's suicide, "Bangzi" / "Loc Tee Kun Tzin," and melodies later employed in *Turandot*.[25]

This threefold introduction of Butterfly in generic terms as Japanese, then as an offstage voice, and finally as a visible figure with an individual melody does not, however, lead directly to an introductory aria. Instead, it is followed by a discussion defining her in terms of Western male interest, first through a series of answers to Sharpless's questions, then—after the arrival of the Imperial Commissioner and her relatives—through a more personal conversation with Pinkerton. These exchanges confirm the relative bias between West and East in the representation of the hero and heroine: whereas Pinkerton can express himself in his breezy American aria, Butterfly is limited to defining herself in response to the Consul's questions and then in terms of her putative husband-to-be's preferences and expectations.

At the same time, this limitation is also represented as imposed from within by a Japanese emphasis on group identity. After Sharpless comments on her name to a reprise of "Shiba mo," the heroine's third and "individual" entrance melody (rehearsal number 43 + 4 mm.), his inquiry turns to family origins and Nagasaki. Since Cio-Cio-san's response is entirely in terms of group identity, without a first-person pronoun or verb—"Signor sì. Di famiglia assai prospera un tempo" (Yes, sir. From a once prosperous family)—the melody to which she recites her family history reinforces its generically Japanese nature: "Echigo jishi," used moments previously for Goro's announcement of Butterfly and her friends. But as the Consul continues, another "oriental" melody emerges, this one of far greater significance for Butterfly, even though it is not hers. When Sharpless inquires about her father, the most important family member of all, the shocked Butterfly answers, "Dead!"—and there is an embarrassed silence while the orchestra moves softly through several bars of oriental-sounding music before ending in a fermata (Example 3). This melody, recently identified as the Chinese "Bangzi" (previously associated incorrectly with the koto piece "Ume no haru"),[26] has a significance of singular importance, involving Butterfly's father and ultimately the power of patriarchy and religion in her destiny.

Sharpless eventually focuses on the heroine herself with a question about age. While Cio-Cio-san turns the answer into a guessing game "con civetteria quasi infantile" (with almost infantile coquettishness), the questions and responses narrow to her actual age, which is followed by a rapid staccato passage for oboe and then oboe and flute reminiscent of childish giggling (rehearsal number 55 +1 measure). Sharpless and Pinkerton exclaim "Fifteen!," each drawing a different conclusion, the Consul emphasizing Butterfly's childishness and the hero eagerly asserting her maturity, foregrounding another ambiguity about her character that is again interrupted, this time by the entrance of the wedding party.

Example 3. *Madama Butterfly*, Act 1, "E vostro padre?"

Puccini soon directs attention to the heroine in a conversation with Pinkerton, who narrows the discussion to the private sphere. Setting the agenda with "Amor mio!" (My love!), which he sings to the entrance melody with which the heroine celebrated the "richiamo d'amor" (call of love), the request reveals his underlying sexual eagerness. As she will do in the duet, the heroine does not respond directly to this overt invitation: accompanied by a 2/4 staccato "Japanese" pattern in rising and falling octaves, Cio-Cio-san instead requests permission to keep a few possessions from her past life. Pinkerton's questions about these objects eventually broach a far more serious subject: a long narrow box, which she gravely characterizes as "cosa sacra e mia" (something sacred and mine), refusing to show it while "Bangzi" returns in a staccato octave harmony marked *misterioso*, swelling suddenly to *fortissimo* and diminishing just as suddenly as Goro whispers:

È un presente	It's a present
del Mikado a suo padre …	from the Mikado to her father . . .
coll'invito …	with an invitation . . .
(fa il gesto di chi s'apre il	(*makes a gesture of someone*
ventre)	*slitting open his stomach*)

The accompaniment then subsides for the last group of items among Butterfly's collection of objects: the *ottokè* or "statuettes" of her ancestors. This graduated progression from items of personal use to mementos of the dominant cultural forces in her life, patriarchy and religion, grounds the heroine's character in her ethnicity.

At the same time, it also suggests the enormity of the change involved in her intended transformation from Madama Butterfly to Mrs. B. F. Pinkerton. As the last item in this progression, religion represents a major difference between West and East, and it therefore becomes the point of departure for Butterfly's imagined construction of a "new life" in the arioso "Io seguo il mio destino." The heroine's revelation of her visit to the mission the previous day narrates her desire to convert, which is intended as a personal turn from "my people" to Lieutenant Pinkerton, from Japanese child-bride to Western wife. The product of extensive revision throughout the early production history of the opera,[27] this confession of her desire to construct a Western identity culminates in her first approach to an aria:

Io seguo il mio destino	I follow my destiny,
e piena d'umiltà,	and full of humility,
al Dio del signor Pinkerton	I bow to the god of Mr.
m'inchino.	Pinkerton.
È mio destino.	It is my destiny.
Nella stessa chiesetta	In the same church
in ginocchio con voi	on my knees with you
pregherò lo stesso Dio.	I will pray to the same God.
E per farvi contento	And to make you happy,
potrò forse obliar la gente	I will perhaps be able to forget
mia.	my people.
(si getta nelle braccia di	(*throws herself into the arms of*
Pinkerton)	*Pinkerton*)
Amore mio!	My love!

Puccini's setting begins in A major, drawing attention to the proposed identity formation by using "Shiba mo," the individual melody associated previously with Butterfly's entrance and Sharpless's comment on her name, suggesting the emotion behind its unexpected outburst of subjectivity with rapid arpeggiations and a string accompaniment marked *dolcissimo*. As Butterfly finally answers Pinkerton's "Amor mio!" by throwing herself into his arms with the response "Amore mio!," the music slips into A minor and the melody of "Bangzi" bursts forth *fortissimo*, making

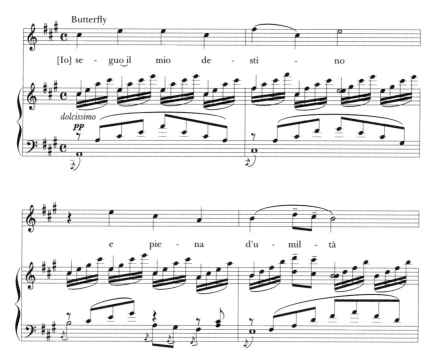

Example 4a. *Madama Butterfly*, Act 1, "Io seguo il mio destino."

the heroine suddenly pause "come avesse paura d'essere stata udita dai parenti" (as if she were afraid of having been heard by her relatives) (see Examples 4a and 4b).[28]

Butterfly's would-be aria about her desired identity as an American wife and its interruption by "Bangzi" vividly illustrate the opera's implicit conflict between West and East, and also suggest that this conflict is being fought within Cio-Cio-san herself. Already presented twice and associated with mysterious power, "Bangzi" also has a more particularized function here, suggesting that the heroine's essential "nature" as a Japanese woman, dominated by the forces of patriarchy and religion, interferes with—indeed, prevents—her desired identity as an American wife. In spite of the intense desire to cast off her "native" ethnicity and construct a new existence as Mrs. B. F. Pinkerton, Butterfly seems destined to remain inescapably her father's daughter, inescapably Japanese.

Of course, Cio-Cio-san's desire is both tragic and ironic, since it is based on Pinkerton's deception, and in fact the music does not support her assumption that the "pseudo-wedding" effects the desired change of

Example 4b. *Madama Butterfly*, Act 1, "Amore mio!"

identity. Immediately after the ceremony, she corrects the girlfriends' congratulatory "Madama Butterfly" to "Madama B. F. Pinkerton," drawing attention to her putative new status. The orchestra, however, prefaces the girlfriends' felicitation with a Japanese melody, "O Edo Nihon bashi," then undercuts the heroine's insistence on her new identity by repeating the same melody, implying that the ceremony has not changed anything at all (rehearsal number 86 + 6 mm.).

Cio-Cio-san's entrance(s), her attempted self-fashioning in "Io seguo il mio destino," and her "wedding reception" raise important problems of characterization beyond this dramatic irony. Even if we discount Pinkerton's deception, the opera does not suggest much latitude for realizing the heroine's desires, which seem limited at best. We might illustrate this with two vivid images associated with the names Butterfly/Cio-Cio-san ("Chô" means "Butterfly" in Japanese), each of which clearly refers to the heroine's unhappy destiny. In the first, where "butterfly" is clearly a metonymy for Cio-Cio-san, the heroine anxiously interrupts the Act 1 love duet, responding to Pinkerton's exclamation of her name by asking whether across the ocean every butterfly that falls into the hands of men is "transfixed by a pin and mounted on a board" ("da uno spillo è trafitta

/ ed in tavola infitta"). In the second, which introduces the suicide scene at the end of the opera, Butterfly's servant Suzuki rushes in to revive the heroine, commenting that the wings of her little heart are beating "come una mosca prigioniera" (like an imprisoned fly).

The image of a transfixed butterfly on a mounting board suggests Cio-Cio-san as a passive victim of a foreign agency that destroys an entire order of things: "*every* butterfly." It derives from Illica's initial draft of the libretto,[29] and articulates his simultaneously orientalizing and anti-colonial conception of the plot in terms of the unequal power relationship between East and West. The simile of the imprisoned fly, in contrast, unappealing as the demotion from Lepidoptera to household pest may seem, none-theless grants the insect a modicum of agency even though it cannot escape. It derives from the other librettist Giuseppe Giacosa's revision, with its conceptual shift away from conflicting historical forces to charac-ter drama and the poet's own specialty in domestic tragedy.

The implications of such multivalent images for the opera as a whole are far-reaching. If we based an interpretation on the "transfixed but-terfly," the opera might be an exotic melodrama about the victimization of the heroine, but if we focused on the "imprisoned fly," *Madama Butterfly* might concede tragic stature to her struggle. This double voic-ing of the libretto is partly a result of the different conceptualizations by Illica and Giacosa, and partly a result of genre expectations inherent in Italian opera. As we saw above, Illica had no difficultly formulating a draft libretto that foregrounded "little details to embarrass Butterfly," representing her inability to construct a "Western" identity as part of a larger tragi-comedy of sexual colonialism. But Giacosa had the addi-tional responsibility for versifying the principal musical "numbers" after Pinkerton's and Butterfly's initial arias, rewriting the love duet and her aria "Un bel dì" as well as creating another aria for her, "Che tua madre," and the suicide scene. Inasmuch as such numbers traditionally consti-tuted the emotional high points of an opera, they presupposed emotional depth, that is, a Western idea of character, which Illica's conception had largely denied to Cio-Cio-san. In short: Illica's drama demanded limita-tions on Butterfly's character as Japanese and a victim, while Giacosa's musical highpoints required tragic stature and therefore something approaching Western interiority.

It is a testimony to the strength of the team's collaboration that Illica, Giacosa, and Puccini turned this contradiction to their advantage, creat-ing a complexity of character unmatched in fin-de-siècle Italian opera. This complexity also helps explain why the heroine has a variety of melodies associated with her during the extended entrance in Act 1. The offstage melodies of "Echigo jishi" and "Spira sul mare" present a Cio-Cio-san who is Japanese as well as young and infatuated, as someone with an alien group identity *and* interiority. The latter quality makes her seem almost Western—hence Puccini's reference to her entrance as "un po' italiana" (a bit Italian)[30] or the audience's objections to it at the La Scala premiere as too similar to Mimì's entrance.[31] Similarly, the third motive foregrounded at the conclusion of Cio-Cio-san's entrance and associated with her name is also ambivalent. Derived from the Chinese melody "Shiba mo" and orientalized as she genuflects before Pinkerton, it returns with prominent arpeggiation in "Io seguo il mio destino," invested with an interior emotional depth appropriate to a Western bride, only to be cut short by the motive of her father's suicide, proleptically looking ahead to her own death. Cio-Cio-san exists in a no-man's-land, an inter-national space: essentialized as Japanese, but ostracized by her friends and relatives; desiring to construct an American identity as the putative Mrs. B. F. Pinkerton, but incapable of attaining that illusory goal.

To this we should add an important but often ignored facet of Cio-Cio-san's character: she has been trained as a geisha (however improbably for a fifteen-year-old), and is adept at pleasing men through her conversation as well as through song and dance. This makes her actions susceptible to interpretations ranging from the involuntary to the carefully staged, a spectrum that frames the beginning and conclusion of her entrance. Goro introduces the approaching group of Butterfly and friends as a "feminine swarm"; once on stage, however, she choreographs her friends' motions so that they all genuflect to the same beat,[32] then begins her geisha shtick with a "molto raro complimento" (very rare compliment) directed at Pinkerton, hinting at further conversational ploys: "Dei più belli / ancor ne so" (I know even better ones). The potential for performativity adds complexity to her behavior: it may not always be clear whether she is essentially immature/childish/"primitive"/Japanese, or is acting this way for an interlocutor, especially when he is male, and above all when the male is Pinkerton. As we will see, in Acts 2 and 3 she makes her strongest argument against her destiny through performing first Pinkerton's imagined return for Suzuki in her aria "Un bel dì," and then a dialogue between a husband and a judge in an American divorce court for Sharpless. Later on, she will even act out for her son Dolore the itinerant dancer she refuses to become in another aria, "Che tua madre," before finally performing ritual suicide in front of her blindfolded son (and for the late-arriving Pinkerton).[33]

III

Act 1 begins *in medias res* with a fugato; Act 2 begins the same way three years later, introducing a parallelism in the action. Indeed, the previous insinuations of the heroine's limited capacity for assuming a Western identity become explicit almost immediately with scenes featuring "little details for embarrassing Butterfly." The action opens with Suzuki's prayer, garbling names of the primal deities to the popular melody of "Takai yama."[34] Butterfly distances herself from this useless effort, but despite having imagined a new life praying with Pinkerton in church, she does not appear to have converted, situating herself "in between" Eastern and Western deities:

Pigri ed obesi	The Japanese Gods
son gli Dei Giapponesi.	are lazy and fat.
L'americano Iddio son persuasa	The American God, I'm persuaded,
ben più presto risponde a chi	answers those who implore him
l'implori.	much more quickly.

Moreover, her stance toward religion remains "primitive" or infantile at best: she anthropomorphizes the deities of both religions, rejecting the Japanese gods while fearing that the American counterpart has neglected to note her address, "Ma temo ch'egli ignori / che noi stiam qui di casa" (I am afraid he doesn't know that we live here).

Behaving like an American housewife also seems beyond Cio-Cio-san, as Sharpless's entrance and conversation with her reveal, in ways that make some spectators squirm. Correcting the Consul's greeting, "Madama Butterfly," to "Madama Pinkerton" (ironically prefaced again by the Japanese melody "O Edo Nihon bashi"), she welcomes him to an "American house," the pretensions of which are immediately undercut as he falls "grotesquely" onto a cushion—there being no Western-style furniture. Her conversation begins with Japanese indirection, inquiring about his ancestors before she lights and inhales a pipe to offer him, then thinking of stale American cigarettes only after he refuses. In spite of its light tone, this exchange reiterates the problem of Cio-Cio-san's intermediate status as well as Western premises of Eastern inferiority intimated in Act 1: Cio-Cio-san's acculturation will not progress beyond a degenerate mixture of Japanese and American customs.

Puccini emphasizes the essentially "oriental" basis of Cio-Cio-san's domestic conversation here and in the ensuing minutes with "Miya sama," probably the best-known Japanese melody at the fin de siècle, thanks to its appearance in Gilbert and Sullivan's *The Mikado* (1885). The melody's somewhat ceremonial and repetitious nature, not to mention its reception via operetta, gives "Miya sama" a comic edge that provides an apt accompaniment to Butterfly's faux pas of lighting her pipe and offering it to the Consul (rehearsal number 20 + 6 mm.),[35] or to Suzuki's preparation of tea while the heroine unexpectedly asks whether robins nest as frequently in America as in Japan. When Sharpless attempts to avoid embarrassment by saying that he has not studied ornithology, she can only repeat the first two syllables:

> BUTTERFLY: Orni …
> SHARPLESS: …. tologia.

During this exchange, Goro appears and "fa una risata" (lets out a laugh), a pointed gesture by a partly westernized male that cruelly exposes this girl-woman's inability to make generalizations about the natural world or grasp abstract concepts.

Furthermore, the fact that Prince Yamadori also enters and exits to "Miya sama" (rehearsal nos. 28 + 1 measure and 39 + 1 measure) suggests some connection between the two characters. Puccini's fascination with Yamadori as a "debauched American millionaire" at the beginning of the opera's genesis finds its most obvious reflex in the stage direction for the La Scala premiere, which has him express his degenerate hybridity through a mixture of exaggerated Western manners and Japanese habits:

> Prince Yamadori crosses the garden followed by two servants who carry flowers. . . . Yamadori enters with great solemnity, dressed in European style in the fashion of high society: he gives a ponderous handshake to Sharpless as between persons who know each other, makes a most gracious bow to Butterfly. The two Japanese servants deposit the flowers with deep bows and withdraw. Goro, with great servility, carries a cushion to Yamadori.[36]

"Miya sama" thus draws attention to Butterfly and Yamadori as partially westernized Japanese who imperfectly imitate Western customs. In this regard, at least, they are a perfect match, and this furnishes the ensuing "comedy" of their interaction.

The fact that Yamadori, who has married and divorced many wives in "Japanese" fashion, also woos Cio-Cio-san with a promise to be faithful to her alone, that is, in the "Western" way, not only accentuates the intercultural comedy of manners but also raises a more fundamental issue. Their discussion, framed by languishing Tristanesque music at Butterfly's greeting and Yamadori's exit (rehearsal nos. 29 + 1 measure and 40 + 1 measure), is presented as a Japanese imitation of Western discourse on love. Yamadori's excessive sighs conflate romantic passion with marriage, a conflation rendered even more comic by the Japanese mise-en-scène, whose unintentional replication of a European salon is suggested by Suzuki's pouring tea to a deliberately slow, waltz-like accompaniment marked Molto moderato quasi Valzer lentissimo (rehearsal number 36 + 5 mm.). More ominously, Yamadori's romantic excess also presents a distorted mirror image of Butterfly's own delusion. Their opening exchange about Yamadori's offer of "constant fidelity" even presents a proleptic parody of the opera's conclusion, in which Butterfly's ridicule of his effeminate delusion and threat of suicide reflects not only her own blind faith but also foreshadows her death:

Yamadori, ancor ... le pene	Yamadori, still . . . the sufferings
dell'amor, non v'han deluso?	of love haven't disappointed you?
Vi tagliate ancor le vene	Will you still cut open your veins
se il mio bacio vi ricuso?	if I refuse you my kiss?

Deluded by what Sharpless calls "piena cecità" (complete blindness), Cio-Cio-san will take her own life in this way—not in the samurai ritual of disembowelment (*seppuku*), to be sure, but in the manner appropriate for a woman by slitting her carotid artery with a knife (*tantō*).

One further episode should be considered before we turn our attention to Butterfly's famous numbers—the introduction of her son Dolore, an unusual moment in opera generally, which rarely presents heroines as mothers.[37] Until this moment, the action has progressed from the love relationship, with Butterfly as the object of Pinkerton's desire, to her expectation of his return three years later. While the heroine's deluded faith in him continues almost to the end, the musical action increasingly includes her son. In fact, Butterfly's last two solos, "Che tua madre" and the suicide scene, are addressed specifically to the silent and then blindfolded Dolore.

The child adds an important complication as a visible reminder of Orientalism's simultaneous attraction to racial otherness and fear of racial miscegenation.[38] In Act 1, for example, Pinkerton's desire for Butterfly is driven partly by "exotic" difference. Indeed, eyes, an obvious marker of difference in a Japanese-American couple, figure prominently in Pinkerton's opening gambit in the love duet, which begins with the evocation of difference, "Bimba dagli occhi pieni di malìa" (Child with your eyes full of magic), and concludes with the "gioie celestiali . . . nei tuoi lunghi occhi ovali" (celestial joys in your long oval eyes). This first part of the duet foregrounds difference in other ways as well: Pinkerton begins with three passionate advances to Butterfly in the A major of her "Io seguo il mio destino," to which she responds with Japanese indirectness. Even when they begin to sing together at the end, their differences are unresolved, at least on the verbal level, with Pinkerton ardently claiming Butterfly while she deflects attention to the starry night filled with fireflies, and the orchestra cadences with an extended reminiscence of her entrance and its ambiguous I^{sub6} chord conclusion (rehearsal nos. 41 and 136).[39]

In Act 2, racial difference becomes an explicit problem in the figure of Dolore, whom the heroine triumphantly shows to Sharpless as proof of her binding union with Pinkerton, with citations from Japanese and American music attesting to his mixed parentage (rehearsal number 50 + 7 mm.). What seems surprising (and biologically improbable) to today's audiences, though, is the visual absence of genetic hybridity, the lack of Asian features in what appears to be a "racially pure" Caucasian child:

Chi mai vide	Who ever saw
a bimbo del Giappone occhi azzurrini?	a Japanese child with blue eyes?
E il labbro? E i ricciolini	And his lips? and curls
d'oro schietto?	of pure gold?

Here the fin-de-siècle Western presumption of a hierarchical relationship between Caucasian and Asian races is mapped onto one between genders: while Butterfly, as a Japanese woman, remains trapped between her Japanese origins and her desired Western identity, the white male hero miraculously engenders through her a male child who can pass as Caucasian.

The scene with Dolore marks the culmination of a series of episodes that progressively exclude Butterfly from her goal, beginning with the cultural variable of religion and ending with the immutable essence of race. Indeed, the presumption of "essential" racial inferiority may under-lie a cumulative sense of childishness in Cio-Cio-san's approaches to religion, foreign customs, natural science—"orni . . . tologia"—and legal systems—the imaginary judge in divorce court—treating events with a lively but naïve subjectivity, often described in the stage directions with *infantile,* that continually lapses into what Sharpless calls "miraggi ingannatori" (deceptive mirages). Her ingenuousness can also turn violent, as when she tells Suzuki "*(furibonda)* Taci, o t'uccido" (*[furiously]* Shut up, or I'll kill you) or emits a "savage" cry at Goro's suggestion that Dolore will remain an outcast, running to get her father's knife and threatening him, "Dillo ancora e t'uccido" (Say that again and I'll kill you). Given Pinkerton's reference to Butterfly's relations as a "tribe," this alternately infantile and savage instability may reflect a fin-de-siècle prejudice considering the Japanese as a still "primitive" people.

IV

The initial scenes of Act 2, with their episodes "to embarrass Butterfly," seem to offer bleak prospects for the heroine's imagined future as Mrs. B. F. Pinkerton. Nonetheless, these little scenes also provide the setting for Cio-Cio-san's struggle to escape the prison-house of Orientalism in "Un bel dì," "Che tua madre," and "Tu, tu, piccolo Iddio!," shifting the libretto's frequent comedy of failed assimilation toward moments of intense operatic pathos. It may be, of course, that Illica, Giacosa, and Puccini themselves did not escape the trap in which they placed their heroine, also achieving something "in between" comedy and tragedy, which may help explain the opera's controversial failure at its La Scala premiere as well as the success of its revision in Brescia shortly thereafter.[40]

Puccini contextualized "Un bel dì," Butterfly's most important solo number, with particular care. Set as a 3/4 Andante molto calmo in G-flat major, it shares both meter and key with Pinkerton's "Dovunque al mondo." Moreover, both pieces are the first major numbers in Acts 1 and 2 respectively, beginning shortly after an introductory fugato and a brief exchange with a confidant of the same race, ethnicity, and gender. Both share the dominant metaphor of a ship's voyage, although the disjuncture between Pinkerton's stormy adventure and Butterfly's vision of his stately return underscores the radical differences between hero and heroine. Given the implicit binarism of West and East, both the parallelism and the difference are hardly fortuitous: "Dovunque al mondo" presents the heedless sexual adventurism with which Pinkerton undertakes his "pseudo-wedding," and "Un bel dì" reveals the consequences of his action. Since Butterfly has both rejected and been rejected by her relatives, her attempted identity formation as an American wife is based largely on Pinkerton's deception, and the irony of his absence figures prominently in this number and throughout Act 2.

At first glance, the situation seems to place "Un bel dì" in the well-known operatic context of a heroine awaiting the hero. But unlike nineteenth-century arias of this genre type (such as Elvira's "Ernani, Ernani, involami" in Verdi's *Ernani*), which articulate the heroine's desire to hasten the hero's arrival, Butterfly's aria lacks a crucial ingredient— Pinkerton himself, who is replaced by a fantasy of his arrival. As such, the aria is less an expression of desire for a hero actually *in arrivo* than a performance of delusion.[41] Not surprisingly, it is preceded by a reproach of Suzuki's lack of faith, "Ah la fede ti manca," and concludes with an emphasis on her own belief:

Senti.	Listen.
(fa la scena come se realmente vi assistesse)[42]	(*acts the scene as if she were actually witnessing it*)
– *Un bel dì, vedremo*	One fine day we'll see
levarsi un fil di fumo sull' estremo	a thread of smoke rise on the farthest
confin del mare.	edge of the sea.
E poi la nave appare.	And then the ship appears.
E poi la nave è bianca.	Then the ship is white.
Entra nel porto, romba il suo saluto.	It enters the port, thunders its salute.
Vedi? E venuto!	Do you see? he's come!
Io non gli scendo incontro. Io no. Mi metto	I don't go down toward him. Not I. I stand
là sul ciglio del colle e aspetto, aspetto	there at the edge of the hill and wait, and wait
gran tempo e non mi pesa la lunga attesa.	a long time and am not bothered by the long wait.
E … uscito dalla folla cittadina	And, coming from the city's crowd
un uomo, un picciol punto	a man, a little dot
s'avvia per la collina.	moves up the hill.
Chi sarà? chi sarà?	Who will it be? Who will it be?
E come sarà giunto	And when he has arrived,
che dirà? che dirà?	what will he say? What will he say?
Chiamerà Butterfly dalla lontana.	He will call Butterfly from afar.
Io senza far risposta	I, without giving an answer,
me ne starò nascosta	will stay hidden,

un po' per celia, un po' per non morire	a bit to tease and a bit so as not to die
al primo incontro, ed egli alquanto in pena	at the first meeting, and he, rather worried,
chiamerà, chiamerà:	will call, he will call:
"Piccina – mogliettina, olezzo di verbena"	*"Tiny little wife, verbena perfume,"*
i nomi che mi dava al suo venire. (a Suzuki)	the names he gave me on his arrival. (*to Suzuki*)
Tutto questo avverrà, te lo prometto.	All this will happen, I promise you.
Tienti la tua paura – io con sicura	Keep your fear to yourself. I, with certain
fede lo aspetto.	faith, wait for him.

Several features seem to imply that this variant of the "heroine in waiting" is also an aria manqué, reflecting a lack in Butterfly herself. The fantasy of arrival it tells is an aggregate of individual moments, represented with varying degrees of detail. Butterfly's vision connects imagined events sequentially—"and" or "then"—pausing to focus on a single detail, adding shape and then color, for example, as Pinkerton's ship approaches, then repeating the process as a diminutive figure climbs the hill and becomes recognizable as Pinkerton himself. Inasmuch as Butterfly reverts to the infantilism of her wedding day, playing guessing games about the approaching figure or imagining a game of hide-and-seek, the narrative's additive composition seems grounded in her childish or "primitive" subjectivity.

Butterfly also performs this narrative as an extended fantasy, acting out the approach of Pinkerton's ship and then Pinkerton himself in spite of all indications to the contrary. The stage direction added to the first piano-vocal score suggests that the scene is to be acted "as if she were actually witnessing it." As was the case with her attempt to assert a Western identity in "Io seguo il mio destino," the unfounded basis of this scenario intrudes on Butterfly's inability to control the action. Cio-Cio-san begins the aria with a first person plural involving Suzuki in the fantasy, "we will see," but cannot resist stepping outside the fantasy to assert its validity: "You see?" Unable to remain within the narrative, she interrupts the ship's and then Pinkerton's arrival with repetitive asides, in the latter instance even imagining his words on entering the house. Butterfly's inability to separate fantasy from reality emerges in her use of verb tenses, which proceed from future to present—"we will see," "appears . . . enters . . . thunders"—while the tenses for Pinkerton's imagined coming, *venire,* slip from her grasp, moving from the certainty of an action completed, "He's come!" to the never completed moment of his arriving, "al suo venire," with which the fantasy ends. At the same time, the most important verb for Butterfly's inaction inadvertently reveals her dependence on the hero and ominously supplies the open-ended final word in the aria, "lo aspetto" (I wait for him), displacing her passivity into the remainder of the act, which ends, appropriately enough, with the infinitive "ad aspettar" (to wait).

Puccini's setting also renders the narrative largely as a sequence of distinct segments, albeit with prominent modifications not suggested by the libretto. The famous opening phrase suggests the initial sequence of the fantasy with great ingenuity, rendering the "thread of smoke" on the horizon with an accompaniment for solo violin and clarinets marked "come da lontano" (as if from afar), adding violas and cellos for the appearance of the ship, then increasing the tempo and adding unison winds and cellos for "then the white ship," and finally marking the ship's salute with a bass drum. At the same time, the orchestra underscores the subjectivity of Butterfly's vision by adhering largely to a unison accompaniment of her vocal line, which moves in a slow octave descent.

Ensuing sections often begin at unexpected places in the middle of verses, and thus partly occlude the heroine's verbal narrative, interrupting the momentum of her fantasy or calling attention to her waiting in vain. The announcement of Pinkerton's imagined arrival is marked *con passione* and pauses on f^2 for the final syllables of "he has come," undercutting the sense of having arrived implied by the text. The next musical phrase on "[mi] metto," sung *con semplicità* in a "Japanese" 2/4 meter, begins on f^1 and gradually rises an octave before falling again, the high and low pitches emphasizing Butterfly's obsession with waiting on the words *aspetto* and *attesa* to a static ostinato.[43] Subsequent phrases repeat this pattern, with Butterfly's whole-tone portrayal of Pinkerton's ascent eventually acquiring unison octave support as he climbs the hill; but a nearly empty accompaniment refuses to support the guessing game with her own reactions: "Chi sarà?" Even more ominously, the belief that Pinkerton will call her from afar (Example 5)—the musical worm in the apple of her fantasy—quotes her earlier citation of his deceitful promise to return when the robins nest again (rehearsal number 10 + 7 mm.), something she repeats later with stubborn insistence in asking Sharpless about the nesting habits of robins.

The most striking musical intervention, a powerful return of the initial melodic phrase, occurs not only in the middle of a line but in the middle

Example 5. *Madama Butterfly*, Act 2, "Chiamerà Butterfly dalla lontana."

of "mo-rire," sung *con forza* and *con molta passione* while the orchestra accompanies largely in unison. The break in the word as well as the sudden shift in meter and in dynamics imbue the beginning of this reprise on "to die" with something unexpected and close to hysteria, as Butterfly suddenly blurts out her anxiety on a word foreshadowing her fate (recall her interruption of the love duet to inquire about transfixing butterfly specimens with pins). Although she seems to reassert control in a description of Pinkerton's calling to her, the diminutive nicknames have a vocal line not far removed from patter.

In fact, at the same time that Butterfly completes the reprise, giving her imagined narrative a circular structure that reflects the circularity of basing her faith in Pinkerton's return on his previous arrivals, the accompaniment moves into a concluding section, "Tutto questo avverrà," in which Cio-Cio-san turns to Suzuki and asserts the certainty of this event by contrasting the servant's fear with her own "certain faith." The music, however, again undercuts Butterfly's distinction, articulating Suzuki's fear as well as her own certainty with the same sequence of pitches. Moreover, while the heroine promises to demonstrate her faith in continued waiting with an assertive b♭², the orchestra cadences for her, intimating the discrepancy between her imagination and events over which she has no control.

V

The defining moment for the subsequent musical drama of Cio-Cio-san's disillusionment and suicide occurs when Sharpless forces the heroine to face the possibility of Pinkerton's not returning, and she responds:

(immobile, come colpita a morte,
   china la testa e dice con
   sommessione infantile)
     Due cose potrei fare:
     tornare a divertire
     la gente col cantare
     oppur, meglio, morire.

(*immobile, as if struck by a mortal*
   blow, bows her head and responds
   with infantile submission)
     I could do two things:
     return to entertaining
     people by singing,
     or—better—die.

This sudden confrontation with a fate different from what she has imagined presents the limited options left to her, reverting to her role as entertainer or dying, options that dominate her remaining solos, "Che tua madre" and "Tu, tu piccolo Iddio!"

"Che tua madre," set as an Andante molto mosso in A-flat minor, is another narrative of imagined events, answering a rhetorical question addressed to Dolore. Another game of fantasy, it is also a performance of the heroine's desperate struggle, acting out the first option mentioned to Sharpless even while passionately resisting it. Accompanied by a bleak orientalizing ostinato of arpeggiated octaves and chords, the much-revised 1907 version presents a dystopian fantasy of having devolved to an impoverished itinerant performer, acquiring a Japanese melodic shape and then verbal intensity, underpinned by bass drum and cymbals, as she imagines extending her hands to beg an audience's pity:

Che tua madre dovrà
prenderti in braccio ed alla
   pioggia e al vento
andar per la città

That your mother will have to
take you in her arms and, in the
   rain and wind,
go about the city

a guadagnarti il pane e il vestimento.	to earn your bread and clothing.
Ed alle impietosite	And toward the pitying
genti ... la man tremante	people . . . she will hold out her
stenderà ...	trembling hand . . .
gridando, Udite, udite	crying, "Hear, hear
la triste mia canzon.	my sad song.
A un'infelice madre	Charity for an unhappy mother,
la carità, muovetevi a pietà ...	be moved to pity."
(si alza, mentre il bimbo rimane seduto sul cuscino giocando con una bambola)	(*stands up, while the child remains seated on the pillow, playing with a doll*)
E Butterfly, orribile	And Butterfly—horrible
destino, danzerà per te ...	fate—will dance for you . . .
E come fece già	And as she did before
(rialza il bimbo e colle mani levate lo fa implorare)	(*raises up the child and has him implore with uplifted hands*)
la Ghesha canterà!	the geisha will sing!
E la canzon giuliva	And the merry, happy song
e lieta in un singhiozzo finirà!	will end in a sob!
(buttandosi a' ginocchi davanti a Sharpless)	(*throwing herself down on her knees before Sharpless*)
Ah no, no! questo mai!	Ah, no, no! Never this!
questo mestier che al disonore porta!	This profession that leads to dishonor!
Morta! morta! Mai più danzar!	Dead! Dead! Never dance again!
Piuttosto la mia vita vo' troncar!	Instead I'd rather cut short my life!
Ah! ... morta!	Ah! . . . Dead!
(cade a terra vicino al bimbo che abbraccia strettamente ed accarezza con moto convulsivo)	(*she falls on the floor beside the child, whom she embraces tightly and caresses with a convulsive motion*)

Although Butterfly interrupts the narrative to comment on the "horrible destiny" of performing again, the dance-like orchestral accompaniment assumes a life of its own to the Japanese melody "Suiryo bushi," driven by alternating bass drum and cymbals, with pizzicato strings in unison "battendo il legno dell'arco sulle corde" (striking the wood of the bow on the strings). After a brief B-major evocation of the "merry, happy song," Butterfly throws herself on her knees in front of Sharpless, simultaneously rejecting the deceptively pleasant option by negating the entire vision and forcing the music back into A-flat minor, where she resists the fate she has imagined with violent denials, twice interjecting the word *morta* (dead) on passionate octave descents from ab^2 and bb^2 before first refusing to dance and then preferring to cut short her own life (thus answering Sharpless's question). As Butterfly hugs her baby, the dancing fate suggested by "Suiryo bushi" powerfully reasserts itself in parallel octaves in the orchestra, cadencing on a fermata, which the heroine joins with a fortissimo "Ah!" on a tonic ab^2 before falling back an octave to a quiet "morta!" (see Example 6). It is Cio-Cio-san's most intense moment in the struggle to assert herself in the face of increasingly bleak prospects.

VI

Perhaps because Puccini's characterization leaves much to the acting abilities of the soprano, Butterfly's death seldom receives more than cursory critical attention—as if the end were a foregone conclusion. Although a tragic denouement has been an explicit option ever since her offstage voice announced a summons to love for those who live and those who die, the Orientalism that has organized much of the opera's action does not prepare us for what actually happens: a death scene with two distinct episodes and two suicide attempts.

The first episode, musically part of a larger structure that begins immediately after Butterfly agrees to surrender her child, opens with a dramatic ostinato on the timpani to reminiscences of the Bonze's curse as Cio-Cio-san genuflects before the statue of Buddha, followed by a reminiscence of her Act 1 entrance as she remains motionless, absorbed in thought. Coming after her instructions to Suzuki to close off and darken the house, these two reminiscences recall the process of Butterfly's isolation, the ostracism that alienated her from her Japanese relatives and the "pseudo-wedding" that never validated the "new life" in her empty "American house."[44]

This isolation seems to announce the suicide that we have been expecting ever since allusions to her father's death revealed that she possessed his knife and her threat to Goro demonstrated that she was capable of using it. The action begins in a ritual manner as Butterfly kneels in front of the Buddha and proceeds to take the weapon from a lacquered case near the statue. As "Bangzi" resounds *fortissimo* in unison from the orchestra, the heroine kisses the blade "religiously" and reads the words inscribed on it: "Con onor muore / Chi non può serbar vita con onore" (He dies with honor who cannot continue living with honor).

Example 6. *Madama Butterfly*, Act 2, "Piuttosto la mia vita vo' troncar!"

This appears to place Butterfly's death in a purely Japanese ambience with no option but to follow her father in death. This is the point to which Illica directed his vision of the drama, and it follows his draft in being wordless except for reading the inscription. The absence of speech and interiority removes the action from the personal sphere, placing it instead amid impersonal forces of conflict. While the heroine is initially a victim of Pinkerton's deception, she also seems to have become a victim of a rigid patriarchal and religious code that she will literally re-inscribe on her body by performing ritual suicide with her father's knife. An opera that ended here would thus have the dubious distinction of making the heroine a double victim, indirectly confirming the negative perspective on the feckless American hero as well as the inability of the heroine to escape from fixed racial and ethnic behavioral patterns.

But this "Japanese tragedy" is precisely what does *not* occur. Instead, the action continues into a second and very different death scene. As Butterfly points the knife toward her throat, the music shifts to B minor while the door opens and Suzuki pushes Dolore into the room, distracting the heroine's attention and occasioning the last of her solo numbers, directed entirely at her three-year-old son. The change of focus transposes the tragedy from East-West conflict to the personal sphere "in between," providing Butterfly a chance to recuperate something from her own death through Dolore's racial hybridity:

Tu, tu, piccolo Iddio!	You, you, little God!
Amore, amore mio,	Love, my love,
fior di giglio e di rosa,	flower of lily and rose,
[qui la tua testa bionda	[put your blond head here,
qui, ch'io nasconda	here, so that I may hide
la fronte dolorosa	my sorrowful face
ne' tuoi capelli.] Non saperlo mai:	in your hair.] Never know it:
per te, per i tuoi puri	for you, for your pure
occhi, muor Butterfly	eyes, Butterfly dies
perché tu possa andare	so that you may go
di là dal mare	beyond the sea
senza che ti rimorda ai dì	without being tormented, when
maturi,	you are grown,
il materno abbandono.	by your mother's abandonment.

"Tu, tu, piccolo Iddio" initially emphasizes the child's biracial heritage as a "flower of lily and rose," attempting to deny him the guilt of knowing her sacrifice, disrupting the causal chain linking her father's suicide to her own and thus enabling him to pass as a Westerner unburdened by his Japanese past. The invocation of Dolore originally contained a more extended passage attesting to his "blond head" and Caucasian appearance (in brackets above); the generally performed 1907 revision merely alludes to the apparent racial difference between mother and son through the reference to his "pure eyes," that is, blue and Western.[45]

On the heavily laden word *abandonment*, however, Butterfly's intended sacrifice on behalf of her son's racial otherness takes a new direction, sung *con esaltazione* as an Andante sostenuto in a firm B minor. Desperate to avoid repeating her own abandonment, she affirms the maternal bond, impressing a trace of her visage on his memory:

guarda ben fiso, fiso	look carefully, carefully
di tua madre la faccia! ...	at your mother's face! . . .
che t'en resti una traccia	so that a trace of it may remain with you

The concluding unison Japanese melody, played *tutta forza*, seems to shroud the opera again in oriental mystery. This melody, however, is not "Bangzi," which provided the motive of her father's suicide, but rather "Suiryo bushi," heard previously in "Che tua madre," which is also addressed to Dolore. The recurrence of "Suiryo bushi" thus draws attention to the modicum of tragic freedom a heroine trapped between East and West has been allowed in choosing death: the freedom to assert her maternal love even while sacrificing herself for a future denied to her—her son's assimilation into a Western race and culture.

But does a postcolonial reading of *Madama Butterfly* leave contemporary audiences also trapped in a musical and cultural quandary of their own? Most listeners simply want to hear and enjoy beautiful music by a great composer. (Indeed, the next Olympic Games held in Japan will probably feature "Un bel dì" again as agreeably conciliatory and international theme music for the opening ceremony.) Others might choose to reject the opera because of the orientalizing biases that inform the portrayal of Cio-Cio-san and the Japanese. One can hope, however, that a critically informed approach to Puccini and his world can enable us to enjoy *Madama Butterfly* with a deeper understanding of the complex and even contradictory historical discourses in which it is imbricated, even as it remains one the most enduringly popular operas in the repertory.

NOTES

1. See Puccini's letter to Elvira of 22 June 1900, in Cesare Garboli, "'Sembra una figura da paravento,'" *Quaderni pucciniani* 1 (1982): 98.

2. Interview of 11 September 1902, repr. in Carlo Paladini, *Giacomo Puccini*, ed. Marzia Paladini (Florence: Vallecchi, 1961), 101.

3. See my "Luigi Illica's Libretto for *Madama Butterfly* (1901)," *Studi pucciniani* 2 (2000): 91–204, quote at 92–93.

4. *Giacomo Puccini. Epistolario*, ed. Giuseppe Adami (1928; repr. Milan: Mondadori, 1982), 143.

5. See the letter to Illica of March 6 in the *Epistolario* for the opera edited by Dieter Schickling and Gabriella Biagi Ravenni, in: *Madama Butterfly: Fonti e documenti della genesi*, ed. Arthur Groos et al. (Lucca: Centro studi Giacomo Puccini/Maria Pacini Fazzi, 2005), 310.

6. On Orientalism and the opera, see *Madama Butterfly: L'orientalismo di fine secolo, l'approccio pucciniano, la ricezione*, ed. Arthur Groos and Virgilio Bernardoni (Florence, IT: Leo S. Olschki, 2008); Ralph Locke, *Musical Exoticism: Images and Reflections* (Cambridge: Cambridge University Press, 2009), 202–13; and Domingos de Mascarenhas, "Beyond Orientalism: The International Rise of Japan and the Revisions to *Madame Butterfly*," in *Art and Ideology in European Opera: Essays in Honour of Julian Rushton*, ed. Rachel Cowgill et al. (Woodbridge: Boydell, 2010), 281–302.

7. In Italian, *commedia* can mean drama as well as comedy, but see my "*Madama Butterfly* Between Comedy and Tragedy," in *Madama Butterfly: L'orientalismo di fine secolo*, 159–81, esp. 161–62.

8. Letter of 11 March 1901, *Madama Butterfly: Fonti e documenti*, 312.

9. *Carteggi pucciniani*, ed. Eugenio Gara (Milan: Ricordi, 1958), 209.

10. Letter of 16 November 1902, *Madama Butterfly: Fonti e documenti*, 349.

11. The best recent discussions of the opera as a whole are Michele Girardi, *Puccini: His International Art*, trans. Laura Basini (Chicago: University of Chicago Press, 2000), 195–258; and Julian Budden, *Puccini: His Life and Works* (New York: Oxford University Press, 2002), 223–73. For earlier research, see Linda B. Fairtile, *Giacomo Puccini: A Guide to Research* (New York: Garland, 1999), 149–64.

12. "A hill near Nagasaki. Japanese house, terrace, and garden. Below, in the background, the bay, the harbor, and the city of Nagasaki." All quotations from the libretto are taken from my synoptic edition in *Madama Butterfly: Fonti e documenti*, 195–294.

13. Mosco Carner, *Puccini: A Critical Biography*, 2nd ed. (London: Duckworth, 1974), 391.

14. Puccini did not set the Consul's verses in the 1904 La Scala version of the libretto: "*How-exciting!* Giudizio: / o il pseudo sposalizio / vi mena al precipizio." ("How-exciting" originally in English and with hyphen.) Translation: "*How exciting!* Careful, or the pseudo-wedding will lead you to a precipice" (literal), or "will lead to your downfall." *Madama Butterfly: Fonti e documenti*, 217.

15. Ibid., 203 and 215–16.

16. See my "Lieutenant F. B. Pinkerton: Problems in the Genesis and Performance of *Madama Butterfly*," in *The Puccini Companion*, ed. Simonetta Puccini and William Weaver (New York: W. W. Norton, 1994), 169–201.

17. *Madama Butterfly: Fonti e documenti*, 163.

18. On "temporary marriages," see my "*Madame Butterfly*: The Story," *Cambridge Opera Journal* 3 (1991): 125–58, esp. 148–52.

19. Puccini did not set "Donna o gingillo."

20. The Japanese chorus in Gilbert and Sullivan's *The Mikado* (1885) already describes themselves as having been seen "On many a vase and jar— / On many a screen and fan."

21. See Helen M. Greenwald, "Character Distinction and Rhythmic Differentiation in Puccini's Operas," in *Giacomo Puccini: L'uomo, il musicista, il panorama europeo*, ed. Gabriella Biagi Ravenni and Carolyn Gianturco (Lucca: LIM, 1997), 495–515, esp. 500–504.

22. For a succinct presentation of Puccini's use of Japanese melodies, see Girardi, *Puccini*, 216–23. The standard inventory of melodies is Kimiyo Powils-Okano, *Puccinis "Madama Butterfly*," Orpheus-Schriftenreihe zu Grundfragen der Musik, vol. 44 (Bonn: Verlag für systematische Musikwissenschaft, 1986), 44–62.

23. See my "Cio-Cio-san and Sadayakko: Japanese Music-Theater in *Madama Butterfly*," *Monumenta Nipponica* 54 (1999): 41–73, esp. 48–55.

24. Ibid., 45–46, now also in *Madama Butterfly: Fonti e documenti*, 68–69; but see the criticism of David Rosen, "'Pigri ed obesi Dei': Religion in the Operas of Puccini," in *Madama Butterfly: L'orientalismo di fine secolo*, 257–98, esp. 263–65.

25. As this chapter was being copyedited for publication, an important article by W. Anthony Sheppard appeared: "Puccini and the Music Boxes," *Journal of the Royal Musical Association* 140 (2015): 41–92, esp. 52–70. I have been unable to engage with the ramifications of this suggestive article, but have changed the names of the melodies associated with Butterfly and the father's death to accord with Sheppard's discovery.

26. Powils-Okano, 59, cites the *Collection of Japanese Koto Music* (Tokyo, 1888), which, however, does not contain it. On the new identification, see Sheppard, "Puccini and the Music Boxes," esp. 64–68.

27. See *Madama Butterfly: Fonti e documenti*, 226–27.

28. The current version differs substantially from the La Scala and Brescia versions, where the reminiscence of her father's suicide accompanies her discarding the ottoké. *Madama Butterfly: Fonti e documenti*, 226–27.

29. See Groos, "Illica's Libretto," 147.

30. Puccini to Ricordi, 3 May 1902, in Adami, *Epistolario*, 146.

31. See *Madama Butterfly: Fonti e documenti*, 458 and 462.

32. Illica's draft called for gestures "as composed and exact as a military drill." See Groos, "Illica's Libretto," 121.

33. Her suicide performance seems intended to include Pinkerton; see the careful repetition of the whole-tone phrase "s'avvia per la collina" (climbs the hill) from "Un bel dì" in the last scene (Locke, *Musical Exoticism*, 204). Giacosa's penultimate draft of the libretto even had the dying Butterfly tell him: "Tardi sei giunto!" (You're late!).

34. A popular tune of the late Edo period. See my "Return of the Native: Japan in *Madama Butterfly*/*Madama Butterfly* in Japan," *Cambridge Opera Journal* 1 (1989): 167–94, esp. 175–77.

35. Libretti for the first and second productions emphasize that it is an opium pipe. *Madama Butterfly: Fonti e documenti*, 248n5.

36. Ibid., 252.

37. See Jennifer Barnes, "Where Are the Mothers in Opera?," in *Girls! Girls! Girls!: Essays on Women and Music*, ed. Sarah Cooper (New York: New York University Press, 1995), 86–97.

38. See, for example, Robert J. C. Young, *Colonial Desire: Hybridity in Theory, Culture, and Race* (London: Routledge, 1995).

39. See Rosen, "'Pigri ed obesi,'" 265 and note.

40. See Groos, "*Madama Butterfly* Between Comedy and Tragedy," 178–81. Some material in Act 1 thought to resemble operetta was deleted after the premiere. The progressive changes are listed in Dieter Schickling, *Giacomo Puccini: Catalogue of the Works*

(Kassel: Bärenreiter, 2003), 255–87. See also discussions by Schickling, "Criteri per un'edizione critica di *Madama Butterfly*," in *Madama Butterfly: L'orientalismo di fine secolo*, 317–24; and Linda B. Fairtile, "Revising Cio-Cio-San," in ibid., 301–15.

41. See James A. Hepokoski, "'Un bel dì? Vedremo!' Anatomy of a Delusion," in *Madama Butterfly: L'orientalismo di fine secolo*, 219–46.

42. This stage direction was added to the first piano-vocal score; *Madama Butterfly: Fonti e documenti*, 246n5.

43. On ostinato as a stylistic feature in Puccini, see Andrew Davis, *"Il Trittico," "Turandot," and Puccini's Late Style* (Bloomington: Indiana University Press, 2010).

44. On the interior space, see Helen M. Greenwald, "Picturing Cio-Cio-San: House, Screen, and Ceremony in Puccini's *Madama Butterfly*," *Cambridge Opera Journal* 12 (2000): 237–59.

45. See *Madama Butterfly: Fonti e documenti*, 292n5.

Laggiù nel Soledad:
Indexing and Archiving the Operatic West

ELLEN LOCKHART

The archive is always a wager about the future.
—Mary Ann Doane,
The Emergence of Cinematic Time

Over the past two centuries, the Milan-based music publisher Ricordi accumulated a veritable gold mine of historical artifacts relating to nineteenth-century Italian opera. The archives of Casa Ricordi—once the mighty firm associated with Rossini, Bellini, Donizetti, Verdi, and Puccini; now a modest wing of the pop-music powerhouse Universal Music International—were long inaccessible to all but a very small inner circle. This situation underwent a sudden and fortuitous reversal beginning in 2003: first, the Archivio Storico Ricordi separated from Casa Ricordi and was relocated to the Biblioteca Nazionale Braidense in Milan; more recently, much of this material was made available online, as part of the Italian National Library's extraordinary digitization initiative. These events have the potential to transform the landscape of Italian opera scholarship, particularly that relating to composers like Puccini who had a lifelong and nearly exclusive relationship with Ricordi. Only ten years ago, for instance, Annie Randall and Rosalind Gray Davis had to publish their otherwise comprehensive documentary study of Puccini's 1910 opera *La fanciulla del West* without having been able to consult any of Ricordi's materials.[1]

Looking through the portion of these newly available Ricordi archives that relates to *La fanciulla* is a bit like emptying a suitcase packed long ago for a voyage that never happened. Or it is like the "extraordinary collection of articles" discovered in the locked closet of Farmer Boldwood at the end of Thomas Hardy's *Far from the Madding Crowd*: its materials were gathered, sorted, and labeled in anticipation of a successful outcome that never was—acquisitions fired by a desire that was no less acquisitive for having ultimately been unreciprocated. Premiered in 1910, at the height of Puccini's powers—after the lessons of *Manon*, *La bohème*, *Tosca*, and *Madama Butterfly*, but before his health began its long decline—*La fanciulla* was his most ambitious score to date in many senses. Moreover, it was an opera on an American subject—*The Girl of the Golden West*, a play by David Belasco, who had also written *Madame Butterfly*—which was composed for the foremost American venue, New York City's Metropolitan Opera. Set in California during the Gold Rush of 1848, *La fanciulla* featured a gun-toting saloon maiden, Minnie, as its main character; and boasted a manhunt, a snowstorm, and in the premiere no fewer than ten live horses, as well as the vocal talents of Emmy Destinn, Pasquale Amato as the sheriff Jack Rance, and even Enrico Caruso himself as the bandit Dick Johnson. Its creators were understandably ambitious on its behalf; surely, they imagined, this opera could not fail. Yet with *Fanciulla* (as in Hardy's novel), the full extent of its creators' ambitions can be observed only after the last shots have been fired, when the secret closet is unlocked.

I would like to begin here by sorting through the treasures hidden in this secret closet, which have sat in mostly undisturbed quiet for a hundred years. My motivations are partly practical. As the editor of a forthcoming critical edition of the opera, to be published by Ricordi, I need to locate and ascertain the authority of the opera's early musical scores, both those that are handwritten and those that are engraved. This endeavor also requires me to assess what staging materials (if any) survive from the original production, and whether these were considered essential to the opera or merely incidental. For *La fanciulla* historical and philological questions of how exactly the opera was supposed to look and sound at its premiere have an added fascination; and this is because, of all Puccini's mature works, his Wild West opera most evokes a life-world now largely inaccessible to us. My hope, ultimately, is that these materials will reveal something about how meaning was created in this opera and that through this process *La fanciulla*'s life-world will become, if not accessible, then at least a degree more knowable. In other words, I peer into this Boldwood's-closet archive not merely from an antiquarian impulse, or in the hope of finally effecting a union between *La fanciulla* and the Puccini-admiring public (by way of its most literate wing), but because it might shed light on an opera that still does not seem to yield itself, even to the willing.

Puccini Preserved

First there are the three enormous volumes of Puccini's autograph score; and the three volumes of proofs used by Arturo Toscanini to conduct the premiere, annotated lightly by Puccini during the final rehearsals. These materials are the most important in the collection, both from an anti-quarian perspective—even the briefest of letters from the composer can fetch well into the four figures at auction—and from an editorial one.[2] Together, these documents allow us to ascertain more or less how Puccini wanted the opera's score to look, a matter that seems simple enough but is, in fact, almost impossibly complicated.[3] After all, unlike almost every other major composer, Puccini continued to revise his operas after the engraving had begun, sometimes even well after the premiere, but he did not record these revisions in his autograph. The current circulating versions differ from his handwritten ones in many thousands of details: some of these are significant enough that they can only have come from the composer, despite the lack of a documentary trail; a few are revisions done for later stagings, and a handful are engravers' errors, but most are of unknown provenance. Together, the autograph and first "Toscanini" proofs form the basis of my critical edition of the opera. I was assisted in this endeavor by other items in *La fanciulla*'s archive: a few letters from the composer to his publisher, and manuscript copies of the libretto by Guelfo Civinini and Carlo Zangarini.

Next in our itemized list of *La fanciulla*'s archive come the staging manuals: two mise-en-scènes, in French, for which the author is identified as one Jules Speck. These two booklets are nearly identical in content: one is in the very tidy script of two copyists, and the other is in a mess-ier hand, presumably Speck's own.[4] Staging manuals like these are not uncommon for nineteenth- and early twentieth-century operas: French operas from the 1830s onward often have them; Ricordi published them for Verdi's operas beginning with *Les vêpres siciliennes*.[5] The staging man-ual for *La fanciulla* supplies detailed descriptions of its sets, props, and costumes, as well as instructions relating to lighting and other spectacu-lar effects, and the movements of singers and chorus around the stage, and some suggestions about character interpretation. The purpose of the mise-en-scène was to ensure that an opera was always staged more or less the same way. Though few today share this ideal of uniformity in opera production, scholars and editors have increasingly argued for the textual relevance of these mise-en-scènes: if an opera's staging manual can be shown to represent its first production, or there is evidence that the composer (in particular) considered it to be definitive, then it should be considered part of the opera's text—equal in status, that is, to its words and its music.

The staging manual in the *Fanciulla del West* archives was long considered to be of only peripheral interest, on the assumption that the locale of its publication (Paris, ca. 1912) and that it was written in French made it unlikely to represent that all-important first production at the Metropolitan Opera.[6] We now know, however, that it can be traced directly to the premiere, a fact that makes it unique among Puccini's operas; we also know that Puccini considered the premiere production of *La fanciulla* to be definitive, something other opera houses must copy.[7] Little is known about its credited author, Jules Speck, who was stage director for French and Italian productions at the Metropolitan Opera House between 1908 and 1917, during the first decade of Giulio Gatti-Casazza's directorship. He had been brought to New York from Paris, where he worked at the Opéra-Comique and the Opéra.[8] In 1914 the *New York Times* lauded Speck as one of two "Invisible Men Who Make Grand Opera Succeed" at the Metropolitan; the other was the chorus master, Giulio Setti. A photograph published with that article reveals him to be a dapper man of middle age, fair-haired or perhaps prematurely gray.[9] Despite the official credit given Speck, Belasco was widely proclaimed to be the true author of *La fanciulla*'s first staging; he attended rehearsals in the days leading up to the opera's premiere on 10 December.

It seems indeed likely that, though Speck is the only credited author, this mise-en-scène features a lot of Belasco as well. In addition to meticulously describing the sets and props, which were re-created from the original 1905 staging of the spoken play, the booklet reflects Belasco's instructions to the singers about how "real Americans" behaved. It tells us, for instance, that when Johnson arrives at Minnie's cottage in Act 2, he not only puts his lantern down on the table, but must also pull revolvers out of the pockets of his trousers and put them into his coat, without Minnie noticing. In the staging manual, as in the libretto, it is noted that he then attempts to embrace her and is rebuffed. But Speck also recorded that Minnie should watch, blush, and bat her eyelashes as Johnson removes his coat and offers her his hand; and when they finally join hands, the characters perform "an energetic handshake in the American style."[10] They sit down simultaneously, Minnie "a bit gauchely." The manual also tells that Minnie should perform the first several lines of her Act 1 aria "Laggiù nel Soledad" (Down There in Soledad) while seated at the round table just to the right of center stage: a pose she strikes (according to Speck) precisely at the fermata after Rance's exclamation "Poesia!" As the aria approaches its climax, at "Si amavan tanto," she stands and faces

Figure 1. Giacomo Puccini on the Brooklyn Bridge.

the audience; as it concludes, she turns back to Rance, "walks up to him and pats him gently on the left shoulder as if to calm him, with the air of saying 'good boy, run along, Rance,' and then passes in front of him and goes to stand behind the counter."[11] In other words, the staging manuals that Ricordi preserved in its collection for *La fanciulla del West* provide a fascinating glimpse into the history of theatrical practice. What is more, they have a demonstrable relevance to ongoing endeavors in critical editing, which are increasingly concerned with documenting and making available the operatic work in its full historical scope.

So far, though, this accounts for only a small fraction of the items in the *Fanciulla* archive. The remainder of the catalog—also its majority by a wide margin, at least in terms of number—is composed of photographic records dating from the late nineteenth century through the 1920s. These range from the predictable to the downright strange. A publicity shot from around the time of the opera's premiere shows the composer posing on the Brooklyn Bridge, captured in panorama; a pedestrian in the distance glances backward over his shoulder (Figure 1). There are also two views of a felled giant sequoia, or "Bigtree," in California, reproduced here as Figures 2 and 3: the documentarians have arranged a series of men on horseback to show the size of the tree. These feature in the catalog as "Paesaggio Americano: Bigtree Mariposa Grove" and "Stump of Bigtree" and are almost certainly the photographs of the California landscape on which Puccini gazed for inspiration during the opera's writing.[12] They provide an immediate source for the composer's notion to set the opera's final act in the California forest, rather than, as in the play's third and fourth acts, "the interior of a typical mining-camp dance hall of the period," followed by "the boundless prairies of the West."[13] "I am *determined* that [the third act] must be in the open air in a large clearing of a forest with colossal trees and with ten or more horses and sixty men," he wrote to Zangarini on 27 August 1907.[14] Also, there are several pictures

Figure 2. "Paesaggio Americano: Bigtree Mariposa Grove."

Figure 3. "Stump of Bigtree."

of a forest near Pistoia, perhaps those taken by Puccini at the time of the preceding letter, while he was on vacation in the Apennines.[15]

The rest are theatrical photographs. A few record empty sets: the carefully constructed chaos of the Polka Saloon in Act 1, complete with stuffed grizzly holding a parasol; the no less carefully constructed chaos of Minnie's cottage in Act 2; the California forest in Act 3, featuring a central stump for Johnson's intended hanging (the stump is more on the Pistoian scale than the sequoian, it must be admitted). There are two props cards, or *tavole di attrezzerie*, relating to the first two acts of the opera: the card for Act 2, reproduced as Figure 4, shows a tablecloth, a bearskin rug, Minnie's dressing gown, a ladder, a Navajo-style blanket, and other furniture items from the heroine's cottage. Then there are stills of Minnie, Johnson, Rance, and the boys in various poses and incarnations. I have written elsewhere about how *La fanciulla* was one of the first operas to rely on photographic records for its staging; the Metropolitan Opera archives attest that the stages and costumes for the premiere were carefully re-created from those done for the original 1905 production of Belasco's *The Girl of the Golden West* at the New Belasco Theatre in Pittsburgh.[16] It turns out that these represented only the tip of the iceberg. For reasons we can only speculate about, Ricordi also began to compile a much larger collection of stills for the opera.

Many of the stills are from the premiere of Belasco's play, starring Blanche Bates as Minnie, but they have been catalogued according to the closest lines in the libretto, which are occasionally only a close approximation. For example, Figure 5 shows Bates as Minnie and Robert Hilliard as Johnson, conversing in the Polka Saloon near the end of Act 1; it is labeled "Su, su, come le stelle." In Figure 6, "Ecco padrona," Minnie brings her white shoes to the attention of Wowkle, an "Indian woman" who seems to have been a much more imposing figure in the play than in the opera. Figure 7—"Non è vero! Mentite!"—shows Minnie refusing to believe that Johnson is the bandit Ramerrez. Intriguingly, Ricordi seems to have begun to prepare these photos for publication. Among these archival photographs are some thirty pages or so of a numbered series, featuring these photographs from the play along with their Italian captions and the relevant page of the score, with Puccini's name and the opera's title given at the top of each page, and the Ricordi trademark at the bottom. Figure 5 here is drawn from this series.

We do not know whether the publishing house was intending a photographic booklet to supplement the mise-en-scène, or something more ambitious, like a series of projected slides or even a film. At any rate, the project was abandoned before it was completed. There are no stills to

Figure 4. Props card, *La fanciulla del West*, Act 2.

Figure 5. Ricordi Archive still from Belasco's 1905 production of
The Girl of the Golden West, "Su, su, come le stelle."

Figure 6. Ricordi Archive still (1905), "Ecco padrona."

represent Act 3; one photograph in the collection, representing Act 4 of the spoken play (Figure 8), is catalogued under the phrase "Noi dobbiamo guardare avanti," a direct translation of Belasco's line for Johnson, "We must look ahead, Girl," which has no equivalent in the opera libretto. There are good reasons why this series was left unfinished. Most obvious among them—as the photographs of California sequoias remind us—is that after Act 2 the opera diverged sharply from the course set by the play; the 1905 stills from Pittsburgh's New Belasco Theatre could not serve the purpose. Ricordi probably planned to acquire the rest of the photographs in its series from the first production of the opera, and certainly the Metropolitan Opera's usual firm, White's, was documenting the premiere. The famous tableau of Minnie halting Johnson's execution, for instance, might have been included in Ricordi's photographic series. However, as Figure 9 makes clear, though their costumes were identical in nearly every detail, the original singers hardly passed as doppelgangers for the actors in the play. Minnie was a particular problem: few

Figure 7. Ricordi Archive still (1905), "Non è vero! Mentite!"

Puccinian sopranos were likely to slouch across the boards like Bates, a skeletal if charismatic stage presence. Ricordi seems to have continued to search for a suitably photogenic Minnie as late as 1912, when it acquired several shots of the willowy Vittorina Peruzzi gesticulating broadly in that now-familiar costume (see Figure 10).

By 1912, though, Ricordi may already have concluded that the eventuality for which these materials were being accumulated would not come to pass. For the first time since *Edgar* of 1889, Puccini had written a flop. Touring the world's foremost opera houses in the United States and Europe in the two years after its premiere, *La fanciulla* inspired only a lukewarm affection among audiences, and predominantly negative reviews; it disappeared from stages soon after. What is more, the very ideals of theatrical realism and staging uniformity that motivated Ricordi to acquire all these photographs and plan an elaborate apparatus for the standardization of *La fanciulla*'s staging did not long outlive the first production.

Puccini Forgotten

Oddly, the considerable scope of *La fanciulla*'s archive may seem to invert what is most often said about the opera's music, which is that it seems

Figure 8. Ricordi Archive still (1905), "Noi dobbiamo guardare avanti."

to elude recollection. Unlike the rest of Puccini's full-scale operas, from *Manon* onward—and even *La rondine*, thanks to the protagonist's aria "Che il bel sogno di Doretta"—*La fanciulla* fails to leave melodic traces in the memory of its listener. This critical strain was pervasive when the opera was revived for centenary productions. "*Fanciulla* does not quite win us over," proclaimed *Opera Today* in December 2010, noting that Minnie in particular has "so much to sing but *no memorable tune*. [. . .] The unforgettable tune is also a necessity, and it's not here."[17] "Forgettable Puccini"; "there aren't many memorable musical moments"; "this is the only Puccini opera that contains no memorable tunes," shouted voices from the blogosphere.[18] When *La fanciulla* was done by Opera

Figure 9. *La fanciulla del West*, Act 3,
Metropolitan Opera still taken by White's.

Holland Park, London, Rodney Milnes lamented that the opera made "less recourse to hit numbers and the use of recurring themes"; when it was staged by Opera Minnesota, the *Star Tribune* noted that "it lacks this composer's usual string of memorable tunes."[19] The list goes on. These critics frequently, if unwittingly, give further evidence of *La fanciulla*'s lack of memorability by misremembering it. Milnes's suggestion that the opera lacks recurring themes is made often, but it is wrong: the orchestra remembers, even if the spectators do not. Also notable in this regard is the assertion (in the above-quoted article from *Opera Today*) that Destinn did not record any of the opera because there was "no proper aria to fit the three-minute 78rpm format of the day"—the reviewer having evidently forgotten "Laggiù nel Soledad," her aria in Act 1, which clocks in at a bit more than two and a half minutes.

The opera's forgettableness has also featured in the musicological literature, however, despite a substantial following among opera scholars. No less a figure than Gary Tomlinson has proclaimed that the first act of *La fanciulla* is "the best single act Puccini ever wrote."[20] Mosco Carner suggested that Puccini's failure to identify (erotically) with his heroine resulted in a lack of "memorable music"; "the vocal writing is as

Figure 10. Vittorina Peruzzi as Minnie.

technically proficient as it is unmemorable," wrote John Russo.[21] More recently, and more defensively, Shelby Davis suggested that "the opera has no memorable arias because they are integrated into the surrounding music."[22] Alan Mallach, while noting that "in many respects it may have become the musicologists' favourite Puccini opera," also admitted that he found *La fanciulla* to have "no memorable tune [. . .] soaring melodies or memorable motifs."[23] A few scholars have attributed these absences to the opera's perceived Wagnerianisms: its supposed leitmotifs that return in the wrong places and bleed into one another, its unfortunate *unendliche Melodie*.[24]

All of this might seem like an elaborate setup on my part: evidence-gathering for an accusation of intellectual laziness against Puccini's erstwhile defenders. It is not. I take seriously these claims about the forgettableness of *La fanciulla*'s melodies—not least because, at least in recent reception history, they usually constitute a lone source of ambivalence about an opera that is otherwise found to be exciting, dramatically effective, and technically flawless in its music (the latter a claim that is often repeated and conveniently never explained). The central gambit of this essay holds that there is indeed something peculiarly elusive about Puccini's

Wild West, something different about its appeals to memory, even when it seems to have most of the features of the composer's trademark lyricism.

Take, for instance, the high notes. *La fanciulla* has as many as the rest of them: indeed, even more, and longer ones, after the composer made some small but noticeable revisions for a revival of the opera in Rome in 1922. Yet these changes present themselves with such suddenness as to be brutal, making the entire vocal line seem severe and angular, unmoored from melodic conventions that equate erotic tension with vocal ascent, extremes of register with extremes of passion.[25] Such conventions were essential in determining musical ebb and flow in the relative absence of generic formal patterns between, say, late Verdi and final Puccini. For paradigmatic examples think of the love duet from the first act of *Otello*, or Calaf's orgasmic ascent to the last high note in "Nessun dorma." From her first entrance in the opera Minnie shows a tendency to leap around suddenly in her vocal line. Note, in "Laggiù nel Soledad" (the above-mentioned aria in which she rejects the advances of the baritone, Jack Rance), the way she jumps upward a ninth for the first "Ah!" just as the orchestra has relaxed into silence; and the angular setting of her recollection that "qualche volta giocava anch'essa" (sometimes even Mama would join the gambling). She first reaches the high C near the end of the aria when she notes that her parents "si amavan tanto" (loved each other so; see Example 1). But the speed of her ascent, the triadic contours of the melody, and the absence of harmonic tension to support it, undermine the moment as a point of arrival. A similar pole-vault occurs later in the first act, at Minnie's line "Su, su, su, come le stelle" (Up, up, up, like the stars; Example 2); and then there is all the unprepared shrieking at the climax of Act 2. Deborah Voigt, who performed the heroine at the Met's centenary revival, noted that the role "has a couple of really perilous high Cs that come out of nowhere. The word 'voice-wrecker' comes up a lot when people talk about Minnie's arias."[26] Even more extreme in this respect are the "sixteen warm measures that had been lacking," which Puccini added to the love duet between Minnie and Johnson in Act 2. Few have found these warm, consisting as they do of a punishing ascent in unremitting unison, culminating in tied high Cs lasting five-and-a-half slow quarter notes. The singers in the Rome revival of 1922 refused to sing them.[27] Such moments protrude from a musical unfolding that is brutal and jagged at the level of the moment, while being preeminently continuous at the level of the act; the musical style of *La fanciulla* thus gives rise to these vocal shards yet refuses to integrate them. They are memorable, I would argue, much in the way that any sudden, piercing stimulus sits in the memory—that is, without the warm embrace of context.

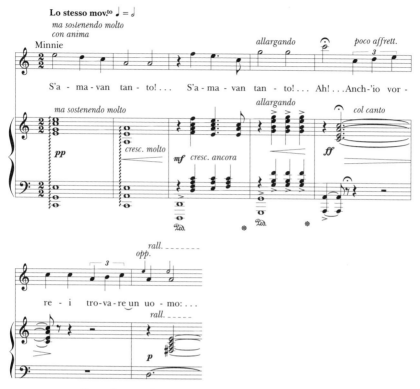

Example 1. *La fanciulla del West*, Act 1, "S'amavan tanto."

The high notes emerge so suddenly in *La fanciulla* in part because of the harmonic idioms that predominate in the opera. Except at the moments of highest character drama, when "local color" usually yields to a more familiar chiaroscuro, Puccini rendered the American West in whole-tone, Dorian, and pentatonic scales. Lacking in leading tones and dominant harmonies, this palette is unlikely to generate the kind of long-range harmonic tension that might otherwise assimilate vertiginous vocal heights into a slowly rolling landscape of musical highs and lows. It is also less likely to generate distinct melodic profiles, since all the stepwise intervals are identical (few or no semitones among the tones, in other words). This harmonic language has inspired many commentators to wax on about the opera's debts to French Impressionism and to prefabricated techniques of the musical exotic, more often used to depict Eastern peoples and locales—an "Eastern western," Stravinsky called the opera.[28]

I believe these to be dead ends. It is more productive to read *La fanciulla*'s music in light of the opera's engagement with a peculiarly extreme,

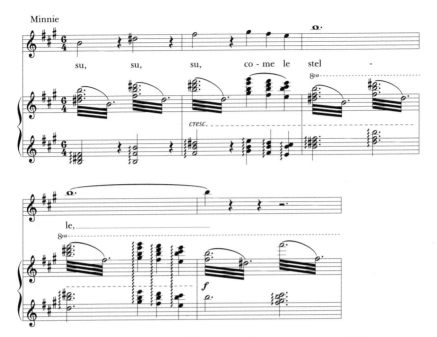

Example 2. *La fanciulla del West*, Act 1, "Su, su, su, come le stelle."

American theatrical practice known as "Belasco realism."[29] This avenue of investigation may encompass not just a preoccupation with reproducing the real—a matter for which Belasco represented an extreme point—but also the means by which historical realities were documented, reproduced, and archived for future study. Speck's mise-en-scène and the photographs shown here attest to an acquisitive impulse in the staging itself of *La fanciulla*, the urge to accumulate vast quantities of details— seemingly accidental and mutually nonadhesive—that would clinch the historical illusion precisely through their randomness. Minnie's cottage, for instance, must feature a bearskin rug, a canopy bed with a floral design on the curtains, a rocking chair made of an old barrel, cut in half and mounted on two pieces of wood shaped like half-moons, painted, and with two cushions on top (to emphasize, all of these details were declared mandatory); her oil lamp must lack a globe, and her armoire must be made of pine, and its doors should be ajar throughout the entirety of Act 2; the curtains on the windows are checkered white and blue. The orchestrated clutter of the opera's props and sets have their analog in the vast stretches of unassimilated (and unassimilable) notes in the score of *La fanciulla*—particularly those at the beginning of each of its acts, when each "scene" of music shares with its immediate neighbors only the weak bonds of adjacency—rather than attraction, or kinship, or narrative drive.

The opera's fascination with chance is manifest in its prominent scenes of gambling and references to card-playing: the boys play cards in the Polka Saloon; Minnie gambles with Rance for Johnson's life; she remembers her parents playing cards in Soledad. After all, as the adage goes, in a world defined by accident "a game passes the time more quickly as chance comes to light more absolutely in it."[30] Not coincidentally, in the first true gambling scene the atomization that characterizes much of Puccini's music for *La fanciulla* is present at its most extreme. It begins with the return of the first five notes of the miners' motive, in G-minor—an upward leap of an octave, followed by an arpeggiated descent—but this is subject to near-immediate dissolution as it is passed quickly between voices. There follows a snatch of the "doo-da day" melody, first heard just after the opening of the curtain, but this too breaks down into its constituent parts; then something else, for just two measures. The orchestra stutters into silence, punctuated by eighth notes that are at once featureless (simple ascending and descending scalar motion) and absolutely emphatic (all of them played with accents and as loudly as possible). Vocal interjections are short, brutal, and rhythmically unpredictable—Queen! Ace! King!—and assigned to indeterminate choristers. The musical momentum only resumes when a character cheats, and the game is thrown.

The contingency on display in Puccini's Wild West opera has been most compellingly theorized in relation to the photograph. The photograph —and, by extension, what I am calling "photographic" music—registers neither meaning nor subjectivity, nor depth of experience, but merely an array of surface details. Form is a mere by-product of an array of contingent happenings, accidental arrangements. It lays claim to reproducing time, but the time that gives rise to it is what theorists have called a homogenous (as opposed to auratic) time: defined by an overabundance of surface phenomena, it refuses interpretation and is resistant to what Mary Ann Doane calls "the depth of experiential meaning."[31] Herein may reside a key to the opera's forgettability. As Freud tells us, the mind that parries an excess of surface phenomena does not remember.[32] This is why *La fanciulla del West* offers no madeleines.

Figure 11. Ricordi Archive still (1905), "Del biscotto alla crema?"

Minnie's Finger

The opera may not offer madeleines, but its protagonist does, however, have tea and cookies, or "del biscotto alla crema," as the libretto informs. They are laid out in preparation for Johnson's visit to Minnie's cottage in Act 2: note, in Figure 11, how she points down at the cookies as she offers them. The gesture might seem laughably redundant given the context—unless we consider that Johnson's gaze may be inclined to wander, either toward Minnie's own charms or, less fortunately, in the direction of her décor. This photograph provides perhaps the most vivid glimpse into Belasco's "photographic" staging, wherein chaotic details—inside patterns, inside layers, inside details—accumulate in pursuit of a historical reality.

I want to linger on the pointing gesture, because I believe that it says something important about how meaning is created in this play and the peculiar opera made in its image. As the photographs in the Archivio Storico Ricordi attest, the characters in *The Girl of the Golden West* loved to point at things. Minnie points at her cookies; she also points at her white shoes, to bring them to Wowkle's attention (Figure 6). She points at Rance to accuse him of lying (Figure 7). She points at something in the saloon to bring it to Billy's attention (Figure 12). She points at the

Figure 12. Ricordi Archive still (1905), Minnie and Billy.

stars, telling Johnson she wants to ascend to the level of Johnson's clev-
erness, "Su, su, su" (Figure 5), while Johnson points to what he wants.
Rance points at Castro, the traitor, in Figure 13, and toward Johnson in
the noose in Figure 9. Johnson points at the horizon—"Noi dobbiamo
guardare avanti" (Figure 8). The miners point together toward Minnie
(Figure 14). Only the Indians are not shown to point: a measure (surely)
of their inability to direct attention.

These gestures show *The Girl*'s characters enthusiastically telegraph-
ing the heavy-handed system of signs that Belasco created for them: the

Figure 13. Ricordi Archive still (1905), Rance accuses Castro.

shoes to which Minnie points, for instance, and in which she can only wobble, represent a coy femininity that she keeps hidden from the miners; Johnson indicates the direction of his desires, while Rance fingers the guilty party. "Interpret this!" the gesture seems to shout. Yet it is also a deictic category of expression—*this* is the traitor; *these* are my shoes; *here* is your tea; *there* is where I will go—that relies on the presence of the object. As such, this collection of photographs records a peculiarly graphic instance of what Charles Sanders Peirce called "indexicality": the category of sign that points to its object, and has historically been associated with epistemologies of contingency, singularity, chance.

Such visual indices have analogs in opera's many instances of word painting. Indeed, given that Puccini—unable to read his English-language source play but keen to direct his wayward librettists—studied the theatrical stills carefully while composing, the pointing gestures recorded in the photographs may have given rise to the abundance of musical indices. Many of these are given to Minnie, who is, after all, at the opera's center. The rising arpeggio on "Su, su, su, come le stelle" is one, and here Puccini supplied a bald pictorialism to match an artless locution in the libretto. Other memorable ones occur in her Act 2 aria "Oh, se sapeste": when she describes riding her horse, the vocal line assumes a

Figure 14. Ricordi Archive still (1905), the miners.

sequence of galloping melismas (Example 3); when she turns her gaze
to the mountains and the sky, the melody rises again. Her signature aria
even begins with a pointing gesture, "Down there in Soledad," the vocal
line uncharacteristically sinking downward when she names her hometown (Example 4). Emanuele Senici has taken these details to represent
Minnie's extraordinary sensitivity to the landscape.[33] But the orchestra
points too: indeed, as in Senici's notion of a "particularly powerful ear, a
giant one," that perceives the offstage action in Act 3's manhunt scene,
we might imagine a giant index finger in the score. It gestures at times
to the objects and places named by the characters, whether distant or
merely imagined: there are the brays of the donkey in the lesson scene of
Act 1, and the sound of the triangle when Minnie mentions "the East."[34]
But more frequently, and in perhaps more fitting analogy to the indexical
gestures onstage, the orchestra warps its posture into Blanche Bates–like
contortions and hollers out emphasis: THIS! THIS! THIS!

My wager here is that this accumulation of indices makes *La fanciulla*
into an archive of sorts: a catalog of *this* plus *this* plus *this* (etc.) that slide
past the memory and go straight for the record, where they are logged
and registered for future interpretation. If the archive has always been
"a protection against time and its inevitable entropy and corruption," as

Example 3. *La fanciulla del West*, Act 2, "Che mi porta a galoppo."

Doane suggests, it is also something of a resting place for the gently aging ciphers that are too common or unshapely for museums.[35] They sit there and wait. Jacques Derrida identified what he called a "spectral messianicity" in his foundational text of archive studies: "If we want to know what that will have meant, we will only know in times to come."[36] Yet the archive-messiah can fill in *this* or *that* with anything whatsoever; it can be any he or she—it hardly matters. The storing of the "once present and unique" for future interpretation is above all a shoring up against the rule of accident.[37] After all, characters in *La fanciulla* may gamble to pass the time—or to determine matters of life and death—but the games are never allowed to unfold according to true chance: someone always cheats.

Example 4. *La fanciulla del West*, Act 1, "Laggiù nel Soledad."

NOTES

1. "Once archival materials that have been severely restricted have been made available for study, cross-checking will be possible." Annie J. Randall and Rosalind Gray Davis, *Puccini and the Girl: History and Reception of "The Girl of the Golden West"* (Chicago: University of Chicago Press, 2005), 8.

2. On 19 June 2012 Christie's auction house fetched £1,375 for a two-page letter from Puccini to Diaghilev, confirming the composer's attendance at an event in London the following evening.

3. On the discovery of Toscanini's conducting score among the archives of Casa Ricordi, and for an insightful study of the authorial entanglements to which it attests, see Gabriele Dotto, "Opera, Four Hands: Collaborative Alterations in Puccini's *Fanciulla*," *Journal of the American Musicological Society* 42 (1989): 602–24. For a more recent assessment of the editorial challenges related to Puccini's operas, see Philip Gossett, "Some Thoughts on the Use of Autograph Manuscripts in Editing the Works of Puccini and Verdi," *Journal of the American Musicological Society* 66 (2013): 103–28.

4. The copyists' version was published as *La fille du West: Mise-en-scène de Monsieur Jules Speck* (Paris: Ricordi, ca. 1912).

5. For more on staging manuals, see Michele Girardi's introduction to the excerpts from Albert Carré's staging manual for *Madama Butterfly* in this volume.

6. Even Michele Girardi wrote as recently as the late 1990s that the staging manual for *Manon*, published in 1893, was "the last important staging manual published by Ricordi." Girardi, *Puccini: His International Art*, trans. Laura Basini (Chicago: University of Chicago Press, 2000), 83.

7. See Mercedes Viale Ferrero, "Stage and Set," in *Opera on Stage*, ed. Lorenzo Bianconi and Giorgio Pestelli, trans. Kate Singleton (Chicago: University of Chicago Press, 2003), 1–223, esp. 105–8.

8. Speck is credited with the staging manuals for a number of works that premiered at the Opéra, including Emmanuel Chabrier's *Gwendoline*, Georges Marty's *Daria*, and Jules Massenet's *Ariane*. He also did lighter fare, such as Émile Pessard's *Les folies amoureuses* (Opéra-Comique, 1891) and canonical works such as Gluck's *Iphigénie en Tauride*, remounted in Paris ca. 1900. See H. Robert Cohen and Marie-Odile Gigou, *One Hundred Years of Operatic Staging in France (ca. 1830–1930)* (New York: Pendragon, 1986).

9. The correspondent describes Speck intervening at a rehearsal for *Boris Godunov* when the "stage crowd" tries to affect holiday merriment: "It doesn't suit Jules Speck at all. Up he jumps from his chair, the score falling to the ground, and into the crowd he takes a header. He soon emerges at the head of a line of serpentiners. In real life Mr. Speck is a quiet, dignified Frenchman. But this is the stage Mr. Speck, the man of a thousand nerves. He is prancing like a young colt in the effort to get some life into the line of chorus people behind him. He is roaring the music in exaggerated emphasis in order to make them accommodate their steps to the rhythm. [...] He mounts a chair and continues his dance on this precarious footing. Mr. Speck was once a great tenor himself in the Paris Opéra, and one realizes it now as he sings the music. [. . .] 'Louder! Louder!' shouts Speck in French from his chair. He is red in the face from exertion." See "Invisible Men Who Make Grand Opera Succeed," *New York Times*, 12 April 1914. It is not clear why Speck left the Met in 1917. The local papers suggested that he was headed back across the Atlantic—"Speck [. . .] has resigned and will return to his home in France," proclaimed the *Times*—but it seems he relocated instead to the Chicago Opera Company.

10. Speck, *La fille du West*, 46 (my translation).

11. Ibid., 26.

12. See Puccini's letter to Zangarini of 26 July 1907; Randall and Gray Davis, *Puccini and the Girl*, 182.

13. Belasco's *The Girl of the Golden West* was published in *Representative American Dramas*, ed. Montrose J. Moses (Boston: Little, Brown & Co., 1925), 50–97. The operatic version condenses its final two acts into a single act. The play was also novelized in 1911.

14. Quoted and translated in Randall and Gray Davis, *Puccini and the Girl*, 183 (original text), and 59 (translation; italics original).

15. The opening of the letter reads: "Increasingly the California mania takes hold of me. I have taken various photographs of the most beautiful part of the forest, where the tallest and biggest trees are and everything [needed] for the scenery of the third act" (translation modified from ibid.).

16. Ellen Lockhart, "Photo-Opera: *La fanciulla del West* and the Staging Souvenir," *Cambridge Opera Journal* 23 (2011): 145–66.

17. J. Y., "*La fanciulla del West*, New York," *Opera Today*, 19 December 2010, available at http://www.operatoday.com/content/2010/12/la_fanciulla_de.php. Italics mine.

18. "Listen: *La fanciulla del West*," Stanley's Reading Listening Watching, 20 June 2011, http://skstrauss.blogspot.ca/2011/06/listen-la-fanciulla-del-west.html; Chloe Veltman, "Debbie Get your Gun," Lies Like Truth: An Arts Journal Blog, June 2010, http://www.artsjournal.com/lies/2010/06/debbie_get_your_gun/; Gyran, "An Opera with Dick and Minnie," http://www.imdb.com/title/tt1736154/; a review of the DVD of the high-definition broadcast of the Met's centenary *Fanciulla*, posted on the Internet Movie Database, 28 May 2012.

19. Rodney Milnes, "Puccini's Golden Girl," Opera Holland Park website, ca. 2014, http://www.rbkc.gov.uk/subsites/investecoperahollandpark/puccinisgoldengirl.aspx; Michael Anthony, "A Western by Puccini: *La Fanciulla del West* at Minnesota Opera," *Star Tribune*, 22 September 2014, http://www.startribune.com/entertainment/music/276130891.html.

20. Gary Tomlinson, "Puccini Turns Respectable," *New York Times*, 15 December 2002.

21. Mosco Carner, *Puccini: A Critical Biography*, 3rd ed. (New York: Holmes and Meier, 1992), 462; John Paul Russo, "Puccini, the Immigrants, and the Golden West," *Opera Quarterly* 7/3 (Fall 1990): 4–27, quotation at 19; both cited in Randall and Gray Davis, *Puccini and the Girl*, 163.

22. Shelby J. Davis, "David Belasco and Giacomo Puccini: Their Collaborations," in *Opera and the Golden West: The Past, Present, and Future of Opera in the USA*, ed. John L. DiGaetani and Josef P. Sirefman (Cranbury, NJ: Associated University Presses, 1994), 129–39, quotation at 136.

23. Alan Mallach, *The Autumn of Italian Opera: From Verismo to Modernism, 1890–1915* (Lebanon, NH: Northeastern University Press, 2007), 272.

24. Randall and Gray Davis, *Puccini and the Girl*, 162–66.

25. On the angularity of the opera's vocal melodies see also Emanuele Senici, *Landscape and Gender in Italian Opera: The Alpine Virgin from Bellini to Puccini* (Cambridge: Cambridge University Press, 2005), 236.

26. Ellis Nassour, "Puccini's *La fanciulla del West*," ca. 10 December 2010, http://www.theaterlife.com/node/4912.

27. On the "16 battute calde che vi mancavano," see Arnaldo Marchetti, "La variante che Puccini non azzeccò," *Rassegna musicale Curci* 29/3 (December 1976): 34–35.

28. Igor Stravinsky and Robert Craft, *Dialogues* (Berkeley and Los Angeles: University of California Press, 1982), 58.

29. On "Belasco realism," see Lise-Lone Marker, *David Belasco: Naturalism in the American Theatre* (Princeton: Princeton University Press, 1975).

30. A fragment from Walter Benjamin's *The Arcades Project*, quoted in Doane, *The Emergence of Cinematic Time: Modernity, Contingency, the Archive* (Cambridge, MA: Harvard University Press, 2002), 223.

31. Doane, *The Emergence of Cinematic Time*, 102.

32. Sigmund Freud, *Beyond the Pleasure Principle*, trans. and ed. James Strachey (London: Hogarth, 1955), 1–64. Freud notes that "consciousness emerges instead of a memory-trace," and the most powerful memories are those "left behind" by events that "never entered consciousness." For a consideration of Freud's ideas of memory formation as they are relevant to turn-of-the-century photography and early cinema, see Doane, *The Emergence of Cinematic Time*, 13–15.

33. Senici, *Landscape and Gender*, 231.

34. Ibid., 255.

35. Doane, *The Emergence of Cinematic Time*, 206.

36. Jacques Derrida, *Archive Fever: A Freudian Impression*, trans. Eric Prenowitz (Chicago: University of Chicago Press, 1996), 36.

37. Doane, *The Emergence of Cinematic Time*, 16.

The Swallow and the Lark:
La rondine and Viennese Operetta

MICAELA BARANELLO

In March 1914, the close-knit world of Viennese operetta received a shock: Siegmund Eibenschütz, director of the eminent Carl Theater, had reached an agreement with Giacomo Puccini for the composition of a new operetta, "a comedy about a courtesan who begins a love idyll with an innocent young man."[1] The news broke publicly in the *Neues Wiener Journal*'s "Behind the Curtains" column, a regular compendium of gossip. "For several days," the columnist emphasized, "the operetta circle has been very energetically occupied with this news."[2] For this small theatrical community, an operetta by Puccini was a tantalizing prospect, but it also would have seemed an intrusion by an outsized interloper. The most surprised of all, the columnist claimed, was preeminent composer Franz Lehár—and not due to the threat of competition or even the existence of the agreement itself. Puccini and Eibenschütz's agreement stipulated a libretto by "Dr. Willner und Reichert," meaning Alfred Maria Willner and Heinz Reichert, two old hands in the industry, and this particular libretto had already been offered to Lehár himself two years prior (Lehár, the columnist noted, usually got first refusal). Lehár had "read it, considered it, and rejected it."

Even at this early point, the columnist doubted that a Puccini operetta would ever come to pass, noting that "now we're only waiting in suspense to find out if the premiere will actually take place in the Carl Theater or whether Puccini won't ultimately decide in favor of an opera house."[3] An opera house it would be, not in Vienna, though, but in Monte Carlo, and not until 1917, in the depths of the Great War. Willner and Reichert's libretto was translated and adapted into an Italian-language sung-through opera by Giuseppe Adami, the title transformed from the German *Die Schwalbe* to the Italian *La rondine* (both meaning The Swallow). The story of a courtesan's attempted romance, set against an idealized backdrop of Second Empire Paris, remained. *La rondine* has been captured in a purgatory between opera and operetta ever since. What may sound, from one perspective, like a pedestrian operetta is also something unique among Puccini's operas: a bittersweet, cosmopolitan romance, whose score is filled with dance rhythms, ending not with death but rather its lovers' separation, and yet, despite this, it is still usually described as a comedy.

When *La rondine* finally premiered in Vienna in 1920, audiences were both mindful and suspicious of its local origins. As critic David Josef Bach wrote:

> Since Viennese operettas are most easily exchanged with operas when they are at their most false, namely in their sentimentality, it seems obvious that the master of all sweetness and sentimentality, Giacomo Puccini, has now foisted himself upon an operetta text in which he has embedded above all products of the Viennese industry.[4]

Bach goes on to argue that despite Puccini's technical brilliance, *La rondine*'s libretto—and its operetta heritage—imposed a distancing, mannered barrier between the events and their telling: "Dr. Willner and Reichert certainly gave him a tear-softened operetta libretto. Operetta, though silenced, is at work: passionate melody is reduced to gestures toward passion, tender sweetness to sentimentality."[5] The vivid passion that the Viennese considered Puccini's greatest, and most Italian, asset was muted, the generically confused text made more awkward by being filtered through multiple translations (from German to Italian and back to German again—except for the Viennese premiere's leading tenor, who sang Ruggero in Italian).[6]

The shadow operetta of *La rondine* allowed—perhaps, when he soured on the contract, forced—Puccini to step outside his customary practices. The story of courtesan Magda's brief departure from her wealthy patron Rambaldo and romance with naïve young Ruggero is not easily given a role in a teleological narrative or a location within any particular national tradition. It is intimate, modest, and largely bereft of dramatic tension. Like its wartime 1917 premiere in Monte Carlo, it seems to exist outside of its place in history. For many scholars, *La rondine* is a failed experiment, primarily due to a mix of musical styles that were simultaneously derivative and faddish. Puccini's early Viennese biographer Richard Specht found it "feeble from beginning to end. [. . .] There is not a single bar in it that does not echo something he has said before," and describes the story as warmed-over *La bohème* and *Manon Lescaut*.[7] Arnaldo Fraccaroli agreed, adding that it was not only second-rate Puccini, it was also faddish rather than classic, with "banal and overused self-repetitions of situations and episodes characteristic of fashionable scale-models of light opera."[8] Julian Budden faulted its originality and dramatic gravity, calling it a "*Traviata* from which all the larger issues have been banished."[9] After multiple revisions of the opera—three versions in total—Puccini was himself inclined to agree, referring to *La rondine* as "this pig of an opera."[10]

What *La rondine* is usually not called is an operetta. For all the explicative weight its origins have been made to bear, they have rarely been explored in detail. *La rondine* is inevitably compared to *Die Fledermaus* (one of the few operettas familiar to modern audiences) in its characters and some plot events, its many waltzes are noted, and the third act's convoluted melodrama is considered at odds with the lightness of the first two.[11] But the milieu, characters, and plot of *La rondine* are not derived from the nineteenth-century *Fledermaus* but rather are highly typical of work of twentieth-century "Silver Age" Viennese operetta in general and librettos by Alfred Maria Willner in particular.[12] The rumor that the libretto was originally intended as a straightforward operetta for Lehár is, though, entirely plausible. Yet Willner and Reichert have often been discounted; Michele Girardi, for example, refers to them in terms of "influence" rather than authorship.[13] William Ashbrook argues that the libretto is Adami's, not Willner and Reichert's.[14] Primary responsibility for this disavowal surely goes to Puccini himself, who shortly after the Monte Carlo premiere attested to *La rondine*'s Italian credentials and gave no credit to Willner and Reichert. This repudiation, however, was prompted not by aesthetic confusion but rather political pressure.

Puccini's renunciation is nonetheless convenient, normalizing a problem work by assigning *La rondine* an Italian lineage. His equivocations have been given too much credit, however, particularly given the wartime circumstances in which they were made. It is the work of Willner and Reichert, and the world of operetta, that gives *La rondine* its otherworldly air, its lack of national affiliation, and, in that time of war, even its Second Empire nostalgia. Examining *La rondine* as a hybrid operetta reveals many of these features as standard features. Yet a hybrid of opera and operetta also defies conventional analytic frameworks. In the first section of this essay, I will trace *La rondine*'s history as operetta, placing it in the context of Viennese work of its time. I then will examine how and why this history has been concealed.

Genesis

In 1923, Puccini told journalist Desiderius Papp, again in the *Neues Wiener Journal*: "I never think to seek out operetta theaters in Italy. But when in Vienna, I never neglect to see two or three performances."[15] For many Viennese, a fusion of local operetta and Italian opera seemed only natural. According to many histories of operetta, Vienna's proximity to Italy and Viennese audiences' fondness for Italian opera marked, for better or worse, an important stage in the genre's development. Alluding to the long reign of Italian opera in Vienna, Lehár credited Viennese audiences with a "love for aria, which often places great demands on the singers' vocal abilities."[16] For Puccini, operetta seems to have been emblematic of the importance of music in the city's cultural life.[17]

Work on *La rondine* began in 1913, when Puccini was in Vienna for the local premiere of *La fanciulla del West*. As usual, he went to see some operettas. The *Fremden-Blatt* chronicled Puccini's theatrical adventures in Vienna, a series of performances in the company of Ricordi agent Carlo Clausetti. These included Paul Ottenheimer's short-lived *Der arme Millionär* (The Poor Millionaire) at the Johann Strauss Theater and Lehár's *Die ideale Gattin* (The Ideal Wife) at the Theater an der Wien. Puccini, the paper noted, had a "particular predilection" for Lehár's music.[18] The two were personal friends; Lehár often attended Puccini's premieres and entertained him when he was in Vienna. Stefan Frey argues that the importance of this relationship has been discounted by many Puccini scholars, even though much of the evidence is drawn from promotional press features.[19] Such publicity was mutually beneficial: Lehár profited from Puccini's operatic credentials and Puccini could avail himself of Lehár's local popularity.

During his stay in Vienna, Puccini attended, possibly at Lehár's invitation, a party hosted by Siegmund Eibenschütz at a *Heuriger* (vineyard inn). There, Eibenschütz proposed that Puccini write an operetta for his theater, which would not only premiere there but also be published by Eibenschütz's own firm of Eibenschütz & Berté. The sum offered was enormous: 200,000 *Kronen* ($40,500).[20] In comparison, leading operetta composer Leo Fall's 1916 contract for a new work with the rival Theater an der Wien included a guarantee of only 30,000 *Kronen*.[21]

Some kind of informal agreement was reached, yet Puccini's enthusiasm quickly cooled. Upon receiving the proposed subject in December—whose authorship remains unknown—he wrote to his Viennese agent, Angelo Eisner:

The subject you sent me doesn't suit me at all. It's the usual
crude and banal operetta, with the usual contrast between
Orient and Occident, balls and occasions for dancing, without character studies, without originality, and finally without
interest (the most serious thing). So? An operetta I will never
do: comic opera, yes, like *Rosenkavalier* but funnier and more
organic. Or if they want a lyric opera, not large but interesting and varied, nothing even close to operetta, I would do it
more willingly and it would be more seemly for me. So the
subject sent to me is definitely discarded.[22]

In this letter, Puccini seems to realize what he has committed to and does
not like the idea at all. His description of the "usual" Viennese operetta is, for 1913, entirely accurate. East-West contrast had been a staple
since Johann Strauss's 1881 *Der Zigeunerbaron*, and generalized character
types, to be filled in by celebrity actors, were the order of the day.

Puccini received a second subject in the spring, this one by Willner
and Reichert, which he accepted.[23] *Die Schwalbe*, the future *La rondine*, was
not a model of originality either. According to "Behind the Curtains," it
was originally the work of Willner and Robert Bodanzky, one of the most
prominent librettist duos in operetta.[24] Their previous work included
three major operettas for Lehár: first the enormously successful *Der Graf
von Luxemburg* (*The Count of Luxembourg*, 1909), a marriage comedy about
Parisian bohemians; then the ambitious, operatic *Zigeunerliebe* (*Gypsy Love*,
1910); and, finally, *Eva* (*Das Fabrikmädel*) (*Eva* [*The Factory Girl*]), which
premiered at the Theater an der Wien on 24 November 1911. *Eva* had
been a successful but controversial piece: a sentimental fairy tale of a
naïve, orphaned factory worker who falls in love with her cynical Parisian
boss.[25] The operetta was heartily criticized, not only for its staging of a
brief workers' revolt in Act 2, but for the perceived implausibility of its
plot, which combined a gritty factory setting with a Cinderella story.[26]

Die Schwalbe, then, was plausibly written as a follow-up to *Eva* and
would have been presented to Lehár at or around *Eva*'s premiere. The
Theater an der Wien's intendant, Wilhelm Karczag, had reportedly
gone so far as to buy the rights to *Die Schwalbe* for his publishing company for Lehár's use and, after Lehár's rejection, was obliged to ask for
a refund.[27] *Die Schwalbe* would have been a fitting continuation of the
Willner-Bodanzky-Lehár partnership. The story—a jaded courtesan falls
in love with a naïve boy from the country—inverts *Eva*'s pairing of a
simple girl with a nightlife-addled man. This time it is the woman who is

urban and world-weary while the man is a young romantic. The gender reversal is not simple: in both cases the man occupies the more socially stable position. The naïve Ruggero is a respectable member of the provincial bourgeoisie while courtesan Magda has an even more dubious status than orphan Eva. But the underlying mismatch is similar.[28] (The name of *Eva*'s secondary male lead, Prunelles, also strongly recalls *La rondine*'s secondary lead, Prunier.)[29]

The sad ending of Puccini's opera might seem the work's least operetta-like feature, and indeed unhappy endings were rare in operetta before the 1920s. Yet there is one prominent example and it is Willner and Bodanzky's *Zigeunerliebe*. The ending, extended dream sequence, wild dramatic landscapes, and "Gypsy passion" of *Zigeunerliebe*, as well as the thin social realism of *Eva*'s factory setting, were all part of Lehár and Willner's mission to make operetta more than a frivolous entertainment and stake a claim to art. The irony didn't escape Viennese critics' notice, and is evident in Bach's review of *La rondine*, quoted above: even as Puccini looked at operetta as a chance to escape into light music, Lehár and Willner were working to transform operetta into something more Puccini-like. The *Neue Freie Presse* specifically referred to *Eva*'s score as "in the style of Puccini or a post-Wagnerian music drama," and it and *Zigeunerliebe* were routinely referred to as operas.[30] After *Die Schwalbe*, Willner and Bodanzky would continue on this path with *Endlich allein*, a dramatic Alpine operetta again written for Lehár (1915). And after Puccini's death, Lehár was even proposed as a candidate to complete *Turandot*, presumably due to his Chinese-themed operetta *Die gelbe Jacke* (The Yellow Jacket, 1923), the first version of *Das Land des Lächelns* (The Land of Smiles, 1929).[31]

La rondine is a much more conventional Silver Age operetta than *Eva*. Especially since Richard Heuberger's 1898 hit operetta *Der Opernball* (The Opera Ball), Paris had stood for sex and modernity in a way Vienna did not.[32] The demimonde of the Second Empire in particular coincides with operetta's generic origins. The characters of *La rondine* correspond to the Fach system used in operetta, and not usually in opera: one leading couple, Magda and Ruggero (lyric soprano and tenor or light baritone); a lighter-voiced, younger "second couple," Lisette and Prunier (soubrette and comic tenor); and various minor supporting roles. Other elements reference operatic precedents: although the bohemian atmosphere of the nightclub Bullier recalls Willner's earlier operetta for Lehár, *Der Graf von Luxemburg*, the busy ensemble scene complete with flower sellers and drinking students is an obvious nod toward *La bohème*. Similarly, the plot of a courtesan seeking true love unmistakably echoes Verdi's *La traviata*. Magda's patron, Rambaldo, recalls Geronte of Puccini's *Manon Lescaut*, and Ruggero echoes Des Grieux. As many have noted, Lisette's masquerade in Magda's clothing for a night on the town recalls Act 2 of *Die Fledermaus*. For a Viennese operetta such lack of originality was not a deficit: popular elements were habitually recycled for years, if not decades. Canny pacing, jokes, and well-placed musical numbers were more important than formal or thematic originality.[33] Even an innovator like Willner or Victor Léon relied on tried-and-true formulas to make their work legible as operetta.

Both Julian Budden and Michele Girardi have proposed another inspiration for *La rondine*—Massenet's opera *Sapho* (1896). *Sapho* also concerns a provincial man "who falls in love at first sight with a worldly woman. [. . .] She [Sapho, the equivalent of Magda] flees with the unwitting Jean, living with him for a year in idyllic happiness in the suburbs of Paris until the young man learns the truth from two of the woman's ex-lovers."[34] The similarities are striking. Yet, while scholars have largely been concerned with Puccini's awareness of *Sapho*, Willner and Reichert's knowledge seems far more salient. *Sapho* had no Viennese performance history at the time of *La rondine*'s composition, but this does not mean Willner did not know it; operetta composers habitually drew from a wide range of preexisting sources, often without credit or with sources actively concealed (in order to avoid paying royalties), the more obscure the better.[35] French subjects were so popular that when describing the process of composing a libretto, Willner said that he began with a concept, either from a French source or by inventing one himself.[36] It seems more likely that if Willner knew *Sapho*, it was through Massenet's source, a novella by Alphonse Daudet dating from 1884.[37] *Sapho*'s influence on *La rondine* is impossible to prove or disprove, but the similarity is nonetheless profoundly ironic: Alphonse Daudet's son, Léon Daudet, would become *La rondine*'s most vociferous critic.

Willner's approach to *Die Schwalbe* does not seem to have differed from his working process for any other of his librettos. Even Giuseppe Adami's Italianized version is for the most part an utterly typical Silver Age piece—sweet, wistful, and gently comic, and largely lacking in dramatic tension. Set by a conventional operetta composer for the ensemble of an operetta theater, it could be cast in five minutes. It lacks the class conflict, aristocrats, and farce of a nineteenth-century Golden Age operetta, and its romance and sincerity mark it as a twentieth-century work.

Figure 1. Lucrezia Bori as Magda in *La rondine*'s
American premiere at the Metropolitan Opera, 1928.

Despite Puccini's evident enthusiasm for Silver Age operetta, his interest in *Die Schwalbe* quickly cooled. He wrote to Eisner on 26 May, only a few months after accepting the commission, that he was "not terribly pleased" with the libretto.[38] That summer he began to adapt it into more conventional operatic form with the assistance of Giuseppe Adami. It is evident that he never intended to write a real operetta: "Like Leoncavallo!! [. . .] I couldn't manage to do it like him even if I tried," he wrote dismissively to Eisner.[39] The point at which Puccini stopped writing an operetta and started writing an opera remains unclear. William Ashbrook claims that he never had any intention of writing the former, citing the letter to Eisner and a much later letter from Willner criticizing Adami's work.[40] The commission obviously specified an operetta, however, implying that this difference of purpose had not been fully clarified by Eisner, perhaps opportunely. Nevertheless, it seems strange that Puccini would sign a contract so cavalierly—placing himself in such a tight bind, as the history of *Rondine* attests, that not even a war could prevent its fulfillment.

Other evidence suggests that the Carl Theater management was convinced they had commissioned an operetta: on 21 March 1914, *Musical America* reported that Andreas Dippel, German tenor and erstwhile joint manager of the Metropolitan Opera, had bought the American and Canadian rights.[41] Dippel had recently left a position as manager of the Chicago-Philadelphia Grand Opera and one condition of his resignation was a non-compete clause. Forbidden to produce opera, he founded the Dippel Opera Comique Company in New York. Dippel's acquisition of *La rondine* for this company—presumably via Eibenschütz & Berté, who held the American rights—strongly suggests that the contract had indeed stipulated that Puccini would compose an operetta.[42]

Contrary to Ashbrook's interpretation, Willner's letter to Puccini suggests that the eventual work was actually rather close to his own original scenario. The letter objects to relatively small-scale issues of construction, most having to do with etiquette and character motivations, none of which imply that Adami made major, wholesale changes.[43] If anything, Willner's letter is strong evidence that Adami's interventions were anything but drastic, and many of the points are minor. For example, Lisette is judged as far too forward for a maid—Willner says that in the original, it was Prunier who described the wonders of Parisian nightlife. The description itself, however, can be found in Willner's original. Puccini, it is clear, set an operetta libretto.

The composer's waning enthusiasm was only the beginning of *La rondine*'s problems. As with most plans made in early 1914, the future of the

Figure 2. Beniamino Gigli (Ruggero), Lucrezia Bori (Magda),
Editha Fleischer (Lisette), and Armand Tokatyan (Prunier) in
Act 2 of *La rondine*, Metropolitan Opera, 1928.

project was thrown into disarray by the outbreak of the Great War. On 23
May 1915, Italy declared war on Austria-Hungary, and a premiere across
enemy lines was impossible. Ricordi had no interest in publishing *La rondine* and Puccini signed an agreement for the Italian publishing rights
with rival Sonzogno—his first and only work placed with another publishing house. After protracted negotiations with the initiating Viennese
publishers, some of which took place in person with Berté in Switzerland,
the premiere of *La rondine* was relocated to Monaco, neutral territory and
an oasis of leisure seemingly perfectly suited to *La rondine*'s delicate charm.

"The *Rondine* Affair"

The Opéra de Monte-Carlo was a fitting location for *La rondine*'s premiere. Since 1892 the Opéra had been run by the enterprising Raoul

Gunsbourg, a French-Romanian Jew whose career had begun in St. Petersburg, where he had founded an operetta theater before running the private theater of Tsar Alexander III. Gunsbourg's own cosmopolitanism was ideally suited to the internationalism of Monte Carlo and was in turn reflected in his eclectic, adventurous programming.[44] For *La rondine*, the intimate Second Empire theater located in neutral territory was practically and symbolically apt. In the midst of the war Monaco's relative isolation and peace made it one of the few places where a sad, nostalgic visit to an imperial past might seem wistful rather than blind. For Puccini and his Austrian publishers, it was an attractive compromise.[45]

Although Monaco made the premiere possible, the contract between Puccini and Eibenschütz & Berté still crossed enemy lines. French criticism of the premiere's financial terms—that the performances were enriching the Viennese enemy—would prove decisive for the reception of the work and for Puccini's own stance toward it. Though this controversy has received little attention from scholars, it is a key stage in the erasure of operetta from *La rondine*, as well as an illustration of how far the work had strayed from wartime norms. The instigator of the "*Rondine* Affair" was Léon Daudet, one of the editors of the far-right newspaper *L'Action française*.[46] As a political movement, the archconservative Action Française was never influential; its plotted coups d'état to restore the monarchy were fatally—and, considering the group's name, ironically—undermined by indecision.[47] Yet as propagandists the group was successful. Puccini had already been briefly a subject for *L'Action française*'s wrath when he failed to sign a letter protesting the bombing of Rheims.[48]

Being Romanian and Jewish, Raoul Gunsbourg was an obvious target for a movement founded during the Dreyfus Affair. In a series of front-page essays that appeared some weeks before the premiere of *La rondine*, Daudet condemned Monte Carlo as a hotbed of German espionage and called Gunsbourg not only a *métèque* (a derogatory term for a foreigner) but also German (probably really named Gunzburg) and a spy.[49] His cosmopolitanism, a boon for his opera house, now made him a convenient object of suspicion. On 25 March, only a few days before the premiere, Daudet reported that the commission for *La rondine* came from the Viennese, neglecting to specify that the contract originated before the war began. He then described with considerable embroidery Swiss negotiations between Gunsbourg, Puccini, Sonzogno, and Weinberger (another Viennese publisher, which he confuses with Eibenschütz & Berté) to bring *La rondine* to Monaco. The very existence of these negotiations, he said, was proof of commerce with the enemy. As additional evidence, he cited a 1916 interview with Puccini from the magazine *Noi e il mondo*, in which the composer despaired over his "contrat malheureux" (unfortunate contract). Gunsbourg's plans to donate the premiere's box office take to wounded Allied soldiers was an ignominy worthy only of a traitor, Daudet claimed.[50] Most important, Daudet implored Puccini to renounce any influence Willner and Reichert may have had on the libretto and proclaim it as solely the work of Adami. Daudet's condemnations of the Jewish Gunsbourg, Willner, and Reichert had an anti-Semitic subtext.[51]

The implication that the premiere constituted treason and would financially benefit the enemy was a grievous charge against Puccini. A planned onetime performance at the Opéra-Comique in Paris was canceled, a turn of events for which Daudet took credit (later denied by Puccini). Daudet added a litany of other claims: that while in Switzerland, Sonzogno had acquired for Gunsbourg a number of Viennese operas and operettas to be performed as the work of Italian composers with the idea of laundering the money back to Vienna; that Gunsbourg was leading tours to Berlin for the purposes of selling information.

Daudet's accusations were not a matter of aesthetics; nor would they have been possible without *La rondine*'s internationalism and hybridity. The terms by which Daudet attacked Gunsbourg and Puccini are familiar, and telling: Gunsbourg is effeminate—a "danseuse"—more international than nationalist. *La rondine*'s lack of clear national credentials made it inappropriate wartime entertainment.

Puccini's vociferous, thorough, and sweeping responses to Daudet's charges betray just how perturbed he was by them. He first gave a statement to Parisian critics, printed in the "Courrier des théâtres" in *Le Figaro* on 29 March and on 1 April alongside the reviews of the premiere in *Le Matin*. Puccini proclaimed that he wrote *La rondine* in 1912 on an "Italian libretto by the Italian poet Giuseppe Adami," that the opera was to be premiered in Vienna, and that despite his best attempts he could not fully escape his obligation.[52] On 10 April he published a more extended essay in the *Corriere della sera*. This account contains a somewhat more truthful description of the operetta's origins, though Puccini still insists that he rejected Willner and Reichert's libretto in favor of what is implied to be a completely different one by Adami, writing that "thus, the libretto was born of a continuous and assiduous collaboration between Adami and me, to which Messrs. Willner and Reichert remained extraneous."[53] Willner and Reichert, on the other side of the front, were discarded. His defense of his patriotism had required the renunciation of his Viennese collaborators, a denial that erases *La rondine*'s early history and leaves concealed the importance of Willner and Reichert's work.

Doretta and Prolepsis

After the war, when *La rondine* made its belated Viennese premiere in the autumn of 1920, Willner and Reichert returned, translating Adami's libretto back into German and evidently working with Puccini on the revisions. When Eibenschütz & Berté finally published the opera, it was in this second version.[54] Now it was Adami who had vanished, his name nowhere to be found on the printed score. The publishers also took the operetta-like liberty of dividing Puccini's score into numbers, some-thing not found in German-language editions of other Puccini operas, none of which were, of course, published by Eibenschütz & Berté.[55] The vestigial operetta structure is evident: the act begins with an ensemble introduction, then contains entrance songs for both the leading lady and man, Ruggero/Roger's romance "Paris, ja das ist die Stadt" being a new addition to the score;[56] followed by Magda's waltz song, "Nur Geld, immer Geld" in the German version. The list is too short (and sections are accordingly too long) for an operetta table of contents, but the same organizational principle is at work.

One of *La rondine*'s most operetta-like features is the diegetic song "Che il bel sogno di Doretta," found early in the opera, begun by Prunier as an incomplete song, then completed by Magda. Such narrative "story num-ber" songs had been a standard feature of Silver Age operetta ever since the massive success of *The Merry Widow*'s "Vilja-Lied" in 1905. Usually lyrical and strophic, the songs relate a fairy-tale parallel to the operetta's plot, giving depth to the characters' feelings and implying that they are participating in an archetypal scheme. "Che il bel sogno di Doretta" is unusual, however, in that it appears not at the customary place at the beginning of Act 2 but rather near the start of Act 1, presenting a situation that is not reflective but prophetic. Puccini's setting begins with Prunier's incomplete song set in fragmentary fashion—Prunier playing incantatory arpeggios on an onstage piano, introducing one motive, but offering few indications of tempo or affect. Prunier introduces the fictional Doretta, a girl who turns down a romance with a king. After singing only a few lines of regular four-measure phrases, Prunier breaks off and begins speaking at "Ah! Creatura! Dolce incanto!" (Ah, child! Sweet enchantment!); his sentiments seem to betray as much enchantment with his own words as with the imaginary Doretta. A solo violin playing under Prunier's words seems to hint at the song's completion, with a high-pitched, conjunct, and long-breathed theme, particularly compared to the opening theme's disjunct, short phrases. But the violin's theme, a voice from outside the song's diegetic space, does not yet have words to give it semantic meaning.

Magda takes up Prunier's challenge to finish the song. She provides an explanation for Doretta's rejection of her royal suitor: a genuine romance with a student, sung to the same music of Prunier's opening. But she also completes the song by finding words to sing the violin's theme. Beginning on a high A marked *dolcissimo*, Magda echoes Prunier's enchantment in more specific terms: "Folle amore! Folle ebbrezza!" (Mad love! Mad intoxication!). She takes what existed for Prunier as pure sentiment and moves it gradually into dramatic reality. Her vocal line extends the theme from its previous appearance, finally transitioning back into non-diegetic space as the three-note love theme from the opera's opening returns in the orchestra, linking Doretta's love to the opera's larger plot.

The equation of Magda and Doretta is explicit: first in the use of the love motive, then later in Prunier's reference to Magda as "the real Doretta."[57] Shortly after this number, Magda reminisces to her friends Bianca, Yvette, and Suzy an incident initially identical to the one she allegorized in the song "Ore dolci e divine di lieta baraonda," (Sweet and divine hours of happy chaos; rehearsal number 23), now given some temporal specificity—the evening Magda ran away from her aunt—and a location in the restaurant Bullier, as well as dramatic details (she and her mysterious lovers write their names on their table). But now her romance has an end point: she heard a distant "strange music" and a voice warning her that her romance would end in tears. Unlike the first story, this time the music is not explicitly diegetic. It is, however, a waltz, and the score's most extended exercise in popular music up to this point, giving the "strange music" described by Magda a self-referential quality.

The entrance of Magda's future suitor, Ruggero, follows this number and could hardly be more portentous. Magda is concealed behind a screen, having her fortune read by Prunier. He speculates "like the swallow," she may fly to a "land of dreams" and love.[58] Simultaneously, Ruggero chats with Rambaldo, their dialogue trivial in comparison but its significance obvious—even heavy-handed. Like his song, the fortune Prunier provides Magda lacks an ending. Magda, however, knows her fate, having already given it away in her waltz. Acts 2 and 3 largely consist of the actions that have already been foretold, right up to Magda writing her (assumed) name on a table at Bullier. Magda's and Ruggero's predicted separation eventually follows.

The opera's plot, therefore, is proposed as a fantasy or a dream, begun by a poet and completed by a courtesan. As Rambaldo suggests before "Doretta," the subject of love is "un po' appassito" (a bit passé), but simultaneously, as Magda replies to him, "sempre nuovo" (always new). Magda's romance does not arise naturally but is adopted temporarily and self-consciously as an "argomento," a plot, one whose moves she knows even as she performs them. Magda's actions are as if preordained, as if having already occurred. This predestined nature of the plot gives the entire romance a tinge of fateful despair—something more complex and melancholy than what Budden described as a "*Traviata* from which all larger issues are banished."[59] As Viennese critic David Josef Bach described, the dictates of operetta structure and the diegetic elements of the music confer a degree of remove from the events as depicted. For *La rondine*, operetta's formulas are not a straightjacket, but the source of its strange inevitability.

The Swallow Returns to Vienna

The Vienna premiere of *Die Schwalbe* also marked the first outing of a reworked third act, the second of three versions. This was an act that had long been troublesome; in November 1914, Puccini wrote to Adami that "the third act makes me suffer horribly . . . perhaps *La rondine* will remain two acts and a postlude." The third act, however, seems indispensable, since it contains the most serious action of the opera: Ruggero's discovery of Magda's past and their parting. The mechanics of this separation, however, were never completely worked out to Puccini's satisfaction and play out very differently in each of the opera's three versions. That Magda and Ruggero part in each version gives the opera its poignancy: one way or another, the bourgeois morality of Ruggero's family will not permit their relationship to last. That Adami, Willner, Reichert, and Puccini found it surprisingly difficult to maneuver their separation—prompted variably by an anonymous letter, an injunction from Rambaldo, or a revelation by Prunier and Lisette—perhaps indicates how the work fails to conform to any generic pattern.

In comparison, operetta was freewheeling and even, at the time, forward-looking, even beyond *Eva*'s pairing of industrialist and orphan.

One of the biggest successes of the war period, Emmerich Kálmán's *Die Csárdásfürstin* (*The Gypsy Princess*), presents a couple with a very similar problem: the aristocratic Edwin is engaged to a *Tingeltangldame* (night-club singer) named Sylva. By the end of the operetta, the social mores that kept the two apart are revealed to be hypocritical, because Edwin's mother had, early in her life, also spent time as a *Tingeltangldame*. Stephen Beller argues that this kind of progressivism, particularly in regard to class, was typical of wartime operetta, "stressing not only its ability to divert from life's realities but also its emancipatory and even assimilatory potential."[60] *La rondine*'s affirmation of nineteenth-century ideals of virtue and morality is comparatively anachronistic; it is part of what makes the opera old-fashioned and, for 1917, tone deaf.

If this were a typical Silver Age operetta, a discussion of the third act would need to begin at the end of the second—which would end with a denouement in which a secret is dramatically revealed, leading to a crisis and cliffhanger, the so-called tragic second act finale. In *Die Csárdásfürstin*, for example, Sylva's sordid professional life is revealed in front of Edwin's aristocratic family. The ending of *La rondine*'s second act is comparatively placid. A distant, anonymous woman sings an ominous warning: "Mi vuoi dir chi sei tu? . . . Nell'amor non fidar" (Do you want to tell me who you are? . . . Do not trust love) as Magda and Ruggero declare their love. But it is easy to imagine what a more typical second act finale would be: Magda's true identity is revealed to Ruggero in public at Bullier, possibly by Rambaldo, or in anger by Lisette or Prunier. Ruggero condemns Magda publicly (like Alfredo in *La traviata*), recapitulates one of his declarations of love in bitter irony, and the chorus loudly expresses its confusion and shock. Then, in Act 3, the situation would be harmlessly resolved: Ruggero and Magda would reunite and together live happily ever after.

Instead, *La rondine* moves this revelation and accompanying denouement to the end of the opera, where there is no space for resolution. The usual operetta structure is present but drawn out and, finally, truncated. The opera has been frequently criticized for its low stakes, but perhaps this seemingly trivial ending could be better understood as an operetta Act 2 finale in search of its final resolution. Willner's letter to Puccini reveals the original Act 3: no letter from Ruggero's mother, but rather a dramatic scene in which Ruggero confronts—and, presumably, condemns—Magda in a "virile and dramatic" fashion, ending with Prunier speaking to Magda "to raise her up from her disaster."[61] Though more heated, Puccini's three versions all lead to the same result: Magda's

Figure 3. Set design for Act 3 by Joseph Urban, Metropolitan Opera, 1928.

return to her courtesan status quo. Magda's romance evaporates as if it had never happened at all, the proof that "Che il bel sogno di Doretta" was, in fact, nothing more than a dream.

The Lark

In the waning days of the war, slightly after *La rondine*'s premiere, Franz Lehár embarked on another Willner and Reichert libretto, this one titled *Wo die Lerche singt* (*Where the Lark Sings*). Whereas the swallow had sung in a nostalgic, urban Paris, the lark belonged to the Hungarian countryside. The protagonist, the suggestively named Margit, makes the opposite journey from Magda: a brief and unsuccessful idyll in the city. A young farm girl, Margit is betrothed to a neighbor but lured by a visiting artist, Sándor, to Budapest, to have her portrait painted. There Margit embarks on a romance with Sándor and tries and fails to become a sophisticate. When Sándor's portrait of Margit wins a prize, he realizes he was only in love with her image, and leaves her for a more suitable and cosmopolitan woman. Margit is relieved to return to her country home and former fiancé.[62]

Lerche is "freely adapted" from Charlotte Birch-Pfeiffer's 1847 novel *Dorf und Stadt* (Village and City). Its similarities to *La rondine* are self-evident, yet much has changed. Margit, the provincial innocent, momentarily seeks the excitement of big city life, but after a brief romance finds only infidelity and homesickness. In *La rondine*, the city is a place of pleasure and beauty, in *Lerche* it is responsible for Margit's alienation. The score is defined not by the urban commercial music of *La rondine* but rather by pastiche Hungarian folksongs and dances. Even as *Lerche* played in various urban theaters—first in Budapest, then in Vienna, then around the world—it presented a romantic, pastoral vision. For the audience's members, many of whom may have made their own Margit-like migration, the story was only too personal, particularly when performed amid the wreckage of the war, a kind of Habsburg *Oklahoma!* In contrast, *La rondine* would have been impossibly distant for a Viennese audience during the war. If *La rondine* celebrates sophistication, internationalism, and romance, *Lerche* exalts fidelity, (Hungarian) patriotism, and simplicity. *Lerche* was a canny choice for its time, a tribute to the virtues of the common peasant for a homesick audience.

In 1919, Puccini was in Vienna in preparation for the premiere of *Il trittico*, and probably saw *Wo die Lerche singt*. The *Neues Wiener Journal* printed what claimed to be an effusive letter he sent to Lehár. Puccini wrote, "I saw your exquisite new operetta *Wo die Lerche singt* and can only say, 'bravo, master!' Oh, what memories of the days in Vienna in 1913! I will come back with new music, return with a new work."[63] *Lerche*, like *Rondine*, cast Puccini back into the happier days before the war. Margit, after her traumatic modern adventure, returned to an intact prelapsarian countryside. Magda's journey from a world of glamorous commerce to provincial romance is similarly temporary; like Margit's groom, Rambaldo welcomes her back. For Puccini, the flight from opera to operetta was equally brief. However incompatible operetta might have seemed, it nonetheless cast a long shadow. As Puccini struggled to reconcile the conventions and expectations of a "Viennese product" with his own poetics, so have subsequent listeners puzzled over *La rondine*'s carefree melancholy. *La rondine* may never fit in, but its own strange history reveals fault lines between genres, national schools, and even war and peace. That history remains integral to its enduring charm.

NOTES

1. This chapter is an expansion of an earlier essay, "Puccini's Crossover Dalliance," *New York Times*, 5 January 2013. My thanks to James Oestreich and Zachary Woolfe for their support.

2. "Hinter den Kulissen. Der Puccini-Rummel," *Neues Wiener Journal*, 21 March 1914.

3. After this note of skepticism, the columnist turned his attention to the next pressing issue, a lawsuit between the Theater an der Wien and Lehár regarding the production of the latter's latest operetta, *Endlich allein*.

4. David Josef Bach, "Puccinis 'Schwalbe,'" *Arbeiter-Zeitung*, 10 October 1920.

5. Ibid.

6. Bach even claims that the Viennese premiere was translated from Italian to French and then to German. There is no evidence that Willner and Reichert, who wrote the original libretto as well as the translation, were working from a French version, but it is possible.

7. Richard Specht, *Giacomo Puccini: The Man, His Life, His Works*, trans. Catherine Alison Phillips (New York: Knopf, 1933), 213.

8. Arnaldo Fraccaroli, *La vita di Giacomo Puccini* (Milan: Ricordi, 1925), 192.

9. Julian Budden, *Puccini: His Life and Works* (New York: Oxford University Press, 2002), 392.

10. The first version is the one most commonly performed today. The phrase "questa porca opera *Rondine*" is in a letter from Puccini to Riccardo Schnabl, 8 October 1922, in Eugenio Gara, ed., *Carteggi pucciniani* (Milan: Ricordi, 1958), 529.

11. See, for example Budden, *Puccini: His Life and Works,* and John Champagne's recent analysis. Champagne considers the *Rondine*'s much-revised third act to reflect the difficulty of marrying melodrama to operetta, but I argue that these two modes are far from diametrically opposed. John Champagne, *Italian Masculinity as Queer Melodrama: Caravaggio, Puccini, Contemporary Cinema* (New York: Palgrave Macmillan, 2015), 115–46.

12. The Silver Age of Viennese operetta began with the premiere of *Die lustige Witwe* (*The Merry Widow*) in 1905 and stretched to the genre's decline in the early 1930s. Silver Age works are more cosmopolitan and serious than their nineteenth-century Golden Age predecessors. The Silver Age's generation of composers was led by Lehár, Oscar Straus, and Emmerich Kálmán. For more on the conceptualization of the Silver Age, see Micaela Baranello, "*Die lustige Witwe* and the Creation of the Silver Age of Viennese Operetta," *Cambridge Opera Journal* 26/2 (July 2014): 175–202. Willner is occasionally identified as "Arthur Maria" rather than "Alfred Maria." The Deutsche Nationalbibliothek has identified "Alfred" as the standard form.

13. Michele Girardi, *Puccini: His International Art*, trans. Laura Basini (Chicago: University of Chicago Press, 2000), 340.

14. William Ashbrook, "*La rondine*," in *The Puccini Companion*, ed. William Weaver and Simonetta Puccini (New York: W. W. Norton, 1994), 260.

15. Desiderius Papp, "Bei Giacomo Puccini," *Neues Wiener Journal*, 11 May 1923. During this visit he saw Lehár's *Die gelbe Jacke* (the first version of *Das Land des Lächelns*) and *Libellentanz*, as well as Jean Gilbert's *Katja, die Tänzerin*.

16. Franz Lehár, "Die Zukunft der Operette," *Die Wage*, 10 January 1903.

17. In 1921, the *Neues Wiener Journal* printed a letter claiming to be from Puccini to Lehár in which Puccini exalted Vienna as "that city where music resonates in the soul of every person and even inanimate objects seem to have rhythmic life." "Puccinis letzte Grüße an Wien," *Neues Wiener Journal*, 7 December 1924.

18. Puccini also attended the Intime Theater, a small venue in the Nestroy-Platz that performed one-act plays because, the report specifies, "he is looking for subjects for an evening of three one-act operas," the future *Il trittico.* Since Puccini's German was, by most accounts, rudimentary, it perhaps should not be surprising that he did not find anything. The report goes on: "The first act of the triptych will be tragic, the second lyrical, the third comic; the tragic act will be based on *Houppelande* [The Cloak, the future *Il tabarro*], which he discovered in a suburban Parisian theater." "Aus der Theaterwelt," *Fremden-Blatt,* 19 October 1913.

19. Stefan Frey, *Was sagt ihr zu diesem Erfolg: Franz Lehár und die Unterhaltungsmusik des 20. Jahrhunderts* (Frankfurt: Insel, 1999), 141–42.

20. These details of origin were provided by Eibenschütz's son Karl to Michael Kaye. Budden specifies without source that Lehár introduced Puccini to Eibenschütz. Michael Kaye, *The Unknown Puccini* (New York: Oxford University Press, 1987), 193; Julian Budden, *Puccini: His Life and Works,* 333. Later Puccini claimed that the fee was 250,000 *Kronen* ($50,650). Exchange rate of $0.2026 in 1912 is from U.S. Department of Commerce, Bureau of Foreign and Domestic Commerce, Division of Statistical Research, *Handbook of Foreign Currency and Exchange,* by James R. Mood (Washington, D.C.: United States Government Printing Service, 1930), 13.

21. Both Fall and Puccini also received a cut of the box office proceeds. The Fall contract is for *Die Rose von Stambul (The Rose of Stambul)*, which was one of the biggest successes of the decade and ultimately proved very lucrative. Österreichische Nationalbibliothek, Musiksammlung F88 Leo Fall, Folder 283.

22. Puccini to Eisner, 14 December 1913, in Gara, *Carteggi pucciniani,* 417.

23. Willner described his compositional process in 1905: first a concept, then a plot outline with moments for diegetic music, followed by a full draft, then a go-through by the theater management to adjust the distribution of the musical numbers among their cast. "Wie entsteht eine Operette? Eine Rundfrage," *Neues Wiener Journal,* 11 June 1905.

24. Viennese operettas were customarily written by pairs of writers, one responsible for the overall planning and spoken dialogue and the other for the verse of the song texts. Alfred Maria Willner (1859–1929) fulfilled the former role and the replacement of Bodanzky with Heinz Reichert (1877–1940), described speculatively by the *Neues Wiener Journal,* would not be significant for the work's larger plan.

25. The uproar over *Eva* had largely centered around a scene in which the factory workers revolt in defense of Eva's virtue, a scene that some critics saw as threateningly similar to several real workers' protests in Vienna around the same time.

26. See Frey, *Was sagt ihr zu diesem Erfolg,* 141–45.

27. Both Eibenschütz and Berté of the Carl Theater and Karczag of the Theater an der Wien operated publishing firms in conjunction with their Viennese theaters. This enabled them to develop new operettas for their stage and then further profit from royalties as other theaters produced the work, as well as sell sheet music and arrangements to salon orchestras and to the general public.

28. They are called Madeleine and Roger in the German version; I use the Italian names for consistency.

29. Giuseppe Adami had even translated *Eva* for its Italian-language premiere in Milan, a translation that was subsequently published by Sonzogno, the eventual Italian publisher of *La rondine.* A. M. Willner, Robert Bodanzky, and Franz Lehár, *Eva: Operetta in tre atti,* trans. Giuseppe Adami (Milan: Casa Musicale Sonzogno, 1911).

30. "Franz Lehars Operette 'Eva,'" *Neue Freie Presse,* 25 November 1911.

31. Frey, *Was sagt ihr zu diesem Erfolg,* 188–93. The relationship is also chronicled in Jürgen Leukel, "Puccini und Lehár," *Schweizerische Musikzeitung / Revue musicale suisse* 122/2 (1982): 65–73.

32. After *Der Opernball*, *Die lustige Witwe* also takes place in Paris, as does Willner's *Der Graf von Luxemburg*. Moritz Csáky examines the symbolism of Paris for Viennese operetta in Csáky, *Ideologie der Operette und Wiener Moderne: Ein kulturhistorischer Essay zur österreichischen Identität* (Vienna: Böhlau, 1996), 129.

33. Libretto design is examined in Heike Quissek, *Das deutschsprachige Operettenlibretto: Figuren, Stoffe, Dramaturgie* (Stuttgart: J. B. Metzler, 2012).

34. Girardi, *Puccini*, 339. Girardi credits Budden.

35. As a theatrical joke book put it, "Why does he write 'from the French' on all his librettos? So it doesn't come out that they're all from the English!" Alexander Engel, *Vorhang auf! 250 Witze und Anekdoten vom Theater* (Vienna: M. Perles, 1910), 94.

36. A. M. Willner, "Wie eine Operette entsteht? Eine Rundfrage."

37. A play adaptation of the novel was performed in Vienna to great fanfare by the touring French actress Gabrielle Réjane at the Raimund Theater on 31 October 1899. Alphonse Daudet, *Sapho: Moeurs parisiennes* (Paris: Charpentier, 1884). Despite Massenet's popularity in Vienna, *Sapho* was never performed at the Hofoper or the Volksoper, nor was it published in German.

38. Puccini to Eisner, 26 May 1914, in Gara, *Carteggi pucciniani*, 425–26.

39. Puccini to Eisner, 25 March 1914, ibid., 421–22. Cited in Girardi, *Puccini*, 334.

40. Ashbrook, "*La rondine*," 248.

41. *Musical America*, 21 March 1914, cited in Kaye, *The Unknown Puccini*, 175. W. J. Henderson references the deal again in his review of the American premiere of *Rondine*, but he credits Dippel with the commission of *La rondine*, which, he says, was written for Broadway! W. J. Henderson, "*La rondine* is presented here," *The Sun* (New York), 11 March 1928

42. Ashbrook places the word *operetta* in scare quotes without mentioning the terms of Dippel's company; there is no evidence to believe that the Carl Theater management did not believe they would get what they were playing for.

43. The letter's exact provenance is unclear; it was published in a program produced by the Teatro Comunale. Ashbrook quotes it in full, in "La *rondine*," 260–62.

44. The company's repertoire was extraordinarily heterogeneous. Under Gunsbourg, they performed some of the first Francophone productions of Wagner, a number of rediscoveries of works by French composers such as Lalo and Bizet, premieres of works by Massenet and Franck, a large variety of Russian operas harkening back to Gunsbourg's St. Petersburg years, and even some of the first modern Baroque revivals of Monteverdi, Rameau, and Lully. Albert Gier, "Die 53 Spielzeiten des Raoul Gunsbourg, oder: Die Oper Monte Carlo zwischen Belle Epoque und Occupation," in *Das (Musik-)Theater in Exil und Diktatur*, ed. Peter Csobádi, Gernot Gruber, and Jürgen Kühnel (Anif: Mueller-Speiser, 2005), 333; Michael Scott, "Raoul Gunsbourg and the Monte Carlo Opera," *Opera Quarterly* 3/3–4 (Winter 1985): 70–78.

45. The premiere received no coverage in the Viennese press. A report in the *Fremden-Blatt* on 20 June 1917 even described the first Bologna performances as the world premiere.

46. Daudet was the son of Alphonse Daudet whose novella *Sapho*, as mentioned, may have inadvertently supplied one of *La rondine*'s sources, though the resemblance evidently went unnoticed.

47. Stephen Wilson, "The 'Action Francaise' in French Intellectual Life," *Historical Journal* 12/2 (1 January 1969): 328–50; Eugen Weber, *Action Française: Royalism and Reaction in Twentieth-Century France* (Stanford, CA: Stanford University Press, 1962).

48. See Ashbrook, "*La rondine*," 250.

49. This would be correctly spelled Günzburg; Daudet did not include an umlaut. Gunsbourg's name came from his French father. See Léon Daudet, "Mesures contre le

gaspillage: Sauf contre les Jeux de Monaco," *L'Action française*, 9 February 1917; and Léon Daudet, "De Verdun à Jeux de Monaco," *L'Action française*, 22 February 1917.

50. Léon Daudet, "L'Affaire de la 'Rondine': Gunsbourg pris la main dans le sac," *L'Action française*, 25 March 1917.

51. At one point Daudet claimed that Gunsbourg conspired with a certain "Finkalstein" to communicate intelligence to Berlin. Daudet also consistently refers to Gunsbourg as a "danseuse," in quotation marks, simultaneously impugning his masculinity and crediting him with a dance career he never had. Léon Daudet, "Etranges Avatars du 'danseuse' Gunsbourg," *L'Action française*, 16 February 1917.

52. "J'ai écrit *La rondine* en 1912 sur un livret italien du poète italien Giuseppe Adami." The identical text appeared in *Le Matin*, 1 April 1917, and *Le Figaro*, 29 March 1917.

53. "Il libretto di *Rondine* nacque quindi da una continua ed assidua collaborazione tra me e l'Adami alla quale i signori Willner e Reichert rimasero estranei." Giacomo Puccini, "Le polemiche per la *Rondine*," *Corriere della sera*, 10 April 1917. Michael Kaye speculates that the "15,000 lire in cash to the *Corriere*," referenced by Puccini in a letter to Carlo Paladini on 11 November 1919, was payment for printing this essay. Kaye, *The Unknown Puccini*, 187.

54. The second version had premiered in Italian in Palermo in the spring of 1920.

55. Giacomo Puccini, Dr. A. M. Willner, and Heinz Reichert, *La rondine (Die Schwalbe)* (Vienna: Eibenschütz & Berté, 1920), 2.

56. The music is based on Puccini's song "Morire?"; for more on this see Kaye, *The Unknown Puccini*, 194–96.

57. "La Doretta della mia fantasia non si turba, ma, in verità, mi pare che vacilli quella della realtà!" (The Doretta of my imagination was not troubled, but it seems to me that the real one is yielding!).

58. "Forse, come la rondine, migrerete oltre il mare, verso un chiaro paese di sogno, verso il sole, verso l'amore."

59. See Budden, *Puccini: His Life and Works*, 392.

60. Steven Beller, "The Tragic Carnival," in *European Culture in the Great War: The Arts, Entertainment, and Propaganda, 1914–1918*, ed. Aviel Roshwald and Richard Stites (Cambridge: Cambridge University Press, 1999), 154–59.

61. Ashbrook, "*La rondine*," 260–61.

62. A complete recording from a performance at the Lehár-Festival in Bad Ischl is available on CD from CPO , CPO 777 816-2 (2014).

63. Puccini to Lehár, in *Neues Wiener Journal*, 18 November 1919.

Puccini's Things: Materials and Media in *Il trittico*

ALESSANDRA CAMPANA AND CHRISTOPHER MORRIS

In Puccini's late operas and *Il trittico* in particular, music and stage action seem to deal differently with the work of representing. According to Michele Girardi, for instance:

> Only after *La fanciulla* did [Puccini] decide to dedicate a different type of space to the atmosphere of an opera. Functional music and dramatic interaction between event and place allowed him to bring about the new musical structures that he had had in mind ever since he had become aware of the symptoms of the twentieth-century crisis.[1]

From *Fanciulla* onward the composer appears to have been on the verge of elaborating a radically new dramaturgy for modern opera—a project never quite realized and marred by an incapacity to sever the connection with tradition and, even more, by a naïve national-popular agenda that implicated the composer's late works in the fascist program to come. Against this background, interpretations of the formal and dramaturgical features of the late operas have stressed the citational, both in dramatic content and musical style: the antiquarianism or exoticism of the libretti and the eclecticism or "marked" styles of the scores.[2] The late operas have then been measured against the wealth of contemporary reactions and understood as cultural objects reflecting (on) issues of nationalism, imperialism, fascism. These last works therefore seem to outline a historiography of climactic closure to the "great tradition" of Italian opera. Their marked stylistic features are taken as signs of exhaustion of their creative potential: a state of almost posthumous life, turned toward the past but without a future.

Here we want to take another look at Puccini's late operas and register the possibility of a less straight-laced purview. Puccini's "awareness" of the need to find new ways for opera in the twentieth century appears most overtly, we argue, in a purposeful and patent foregrounding of opera's medial capabilities, of its representational and aesthetic goals and devices, which are simultaneously restated and tested. In order to take the aesthetic project of these late operas seriously we follow the trail left by theatrical matter that is seemingly marginal but in fact traces the very semiotic borders of musical-theatrical signification. These are the "things" that travel between, on the one hand, an indexical value—which connects the stage with outside reality—and, on the other, a symbolic role attached to anything once on a stage, behind the proscenium arch, or emanating from the pit (sound effects, props, musical motives). *Trittico* in particular seems to make a point about musical-theatrical things, and the small scale of its three one-acters condenses and amplifies its experimental ambition. We start with an exploration of how *Trittico* reconfigures the aural regime with an intrusive and self-advertising sonic materialism onstage, then turn to modes of repetition that seem first to reinforce but then unravel the traditional dramaturgical and musical functions of motives in the orchestra. Finally, we consider a prop and ask what it means—or if it means—in the new music theater of late Puccini.

Bells and Whistles

The stage of *Trittico* is a noisy one, and the effort to give sonorous density to its three worlds—a humble barge on the Seine in early twentieth-century Paris, a garden in a seventeenth-century monastery, the bedroom of a thirteenth-century Florentine merchant—exceeds the well-tested operatic techniques of *couleur locale*. What becomes obvious very quickly is that sound and music here are not just about "representing" place. The proliferation of environmental sounds, the richer definition of soundscape by way of diegetic noises, simulates the creation of a separate aural channel, noticeably autonomous from the orchestral utterance. The effect is to release the orchestra, at least in part, from one of the roles it had acquired in the nineteenth century—mimetic spatialization—and allow it greater mobility and freedom to weave in and out of the fictional world and its dramas.

All three one-acters begin with a theatrical gesture of separation between stage and pit, using the curtain as a diaphragm. *Tabarro* starts with a silent set, showing *a tranche de vie* of the unhappy couple on their barge, onto which is layered the orchestral rendition of the Seine's movement (a rendition that is mimetic only insofar as it is historical and conventional). Reversing this order, in *Suor Angelica* offstage bells resonating in an invisible space from behind the closed curtain anticipate the motive that will be continued in the orchestra once the set is shown, as if the bells' indexical sound alone generated the vignette of the convent life. In *Gianni Schicchi* what may seem a traditional orchestral prelude in front of a closed curtain, outside the fiction and yet introducing and suggesting it, falters and recedes after only a few energetic measures (*diminuendo e rallentando*) to leave room for the sound of a funereal drum, which, indexically but from the pit, triggers the opening of the curtain on Buoso Donati's deathbed, which is surrounded by his lamenting relatives.

These theatrical gestures of separation and repartitioning of labor do not just restate sound's visual content—hardly a novelty in the theater —but autonomize music from its traditional task of giving voice to place, actions, events. The so-called Seine motive soon becomes the very narrative thread of *Tabarro*, metaphorically running through the tragedy on the barge, unencumbered from the need just to "sound" the place. Similarly, in *Suor Angelica* the orchestra picks up and mimics the offstage bells and transforms them into the nuns' prayer, saying much more, as it does so, about the cloistered life and the sealed-off temporality of the opera; and in *Gianni Schicchi*, the motive that was halted by the *tamburo funebre* restarts unfettered—as if triggered by the opening of the curtain—to become, obsessively and on its own terms, the very musical fabric of the final one-acter. Released from its mimetic role, the orchestral music here is treated as a medium allowed continually to move from within to without the events, and vice versa, and is endowed with the possibility of complete externality. On the other end, the unprecedented variety and multiplication of sound effects—car horns, tugboat whistles, stevedores' voices, songs of passersby, church bells, organ and sung prayers, birdsong, funeral drum, and more—come to define spatial-temporal coordinates in the aural register that intersect but do not completely overlap with those of the drama. Made out of these sound objects, the rich soundscape of *Trittico* constitutes a temporalized space that runs parallel to the dramatic space inhabited by the characters.

The organization of the stage is therefore essential to keep in balance this kind of new spectacle based on separation and layering. The shallow sets of the three operas avoid a rigid split into foreground-background, first of all by narrowing the distance between the characters

Figure 1. Vittorio Rota's sketch for *Tabarro*.

and the events around them, so that events seem to traverse rather than just frame their stories. The composer voiced his preoccupation with finding the appropriate way to stage all this in his letters to the publisher Tito Ricordi in the days leading to the premiere. For instance, in a letter of July 1918 Puccini insists that the main action of *Tabarro* has to take place entirely on the barge. Then, about a month later, he protests that in the sketch he just received,

> The set is designed as usual to have an outlet [*sfogo*] only toward the audience, and as I have to tell you for the 1000th time, this will not do. As if you do not know how this *Tabarro* is built! Of the utmost importance are the episodes and details arriving from the back. [. . .] The problem with this sketch, probably designed by Rota, is that the practicable embankment is too far to accommodate characters proportionately—Frugola, storyteller and "midinettes," traveling musician, etc.—and they all have to arrive or act from there, there is no other way. So the whole foreground has to be smaller: passageway, rampart, and ascending street, because

Figure 2. Pietro Stroppa's sketch for *Tabarro*.

they distance the place of the action: the barge. It may be gloomy, a dead river bend, it will be what it will be . . . not quite the Seine, I don't care, all I need is that the picture is the way it has to be.[3]

Hence the riverbank downstage-right in Vittorio Rota's sketch disappears from the subsequent sketches which instead compress the scene downstage to ensure that Giorgetta, Michele, and Luigi's tragedy is all carried out on the barge, and that the practicable embankment behind them functions as both a second stage and as the site of another indifferent and continually changing audience (see Figures 2 and 3).[4]

As for the other two sets, Girardi notices how they also concentrate the main action within a contained area on the already shallow set. Thus the bed in Buoso Donati's bedroom in *Gianni Schicchi* is the center of the comedy of death and heritage, and an early idea, never realized, places the climactic exchange between Suor Angelica and "la zia Principessa" in an apposite parlor on the set, "in such a way to place the episode into an ever greater relief, thanks to a new spatial dimension created in contrast with the painted scene."[5] However, each episode presents a different topography: in *Tabarro* the river and the city constitute a very present outside, whereas *Suor Angelica* contains everything within the walls of the convent. *Gianni Schicchi* instead condenses the action within the bedroom but as foreground to a distanced and celebrated postcard vista of Florence, a vista that at the very end is invoked as "paradise" and that becomes the vanishing point of the entire historicized fantasy of national-popular pride. As a final gesture—and final also for the whole *Trittico*—the two young lovers open the shutters of the window at the back of the room, like a curtain on another stage, to reveal the view of Florence "bathed in glorious sunshine." Their love duet, as Arman Schwartz has observed, is actually a trio, sung to the distant view of Florence, and "their love is presented as an illustration of the golden landscape, and not the other way around."[6] Indeed, the audiovisual reconfiguration of *Trittico* has to do precisely with this kind of reversal.

The proliferation of sound objects also leads to a reorganization of time: bells, car horns, boat whistles, church organs, etc., mark the time of the everyday: repeatable, unexceptional, and most importantly, indifferent to the temporality of the plot. The latter is an overlay: the teleological rushing toward the unavoidable catastrophe, the climactic accident, does not affect nor appropriate the world of the everyday. In general, earlier opera—from, say, *I Puritani* to *Tristan und Isolde* but also *Tosca*—marks and amplifies the catastrophe by way of a confluence of sound and visual effects, all contributing to conveying the force of that instant, as a symbolic convergence of interiority and exteriority. The drama encompasses the whole world of the characters, from thunderstorms to wedding rites, from history to nature, and opera functions as a kind of mediating instrument, with the power to incorporate into its own signification everything that happens to traverse the stage. Even in the *Te Deum* scene in *Tosca*, the belabored spectacle at the end of Act 1 superimposing Scarpia's lascivious evil over the Catholic rites of praising God (church bell, organ, hymn singing, and procession) turns the latter into an amplification of the character's "will to power."[7] Despite the final unison statement of the Ambrosian hymn, Scarpia has indeed managed to make us forget God. In *Trittico*, instead, tragedy or comedy happens as a fold, an imperceptible crease of an indifferent everyday, connected to it but neither as its effect nor its cause.

Girardi, who has so acutely recognized the appearance of a "detachment between the event acted on stage [. . .] and its musical expression" in the operas from *Fanciulla* onward, as well as a trend common to the contemporary European stage to increase "the distance between the

Figure 3. Still from *L'Atalante*, dir. Jean Vigo (1934).

characters' social conditions and the musical expression of their states of mind," tends to develop this argument toward a discussion of realism— and critics' uses and abuses of the term to define Puccini's music.[8] But let us set aside for a moment the question of Puccini's realism and take a detour into an early sound film that appears to stem from the same fluvial world of *Tabarro*: *L'Atalante* (1934), directed by Jean Vigo. Here too a couple living on a barge is separated by the woman's yearning for life on land. She momentarily escapes to stroll the streets of Paris but he sails off and abandons her there. It will be the old mariner working on the barge who will bring her back for the happy ending.

If the story of *Tabarro* is confined to the one set, to the short and final slice of life on the barge, and to a brutal and unavoidable turn of events, *L'Atalante*—similarly foregrounding the capabilities of its own medium— can afford a looser connection of episodes to explore the movement and light of the water, the rhythm of life on the boat, and the juxtaposition of city and river as that of two different worlds, each with its own regime of perceptions, movements, passions.[9] Siegfried Kracauer, in a review of the film published in 1940 while in exile in France and then republished in 1947 in America, explains how Vigo, a director with "a profound concern with truth," manages in this masterpiece to use the specificity of film:

> More important are the conclusions Vigo draws from the fact that the camera does not discriminate between human beings and objects, animate and inanimate nature. As if led by the meandering camera, he exhibits the material components of mental processes. In *Atalante* we experience with all our senses how strongly the fogs of the river, the avenues of the trees, and the isolated farms affect the mind. [. . .] Other film directors, too, have identified objects as silent accomplices of our thoughts and feelings. But Vigo goes still further. Instead of simply revealing the role objects may play in conditioning the mind, he dwells upon situations in which their influence predominates, thus exploring camera possibilities to the full.[10]

Kracauer captures the effect of Vigo's so-called poetic realism in terms of the camera's capacity to take in the world as well as its inhabitants, the characters as well as their things. This in turn is what film can do best to manifest the link—visual, affective, haptic—with ordinary life. Like the "meandering camera" of Vigo, Puccini's "meandering" score seems similarly intent in making room and giving voice to the sonorous matter of the characters' world. The sound or musical objects that animate the three operas aspire to impact the senses in the way of "material components of mental processes." Perhaps, then, the issue of realism can be recast in terms of their insistence on "situations in which [objects'] influence predominates."

Mourning Machine

In one of his many telling observations, Mosco Carner reflects on the semantic ambiguity of a snatch of melody in *Gianni Schicchi*. The passage in question consists of the first two phrases of an aria that occupies a place in the sound world of even the most opera-averse: Lauretta's "O mio babbino caro." These phrases make their debut not in the opera's one and only chestnut but moments earlier as Lauretta's lover Rinuccio exhorts his scheming relatives to enlist the services of Gianni Schicchi, Lauretta's father. As Rinuccio makes the case for Schicchi as embodiment

Example 1. *Gianni Schicchi*, rehearsal no. 31, "Salgon palagi saldi e torri snelle."

of the spirit of Florence and conjures up the city's splendors, the theme bursts forth in the orchestra (see Example 1). It seems, Carner suggests, to be associated with the city itself, and yet it will return, first to introduce Lauretta as she arrives with her father, then famously in her aria, where its lyrical simplicity—marked *andantino ingenuo*—seems the melodic realization of youthful passion. Isn't this, Carner asks, a characteristic moment for a composer with a penchant for "laxity in the strict use of characterizing themes?"[11] If there is a code of characterization, a logic of the leitmotif, he seems to say, Puccini doesn't quite get it. No sooner are our associative habits triggered than the relationship is undermined by excess and slippage. A musical signifier is recoupled with another theatrical signified, its unique semiotic pairing broken: a characteristic theme becomes, in effect, a tune.

Of course this slippage might itself be rescued by the earnest opera scholar, who never knowingly misses an opportunity for theatrical

Example 2. *Gianni Schicchi*, mm. 6–11.

interpretation. Doesn't this slippage of identity parallel—at a meta-theatrical level—the very theme of the opera?[12] And yet Rinuccio and Lauretta seem like the wrong characters on which to pin a reading centered on duplicity and disguise. Besides, as Carner points out, this is standard fare for Puccini, who "will use the same theme to denote now a character, now a situation, now an atmosphere, and now to add a purely musical interest to the orchestral texture, without perceptible reference to the drama on the stage."[13] *La bohème*, for example, closes with the final bars of Colline's "Vecchia zimarra." A sudden highlighting of a sentimental aside? A last-minute reevaluation of a secondary character? Or simply a "found" motive with which to bring closure?

If the Florence/Lauretta theme participates in this characteristic "laxity" (laxity of characterization?), *Gianni Schicchi* also seems to extend the practice in new ways. Again it involves the orchestra and a melodic gesture, and again it involves a proliferation that unwinds theatrical signification. But there the similarities end, for this is not just a case of multiple pairings between music and stage. It is, rather, a matter of repetition. The musical gesture in question is deceptively simple: repeated appoggiaturas embedded in a step-wise descending motive that is itself repeated in sequence (see Example 2). Less simple or expected is the rhythmic placement of the motive, which repeatedly enters half a beat too early and appears, on paper, to subvert the function of the appoggiaturas by displacing them from their expected accented location (on the beat) to an eighth-note pickup. Marked accents over the appoggiaturas effectively render this displacement inaudible —we hear the motive as though it entered on the strong beat—yet, as Andrew Davis points out, the eighth-note shift has audible consequences when voices enter in their "proper" location, placed according to the notated metrical accents.[14] Which is displaced, then: orchestra or voice? The listener has no stable frame of reference, except perhaps to rely on the foundational role of the orchestra and regard voices as aberrant.

Against this uncertainty, a point of reference—at least for the listener who might recognize it— is the historical association of this appoggiatura gesture with sighing and lamentation, beginning with the *pianto* of the madrigal tradition and carrying into the Baroque.[15] A similar gesture for solo cellos in Act 2 of *Turandot*, marked in the score *come un lamento*, punctuates Turandot's recitation of the riddles with an air of melancholy, even pain. That the historical associations of the *pianto* are parodied in *Gianni Schicchi* only makes them more apparent: the comic exaggeration of the *tamburo funebre* and a sudden lugubrious largo for solo bassoon drive the point home.[16] The *funebre* marking is only one of many textual triggers that invite performance in ways that fasten the semantics of the scene. The marking *lamento* a few bars later introduces a further comic effect: headless note stems instruct the relatives to issue sobs rhythmically aligned with the appoggiaturas in the orchestra. It is the beginning of a performance of mourning that will later prompt Schicchi, in an aside, to liken the relatives' playacting skills to those of a jester: "E perché stanno a lagrimare? Ti recitano meglio d'un giullare!" (And why are they crying? They are better actors than a jester!) Those missing note heads represent an invitation to the singer *not* to sing; they are empty spaces into which a singer, guided by a director, can insert sounds laden with mock *lamento* effect and affect. To fill the spaces is to fill them with gesture. Shadowing the rhythm of the repeated mourning motive, the spaces become overdetermined gestures of mimesis, as though both cementing and mocking the process of semantic association. And all this by way of introduction to a scene of feigned sorrow, as relatives outgrieve one another. "Piangerem!" they sing, as the motive repeats, grounding their lamentations in a continuous litany. This is an unlikely candidate, in other words, to become one of Carner's loose Puccinian characterizing themes.

And yet something does happen to it. Or, rather, nothing happens. For the motive will continue its repetitive strains: statement, repeat down a step, statement, repeat down a step. Minor-mode variation, down a step, minor subdominant, down a step. Pause. Back to the beginning. What began as a motive now becomes an ostinato (see Example 3). Davis

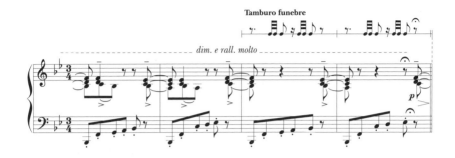

(I parenti di Buoso susurrano una preghiera, mentre Marco, la vecchia Zita e la Ciesca si lamentano addolorati.)

Example 3. *Gianni Schicchi*, mm. 20–31.

is quite right when he characterizes it as an "incessant" figure that "controls nearly the first fifteen minutes of the opera," but even this does not quite convey its pervasive presence.[17] It will also return later, permeating Schicchi's early exchanges with the relatives; underpinning "Si corre dal notaio," Schicchi's outline of the plan to rewrite Buoso Donati's will;

and permeating the relatives' excited reaction to the plan (more on this below). There is no precedent in Puccini's work for the sheer persistence of this figure, and arguably none in opera. Even the celebrated ostinati of Ravel's *L'Heure espagnole* seem localized and contained by comparison, characterized more by their combination into composite patterns of superimposed ostinati than by sheer persistence.[18]

If the motoric duration and repetition anticipates the machine music of the 1920s, and if its origins in a ritualized trope of mourning suggest the litanies of Stravinsky's music, the closest resemblance to the melodic formula and its patterning is surely to be found in a much later body of work, written by a professed admirer of Puccini's operas, Bernard Herrmann.[19] Sequential repetition of short motives over extended periods—David Raksin called Herrmann a "genius with the repeat sign"[20]—became not only a hallmark of Herrmann's film scoring, witness the hypnotic repetition in *North by Northwest* and *Vertigo*, but a blueprint for film scoring in the post-classic Hollywood era of the 1960s. What these short motives seemed to offer formally was a plasticity and flexibility capable of following the sharp contours of filmic editing. Concentrated musical cells could be manipulated more deftly than the expansive lyrical mode characteristic of the classic era (itself arguably Puccinian in its own way), while the arrangement of the motives as ostinati offered a continuity capable of bridging the cinematic cut and generating a sense of coherence.

It was a scoring strategy ideally suited to that much-heralded cinematic art of manipulating tension in the thriller, as exemplified in the Hitchcock-Herrmann partnership. In the archetypical scenario—Cary Grant at the United Nations Building or James Stewart following a car around the streets of San Francisco—the promise of an event or the threat of danger remain just that, concealed for now behind the banal everyday while Herrmann's repetitive gestures, in effect, watch the clock, marking time as empty in a way that invites anticipation of something—anything—happening. This scenario should not, however, conceal the capacity of this mode of scoring to mark time in different ways: the banalities of plot in the opening scenes of a film, again anticipating something, but on the wider arc of plot expectation, or indeed of narrative archetypes linked to different genres. Like *Gianni Schicchi*, the black comedy of *The Trouble with Harry* (dir. Alfred Hitchcock, 1955) centers on the machinations generated by a corpse. Like Buoso Donati's relatives, the inhabitants of a small town are up to no good—the trouble with Harry, of course, is that he is dead—and it is the ostinati of Herrmann's lively score (his first for Hitchcock) that deftly register their busy everyday lives while hinting at something else, precisely because of their repetitive insistence. That so many of Herrmann's ostinati so closely resemble the mourning motive in *Gianni Schicchi* only makes the connection explicit: one of the prominent cues in *North by Northwest*, for example, follows exactly the arrangement of Puccini's motive: a stepwise sequential descent followed by a return to the initial pitch.[21]

The resemblance would come full circle when Alex North, one of Herrmann's contemporaries, scored *Prizzi's Honor* (dir. John Huston, 1985) with a rather more direct reference to Puccini. North's response to the film's unsettling juxtaposition of dark comedy and violent Italian-American gangster drama was to draw on Italian opera, riffing on and directly citing music from Verdi, Donizetti, Rossini, and Puccini. The music of the opening credits, a typically filmic arrangement of short, sequenced motives repeated multiple times, sounds like a film composer's take on Italian opera. It is in fact the mourning motive of the opening scene of *Gianni Schicchi*, here quoted almost verbatim. As Marcia Citron puts it, North presents a "sleight of hand" that makes "literal opera music sound like scored music that sounds operatic."[22] In what amounts to an inversion of the imposter plot of *Gianni Schicchi*, the film seems to pass off as fake what is in fact the real thing.

What should we take from these cinematic resemblances and citations? Drawing on Rebecca Leydon's reading of Debussy's music, Davis wonders whether *Gianni Schicchi* incorporates the editing techniques of early cinematography to forge "modes of continuation"—direct cut, dissolve, matting—between disparate formal sections.[23] So, for example, the angular, "chaotic" musical language of the ongoing argument between Zita and Schicchi shortly after the latter's arrival is twice interrupted in the manner of a "direct cut" by the lyrical "Romantic" mode associated with the young lovers Rinuccio and Lauretta: the duet "Addio, speranza bella" and Lauretta's "O mio babbino caro." If this cinematic account of form in *Gianni Schicchi* is persuasive, it is surely no leap of faith to imagine the orchestra occupying the role of soundtrack (or, more appropriately for early cinema, live musical accompaniment), as though, in retrospect, the opera returned the favor to *Prizzi's Honor*. Provided, that is, that our understanding of the soundtrack role resists the reductive idea of music merely shaping itself mimetically to the needs of the stage picture. To return to our claim that *Il trittico* reimagines the operatic compact between music and sound, the orchestra in *Gianni Schicchi* anticipates cinema precisely in its fashioning of a demarcation between orchestra and soundscape. What is striking in *Gianni Schicchi* is the orchestra's autonomy from the stage, of an orchestral process that unfolds, a trajectory that is precisely not narrative development or teleology but something far more repetitive, cyclical, undetermined, and indeterminate. Still less convincing would be an interpretation of *Gianni Schicchi*, in post-Wagnerian vein, as a staged symphonic poem in which music bends theater to its will. Far from accruing or developing stage associations, the mourning motive in the orchestra seems to shed them. It becomes, through repetition, the musical fabric of the opera in a way that hollows out classic characteristic or leitmotivic meaning.

A notable exception to this independence is the relatives' reaction to Schicchi's revelation of his plan to alter the will. Arman Schwartz draws attention to the strangeness of this cacophonous ensemble, in which the relatives, overwhelmed with the brilliance of the plan, variously cry out with nonsensical expressions of effusive joy, and repeat Schicchi's and their own names over and over. At once overcome with emotion and lacking will or agency, they react, as though under Schicchi's sway. It is, Schwartz concludes, a curious "admixture of affect and automation."[24] From the beginning of the outburst, the four-note stepwise descent of the mourning motive underwrites the scene—it had already featured in Schicchi's narrative of feigned mourning, as though to project him retrospectively as composer of the original scene of mock mourning. It appears first, at rehearsal number 52, in a descending chromatic rendition, though still with the familiar repeated four-note descent, then immediately acquires its familiar appoggiatura before dissolving into whole-tone anarchy. For the first time since the relatives had shadowed the mourning motive with their unpitched *lamento*, the relatives now take heed of the mourning motive and join with the orchestra in delivering it. But only in snatches, loops, and jarring juxtapositions. Only at the point when neo-Aristotelian stage conventions seem furthest away, when cause and effect seem unhinged and dialogue unfolds as a sequence of discrete utterances, does the mourning motive surface from the pit and generate the semblance of its traditional role of vocal support and extension of stage. It is a moment that clarifies what seems to have been happening all along in the orchestra: that the classic modes of reinforcement and congruence have given way to something more channeled and discrete, that insistence and repetition have shaped autonomy into autonomism and music into medium.

Which brings us back to cinema. David Trotter considers the impact of cinema on modernism not merely in its capacity to offer formal models, such as montage, that might be incorporated into literature or music, but in its foregrounding of mediality itself as a relationship to the world based on a "will-to-automatism"—a relationship both technologically mediated, accentuating cinema's distance and constructedness, yet present and immediate in ways that efface its interventions and manipulations. This cinematic "will-to-automatism" was, Trotter concludes, an instrument with far-reaching consequences for modernism, one predicated on "the double desire at once for presence to the world and for absence from it."[25] Cinema's machinic mediation of existence promises, that is, to bypass the subjective and its conventional apparatus of representation by fore-grounding the role of material, objective means; yet it promises that this mediation, unlike its conventional subjective counterpart, will not com-promise but only accentuate immediacy of experience.

Might opera, the very embodiment of the old apparatus, point in the same direction? We contend that the autonomy/autonomism of the orchestra in *Gianni Schicchi* represents a yet more radical gesture, one that partakes of this "will-to-automatism" without resorting to an exter-nal technology (moving camera, celluloid, and projector) but precisely by reorienting the existing apparatus (orchestra, voices, stage as technol-ogy). Here the question of the "thing" returns.

Bill Brown reflects on the growth of interest in things, in creative practice, in theory (Bruno Latour and the new materialism), and specu-lates that it arose in part as a response to the "digitization of our world."[26] Didn't cinema, he asks, trigger a similar response in the 1920s? But in a caveat that chimes with the double relationship identified by Trotter in the "will to automatism," Brown resists the idea that cinema's intervention merely introduced a new separation from things. Rather, it assumed a dual role, introducing, like all new media, "distance *and* proximity."[27] To Brown's historical examples of new media—"perspec-tival painting, printing, telegraphy"—we might add opera, a medium born in the same age as the first item on his list. By 1918, or so the traditional narrative has it, opera was on its deathbed, and in *Turandot* Puccini was about to close its eyes. To suggest that this was not a death-bed—that Puccini had found in opera a new form of animation in tune with the cinematic age—is no act of Schicchi-like deception. In a gesture of persistence and repetition without precedence, musical and theat-rical objects—appoggiaturas, sequences, characteristic motives laden with lamentation—become things. Ostinato—modernism's musical "will to automatism"—exhibits the thingness of musical gestures. We stress "exhibits" because thingness is always a possibility waiting to be recognized, something we might become aware of only when objects shed their customary function. "We begin to confront the thingness of objects," Brown writes, "when they stop working for us."[28] Meditating on the value of attending to musical things, Lawrence Kramer stresses the provisional nature of musical objects: "Musical things are not always content to be reified objects, not always willing to be what they're told to be."[29] That is, the object functions we assign them are not fixed, not inevitable. To attend to things, Kramer adds, is to recognize their "ontological openness."[30] These transformations and resistances need not be tied to historical moments, but we suggest that in late Puccini they are. When *Gianni Schicchi* (or *Il trittico*) accentuates the thingness of theatrical and musical objects, it gestures to a modernist moment as surely as cinema. How telling that it should take as its objects the very fabric of an operatic apparatus honed by tradition.

A Coat and a Cape

Yet, things do turn into objects, raising the suspicion of fetishization, of an aesthetics complicit with commoditization. And such allegations would hardly be new in regard to Puccini's operas: their oft-noted manipulative excesses, their continuing resistance to a critique trained on Teutonic profundities. *Trittico* is predisposed like no other to the logic of commodity fetishism: as a set of three separate units, it anticipates its own piecemeal circulation. The operas, like objects at an exposition, are each perfectly self-contained vignettes in which history, culture, and religion are maximized to become agile and easily transportable merchandise. They were in fact "transported" to the Met as an exotic "foldable" for the New York City premiere and transported back for the Roman premiere as celebrations of national identity with the added prestige of the foreign success.[31] All three operas, moreover, delve into the pleasures of objects in what can be described as garish takes on the catalogue aria. In *Tabarro*, Frugola indulges in enumerating all the "strange objects" contained in the large bag she carries around: a comb, feathers, fabrics, jars, shoes, or in her words, "strange relics, documents of a thousand loves, joys, torments [. . .] making no distinction between rich and humble." In *Suor Angelica*, an episode of the regulated life of the convent is about "the return from the quest," in which the nuns festively attend the arrival of supplies; the "questuants" celebrate with unusual sensuousness all the things they brought back: oil jar, flour, cheese, lentils, eggs, butter, currants. In *Gianni Schicchi* things are the motor of the comedy: Buoso's possessions are enumerated, discussed, coveted, stolen. Most of the stage business is motivated by things: objects in the room are eyed, named, grabbed, hidden, returned, without much regard for their use, form, or material, as far as they can be possessed and exchanged.

After praising Vigo's cinema for its capacity to take in the experiential truth of everyday objects, Kracauer returns to Père Jules—the old mariner in *L'Atalante* whose passion for gathering stuff is similar to Frugola's in *Tabarro*—and to the eccentric collection of objects that fill his cabin to the brim.

> The magic spell they cast over him is revealed in a unique episode in which Père Jules shows Juliette all the mementos he has brought home from his voyages. The piled-up treasures, which crowd his cabin, are depicted in such a manner that we feel they have literally grown together over him. To evoke this impression Vigo focuses on the objects from various sides and on many levels without ever clarifying their spatial interrelationship—using nothing but the medium shots and close-ups made necessary by the narrowness of the cabin. The alarm clock, the musical box, the photograph [. . .] the bric-a-brac emerging little by little, form an impenetrable wickerwork constantly interspersed with fragments of the old man himself: his arm, his tattooed back, his face. How accurately this piecemeal presentation renders his complete submission to the rarities around him can also be inferred from the fact that he preserves in alcohol the hands of a deceased comrade. The idols, on their part, display triumphantly their inherent powers. At the head of their great defile Vigo marches a doll which, when set into motion by Père Jules, conducts mechanical music from a puppet show like a bandmaster. The magical life of the doll is transmitted to the curiosities that follow in the parade.[32]

Objects (and things as objects) acquire magic powers once they turn into mementos: pieces of someone's past (or of a past someone), fragments of a long lost everyday that have been separated from their use value. Their affective hold derives in part from their autonomy (and automatism), and of course, as with Père Jules, from "lack of intellectual awareness"— that is, from an availability or predisposition to enchantment. As if going back a little on his initial enthusiasm, Kracauer ends his review with a note of doubt, wondering if *L'Atalante* wasn't after all a retrogressive turn for Vigo when compared to the earlier film *Zéro de conduite*, a turn the director would have surely corrected, had he lived longer, by pursuing "the task of disenchantment."[33] Hence the celebration of the direct access that objects on film give to the "material components of mental processes" soon becomes wariness for how objects can take over. The solution for Kracauer is to introduce another kind of mediation, that of disenchantment, of intellectual awareness—an apparatus alert precisely to the ethics and politics of objects.

As is quite clear by now, Puccini's *Trittico* raises a similar wariness, and we wonder if this very thingness we have been celebrating thus far as a radical gesture toward modernity may make us too into Frugolas. Aware of the lessons taught by cultural critique, we ought now to turn to a gesture of unmasking and counter the spell with skepticism; too much proximity requires some distancing. But since we promised at the outset a less straight-laced approach, we do not want to yield too easily to skepticism. Instead we will try to pursue this matter a little further and linger on the temporality of the thing and of the object. In a sense both *L'Atalante* and *Trittico* (as well as, to a certain extent, Hitchcock's films by way of Herrmann's scores) study the movement of things into and away from objects, mostly following the movement of desire: the dangerous object is on the other end of an indulgent gaze, shaped and appropriated by desire, nostalgia, and so forth. A thing instead is the before and after of such objects: its past potentiality and its future.

This connection between temporality and things had already been explored by Puccini, especially in *La bohème*, an opera, as Arthur Groos has pointed out, that relies on "little things"—Mimì's bonnet (*cuffietta*) and Colline's coat (*zimarra*) in particular—as the vehicle for an exploration of "historical nostalgia."[34] In Groos's attentive reading of how *cuffietta* and *zimarra* carry their histories into the opera, accrue affective content, and are at the end abandoned, generating a sense of pervasive loss, nostalgia is hardly a retrogressive fetishization. Rather, it appears as a utopian pursuit: "Mimì's death and Colline's '*vecchia zimarra*' thus involve a farewell not only to love and youth, but also to an age in which artifacts still had an individual aura rooted in the uniqueness of their production and the lives of the people who used them."[35]

Despite its historical patina *Trittico* seems to voice a very different appeal to the past. What happened to the nostalgia for the forever lost pre-commodified thing of *Bohème*? The distance between the little things of *Bohème* and those of *Trittico* can be measured by returning to Colline's *zimarra* and considering how it has turned into Michele's *tabarro*. Colline's farewell to his coat in Act 4 is one of the most famous passages of the opera, not least because, as we pointed out, its main theme is briefly but unmistakably recollected in the orchestral final measures, in a gesture that has often been chastised as sloppy desublimation of the tragic end.[36] Just before Mimì's death, in a half-humorous tone, Colline in an aside bids farewell to his coat before taking it to the pawnshop. Addressed directly, the coat is praised for its dignified life and usefulness.

Vecchia zimarra, senti,	Old coat, listen,
io resto al pian,	I'm staying here,
* tu ascendere*	while you have to ascend
il sacro monte or devi.	the sacred hill.
Le mie grazie ricevi.	Please accept my gratitude.
Mai non curvasti il logoro	You never bowed your worn
dorso ai ricchi ed ai potenti.	back to the rich or powerful.
Passâr nelle tue tasche	Through your pockets passed,
come in antri tranquilli	as if in tranquil chambers,
filosofi e poeti.	poets and philosophers.
Ora che i giorni lieti	Now that those happy times
fuggîr, ti dico: addio,	have fled, I bid you farewell,
fedele amico mio.	faithful old friend.
Addio, addio.	Farewell, farewell.

Colline anthropomorphizes his *zimarra* into an interlocutor standing for a younger self. The object here is an extension of the subject, carrying his virtues and pride as a social skin. Bidding farewell to the coat is a way to let go of a past self, to shed the skin of a past identity. The thing, in other words, is subjectivized, saturated with signification into a kind of super-object, in this context the ultimate theatrical object. Rather than losing this baggage once it is exchanged at the pawnshop, the *zimarra* is deemed to continue to accrue history and carry it over to its next owner. Not even its momentary transformation into exchange value seems capable of voiding its history, transforming it into a mere commodity.

Michele's *tabarro* seems to trace an opposite path. Toward the end of the opera, the old seaman tries to rekindle his wife's attentions by launching predictably into a nostalgic recollection of their former familial bliss. Despite her plea not to, Michele summons the memory of how he used to cover his wife and child with his cape to protect them from the night breeze. A banal thing involved in an involuntary memory of a simple instinctual gesture, the cape acquires suddenly all the promise of signification anticipated by the title. Like the *zimarra*, its very fabric seems made out of strands of emotions and desires, its presence made of accumulated pasts. The music in the

Example 4. Michele's recollection, *Tabarro*, three mm. after rehearsal no. 77, "Vi raccoglievo insieme nel tabarro."

orchestra, however, comes in spot on with a strong thematic gesture, assigning to the stressed syllable of Michele's utterance of ta-*bar*-ro the beginning of a slow ominous motive, *Largo doloroso*, obviously at odds with the tenderness brought back by the memory (see Example 4). The motive continues to follow the recollection, halted only at his words "I was so happy." The orchestra evokes an affect quite extraneous to the character's utterance but still appears, as Julian Budden puts it, to be "casting an ever-deepening proleptic shadow over the events on stage.[37] And the cape comes back at the end twice. First Michele strangles his wife's lover and hides the corpse from her with it. Then, in a cruelly ironic turn, it is she who brings it up again, in a remorseful attempt at reconnecting to their shared memories:

Sì ... mi dicevi un tempo:	Yes . . . you once used to tell me:
"Tutti quanti portiamo	"We all wear
un tabarro che asconde	a cape that hides
qualche volta una gioia,	at times a joy
qualche volta un dolore ..."	at times a sorrow . . ."

The motive returns several times during the two men's fortuitous encounter on the dark barge and during their struggle, but is not synchronized with Michele's act of covering the body with the *tabarro*. And again, the motive eludes Giorgetta's memory and is bellowed out by the orchestra—*a tutta forza*—right at the very end, once Michele wildly invites her to join him under the cape and in so doing reveals the copse of her lover.

Rather than intensifying and accruing symbolic weight, like Colline's coat, the cape seems to be getting lighter. With the outrageous gesture of using it to cover his dead antagonist Michele interrupts and vanquishes its history, a history sustained by the character's affective investment and memories. But the musical motive had jumped ship much earlier. Like the musical objects in *Gianni Schicchi,* and affirming once more what Carner referred to as Puccini's "laxity," the motive, which had in the first place gained semantic baggage from mere synchronization, quickly acquires autonomy from its fortuitous semanticization. Both the *tabarro* and the music initially associated with it are progressively emancipated from signification. Death is posited as the severing of the bond: a severing first of all of the object from the subject, from the subject's web of desires and exchanges, from its agency. The first opera of the triptych ends therefore with an overstated theatrical gesture *sui generis*: at the moment when Michele opens the cape on a corpse it declares the death of *zimarra* and creates another sort of theater where objects can be recognized as things, where the final *coup de théâtre* reveals only a *horror vacui*.

In *The Stage Life of Props* Andrew Sofer accuses recent theater theory of indulging in a Colline-like anthropomorphization with its cultural materialist insistence on the prop's social codes. What he seeks instead is an awareness of the materiality of the prop in the context of performance:

> There is a strong risk that the material presence of the onstage object—its movement in concrete stage space and through linear stage time for spectators—will dissolve into the materialist analysis of the anxieties, fault lines, and ideologies that the object may or may not have embodied for the culture. In short, the danger is that we will lose sight of how objects worked, and continue to work, on stage as part of a discrete theatrical event.[38]

Where Sofer insists on a performance-centered materialism as a response to theater theory, we highlight a historical insistence on materiality as challenge to the prevailing traditions of music theater. To understand the impulse toward modernity in *Trittico* we must recover or invent an analytical discourse that loosens and temporalizes the link between the thing and the object. The challenge in *Trittico* to the traditional symbolic theater apparatus anticipates de facto Sofer's call for theorists to "emphasize playhouse practice over cultural signification."[39] But whereas Sofer is concerned with the links to what lies outside the theater—understood as a network of cultural meaning that he partially endorses but finds suffocating—we maintain that even the indexical link to outside reality in *Trittico* is a connection that need not map onto networks of cultural meaning in the classic hermeneutic sense, but rather insists on the prop's own material everydayness, and in a radical way. That is, whereas Sofer's belief in the primacy of performance allows him to assert a materialism based on the autonomy of performance, we highlight a Puccinian materiality that insists on the capacity of the prop—like the orchestra—to question not only its appropriation to the traditional symbolic apparatus of theater but the theatrical imaginary itself. The opaque thing that is the *tabarro* gives the lie to the "discrete theatrical event" by foregrounding attachment to an outside reality, yet its opacity attaches it to reality in ways that preserve its autonomy and thingness.

Its overt trafficking with heritage and antiquarianism may suggest that *Trittico* is foremost a piece of "modernariat," as Paolo Virno would put it, regressively intimating that the present of (Italian) culture depended on its past glories.[40] And yet, this regressive sense of modernity as repetition is combined with a progressive and courageous reconfiguration of what theater and music can do: a radical theater where objects become things, caught in the process of shedding their patrimony of memory, of foregoing their work of nostalgia.

NOTES

1. Michele Girardi, *Puccini: His International Art*, trans. Laura Basini (Chicago: University of Chicago Press, 2000), 377. In a passage a few pages earlier, Girardi also states, à propos *La fanciulla*: "On the surface there seems to be faith that a conventional relationship between text and music was still possible, while the detachment between the event acted on stage [. . .] and its musical expression is, in fact, the most modern trait of the score" (283).

2. For more on the "marked style" in late Puccini, see Andrew Davis, "*Il Trittico*," "*Turandot*," *and Puccini's Late Style* (Bloomington: Indiana University Press, 2010).

3. Puccini to Tito Ricordi, 23 July and 21 August 1918, in *Carteggi pucciniani*, ed. Eugenio Gara (Milan: Ricordi, 1958), 463–65. The translation is ours.

4. Several versions of the set designs are at the Archivio Ricordi and can be viewed at www.internetculturale.it The materials for *Tabarro*, for instance, are collected here: http://www.internetculturale.it/jmms/iccuviewer/iccu.jsp?id=oai%3Awww.internetcultur ale.sbn.it%2FTeca%3A20%3ANT0000%3AMI0285_TABARRO_NY_14121918&mode= all&teca=MagTeca+-+ICCU

5. Michele Girardi, "Giacomo Puccini, regista di suoni," in *Giacomo Puccini e Galileo Chini tra musica e scena dipinta*, ed. Alessandra Belluomini Pucci (Viareggio: La Torre di Legno, 2006), 55–61, quotation at 58.

6. Arman Schwartz, *Puccini's Soundscapes: Realism and Modernity in Italian Opera* (Florence: Leo S. Olschki, 2016).

7. On the *Te Deum* as "grafted onto the Scarpia theme without any break or transitional material," see Girardi, *Puccini*, 164.

8. Ibid., 283.

9. The film's opposition of two systems of perceptions, affections, and actions—that of men on land, and of men of the sea—was famously discussed by Gilles Deleuze in *Cinema I: The Movement–Image*, trans. Hugh Tomlinson and Barbara Habberjam (Minneapolis: University of Minnesota Press, 1986), 79.

10. Siegfried Kracauer, "Jean Vigo," in *Siegfried Kracauer's American Writings: Essays on Film and Popular Culture*, ed. Johannes von Moltke and Kristy Rawson (Berkeley and Los Angeles: University of California Press, 2012), 48–50, quotation at 48.

11. Mosco Carner, *Puccini: A Critical Biography* (New York: Alfred A. Knopf, 1959), 434.

12. And a double imposter at that. Schicchi plays both the relatives' Buoso Donati, who grants them what they wish, and his own Buoso Donati.

13. Carner, *Puccini*, 271.

14. Davis, *Puccini's Late Style*, 148–49.

15. See, for example, Raymond Monelle's genealogy of musical tropes of lamentation, focusing in particular on the *pianto* gesture of chains of falling minor seconds presented as appoggiaturas. Monelle, *The Sense of Music: Semiotic Essays* (Princeton: Princeton University Press, 2000), 66–73.

16. Carner notes the parody element here and lists some of the characteristics of mourning music in Puccini, including the use of appoggiaturas (*Puccini*, 435).

17. Davis, *Puccini's Late Style*, 148.

18. Derrick Puffett identified these constructions in the instrumental music of Debussy and Berg as "ostinato machines" in "Debussy's Ostinato Machine," in *Derrick Puffett on Music*, ed. Kathryn Bailey Puffett (Aldershot: Ashgate, 2001), 231–86; and Puffett, "Berg, Mahler and the *Three Orchestral Pieces*, op. 6," in *The Cambridge Companion to Berg*, ed. Anthony Pople (Cambridge: Cambridge University Press), 111–44, quotation at 136.

19. "Puccini," Herrmann told Royal S. Brown in 1975, "was a very great composer." Royal S. Brown, *Undertones and Overtones: Reading Film Music* (Berkeley and Los Angeles: University of California Press, 1994), 293.

20. David Raksin, in the documentary *Music for the Movies: Bernard Herrmann,* dir. Joshua Waletzky, 1992.

21. The same is true of the whistled sequence that forms the main theme of *Twisted Nerve,* dir. Roy Boulting, 1968.

22. Marcia J. Citron, "Opera and Film," in *Oxford Handbook of Film Studies,* ed. David Neumeyer (New York: Oxford University Press, 2014), 44–71, quotation at 64.

23. Davis, *Puccini's Late Style,* 152–56; Rebecca Leydon, "Debussy's Late Style and the Devices of the Early Cinema," *Music Theory Spectrum* 23/2 (2001): 217–41.

24. Schwartz, *Puccini's Soundscapes.*

25. David Trotter, *Cinema and Modernism* (Oxford: Blackwell, 2007), 10–11.

26. Bill Brown, "Thing Theory," *Critical Inquiry* 28/1 (Autumn 2001): 1–22, quotation at 16.

27. Ibid.

28. Ibid., 4.

29. Lawrence Kramer, *Interpreting Music* (Berkeley and Los Angeles: University of California Press, 2011), 187.

30. Ibid., 189.

31. For the early reception of *Trittico,* see Alexandra Wilson, *The Puccini Problem: Opera, Nationalism, and Modernity* (Cambridge: Cambridge University Press, 2007), 178–84.

32. Kracauer, "Jean Vigo," 50.

33. Ibid.

34. Arthur Groos, "Mimì's Bonnet and Colline's Coat: Bohemian Nostalgia and the Remembrance of Things Past," unpublished paper.

35. Ibid.

36. For Groos this last appearance of the theme signals how the sense of loss expands from Mimì's death to their lives more generally by way of everyday things. Groos, "Mimì's Bonnet and Colline's Coat."

37. Julian Budden, *Puccini: His Life and Works* (New York: Oxford University Press, 2002), 390.

38. Andrew Sofer, *The Stage Life of Props* (Ann Arbor: University of Michigan Press, 2003), 18.

39. Ibid.

40. Paolo Virno, *Déjà Vu and the End of History,* trans. David Broder (London: Verso, 2015), 46–55. For a critique of the historicity of *Gianni Schicchi,* see Chapter Four, "*Gianni Schicchi,* Tuscan Revivalism, War" in Schwartz, *Puccini's Soundscapes.*

Puccini, Fascism, and the Case of *Turandot*

BEN EARLE

How many times did Giacomo Puccini meet Benito Mussolini? Mary Jane Phillips-Matz suggests the two men met twice, within a matter of weeks. She cites a letter from Puccini to Pietrino Malfatti—"an old friend from Torre [del Lago]"—of 1 December 1923, in which the composer mentions a meeting with the Duce that very day. This apparently followed a previous encounter in November.[1] Phillips-Matz's account contradicts the previous understanding, established in the earliest biographies, that the two men met only once.[2] Perhaps her two meetings were one and the same. The date in November has never been confirmed with any precision.[3] The issue may appear of slight importance. But it makes an appropriate introduction to the question of Puccini's relationship with fascism generally. The historical record is confused, sometimes contradictory. Yet our knowledge is not so patchy that we cannot come to some provisional conclusions.

Evidence

Take Puccini's desire to meet Mussolini in the first place. It seems clear that the impulse came from the composer rather than the politician. Phillips-Matz follows Michele Girardi in suggesting that Puccini wanted to put to Mussolini his idea for a national theater.[4] But where was it to be built? Phillips-Matz suggests Viareggio; others say Rome. And was this the only idea Puccini wanted to put to the "President of the Council of Ministers"?[5] Here is Vincent Seligman, elaborating on the composer's correspondence with his mother, Sybil Seligman:

> During his stay in Vienna [in October 1923] Puccini had been much impressed by the report that the Austrian

Government were planning a special season of Viennese opera in London—"Wagner, Strauss, Puccini—with their own orchestra, scenery and singers—including [the soprano Maria] Jeritza." The season never materialized, but on his return home Puccini hoped to be able to persuade the Fascist Government to take similar measures to encourage the spread of Italian music abroad. But the times were not favourable; "I don't think Mussolini is giving a thought to Italian opera at Covent Garden," he writes despondently. [. . .] Shortly afterwards he met the Duce for the first and only time; but he did not succeed in making any headway. "I saw Mussolini," he reports, "but only for a few minutes and I wasn't able to talk much—so there wasn't time to discuss Italian opera abroad."[6]

Was the idea that an Italian National Theater would take its productions on foreign tours, as Girardi suggests? Or were these two separate projects?

Leonardo Pinzauti suggests there was a further scheme on Puccini's mind, involving a state fund financed by the collection of royalties on works already in the public domain.[7] As Fiamma Nicolodi explains, the early 1920s saw a number of attempts to persuade the Italian state to intervene on behalf of the country's opera houses. March 1923 had seen a Congress on Lyric Theater, held in Rome and attended by Puccini's sharpest critic, the musicologist Fausto Torrefranca, and his greatest compositional rival, Pietro Mascagni, among others. As a member of the governmental Permanent Commission for Music, Puccini would have been party to similar discussions.[8] But he would go a step further and put his case to the Duce directly.

In a pamphlet, *Mussolini musicista*, by the journalist and musicologist Raffaele de Rensis, we find a more detailed account:

> Puccini too, the gentle Puccini, [. . .] crossed the threshold of the Office of the President. To whom he wished to set forth his impressions of and his suggestions with regard to the unhappy conditions of our musical theater and to ask for a speedy and generous intervention. Among other things, he requested the bringing into law of an old plan in respect to State's rights to operas that have entered the public domain

and the assignment of the proceeds of these rights to the lyric theater.

In a long and friendly conversation the illustrious maestro also proposed the construction of a National Theater in Rome, but the President, who had himself long dreamed of this splendid project, stressed to him the difficulty at that moment of adding to the balance sheet the many tens of millions that would be required.[9]

This quasi-official document stands in contradiction to Puccini's letter to Sybil Seligman. That the meeting was far from "long" or even "friendly" is confirmed by the most detailed account, which comes from the journalist, musicologist, and friend of Puccini, Guido Marotti. The composer takes up the story himself:

When I entered the *salone della Vittoria*,[10] I saw there, at the back, a table and two enormous globes, one on either side of it. Bent over the table, a man was writing. I remained perplexed for a few moments, then, plucking up courage, walked forward. The man, having raised his head, looked at me, and, getting to his feet, while he fixed me with two big, round, black eyes, which seemed to bore a hole through me, said brusquely:

"What do you want?"

"Nothing! . . . I wanted . . . simply to have the pleasure of meeting you."

He held out his hand and in an affable voice:

"For myself, I am delighted to meet you!"

I had gone to see Mussolini to set forth to him certain of my ideas about the National Lyric Theater to be constructed in Rome. But he, shaking his head and rocking backwards and forwards (he had stayed on his feet), said three times:

"There's no money for that! There's no money for that! There's no money for that! And to carry out Piacentini's plan we need thirty million!"[11]

"If I may, Your Excellency," I ventured, "we could, in my opinion, carry out a more modest plan, but just as—"

He didn't let me finish:

"Either a plan as grand as that, worthy of Rome, or nothing!"

> I felt his power from these few words, and thought that
> Italy had finally found its man . . . and in my confusion, I
> forgot even to speak to him of another thing that was . . . so
> close to my heart![12]

The other "thing" was doubtless the plan for the promotion of Italian
opera abroad, as Puccini told Seligman. The idea that the national theater should be built in Viareggio (which Puccini had discussed with the
town's mayor) had evidently been dropped.[13] In Marotti's account there
is no talk of royalties.

Puccini had one further significant brush with fascism, but the record
here is even more clouded. In a speech to parliament on the afternoon of
29 November 1924, on the occasion of Puccini's death in Brussels earlier
that same day, Mussolini claimed that "some months back" the composer
had "asked for the card" of, that is, asked to join, the Partito Nazionale
Fascista (PNF).[14] It seems the Duce was not quite telling the truth. Even
Marotti, who has no qualms about painting Puccini as a fervent fascist,
tells the story differently. Puccini was "given the fascist card *ad honorem*."
The composer, Marotti adds, "had granitic faith in Benito Mussolini."[15]
Girardi puts a further twist on the episode. In the spring of 1924, he tells
us, "the officials of the Viareggio branch of the Partito Nazionale Fascista
sent [Puccini] an honorary membership card, and for the sake of a quiet
life he did not refuse it."[16] His source is Pinzauti, who writes:

> The truth is that the Viareggio federation of the PNF made
> it known, around the spring of 1924, that it would like to
> offer [Puccini] the card "ad honorem," and Puccini did
> everything he could to avoid this threat to his reputation
> [*compromissione*], even if at home his wife and friends made
> clear to him the inadvisability of a public refusal. And so he
> accepted, ever more perplexed and fearful, above all after
> the Matteotti crime; nor after all would the state of his health
> have put him in the position of being able to be more deci-
> sive in the circumstances.[17]

Which account are we to believe? It is not simply that they do not
tally. None of these writers produces any justification for their assertions.
But what does it matter if Puccini was a fascist? He was hardly alone. As
Seligman puts it, with considerable hyperbole deriving from his own evident enthusiasm for the Duce, Puccini "heartily welcomed" fascism, "in

common with the vast majority of his fellow-countrymen."[18] Nicolodi's archival work has made clear that the record of Italian composers under fascism was nothing to be proud of.[19] And this seems to be the point. The shame of fascism is sufficient to drive commentators not just to disbelieve, but to try to counter testimony such as that of Marotti and Seligman.

So let us lay out the evidence. Puccini's admiration for Mussolini appears plain. Giuseppe Adami, librettist of *La rondine* and *Il tabarro* and joint librettist of *Turandot*, affirms that Puccini was "a fascist from the very beginning [*della primissima ora*]," and that "he had placed all his faith" in the Duce.[20] Here is some more from Marotti:

> "He is greater than Napoleon," [Puccini] said to us one evening, "because Napoleon, you see, didn't have so many difficulties to conquer as Mussolini. And then . . . well . . . Napoleon used canons, which is an easy means, when you are fighting battles, to overcome difficulties!"
>
> "I am for a strong State" was his fundamental credo. "Men like Depretis, Crispi, Giolitti were to my taste because they gave orders instead of taking them.[21] Now there's Mussolini who has saved Italy from falling to pieces!" [. . .] I don't believe in democracy because I don't believe in the possibility of educating the masses. It's like trying to hold water in a wicker basket! Without a strong government headed by a man with an iron fist, like Bismarck in Germany in the past and like Mussolini in Italy now, there is always the danger that the people, who construe freedom as mere licence, will become undisciplined and wreck everything. That's why I'm a fascist: because I hope that fascism will achieve in Italy, for the good of the country, the pre-war German national model.[22]

To be sure, Marotti's account cannot be taken entirely at face value. There is a good deal of novelization here, though it should be remembered that Marotti—unlike Pinzauti, for instance—was frequently in the composer's company. If more solid documentation is required, this too is available, especially from the period immediately following Mussolini's "March on Rome" (28 October 1922).[23] Nicolodi points out how, at the beginning of November 1922, Puccini, uniquely among Italian composers, sent a congratulatory telegram directly to the new prime minister.[24] Three letters to Adami similarly testify to political enthusiasm. "The day after the March on Rome," so the librettist tells us, "he wrote to me as follows: 'Mussolini was undoubtedly sent by God for the salvation of Italy.'"[25] This letter is not included in Adami's well-known collection. But Adami does print letters from 30 October 1922: "What do you think of Mussolini? I hope he will prove to be the man we need. Good luck to him if he will cleanse and give a little peace to our country!"; and from 1 November: "I wonder if Mussolini will introduce a little order into our national economy! I hope so."[26] Even more telling is a further passage, otherwise apparently unknown, but cited by Claudio Sartori, from a letter of 21 June 1924: "Mussolini? I trust that he will reassert himself. If not, better to go abroad." Written at the height of the Matteotti crisis (to be explained below), this certainly undermines Pinzauti's account.[27]

Julian Budden seizes on the letter to Adami of 30 October. "This tells us all," he declares. "Fascist ideology meant nothing to Puccini." He continues with a version of Pinzauti's story about the PNF card, though this time Puccini is held to have accepted it for fear of prejudicing "his chances of being nominated Senator of the Realm."[28] No source is given. Nor does Budden explain what he means by "fascist ideology." That is no straightforward matter, of course. Italian fascism was "a developing, pluralistic, decentralized, even disorderly movement," as the historical sociologist Michael Mann puts it. Yet Mann's own definition is useful, particularly since it focuses on "the rise of fascist movements rather than on established fascist regimes." It is primarily this rise to which Puccini responded. Fascism, writes Mann, is "the pursuit of a transcendent and cleansing nation-statism through paramilitarism."[29] The "bottom-up" movement of armed fascist gangs sought violently—and paradoxically— to institute a "top-down" strong state shorn of elements judged inimical to the national cause (in the Italian case mainly socialism and communism) and capable of uniting all social classes in a single national project.

Much of Mann's definition may seem alien to Puccini. The cosmopolitan outlook evinced by the composer's interests, not least in his choice of subjects for libretti, rarely set in Italy, would suggest distaste for fascism's "organic" nationalism. But there are further clues in the literature. Sartori draws attention to an anecdote told by the priest Dante Del Fiorentino:

> Once when Giacomo was crossing the lake [Lago di Massaciuccoli] in his motorboat, a fisherman shook a fist at him, shouting, "It's yours now, soon it will be our turn!" I was with him at the time. At first he did not seem unduly perturbed by the communist threat. "Let us go home," he said

quietly. But the lines on his face had suddenly deepened, and that sadness which showed when he was in repose was more intense than I had ever seen before.

"There's a new spirit strangling Italy," he complained. "There is a mortal sickness spreading through the world, and it has even come to our peaceful Tuscany. I have never intentionally done anyone any harm. I've tried to make people happy. Then why should that man hate me? There was hatred in his voice and in his face."[30]

Puccini's "mentality" was that of a bourgeois conservative, Sartori explains. Just as the composer could not understand the socialism of 1900, so now, in the aftermath of the First World War, he could not understand communism.[31]

We can go further. Del Fiorentino places the motorboat episode after 1922, yet it resonates more obviously with the period 1919–20, the so-called *biennio rosso*, marked by widespread union activism in the north of Italy, including strikes and factory occupations; in the cities there were also food riots. In rural areas there were similar upheavals.[32] From 7 July 1919 we find the following in a letter from Puccini to Sybil Seligman: "I'm just off to Viareggio in the car; I hope they won't take it away from me, because there are riots there owing to the high cost of living, and it appears that it's half Boshevik." On 3 September 1920, he explains to Seligman that he would not be going to see *Il trittico* at Cento (near Bologna) "because that district is known for the violence of its [leftist] demonstrations—and I've no desire to be made a target."[33] Even more strikingly than in the case of the confrontation on Lake Massaciuccoli (since the standoffs in Viareggio and Cento were imaginary), Puccini recognized himself as a class enemy of the protestors. He evidently feared not just the loss of property but physical injury.

Anyone looking for the explicit "pursuit of a transcendent and cleansing nation-statism" in Puccini's letters will indeed be disappointed. Yet the basis for his support of fascism, as the antidote to class conflict in which he felt personally threatened, is nevertheless clear. The crucial term is "order." As Mann explains, "The triad of property, order, and security, divinely ordained, was the ideological soul of the old regime." In a situation where "order"—inseparably associated with property—is threatened, a bourgeois conservative like Puccini might start to find positive values in "nationalism, statism and class transcendence."[34] Certainly Puccini came to value a strong state. As he wrote to Seligman on 1 July

1920, "Italy is really in a bad way [. . .] it's going to be difficult for me, who am already an old man, to see good order restored in my country." Four days later, he complained to the soprano Gilda Dalla Rizza: "How I miss the days in London! Here everything is rotten, one lives badly, without order, without any state protection, they say Giolitti will get round to it [*Giolitti farà farà*], but for now there's trouble. How I long to live abroad!" And four days later still, to his friend Riccardo Schnabl: "The world is disgusting—you're quite right to stay away. But I still believe in Giolitti and it seems that the *revolts* were repressed with an iron hand."[35] The interest in seeing leftist protests put down with violence is notable. Puccini made no secret of his distaste for socialism. As he put it to Renato Simoni, Adami's co-librettist on *Turandot*, on 21 June 1921, "I very much liked Albertini's speech in the Senate. He really put the socialists straight!" On 22 January 1922, he complained to Schnabl, with irony: "The socialist council [in Milan] is really keeping the city clean! Streets everywhere filthy with snow! Appalling."[36]

These are not the words of a "resolutely apolitical" man, as Phillips-Matz describes him. The notion of apoliticism is in any case misleading. "As with all of those who profess indifference to politics," Budden notes, Puccini "invariably gravitated towards the right."[37] But was he "indifferent" to Italian democracy or in fact opposed to it? Marotti cites a letter from 1898: "I don't want to hear about election demonstrations *et similia*. [. . .] I would abolish Chamber and deputies—that's how much these eternal manufacturers of chatter annoy me. [. . .] Let them elect Mundo or Felice the lifeguard at Viareggio, it's all the same to me."[38] Contempt for parliament, fear and loathing of the revolutionary working class, distaste for socialism, desire for "order" and for decisive state intervention: it all adds up. We should not be surprised to find so much evidence of Puccini's fascism.

Interpretation

A standard critical response, faced with material of the kind collected above, is to insist on the distinction between art and life. Yet musicologists no longer think along such lines, or at least not Anglophone musicologists who write on Puccini. Since the mid-1990s a consensus has developed that *Turandot*, in particular, "is thoroughly embedded in the emerging tropes of fascist discourse."[39] At the most general level, Alexandra Wilson suggests that Puccini's last opera, "a work that looks simultaneously forwards and backwards, was [. . .] a fitting emblem for Fascist Italy, caught between presenting itself to the world as modern and keeping faith with tradition."[40] Fascists could indeed express themselves in such broad terms. Thus Mussolini, in a speech given in Perugia on 5 October 1926, proclaimed:

> Today Italy is a people with great possibilities, and that condition which all the greats longed for, from Machiavelli to Mazzini, has been realized. Today there is more: we are on the point of being unified morally.
>
> Now, on a terrain that has been so well prepared, a great art can be reborn, which can be traditionalist and at the same time modern. We need to create, otherwise we will be exploiters of an old patrimony; we need to create the new art of our times, fascist art.[41]

There are few examples of art from any historical period that could not be described as containing both new and traditional elements. But the generality of Mussolini's remarks was their pragmatic point. The Duce wanted to bind as many artists as possible to the fascist regime. He had no interest in laying down potentially exclusionary stylistic principles.

Commentators keen to view *Turandot* in a fascist light tend to look at the characters and plot. As Arman Schwartz writes, "It is [. . .] surprisingly easy to read *Turandot* as a political allegory, one consistent with fascism's own narrative of the degradation of post–World War I Italy and of Mussolini's heroic rise."[42] Richard M. Berrong takes the line previously suggested by John Louis DeGaetani, according to which the opera's chorus stands for "the desperate, angry Italian crowds that wandered through the street of Milan and other Italian cities during the inflation and unemployment after World War I." Berrong further suggests that the "ice princess" Turandot, in her refusal to submit to a husband, herself allegorizes "the violence of a revolutionary populace." Calaf, the "strongman," wins Turandot over by force. Yet Puccini's final opera is not "an *opéra à clef*." Calaf is not Mussolini, since the message conveyed by the final scene is that "this strongman would need to rule the people, once he had subdued them, not by continued force, but by love."[43]

Michael P. Steinberg and Suzanne Stewart-Steinberg remain unimpressed. The lack of "emotional or ethical conflict" experienced by Calaf at Liù's death (in Act 3) marks him as the typically fanatical subject of fascism. Puccini delivers opera to spectacle, which is also opera's "delivery to fascism, to its aesthetic of power through spectacle."[44] The confrontation of ice princess and phallic strongman in *Turandot* is startlingly misogynistic. As Schwartz points out, studies of fascist culture have suggested that "the opposition of virile hero and demonized woman [. . .] is *the* central node of fascist and protofascist rhetoric."[45] Jeremy Tambling suggests that the "sexist" ascription of "hysterical femininity" to the figure of Scarpia in Puccini's *Tosca* may be recuperated in terms of the undoing of bourgeois patriarchy. But *Turandot* is different: Calaf is non-hysterical. The "fantasy" in this opera "involves the complete victory of the male." "Phallicism" is "central" to an operatic plot that features "Calaf as a fantasy where Mussolini was the reality."[46]

Tambling's musings on "the culture of fascism" were not well received. One of the most disparaging reviews, by H. Marshall Leicester Jr., is also the most thorough: it offers us a way forward. Tambling, we learn, is guilty of "retrospective determinism." Since he knows that fascism was the historical "outcome of the cultural processes he examines," he "reads as if [. . .] fascism *is the meaning* [. . .] of these processes."[47] Instead of throwing current theories of fascism at *Turandot* in an attempt to find a match, and having found one, assuming that the opera was fascist all along, we should investigate the opera's "specifically fascist reception."[48] Leicester urges the employment of a Nietzschean "genealogy," famously celebrated by Michel Foucault as a disruptive method of historical inquiry: "It shows the heterogeneity of what was imagined consistent with itself."[49] We see *Turandot* today and cry "Fascism!"—yet knowledge of the way Italian critics of the 1920s and '30s assessed Puccini's work may make us think twice.

To put it another way: we have seen what fascism meant to Puccini, but what did Puccini mean for fascism? For Mussolini, it was evidently worthwhile to keep the world's most successful opera composer on his side. The Duce might not have been able to offer Puccini a national theater, but he doubtless had a hand in the composer's nomination as "Senator of the Realm," giving him a seat in the upper house of the Italian parliament.[50] As we have already seen, Mussolini did not shy away from exploiting the propaganda value of the composer's name on the very day of his death. The latter half of 1924 had been especially difficult for the Italian government. On 10 June, the socialist deputy Giacomo Matteotti was kidnapped and murdered by a gang of fascist thugs. Matteotti had not only been an outspoken critic of fascism; it seems that he was on the point of disclosing large-scale corruption at the highest level. Though Matteotti's shallow grave was not discovered until 16 August, the authorities arrested the ringleader of the gang, Amerigo Dumini, as soon as

12 June. The following day, one hundred leftist deputies walked out of the parliament to form an "Aventine Secession." Mussolini himself denied responsibility for the murder, instead blaming dissident fascists. But even if he was not directly involved, other high-ranking figures were implicated.[51]

It is in the context of this constitutional turmoil that, on 24 June, Puccini saw fit to reaffirm his support for Mussolini. The Matteotti crisis was still ongoing five months later, when the composer died. The Duce's position had become, if anything, even more difficult after the tit-for-tat assassination by a rogue communist of a fascist deputy, Armando Casalini, on 12 September. For now elements within the Fascist Party demanded a violent response, which Mussolini refused to sanction. The situation was only resolved on 3 January 1925, when the Duce declared himself dictator, putting an end to parliamentary democracy in Italy for twenty years.[52.] At the end of November 1924, however, Italian parliamentary democracy was—just about—still in place. The fascists had won a large majority in elections held the previous April. Thus in his speech on Puccini's death (see Appendix), Mussolini could refer to fascism as "controversial," as if the PNF were a matter for free debate. The general atmosphere of political crisis explains the emphasis he placed on Puccini's party membership. The support given to fascism by the composer of *Madama Butterfly* and *La bohème* offered a much needed legitimacy.

So much for Puccini's name. Wilson tells us that "the Fascist regime" sought also "to appropriate his music for its own political ends."[53] This is most obviously true in the case of a rather minor effort, the *Inno a Roma*, composed in 1919 at the request of Puccini's friend Prospero Colonna, then mayor of the Italian capital. The text, by Fausto Salvatori, is a version of Horace's *Carmen saeculare*, a propagandistic work commissioned by the Emperor Augustus that was a great favorite of fascism, set at least three times in 1935 alone (the 2,000th anniversary of Horace's birth).[54] The following year, which saw Mussolini's triumphant announcement of the foundation of the Italian Empire (that is, the conquest of Ethiopia), Puccini's *Inno* was raised, so Jürg Stenzl tells us, to the status of "a kind of National Hymn."[55] As the youthful critic Renato Mariani put it:

> This long-breathed page of melody is loudly sung today by the people, together with the other national hymns, when there are rallies, rites, ceremonies and anniversaries of victories. And it is particularly beautiful and significant that, in this way, the figure of Giacomo Puccini should always

be present in the spirit of us Italians, who, celebrating and hymning the great events of fascist Italy, thus implicitly celebrate the glory of our unforgettable artist.[56]

In August 1937, the *Inno a Roma* was used to preface open-air performances of opera to mass audiences at the grandiose Roman Baths of Caracalla, a scheme introduced that year by Prospero Colonna's son Piero, who became "governor," the fascist replacement for mayor, of the city in 1936.[57] The first season at the Baths of Caracalla featured a production of *Tosca*; the following year there was *Turandot*, reprised in 1939. The novelist Gore Vidal, present at *Turandot* that summer, left the following account:

> We sit outside in a railed-off box, under the hot dark sky. In the next box, Mussolini, wearing a white uniform. At the first interval, he rose and saluted the soprano. Audience cheered. Then he left the box. As he passed me, I smelled heavy cologne. Onstage, he saluted the audience—Fascist arm outstretched. Vanished.[58]

Puccini's operas remained popular with Italian audiences throughout the fascist period. Between 1935 and 1943 there were eighty-seven productions in the state-subsidized opera houses and major festivals alone.[59] Puccini's operas also featured heavily in the mass theatrical events, such as those held at the Baths of Caracalla, that were such a distinctive feature of the 1930s, the outcome of Mussolini's declaration that fascist culture should "go towards the people." Here is Vincent Seligman in the full flush of his fascist enthusiasm:

> It is scarcely to be wondered at that the Duce should have had other and more pressing problems to attend to at that time [the reference is to his meeting with Puccini]. But no aspect of Italian life, however insignificant, escapes his all-seeing eye for long, and the time was to come, long after Puccini's death, when the operatic stage of Italy received a tremendous new stimulus, not indeed through the financing of costly seasons abroad, but by bringing opera at home within the reach of the slenderest purse at those open-air summer performances where, for a few lire, the people can enjoy first-rate opera to their hearts' content. Only the other

day I chanced in Italy on a number of the *Corriere Della Sera* (August 8th, 1937) which contained three long notices of outdoor performances given on the previous night; in the Castello at Milan *Butterfly* before an audience of 20,000; at Verona *Turandot* before a huge public of 25,000 which included Gabriele D'Annunzio; in Rome an "extraordinary" performance of *Bohème* with Gigli as Rodolfo.[60]

Puccini's operas were also a mainstay of the celebrated *carri lirici*, mobile theaters that took opera on tour to provincial centers from 1930 onward.[61]

At the time of Puccini's death, Wilson writes, Italian critics, "card-carrying Fascists" among them, praised the composer in "extravagantly imperialist terms." The "greatness" of Puccini's music, as Adami unblushingly records, was viewed not just as "artistic" but also as "propagandistic": an advertisement for Italian cultural achievement with a global reach.[62] Wilson points out how *Il popolo d'Italia*, Mussolini's own newspaper, proclaimed that "whenever a Puccini opera was advertised on a theater bill, a 'miracle' of unity occurred, and 'all class divisions ceased.'"[63] This is fascist "class transcendence" in action. Open-air performances in Milan, Verona, or Rome were presumably intended to have this same socially harmonizing role.

Such instrumentalization of Puccini's work says little about its content. In these open-air performances, the Steinbergs suggest, following Jeffrey Schnapp on the *carri lirici*, the medium was the message.[64] Class transcendence was apparently not the message of *Turandot* itself. Both Schwartz and Wilson survey the opera's initial reception. And from a political perspective, there is little to report.[65] Consider, for instance, the lengthy review by Adriano Lualdi, a composer, conductor, and critic who was also a top-level musical bureaucrat under the regime, an ardent fascist with "a great deal of clout," as Harvey Sachs puts it.[66] Lualdi's review is certainly marked by gross sexism, but of the critic's political views there are no more than hints, as when he remarks that the "proof" of Puccini's "qualities as an artist [. . .] of good Italian stock" lies in the manner in which, for the composer, the concept of "life" is indissolubly linked with that of "movement." The reader is presumably to understand a reference to fascism's self-image as unrestingly dynamic.[67] For the most part, Lualdi sticks to matters of primarily aesthetic interest. He compares the libretto to it sources (Gozzi, Schiller, Andrea Maffei), gives a blow-by-blow account of the score, and offers his judgments with respect to the relative success of the opera's various sections.[68]

It seems clear, especially from Wilson's account, that Mussolini's accession to power made little impact on the way critics responded to Puccini's music. Writing about *Turandot*, they worried about the "honesty and homogeneity" of the composer's work, just as they had been doing ever since the premiere of *La bohème*.[69] Wilson in fact expresses some perplexity:

> One might have expected a continuation of the anti-Puccini rhetoric of Torrefranca and the *Voce* circle in the Fascist era, given their use of a proto-Fascist language of virility, misogyny, imperialism and opposition to the bourgeoisie. Rather than emulating such thinkers, however, the most prominent Fascist critics drew instead upon the nationalist hagiography favoured by Puccini's patrons and magnified it.[70]

Wilson attempts to solve this apparent contradiction by noting that while Torrefranca was an intellectual and a progressive, Lualdi was a conservative pragmatist.[71] But Lualdi's review of *Turandot*, though certainly nationalistic in feeling, is far from overblown in this respect. Nor is it hagiographical: the critic maintains his autonomy.

Claudio Casini views the situation differently:

> Fascist musical politics were in the hands of the avant-gardes, who wanted to break precisely with opera and with Puccini. Reserved for opera, and incontestably popular, were the *carri di tespi* [*lirici*], the open-air spectacles at the Baths of Caracalla and the Verona Arena, the prestigious seasons at La Scala, which could not be prised away from the rich Milanese bourgeoisie, and at the Teatro dell'Opera, which would be used for state ceremonies, and the future receptions for Chamberlain and Hitler. But the favourite institutions of the regime would be the Festival of Contemporary Music in Venice, the Maggio Musicale Fiorentino, the season at the Augusteo [the principal concert hall in Rome], where there was no place for Puccini, and where, in various ways, Casella, Pizzetti, Malipiero, Respighi made their names, and the whole constellation that surrounded these four signal musicians of twentieth-century Italy.[72]

Puccini's operas may have retained their popularity, but for many in the Italian musical elite of the 1920s and '30s, his work was passé, at best. In a widely read study of the younger generation of composers, the critic and musicologist Domenico de' Paoli described Puccini as the preeminent musician of the "Umbertine" petty bourgeoisie of the late nineteenth century, the representative of "the sensibility and mentality of this class." With each opera, Puccini's musical language became "ever more refined, rich and varied." But this stylistic development stood in ever greater tension with the composer's sensibility, which did not evolve in a parallel manner, and which, de' Paoli declared, "is no longer ours."[73]

An illustration of how old-fashioned Puccini had come to sound is provided by the critical reception of the only opera premiered under fascism beside *Turandot* that achieved anything like a popular success, though it has now long been forgotten: *Il dibuk* (Milan, 1934) by Lodovico Rocca. This tale of metaphysical goings-on in the Pale of Settlement, based on the celebrated play by the ethnographer, activist, and writer An-Sky, is set by Rocca for the most part in the Mussorgsky/Debussy recitative style that found its leading Italian exponent in Ildebrando Pizzetti. But in the opera's final section, where the young lovers are joined, *Tristan und Isolde*-like, in an otherworldly realm, Rocca responds to the verse of his librettist Renato Simoni (he of *Turandot*) in a manner that clearly harks back to the more lyrical vocal idiom associated with Puccini. Opinion was mixed. As Gian Francesco Malipiero commented, in ironic vein, "There was a little of that divine melody that I consider somewhat too conventional."[74]

Rocca was not given to aesthetico-political pronouncements. It would be inappropriate to read too much into this turn to *verismo* style at the end of his most successful work. The same cannot be said of the music shown in Example 1, from the tenor aria at the start of Act 2 of *I Shardana* (Naples, 1959) by Ennio Porrino. Porrino's previous opera, the one-act *Gli Orazi* (Milan, 1941), was a display of heroic *romanità* in the form of "teatro mussoliniano," originally intended for production at the Baths of Caracalla. The composition of his second opera, set in the prehistoric culture of Sardinia, was financed in part by a onetime payment from the Ministry of Popular Culture, and completed, barring revisions, in 1944 under the Republic of Salò, the Nazi puppet state of 1943–45, to which—in contrast to Rocca in Turin, who refused to sign allegiance—Porrino had moved north from Rome to join.[75] *I Shardana* was doubtless meant to receive the same mass-theatrical treatment intended for *Gli Orazi*. Porrino's shameless cribbing of the distinctive opening harmonic

Example 1. Ennio Porrino, "Aria di Torbeno," *I Shardana*
(*Gli uomini dei nuraghi*), Act 2, mm. 171–76.

progression of Puccini's "Nessun dorma" at the beginning of Torbeno's aria seems fully in line with an attempt to "go towards the people."

Porrino was also active in the late fascist period as a polemical journalist: his target was the neoclassicism of Alfredo Casella, which he denounced as "anti-expressive, internationalized" and productive of "ugliness."[76] In a letter of August 1941, he raved that the "clique" around Casella were "all authentic antifascists [. . .] internationalizing and defeatist."[77] Casella saw things very differently. His writings, in fact, complicate the idea that the Torrefranca line of criticism disappeared under the regime. The history of the last fifty years of Italian music, so Casella declares in a characteristically brazen 1935 piece, is that of the rise of instrumental composition and the concomitant decline of opera.[78] Casella has nothing against Romanticism per se. But *verismo* was decadent with respect to Romanticism, a "false tradition" that expressed "the rhetoric and the academicism of the petty bourgeois and liberal-democratic prewar era."[79] Contemporary Italian composers, Casella declares, have chosen to abandon "romantic positions" in favor of an art that is "constructive and linear."[80] Unlike the *veristi*, who imported a foreign (that is, French) idiom and attempted to Italianize it, they choose purely Italian sources as models, the pre-Beethovenian symphonic and chamber forms of the eighteenth century. This is precisely what Torrefranca was hoping for, it should be added.[81] But there is more. In their gradual throwing off of foreign influences over the course of the twentieth century, Italian composers have followed a path comparable to that of the "national consciousness" generally.[82] "In its sobriety, in its dynamism, in its audacity, in its architectonic sense, in its absence of any rhetoric," Italy's new music exemplifies a truly fascist art.[83]

Casella and Porrino represent extreme positions. And their writings are rather untypical of critical discourse from the fascist period in their explicitly political character. Much more characteristic is the article by Lualdi, cited above, in which the author's politics are soft-pedalled. Marotti presents a similar case. As we saw earlier, he portrays Puccini's political opinions as thoroughly fascistic. But in a "Preludio ad una critica" from 1936, an assessment of Puccini's compositional career as a whole, political concerns are almost entirely absent. Marotti regards the decidedly political pre–First World War critiques by the likes of Torrefranca as laughable. Vociferous condemnation of Puccini's work as either "bourgeois" or "international" simply misses its target. Objectively, Puccini's music is Italian; subjectively it is cosmopolitan. As for his music's "bourgeois" character, this is a mark of its Italianness. Puccini's work is stylistically progressive, but finds no place for arbitrary revolution.[84]

Political reticence in discussing works of art was not confined to musicians. As the cultural historian Ruth Ben-Ghiat explains, "Many literary figures, even those of convinced fascist faith, considered it bad form to

write overtly political works." Nor would they "mandate the style or content of the new national culture."[85] Crucial here was the influence of the
philosopher, historian, and literary critic Benedetto Croce. He may have
been the most prominent public opponent of fascism resident in Italy, but
this fact did not persuade fascist critics to abandon their commitment to
the autonomy of the aesthetic, which frequently took its cue from Croce's
argument that artworks were essentially lyric intuition and thus uncon-
nected, qua art, to the sphere of the practical (where politics resided).[86]
Even the notorious 1932 "Manifesto di musicisti italiani per la tradizione
dell'arte romantica dell'ottocento," a thinly veiled attack on Malipiero and
Casella, which was signed by Lualdi, Pizzetti, Respighi, and others,
and which demanded a return to the tradition of Verdi and Puccini,
makes no explicit mention of fascism at any point. Instead the document
refers somewhat decorously to an "ongoing revolution that is revealing
once again the immortality of the Italian genius."[87]

There seems no evidence to suggest that Puccini himself thought of
Turandot in political terms. To most educated Italians of the 1920s and
'30s the idea would have appeared vulgar, if not simply a philosophical error. Even the crudely politicizing Casella would have found the
notion absurd. *Turandot* he regarded as only partially successful. Though
Puccini's work "certainly testifies [. . .] to a clear desire to break new
ground," this only goes to prove that "the romantic and realist theatrical
forms are past and gone."[88] The best music in *Turandot* belongs to Liù,
Casella felt, but might just as well have belonged to Mimì. And how, he
asked in 1935, could a genuinely fascist art be fashioned from the expressive forms of yesterday's bourgeoisie?[89]

Remove the explicitly political angle, and Casella gives us the standard
line on Puccini held by Italy's "progressive" musical elite of the fascist
period. We have seen this already in de' Paoli; it was given authoritative
expression by the leading critic, editor, and arts administrator Guido M.
Gatti in a lengthy article from 1927. Returning to the topic for the tenth
anniversary of Puccini's death, Gatti saw no reason to alter his views. The
composer's work was "feminine," inasmuch as it "did not set its mark on
its times, but was fertilized and marked by them." Puccini's bourgeois
Romanticism catered perfectly to the Milanese operatic public of the last
quarter of the nineteenth century. To be sure, *Turandot* bears witness to a
desire "to get out of the dead-end of early twentieth-century opera." But
Puccini's powers "failed him when he most needed them."[90]

As Cesare Orselli points out, for a "serious critic" of the 1930s to mount
a defense of Puccini was almost unheard of.[91] Yet there were exceptions.

An article by Renato Mariani, whose thoughts on the *Inno a Roma* are cited above, gives us what we have been looking for: an assessment of *Turandot* in fascist terms by a fascist critic. Turning on its head the opinion of Gatti, who had argued that over the course of his career Puccini's musical language had become increasingly impoverished, Mariani assaults the "mean and limited passion of those many persons who, if they can love and understand the little episode of *Bohème*, are spiritually unable to grasp the elevated, human, collective, choral meaning that is fixed in *Turandot*."[92] Mariani's reading lacks explicit politicization, as is to be expected. Yet it is not hard to catch the political intent of a declaration, in 1936, that *Turandot* expresses "the positive values of healthy, living modernity, of absolute, indisputable contemporaneity."[93] The key here is an interpretation of *La fanciulla del West* as marking a break with the "intimate and restricted drama" of the composer's previous operas.[94] From *Fanciulla* onward, Puccini's work begins to resonate with the "external world" that surrounds it, with "passions of a collectively human and emotional character."[95] Evidently we are meant to understand a parallel to the transition from the atomized individuality of bourgeois liberalism to the organic collectivity of fascism. *Turandot*, in its "great, unitary and choral conception," marks the "victorious" fulfillment of this process.[96] In such terms, we might say, Puccini's final opera stands as a fulfillment of Mussolini's exhortation: "Find a dramatic expression for the collective's passions and you will see the theaters packed."[97] Class transcendence turns out to be the message of *Turandot*, after all.

In Foucault's "genealogical" terms, the investigation has paid off. Mariani's is a "fascist" reading quite unlike those proposed more recently, in which, as we saw, Calaf is dressed (metaphorically) in a black shirt as he takes possession of his princess. For Mariani, the somewhat backward-looking vocal styles given to Calaf and Liù make these characters "less choral" than Turandot herself, whose "new vocality" makes her the "absolute protagonist of the intimate drama and the choral drama."[98] To dress Calaf—this "passionate lover typical of Puccini's theater," as Mariani put it elsewhere[99]—in a real black shirt (as one can hardly believe that no recent director has been tempted to do), is doubtless to produce a political frisson among today's operatic audiences. But it is not, of course, to produce a "fascist" reading of the opera, rather the opposite. And to an Italian audience of the 1930s, one imagines, such a gesture would simply have made no sense.

Appendix:
Mussolini's Speech to the Chamber of Deputies, 29 November 1924

Honorable colleagues!

I have the deep sadness of communicating distressing news to the Chamber.

In a clinic in Brussels, where he had gone once the illness that was afflicting him had assumed an inexorable course, Giacomo Puccini died today. (*The Chamber rises to its feet.*)

I am sure that the sadness that overwhelms us in this moment is profoundly shared by the entire Italian people and, one can say, by the entire civilized world. Each one of us has experienced moments of Puccini's music, each of us has been moved before the unforgettable protagonists whom Puccini brought to the stage, whom he brought to life with the force of his music.

This is not the time to discuss the qualities and the nobility of his creations. It is certain that, in the history of Italian music and in the history of the Italian spirit, Giacomo Puccini occupies the most eminent of positions. Nor do I want at this time to dwell on the fact that some months back this illustrious musician asked for the card of the National Fascist Party. He wanted to make this gesture of adherence to a movement which is controversial, the object of controversy, but which is also the only living thing there is today in Italy.

Having recalled that, we want, affiliations aside, to honor in Giacomo Puccini the musician, the maestro, the creator. His music has moved many generations, including ours; it cannot die, for it represents a moment of the Italian spirit.

Let all the people come together at this time. I believe that the Chamber should make itself the interpreter of all the Italian people, raising a tribute of admiration, of devotion, and of sorrow to the memory of this noblest of spirits. (*Lively approbation.*)

NOTES

1. Mary Jane Phillips-Matz, *Puccini: A Biography* (Boston: Northeastern University Press, 2002), 282–83.

2. See Richard Specht, *Giacomo Puccini: The Man, His Life, His Work*, trans. Catherine Alison Phillips (London: Dent, 1933), 21; Vincent Seligman, *Puccini Among Friends* (London: Macmillan, 1938), 351; Guido Marotti, *Giacomo Puccini intimo*, 2nd ed. (Florence: Vallecchi, 1943), 169.

3. Phillips-Matz cites Michele Girardi, who relies on Leonardo Pinzauti. Pinzauti himself gives no source for the November date, but presumably follows the account of Guido Marotti. See Michele Girardi, *Puccini: His International Art*, trans. Laura Basini (Chicago and London: University of Chicago Press, 2000), 436; Leonardo Pinzauti, *Puccini: Una vita* (Florence: Vallecchi, 1974), 171; Marotti, *Giacomo Puccini intimo*, 169.

4. See Phillips-Matz, *Puccini*, 283; Girardi, *Puccini*, 436.

5. "Presidente del Consiglio dei ministri" was and remains the official title of Italian prime ministers.

6. Seligman, *Puccini Among Friends*, 351.

7. Pinzauti, *Puccini: Una vita*, 171.

8. See Fiamma Nicolodi, *Musica e musicisti nel ventennio fascista* (Fiesole: Discanto, 1984), 37–38; and for Puccini's membership of the Permanent Commission, see Eugenio Gara, ed., *Carteggi pucciniani* (San Giuliano Milanese: Ricordi, 1986), 533.

9. Raffaello de Rensis, *Mussolini musicista* (Mantua: Edizioni Paladino, 1927), 27–28.

10. In Palazzo Chigi in Rome.

11. Marcello Piacentini was the leading architect of fascist Italy. The Teatro Costanzi in Rome was remodeled to his design in 1926–27, reopening in 1928 as the Teatro Reale dell'Opera. Presumably Mussolini had the expenditure for this project in mind.

12. Marotti, *Giacomo Puccini intimo*, 169.

13. Phillips-Matz, *Puccini*, 282.

14. Edmondo and Duilio Susmel, eds., *Opera omnia di Benito Mussolini*, 35 vols. (Florence: La Fenice, 1951–63), 21:188–89. A translation of Mussolini's speech is given in the appendix to this essay.

15. Marotti, *Giacomo Puccini intimo*, 168.

16. Girardi, *Puccini*, 436.

17. Pinzauti, *Puccini: Una vita*, 169.

18. Seligman, *Puccini Among Friends*, 290–91.

19. See Nicolodi, *Musica e musicisti*, passim, but see esp. the documentary section, 306–472.

20. Giuseppe Adami, *Puccini* (Milan: Treves, 1935), 183.

21. Agostino Depretis, Francesco Crispi, and Giovanni Giolitti were all prime ministers of Italy at various times during the "liberal" period, 1871–1922.

22. Marotti, *Giacomo Puccini intimo*, 168–69, 170; translation based on Harvey Sachs, *Music in Fascist Italy* (London: Weidenfeld & Nicolson, 1987), 104.

23. The "March on Rome" was a display of paramilitary strength that accompanied Mussolini's appointment as prime minister. For more details, see R. J. B. Bosworth, *Mussolini* (London: Arnold, 2002), 167–69.

24. See Nicolodi, *Musica e musicisti*, 36. Her source is G. A. Chiurco, *Storia della rivoluzione fascista*, 5 vols. (Florence: Vallecchi, 1929), 5:273.

25. Adami, *Puccini*, 183.

26. Giuseppe Adami, ed., *Letters of Giacomo Puccini, Mainly Connected with the Composition and Production of His Operas*, trans. Ena Makin, rev. ed. (London: Harrap, 1974), 297, 89.

27. See Claudio Sartori, *Puccini* (Milan: Nuova Accademia Editrice, 1958), 334. Sartori does not give the name of the recipient of this letter, but it is clearly Riccardo Schnabl. In the index to Puccini's published correspondence with Schnabl, there is a reference to Mussolini listed for letter 133. But turning to this letter, dated 21 June 1924, one finds not just a lack of reference to the Duce, but also a curious four-line gap in the middle of the page. See Giacomo Puccini, *Lettere a Riccardo Schnabl*, ed. Simonetta Puccini (Milan: Emme Edizioni, 1981), 239. Evidently the text had been cut at proof stage: "Mussolini? Io ho fiducia che si riaffermerà, se fosse il contrario meglio prendere la via dell'estero."

28. Julian Budden, *Puccini: His Life and Works* (New York: Oxford University Press, 2002), 436.

29. Michael Mann, *Fascists* (Cambridge: Cambridge University Press, 2004), 100, 1, 13.

30. Dante Del Fiorentino, *Immortal Bohemian: An Intimate Memoir of Giacomo Puccini* (New York: Prentice-Hall, 1952), 194–95.

31. Sartori, *Puccini*, 332.

32. For a succinct account, see Martin Clark, *Modern Italy: 1871 to the Present*, 3rd ed. (Harlow, UK: Pearson Education, 2008), 247–53.

33. Seligman, *Puccini Among Friends*, 303, 315.

34. Mann, *Fascists*, 63–64.

35. Seligman, *Puccini Among Friends*, 308; Gara, *Carteggi pucciniani*, 491–92; Puccini, *Lettere a Riccardo Schnabl*, 84.

36. Gara, *Carteggi pucciniani*, 509; Puccini, *Lettere a Riccardo Schnabl*, 160. Luigi Albertini was the long-standing editor of the liberal daily *Corriere della sera*.

37. Phillips-Matz, *Puccini*, 284; Budden, *Puccini*, 436.

38. Marotti, *Giacomo Puccini intimo*, 171; the translation is from Sachs, *Music in Fascist Italy*, 102.

39. Arman Schwartz, "Mechanism and Tradition in Puccini's *Turandot*," *Opera Quarterly* 25/1–2 (2009): 32.

40. Alexandra Wilson, *The Puccini Problem: Opera, Nationalism, and Modernity* (Cambridge: Cambridge University Press, 2007), 193.

41. Susmel, *Opera omnia di Benito Mussolini*, 22:230.

42. Schwartz, "Mechanism and Tradition," 32.

43. John Louis De Gaetani, *Puccini the Thinker: The Composer's Intellectual and Dramatic Development* (New York: Peter Lang, 1987), 43; Richard M. Berrong, "*Turandot* as Political Fable," *Opera Quarterly* 11/3 (1995): 70, 72, 74n30.

44. Michael P. Steinberg and Suzanne Stewart-Steinberg, "Fascism and the Operatic Unconscious," in *Opera and Society in Italy and France from Monteverdi to Bourdieu*, ed. Victoria Johnson, Jane F. Fulcher, and Thomas Ertman (Cambridge: Cambridge University Press, 2007), 275, 276.

45. Schwartz, "Mechanism and Tradition," 32–33. See the discussion of the stage direction for the "kiss" in Act 3, in Roger Parker, *Remaking the Song: Operatic Visions and Revisions from Handel to Berio* (Berkeley and Los Angeles: University of California Press, 2006), 96–98. For feminist readings of the opera, see Catherine Clément, *Opera, or the Undoing of Women*, trans. Betsy Wing (London: Virago, 1989), 96–102; Patricia Juliana Smith, "*Gli enigmi sono tre*: The Devolution of Turandot, Lesbian Monster," in *En Travesti: Women, Gender Subversion, Opera*, ed. Corinne E. Blackmer and Patricia Juliana Smith (New York: Columbia University Press, 1995), 242–84.

46. Jeremy Tambling, *Opera and the Culture of Fascism* (Oxford: Clarendon Press, 1996), 126, 151, 149, 157.

47. H. Marshall Leicester Jr., Review of Tambling, *Opera and the Culture of Fascism*, *Cambridge Opera Journal* 10/1 (1998): 122.

48. Ibid.

49. Michel Foucault, "Nietzsche, Genealogy, History," trans. Donald F. Bouchard and Sherry Simon, in *The Foucault Reader: An Introduction to Foucault's Thought*, ed. Paul Rabinow (London: Penguin, 1991), 82.

50. Puccini had been angling for this appointment since 1919; his nomination was approved in the Senate on 23 November 1924. See Budden, *Puccini*, 423; "Le commemorazioni," *Musica d'oggi* 7/3 (1925): Supplement, 50.

51. See Bosworth, *Mussolini*, 192–201.

52. Ibid., 201–3.

53. Wilson, *The Puccini Problem*, 221.

54. See Ben Earle, *Luigi Dallapiccola and Musical Modernism in Fascist Italy* (Cambridge: Cambridge University Press, 2013), 194.

55. Jürg Stenzl, *Von Giacomo Puccini zu Luigi Nono: Italienische Musik 1922–1952: Faschismus, Resistenza, Republik* (Buren: Knuf, 1990), 64.

56. Renato Mariani, *Giacomo Puccini* (Turin: Arione, 1938), 28. The other "national hymns" were *Giovinezza* (the anthem of the Fascist Party) and the *Marcia reale* (the national anthem).

57. For more details on the *Inno*, see Arnaldo Marchetti, "Tutta la verità sull' 'Inno a Roma' di Puccini," *Nuova rivista musicale italiana* 9/3 (1975): 396–408; Michael Kaye, *The Unknown Puccini* (New York and Oxford: Oxford University Press, 1987), 127–41, which includes the music. Both Marchetti and Kaye give the date of the Caracalla performance as 1935, but this is a mistake. See Sandro Carletti, "Istituzione e ripresa degli spettacoli alle Terme di Caracalla," in *Cinquant'anni del Teatro dell'Opera,* ed. Jole Tognelli (Rome: Bestetti, 1979), 92.

58. Gore Vidal, *Palimpsest: A Memoir* (London: Deutsch, 1995), 86; see also Carlo Marinelli Roscioni, "Cronologia," in Tognelli, *Cinquant'anni del Teatro dell'Opera*, 234–36.

59. See Nicolodi, *Musica e musicisti*, 25.

60. Seligman, *Puccini Among Friends*, 351–52n2.

61. See Emanuela Scarpellini, *Organizzazione teatrale e politica del teatro nell'Italia fascista,* 2nd ed. (Milan: LED, 2004), 360.

62. Wilson, *The Puccini Problem*, 190; Adami, *Puccini*, 184.

63. Wilson, *The Puccini Problem*, 186.

64. Steinberg and Stewart-Steinberg, "Fascism and the Operatic Unconscious," 272; Jeffrey Schnapp, *Staging Fascism: 18BL and the Theater of Masses for Masses* (Stanford, CA: Stanford University Press, 1996), 21.

65. Schwartz finds a certain verbal and visual fascist rhetoric in the early reports, but nothing more substantial. See his "Mechanism and Tradition," 33.

66. Sachs, *Music in Fascist Italy*, 21.

67. Adriano Lualdi, *Serate musicali* (Milan: Treves, 1928), 258. For Lualdi's sexism, see p. 248, and the discussion in Parker, *Remaking the Song*, 98–99. On fascism's "futural dynamic," see Roger Griffin, *Modernism and Fascism: The Sense of a Beginning Under Mussolini and Hitler* (Basingstoke, UK: Palgrave Macmillan, 2007).

68. Lualdi, *Serate musicali*, 243–49, 249–58, 258–61.

69. Wilson, *The Puccini Problem*, 218, passim.

70. Ibid., 191.

71. Ibid.

72. Claudio Casini, *Giacomo Puccini* (Turin: UTET, 1978), 449.

73. Domenico de' Paoli, *La crisi musicale italiana (1900–1930)* (Milan: Hoepli, 1939), 33, 34–35.

74. See Luisa Passerini, *Love and the Idea of Europe*, trans. Juliet Haydock with Alan Cameron (New York and Oxford: Berghahn Books, 2009), 258. That an opera with a libretto based on material drawn from Yiddish folklore could be successful in fascist Italy is evidence of the lack of official anti-Semitism before 1938. From 1939, however, the

opera could no longer be performed, despite the protests of the composer (who was not Jewish), and after the war it never regained its initial popularity. See Passerini, *Love and the Idea of Europe*, 260–61. Further discussion of the opera and its sources may be found in Michal Grover-Friedlander, *Operatic Afterlives* (New York: Zone Books, 2011), 115–50.

75. For *Gli Orazi* and the circumstances of the composition of *I Shardana*, see Myriam Quaquero, *Ennio Porrino* (Sassari: Delfino, 2010), 157–79, 207–11, 226–28; Nicolodi, *Musica e musicisti*, 444–46; Giovanni Sedita, *Gli intellettuali di Mussolini: La cultura finanziata dal fascismo* (Florence: Le Lettere, 2010), 209. For Rocca's resistance to Salò, see Passerini, *Love and the Idea of Europe*, 261.

76. Ennio Porrino, "Il problema della musica dotta e della musica popolare," *Il musicista* 5/4–5 (1938): 61–66; repr. in Ennio Porrino, *Questioni musicali 1932–1959*, ed. Giuanne Masala (Stuttgart: Masala, 2010), 41–48, quote at 44–45.

77. Quaquero, *Ennio Porrino*, 182.

78. Alfredo Casella, "Problemi della musica contemporanea italiana," *La rassegna musicale* 8/3 (1935): 161–73; repr. in *La rassegna musicale*, ed. Luigi Pestalozza (Milan: Feltrinelli, 1966), 258–68, quote at 259.

79. Casella, "Problemi," 264.

80. Ibid., 262.

81. Ibid., 258, 262–63; and see, for example, Fausto Torrefranca, "'Per una coscienza musicale italiana," *La voce* 2/38 (1910): 385–86.

82. Casella, "Problemi," 259.

83. Ibid., 264–66.

84. Marotti, *Giacomo Puccini intimo*, 210–11, 212–13.

85. Ruth Ben-Ghiat, *Fascist Modernities: Italy, 1922–1945* (Berkeley and Los Angeles: University of California Press, 2001), 47, 26.

86. For Croce's aesthetics, and a sense of how they fit into his system as a whole, see his *Breviary of Aesthetics: Four Lectures*, trans. Hiroko Fudemoto (Toronto: University of Toronto Press, 2007).

87. The complete text of the "Manifesto of Italian Musicians on Behalf of the Tradition of Nineteenth-Century Romantic Art" can be read in Nicolodi, *Musica e musicisti*, 141–43; excerpts in English translation are available in Sachs, *Music in Fascist Italy*, 24–25.

88. Alfredo Casella, "Puccini's Last Opera," *Christian Science Monitor*, 29 May 1926.

89. Ibid.; Casella, "Problemi," 265.

90. Guido M. Gatti, "Puccini dieci anni dopo la morte," *Pan* 2/11 (1934): 412, 410, 412. The previous, longer article is Guido M. Gatti, "Rileggendo le opere di Puccini," *Il pianoforte* 8/8 (1927): 257–71; repr. in Claudio Sartori, ed., *Giacomo Puccini* (Milan: Ricordi, 1959), 89–108. There is also a version in English, "The Works of Giacomo Puccini," trans. Theodore Baker, *The Musical Quarterly* 14/1 (1928): 16–34.

91. Cesare Orselli, "Verismo e umanità negli scritti di Mariani," in Renato Mariani, *Verismo in musica e altri studi*, ed. Cesare Orselli (Florence: Olschki, 1976), 12.

92. Renato Mariani, "L'ultimo Puccini," *La rassegna musicale* 9/4 (1936): 133–40; repr. in Sartori, *Giacomo Puccini*, 113–21; also in Mariani, *Verismo in musica*, 64–70, quote at 65. For Gatti, see "The Works of Giacomo Puccini," 30.

93. Mariani, "L'ultimo Puccini," 70.

94. Ibid., 68.

95. Ibid., 65.

96. Ibid., 67, 69.

97. See Mussolini's speech of 28 April 1933 to the Italian Society of Authors and Publishers, cited in Steinberg and Stewart-Steinberg, "Fascism and the Operatic Unconscious," 270; the translation is from Schnapp, *Staging Fascism*, 33.

98. Mariani, "L'ultimo Puccini," 69.

99. Mariani, *Giacomo Puccini*, 31.

Music, Language, and Meaning in Opera: Puccini and His Contemporaries

LEON BOTSTEIN

Snobbery and disdain for the works of Giacomo Puccini, once commonplace in academic circles and within a self-consciously sophisticated segment of the opera public, particularly during the two decades that followed the end of the Second World War, are no longer fashionable. The old "Puccini Problem"—the idea that no matter the unrivaled popularity of his operas, and indeed perhaps on account of it, the music was at once somehow manipulative and superficial—has vanished as worthy of serious deliberation. The sheer weight and compelling quality of analytic and historical scholarship during the past half-century, written in a context in which stylistic eclecticism in contemporary music had supplanted high modernism, have demonstrated Puccini's mastery of both tradition and contemporary international compositional practices, as well as his originality.[1]

William Ashbrook published the first comprehensive English-language analysis of the evolution of Puccini's compositional approach to opera. He was respectful of the lingering dismissive majority within the academy circa 1968, politely calling their views "sincere."[2] Michele Girardi, writing some thirty years later, demonstrated with precision and detail Puccini's mastery of harmony, formal structures, orchestration, and dramatic form, as well as the composer's originality and deft appropriation of contemporary compositional practices outside Italy.[3] Girardi was less merciful than Ashbrook with the claims of Puccini's contemporary and posthumous critics.[4]

In 2011, Nicholas Baragwanath took a different approach, concentrating on the line of anti-Puccini criticism that challenged the composer's allegiance to and command of the Italian operatic tradition.[5] By focusing on Puccini's training and appropriation, early in his career, of distinct, long-standing, and sophisticated Italian compositional practices (debunking the most famous of Puccini's contemporary critics, Fausto Torrefranca, without mentioning him), Baragwanath defined Puccini's project as an ambition to breathe new life—artistically and commercially—into the specifically Italian tradition of musical theater.[6] Indeed, in 1882 when Puccini, then an aspiring young composer, penned his own imaginary obituary, he described himself as "great," and the "true successor" to the "renowned" Boccherini, as an artist who breathed new life into "Italian art" with a power equal to the "transalpine echo of Wagnerism."[7]

Much of the critical controversy surrounding Puccini in Italy during his lifetime did concern the manner in which he functioned as a representative of an Italian aesthetic. Despite his unrivaled world-wide fame, skeptical critics at home accused his music of an excessive internationalism and subjected him to almost incomprehensible humilia-tion—consider for example the opening night in 1904 of *Butterfly* at La Scala. In Baragwanath's analysis, however, Puccini's goal emerges as that of reinvigorating a great legacy by modernizing it, and his achievement was the contemporary extension of an Italian compositional heritage. In the end, what Puccini accomplished turned out to have less in common with early twentieth-century "classical" musical culture than with that century's "popular" music. But Puccini's ambition from the start was to connect with and to expand the theater audience, and thereby achieve fame and fortune. He was inspired to bridge the gap between so-called high and low, between the elite and the masses, at a time when fissures between the two were becoming increasingly evident. His success was a rare feat in its own time, and it remains so today.[8]

Nonetheless, nearly a century after his death the implied connec-tion between popularity and superficiality still appears to merit explicit contradiction, for Baragwanath felt it necessary to stress that Puccini's ambition and achievement "should in no way be taken to indicate lack of sophistication and artistic worth."[9] The brilliance and complexity of Puccini's compositional craft may have been securely validated, but given the assumption that legitimate normative categories of superior aesthetic value exist, and that distinctions of meaning and quality—or even of "high" and "low"—can be made persuasively, a residue of discomfort and uncer-tainty remains. Puccini himself sensed that he should somehow widen his range. After *Butterfly* he was not content to repeat himself by relying on the formulas that had brought him earlier success with *La bohème* and *Tosca*. In *La fanciulla del West*, *Il trittico*, and *Turandot* he sought to do more than entertain brilliantly.[10] He was keenly aware that even his staunchest allies, particularly Giulio Ricordi and Arturo Toscanini, shared an ideal-ized notion of the elevated nature of music and opera. Toscanini was, after all, deeply committed to Wagner and Brahms; he revered Verdi as a spiritual and political force and was an advocate of Beethoven's *Fidelio*. Toscanini found no contradiction between an attachment to a German Romantic sensibility that privileged music as a profound art form independent of the linguistic and his own fierce Italian patriotism. Toscanini admired Alfredo Catalani, a composer and sometime rival of Puccini's whose 1890 opera *Loreley* reflected the literary and musical influence of midcentury German practices, and Giuseppe Martucci, Italy's foremost late nineteenth-century composer of non-operatic music.[11]

In Ricordi's view, Puccini would have to rise above melodrama and an inspired but perhaps too facile lyricism if he were to inherit the mantle of Verdi with authenticity. Such urgings may account for Puccini's expansive setting of a moral narrative in *Fanciulla* and the searing and closely argued dramatic density of *Il tabarro*.[12] That Puccini met an untimely death, leaving the score of *Turandot* unfinished, encourages the supposition that, the popularity of his works notwithstanding, he sensed limitations within his own achievement and realized he had yet to match the greatness of Verdi and Wagner.[13]

The intent of this essay is to pick up a long-standing but now discredited thread of criticism and ask: What might be missing? The question of what differentiates Puccini from not only his contemporaries (Richard Strauss in particular) but also from his illustrious predecessors merits examination as long as it is done without the outmoded and condescending trivialization of his work typical of earlier anti-Puccini sentiment.

Surprisingly, the idea that there is something disconcertingly limited about Puccini has long been embedded in even the highest, most genuine praise for the composer. Take the case of Mosco Carner's extensive and admiring biography, first published in 1959. Carner observed:

> Puccini does not engage us on many levels, as do Mozart, Wagner, Verdi and Strauss. Yet he remains an unsurpassed master on his own and most characteristic level, which is where erotic passion, sensuality, tenderness, pathos and despair meet and fuse. Where, then, is Puccini's place in the hierarchy of creative artists? He is unquestionably a major artist, but is he a great one by the highest standards? Perhaps the fairest answer is that he was a potentially great dramatic composer who was prevented from attaining his full stature by the limitations and contradictions in his makeup. He possessed burning intensity of feeling but no profundity and no spirituality.[14]

Carner assumes a familiar dualism within the aesthetics of music—the distinction between emotions and feelings, notably eroticism, on the one hand, and a higher realm of ideas, formal logic and meaning on the other. He ascribes to the most noble in music the capacity to convey and inspire something spiritual and profound.[15] In that respect Puccini's operas fell short of Verdi's for Carner, despite their melodic gifts, harmonic imagination, and brilliant orchestration. Puccini's most "individual" characteristic was the intense rise and fall of a melody expressing "mental pain, suffering and emotional fatigue," whereas Verdi's melodic and dramatic sensibilities made for a musical theater whose impact reached beyond communicating emotion and inspiring delight and enjoyment in beauty. Not even Carner saw in Puccini the "wide and full" "dramatic radius" of Verdi.[16]

However dated and naïve Carner's argument may be, it has noble antecedents. It is reminiscent of a venerable tradition that includes Edmund Burke's privileging of the sublime over the beautiful, leaving beauty as an inferior, temporary, weak, and effeminate characteristic. Puccini is merely beautiful, whereas Verdi is sublime—masculine, dynamic, inspiring, and unsettling. Carner's restrained version of the discourse Fausto Torrefranca exploited against Puccini in his blistering *Giacomo Puccini e l'opera internazionale* of 1912 points to a key factor behind the recent erosion of the too often wrongheaded anti-Puccini line of criticism. A basic shift has taken place within the study of the arts and culture, away from the privileging of "high" art. This has led to the critique of a "canon" or a hierarchy of value, and the elevation of unabashedly popular and commercial art forms directed at mass audiences as worthy of philosophical consideration and the proper objects of scholarship, aesthetic admiration, and analysis. This powerful challenge to the cultural conceits of value assigned to "classical" music during the nineteenth century has accelerated Puccini's gain in critical respectability—precisely because he may have been the most accessible and popular "classical" composer in history, an undisputed master of "crossover" and therefore presciently modern.

Georg Knepler, the eminent music historian of East Germany (as Carl Dahlhaus was in the Federal Republic), observed that writing the history of music requires caution about making invidious evaluative distinctions between the apparently serious and the trivial. Consider the twentieth century in Central Europe. Understanding it as history requires paying at least as much attention to Franz Lehár as to Arnold Schoenberg.[17]

Yet Knepler and Dahlhaus, whatever their ideological differences, both believed there was something qualitatively different in the ambitions and achievements of the two composers, one popular beyond the usual range of classical music, the other unpopular even within the limited public for classical music. This conviction approximates Carner's view that music could—and perhaps should—communicate a profundity and spirituality beyond the accessible lyrical distillation of personal emotion. The current critical consensus is that Puccini accomplished both objectives.

Carner placed considerable faith in psychoanalytic theory (a character-istic of the 1950s) as a key to biography and therefore attributed Puccini's failure to match the greatness of Verdi to his character.[18] Puccini's life may offer a veritable field day for psychological analysis, but the appeal to psychobiography to illuminate the distinctive nature of Puccini's operas remains unpersuasive, as Girardi has argued. Whatever plausibility there is to Carner's kind of criticism of Puccini derives rather from the political history of musical culture and taste in the twentieth century.

In the mid-1930s, aesthetic questions concerning the merits of Puccini were seen from the historical perspective of the political success of fas-cism, with which Puccini's work and popularity have been periodically associated.[19] Theodor Adorno framed the issue of Puccini in terms of the modern phenomenon of "background music"—the music that could be heard in cafés and restaurants. The seemingly non-intrusive, soothing use of music in public gathering spaces that had long been associated with debate and discourse represented the way the aesthetic could be manipulated to diminish the potential of resistance in the public realm. According to Adorno, the music Puccini wrote was one-dimensional, catchy, and ubiquitous. It invited imitation because his melodies func-tioned like "ghosts," creating attachment but no disturbances:

> For they are quoted from the unconscious memory of the lis-teners, not introduced to them. The greater the ecstasies, the more perfect the emotional calm of the hearers over whose heads they drift. There are masters—truly masters—whose greatness first becomes entirely evident in this odd trans-formation of passionate appearance into the cold comfort of reality. One could think that *Bohème, Butterfly, Tosca* were created with the thought of imaginary potpourris that do not emerge until the last tear from the operatic catastrophes has dried up.[20]

Puccini's music, using what Carner regarded as Puccini's unique capacity to evoke "the passionate, ardent and spontaneous," was seen as offering comfort by sentimentalization. For Adorno, Puccini's exceptional melodic gift transformed real and subjective suffering into an experience the spectator could feel good about, shedding tears in apparent sympathy—an act, however, that was ultimately ephemeral and ethically bankrupt. For Adorno, Puccini was a model that could be successfully imitated—and disseminated as background music.

Any attempt to appropriate the music of a great composer such as Schubert for the same purpose, however, would be destined to fail. Such music possessed an inherent, uncompromising, autonomous integrity and a concomitant existential realism. Turning it into background music would be "blasphemous." By contrast, an individual listener to Puccini's melodies, which Adorno characterized as the "best" within the genre of "background" music owing to their great "unbroken arcs," is becalmed and distracted from "his conversation or thoughts"—but at a price. Thanks to the seductively expressive character of the music, the listener is transformed not into an individual who thinks deeply, but into a "suburban dwarf." Puccini's music, for all its astonishing subtlety and refinement (Adorno knew of Berg and Webern's admiration for Puccini's craft) induced thoughtlessness, not a critical dialogue with unvarnished reality, as Schubert's music did.[21]

Adorno's image of the "suburban dwarf" comes from Georg Heym's poem "Die Vorstadt," completed in 1912.[22] The poem describes the miserable conditions of a suburb where humanity, caught in the grip of poverty, makes its appearance as cripples and beggars. The dwarf in the poem has a fancy silk coat and is inclined to a self-delusive and arrogant sentimentality. The dwarf's self-satisfied feeling of pity is a surrogate for candid realism and permits what could be an empathetic suffering to be inverted into a terrifying indifference. For Adorno, Puccini's music triggers this inversion in the listener, inducing thoughtlessness. The only residue left after the curtain falls on the overtly tragic plots of *Manon Lescaut*, *Bohème*, *Tosca*, and *Butterfly* is the self-flattering, fleeting memory of emotional empathy created by a magical, catchy lyricism, empathy for an illusion of human tragedy that remakes the real suffering of daily life into something comforting. Adorno sees Puccini's genius as one that renders conditions of oppression and misery affecting on stage and ironically tolerable outside the theater. Music and spectacle lure the audience into a pathetic complacency.

Adorno's critique, like Carner's, took into account the contrast between early twentieth-century audience expectations for operetta and for opera, even though the two sometimes overlapped. When operetta was at its finest (e.g., Offenbach), its gravity lay in satire and parody, a judgment championed by Karl Kraus and later Siegfried Kracauer.[23] Opera as realized by Mozart, Wagner, and Verdi could be said to retain a persuasive connection to a more penetrating critical construct of realism, and therefore to genuine tragedy and myth. This more powerful connection to the human existential predicament defined how word and music needed to interact in opera. The pinnacle, in this sense, of operatic achievement on the Italian scene was Verdi's *Otello*.

Modern scholarship has helped deepen our understanding of the increasingly affluent, self-confident, and "bourgeois" audience Puccini shared with Wagner, Verdi, and Debussy on the one hand, and with Lehár on the other. Puccini knew he had to please this audience; he held Lehár in the highest esteem and even made his own, still neglected attempt at operetta, *La rondine*.[24] Puccini was unabashedly a man of the theater and, like Verdi and Wagner, deeply concerned that all aspects of the productions of his works conspired to hold the audience's attention. His instincts and facility were uncanny. But the expectations of the late nineteenth- and early twentieth-century audience were a source of heightened anxiety for opera composers after Verdi and Wagner. Despite its surface vitality, visible in the sheer numbers of new works, opera as a popular art form appeared threatened.[25]

By 1918 the moving image—the film—was beginning to pose the greatest challenge to the magical theatrical experience opera provided; the moving image was a spectacular and uniquely modern means of entertaining opera's usual spectators.[26] Opera had been sustained by the arresting melodramatic realism of *verismo* and post-*verismo*, the rapidly changing harmonic palette, and the emphasis on the visual and theatrical spectacle so deftly exploited by David Belasco. (Puccini was moved while watching *Butterfly* and *The Girl of the Golden West*, even though his English was at best rudimentary and he could not understand the texts.)[27] The character of this success, however, may also have paved the way for the decline of opera and the triumph of its ultimate rival and substitute, film.[28]

Puccini was indeed Verdi's successor. He achieved a popular triumph for a distinct and elaborate Italian tradition by utilizing a wide range of techniques derived from Wagner, Debussy, and even Strauss. But perhaps his success depended on using music to leave the audience fundamentally undisturbed and content, the apparent tragedies of the plots notwith-standing (with the exception of *Fanciulla* and *Gianni Schicchi*). But the audience Puccini conquered, at least with the earlier tragedies—Heym's "suburban dwarfs," to use Adorno's term—would later support Mussolini and Hitler. For all of his acknowledged mastery Puccini, in Adorno's estimation, did not know how to disturb a dangerous and banal compla-cency: his music did not inspire idealism or inward or ethical reflection in its listeners, or leave them with a sense of skepticism toward the predica-ments of modern industrial civilization.

The idea that music could or should do so lent legitimacy to Carner's 1950s assessment of Puccini's limitations. Carner (born Cohen) was a refu-gee from fascism, a Viennese Jewish émigré in England. A displaced exile, Carner prized the aesthetic realm. Music in particular seemed the one redeeming cultural remnant from the catastrophe of barbarism that an individual could retain as a reminder of one's humanity and that rep-resented the human capacity for renewal. Music possessed the power to be more than background entertainment. It seemed to be a human attribute that affirmed autonomy, dignity, and freedom. It was therefore a potential means of inner resistance to tyranny and conformism, twin consequences of the spiritual, political, and ethical impotence afflicting the cultured audience of mid-twentieth-century Europe.

It comes as no surprise then that many in the immediate postwar years chose to pay no attention at all to Puccini. Pierre Boulez famously quipped that he "never even gave any thought to Puccini." Later he elaborated, "I can't get very attached to Puccini because it is so easy to understand and that is never very interesting, at least not to me."[29] Boulez shared the prejudice that Puccini's art was popular precisely because it failed to challenge listeners. The lingering doubt about Puccini and a sense of disgust at the behavior of previous generations mirrored a widespread perception that the then-reigning norms of art and culture nurtured a camouflage of evil as benign. They fostered indifference. Complacency or even complicity were encouraged by clichés and thoughtlessness and had been promoted by particular aesthetic preferences. Puccini was understood as exemplary of those preferences. An uncritical reductive taste for a pleasing and briefly engrossing aesthetic—in Puccini's case explicitly derived from musical renderings of emotional suffering—conspired to make the uniquely modern horror and catastrophe of the mid twentieth century possible. This view, expressed in various ways by Carner, Adorno, and Boulez, was contingent on the underlying premise that music, and particularly opera, had the power, if not the obligation, to forge a link between art and ethics.

This criticism emanated from within Italy as well. Both Gian Francesco Malipiero and Ildebrando Pizzetti had attacked Puccini on similar grounds. In Pizzetti's words of 1911, Puccini's success was based on his capacity "sincerely, artistically, to live only the lives of those middling persons"—the turn-of-the-century middle-class opera audience.[30] In 1912 the eminent Italian critic Giannotto Bastianelli derided the "spiritual poverty" and "mediocrity" of Mascagni and Puccini (later he made an exception for *Gianni Schicchi*). Central to Luigi Dallapiccola's postwar ambitions was the creation of an Italian operatic model that achieved the more ambitious and noble ends evident in Verdi's operas and characteristic of the work of older Italian masters such as Claudio Monteverdi and Alessandro Scarlatti.

Much of the anti-Puccini sentiment in Italy was bound up with Italy's highly contested cultural politics, but shortcomings in Puccini were also perceived by adherents of the philosophically grandiose claims of the Hegelian tradition, including Gustav Mahler.[31] German criticism of Puccini was in part a defensive reaction to the enormous popularity enjoyed by Mascagni and Puccini, particularly in Vienna.[32] Writing in 1897, the Viennese writer and critic Max Kalbeck—biographer of Brahms, translator of Mozart and Wolf-Ferrari operas into German, and faithful acolyte of the brilliant anti-Wagnerian Viennese satirist Daniel Spitzer—took aim at *La bohème* from a literary vantage point. To Kalbeck, the opera's libretto and musical setting trivialized the authenticity and power of its literary source, *Scènes de la vie de bohème* by Henri Murger. Although he may be remembered today only through the lens of Puccini's opera (and to a lesser extent Leoncavallo's), Murger was once celebrated as a writer. Kalbeck placed the lion's share of the blame on Puccini's librettists. Not knowing "what to do" with the evocative naturalist realism of Murger, librettists Giacosa and Illica had ruined Murger's "witty and thoughtful study of manners." The reductive plot had turned his arresting material into a spectacle that "flattered the tastes of the time." In the opera, the "worse the society" in which the characters moved, "the more commonplace the events and ordinary their thoughts and feelings" became. By contrast, Murger's text had unmasked "the false pathos of irony" and "the corrosive wit of self-mockery" of the characters. These, Kalbeck argued "evade musical treatment. In vain does one ask again and again: Why do these people sing, and not talk?"[33]

The core of Kalbeck's critique is that Murger's literary material was fundamentally resistant to aestheticization through music. Kalbeck therefore expressed disappointment at the failure of a gifted composer to grasp the unique potential of the operatic medium. For Kalbeck, translating Murger's literary realism into music required an inherent denial of music's essential nature and therefore a reliance on reductive, empty stereotypes. Even the crowd scenes required artistic means inconsistent with music. With a prescient anticipation of the new medium of film, Kalbeck observed: "Would that finally a gigantic sound catcher would be invented to trap and hold the noise of the city, and then play in place of the orchestra. The dramatic part then could be provided by the camera—a new artwork of the future."[34]

Kalbeck was keenly aware of Puccini's gift, musing that even if there were such a new medium, "it would be a shame to miss the pretty music Puccini allows us to hear in his opera, particularly in the two outer scenes. When Rodolfo and Mimì sing of their love they do so in delicate tones that, even if they do not always touch our heart as deeply as the age-old and eternally new revelations of the innermost emotions, they do nevertheless flatter and command the attention of our ear." Kalbeck concluded, "Should the composer ever succeed in liberating himself from his own mannerisms and those of others [. . .] perhaps we finally can expect something better from him than what he had to say and sing in his *Bohème*."[35]

Kalbeck was skeptical about the potential of *verismo*, and thus also of Mascagni and Massenet.[36] To him such lowly subject matter was not adaptable to the morally symbolic and fantastic illusionism of the operatic form. In the age-old debate about the merger of words and music in the theater, Kalbeck located precisely the prejudices that would inform subsequent criticisms of Puccini. For all the lyrical beauty of Puccini's melodic material, the magical deployment of the orchestra and the astonishingly original use of harmonic color and contrast, the music rendered naturalist realism superficial and pat, robbing the literary of its emotional power. The music did not force the narrative into a realm of "age-old and new revelations" of "innermost emotions" but rather "flattered" well-worn clichés about love and death that were, ironically, melodramatic simplifications of the presumed emotional realism of the operatic plots Puccini set to music.

Puccini, like other opera composers in the decades after Wagner and Verdi, encountered two interrelated challenges: first, how to break out of the shadow of these two great nineteenth-century practitioners, and second, how to retain a hold on the audience in the era of the realist novel, naturalist theater, and rapid technological, political, and social change. To better understand, contextualize, and circumscribe the sustained line of criticism that has plagued Puccini, it may be helpful to take an approach inspired *en passant* by Michele Girardi: comparing particular Puccini operas with exactly contemporaneous operas by others.[37] Given the international success of Puccini, and to avoid becoming entangled in Italy's specific cultural politics and personal competitiveness, the comparisons would need to be with non-Italians, from places outside of Italy where Puccini succeeded in capturing the allegiance of the public.[38]

Close historical proximity is crucial to this approach; it creates the framework for an examination of how different contemporary composers construed the opera form during the first two decades of the twentieth century. Three cases present themselves as quite uncanny parallels. *Madama Butterfly* had its disastrous premiere in Milan in February 1904; its second, far more successful version opened in Brescia in May of that year. Leoš Janáček's *Jenůfa* had its premiere in Brno just one month before *Butterfly*, in January 1904. Although relatively obscure at the time, by the 1920s *Jenůfa* had become an international success, and Janáček would emerge as one of the most successful and enduring opera composers of the early twentieth century. In May 1916 in Prague, *Jenůfa*, like *Butterfly*, was revived in revised form to great acclaim, transforming Janáček's career and reputation. By the time of the composer's death, *Jenůfa* had been produced sixty times outside the Czech lands.

La fanciulla del West premiered in New York on 10 December 1910. Richard Strauss's *Der Rosenkavalier* premiered in Dresden on 16 January 1911, just a few weeks later. Both works were quickly regarded as significant turning points, for better or worse, in the artistic development of their respective composers. *Rosenkavalier* went on to be Strauss's best-known opera, somewhat to the composer's dismay. From the vantage point of operatic repertoire in the twenty-first century, Strauss was the only composer in Puccini's lifetime properly comparable to him in terms of productivity, critical attention, and popular acclaim.

The third case has a less immediate contemporaneity, but one sufficient to invite a comparative analysis, particularly in view of the similarity of plot and argument. The second part of *Il trittico*, *Suor Angelica*, was first heard and seen in New York on 14 December 1918. Paul Hindemith's one-act opera, *Sancta Susanna*, also part of a triptych and also set in a convent with a nun as its lead character, was written in 1921.[39] It had its somewhat delayed premiere on 26 March 1922 in Frankfurt. The radical expressionist aesthetic of Hindemith's opera offers a stark stylistic contrast to *Suor Angelica*, but one that forces a reconsideration of the work and of Puccini's relationship to early twentieth-century musical modernism. Hindemith did not share an anti-Puccini prejudice. *La bohème* seems to have been his favorite of all operas in the repertory, perhaps as result of his experience as concertmaster in Frankfurt.[40]

Jenůfa and *Madama Butterfly*

Leoš Janáček held Puccini in the highest regard. *Butterfly* was on his mind while he was writing *Kát'a Kabanová*, a work that premiered in 1921. Janáček's *Kát'a* was in part modeled after Puccini's heroine. In 1919 Janáček described his reaction to "Batrflay": "I am so unsettled by the opera. When it was new I used to go to Prague to see it. Many places still move me deeply." He had seen both the Prague 1908 and the Brno 1919 productions of the work.[41]

Puccini's work was well known in Prague. *La bohème* had been produced there in 1898. Although there is no concrete evidence Janáček heard the production, Jan Smaczny has detected a melodic similarity between the final scene of *Jenůfa* and the closing bars of *Bohème*.[42] *Tosca* is the first Puccini opera that scholars are certain Janáček saw, in its 1903 Prague production.[43] In any event, there is little doubt that an Italian *verismo* approach did have an impact on *Jenůfa*, primarily through Mascagni's *Cavalleria rusticana*, which Janáček saw in Brno in 1892 and reviewed. This fact has led to comparisons between the characters of Santuzza and Jenůfa. Janáček may have been aware of Puccini during the composition of *Jenůfa*, but certainly Puccini had no knowledge of Janáček's music or ideas.

Initial contrasts between the two operas are evident in two arenas: (1) the approach to the nature of love and the suffering it brings, and (2) the connection between the literary text and music. Janáček's approach to psychological and social realism is unvarnished; he therefore retains the language and argument of Gabriela Preissova's play. Preissova explicitly challenged any facile idealization of rural life. The opera's popularity suffered at first, in part on account of criticism directed at Janáček's allegiance to the play's language and diction and its resultant candor about human conduct. In *Jenůfa*, anger, jealousy, and violence and their recognition are not sentimentalized.[44]

Therefore the reconciliation at the end—a nominally "happy end"— becomes plausible, for it is shorn of the dreamy, naïve illusions of Puccini's operatic infatuations (e.g. Butterfly, Des Grieux, or Rodolfo).[45] *Jenůfa* revolves around a female romantic protagonist in the title role, but the complex character of the non-romantic female lead, the stepmother or Kostelnicka, dominates. She evokes horror and sympathy simultaneously. Steva, one of two male leads, is clearly a thoughtless cad, but more flawed than evil. Laca, the closest thing to a romantic hero, is likewise a compelling mixture of self-doubt, violent rage, weakness, and tenderness. Both characters manifest flaws and complexities that are absent in the male protagonists in *Butterfly*. This candid confrontation with the ambiguities of human experience makes Jenůfa and Laca's commitment to each other at the end feel persuasive.

In setting Preissova's unsentimental drama of rural Moravian family life to music, Janáček avoided the temptation to simplify the story, resort to melodrama, or render it conventionally or consistently beautiful. It would have been easy to have Jenůfa commit suicide at the end, like Butterfly. Her stepmother, the one individual who showed her consistent loyalty and affection, murdered her child. Jenůfa is physically disfigured as well as dishonored (like Butterfly), with no place to go. A tragic end would have been operatically ideal; yet the will to survive by forging bonds of affection out of suffering is more realistic and more human, if less conventionally operatic. Janáček not only refused to simplify the story, but drew musical ideas directly from the literary language itself.

Butterfly may be the only multi-act Puccini opera to be set in the contemporary moment, but with respect to the audience the character of Butterfly, in contrast to that of Jenůfa, is cloaked in an unavoidable exoticism. The Moravian specificity of *Jenůfa* does not preclude the opera from inspiring a sense of recognition and empathy in a cosmopolitan audience.[46] Janáček uses evident folk materials to signify the Czech character, but sparingly. Puccini, in contrast, went to great lengths to use authentic Japanese and American musical material to set the theatrical frame.[47] Indeed, the exotic in *Butterfly* is not limited to Japanese elements. The moral critique of the "ugly" callous American is centered on Pinkerton, who may be the most unsympathetic and thinly characterized male romantic lead in the operatic repertoire, a fact that undermines the dramatic persuasiveness of the ravishing duet at the end of Act 1.[48] Kate Pinkerton is hardly an admirable figure and Sharpless—the best American on stage—is hapless in his interactions with Pinkerton.[49]

Butterfly's youth and innocence, her blind hope and ultimately her fate, are cast in a context of explicit foreignness but rendered accessible exclusively through music that, from the first measures, is descriptive, narrative, and decorative: an unmistakable Italianate and French-inspired superimposition on the exotic. Butterfly's emotional development is achieved through music that strategically revels in its self-contained theatricality. Despite the opera's harmonic ingenuity and melodic allure, moments of intensity are carefully calculated (the appearance of her child before the suicide) and the shifts in musical rhetoric are rapid and seductive. The exotic context of the story functions as a platform for a vocal virtuosity of an unambiguous and almost generically expressive nature.[50] Through the music characters are shorn of specificity, ambiguity, and complexity; the exotic is sustained primarily by the visual, despite Puccini's deft use of Japanese elements. The artifice of pacing and staging, as well as the luxurious lyricism, draw attention primarily to themselves. The character of the music emerges from a plot and text that abstract desire, passion, and betrayal. The emotions, passionate and finely drawn as they are in the music, are of a conventional character. They reveal the masterly adaptation of a consistent compositional style. Despite the condescending prejudice in the comment Hugo von Hofmannsthal made to Richard Strauss, noting that in "Mozart and Wagner each work is unique, in contrast to a series of generically identical works like Meyerbeer's or Puccini's," there may be more truth to Hofmannsthal's observation than *Butterfly*'s admirers may wish to admit.[51]

Butterfly's illusions and emotions are transformed into aesthetically recognizable objects, worthy of wonderment, but not any empathy close to the world of the opera's audience, given the exotic and highly exceptional character of her predicament. Jann Pasler has suggested that Butterfly mirrors the barriers to assimilation and acculturation, particularly for Italian immigrants in America, and especially for women.[52] But perhaps the extraordinary popularity of the opera (though notably not with an immigrant audience) and shimmering beauty of the score have led, in recent years, to inspired counterintuitive efforts to blunt the inconvenient fact that *Butterfly*'s appeal may derive from its artificiality and transparently formulaic representation of the tragic consequences of innocence and betrayal.

Puccini brilliantly expands Butterfly's musical canvas, but without deepening her individuality. The opera is framed by theatrical devices—from the flower duet and the humming chorus to the final cry of Pinkerton; these offer moments for the display of successive ravishing musical events. Music illustrates a visual sequence without interrupting the illusion of a naturalistic passage of time. The beauty of the score renders Butterfly's fate purely aesthetic. The transparently melodramatic plot, the unremitting lyricism, and the exotic are more comforting than unsettling to its audience. The music may inspire a sense of pity and compassion in the moment, but hardly a sustained reflection on hope, betrayal, loss, and hopelessness.

Puccini's opera is about theater and music, not about truth or reality. Janáček, in contrast, was obsessed with the potential of music to achieve "truthful expression." Using "a realistic expression of the locality," he fashioned melody from the specificity of the spoken word that brought out "the truest expression of the soul."[53] Puccini set love, desire, despair, regret, and anticipation with uncanny invention and skill, and he illustrated depictions of streets and crowds, all with a recognizable musical and theatrical rhetoric. Janáček sought music in the "melodic motifs of speech." Out of the fragments of Moravian dialect he fashioned motives, musical speech, and extended themes, and integrated them into a continu-ous formal musical structure that shifted with the drama and always emanated from the local, though the music allowed the local to be universally apprehended Janáček was certainly adept at deploying theatrical and operatic conventions; but in *Jenůfa*, the "local" realism, linguistically and musically, is from within, not, as in Puccini, imported. From the eerie opening bars of the xylophone a distinctive musical fabric unfolds, nearly symphonic in character, replete with Italianate lyrical moments, passionate climaxes, *parlando* passages, and folk song and dance. Janáček constructs a disturbingly long dramatic arc, evocative of the particular character of desire, love, cruelty, and the oppressive expectations and limits of village existence that are true to life and cannot fail to provoke.

Indeed, the contrast between the two operas is audible from the orchestral introductions. Puccini's is a tour de force of dramatic energy—a spectacular, almost neoclassical but asymmetrically punctuated piece of imitative writing that rapidly reaches a high point, marked by the composer's unerring sense of rhythmic punctuation and dramatic pacing. Using the opening patterns, the music subsides and sets up a transition to the first scene, revealing the aggressive swagger of the Americans. Janáček cut his initial solution to the start of the opera (a work he published separately with the title *Jealousy*) and settled on a stunning opening that creates a transparent mood of foreboding.[54] Thinly scored, defined by simple ostinato patterns over which dense fragments are gradually extended, the music ambiguously suggests an intimate inner intensity and a desolate exterior. Janáček's mysterious, arresting sound world introduces the fear, anxiety, uncertainty, and vulnerability surrounding the opera's heroine. The prelude leads seamlessly into Jenůfa singing about the approaching evening. Puccini, on the other hand, sets the stage with extroverted theatricality, employing the power of the orchestra and holding the listener through shifts in harmony that underlie a kaleidoscope of seductive melodiousness. Janáček approaches both the vocal line and orchestral support in a more restrained but integrated manner, foregrounding text, framing an economical use of lyricism and accumulating tension toward defined dramatic climaxes.

Janáček learned from Puccini, particularly in terms of the command of the orchestra. In the operas written in the 1920s, he tried to emulate Puccini's condensed melodic rhetoric without sacrificing his allegiance to drawing melody from specific speech. But Janáček's music in *Jenůfa* is neither decorative nor self-consciously theatrical; it does not have, as Max Brod put it, the character of a musical "mosaic" —a word that has been used, in a spirit of praise, to describe the music of *Butterfly*. In *Jenůfa,* "everything seems to flow from the same inexhaustible source, melody upon melody gushes forth, with unforced lightness." Every phrase, Brod observed, gets a "sufficiently powerful melodic line."[55]

Janáček hardly shies away from passion and high drama, as Laca's outburst at the end of the first act indicates, but the music, illustration aside, is consistently integral to the shifting argument of the language: music deepens complexities and invites suggestive meaning beyond the language, derived from the language's musical character, not merely its translatable meaning. It would not be until *Fanciulla* and *Il tabarro* that Puccini would come closer to Janáček's belief in the operatic form as more than a vehicle of melodic expressivity.

Der Rosenkavalier and La fanciulla del West

Late in the spring of 1935, Richard Strauss, frustrated with what he knew were the difficulties of bringing the dense and multilayered (and highly Italianate) musical texture of *Die schweigsame Frau* alive in performance, wrote the young conductor Karl Böhm, "Why was I not brought into the world as Verdi, or for that matter even Puccini? To the devil with German counterpoint!"[56] Strauss, who often turned his fine sense of irony and humor on himself, would express a similar lament to the conductor Clemens Krauss in 1942. He had recently listened to his *Daphne* and had come away with the impression that the German singers lacked a natural cantilena and a "plastic, expressive recitative." But perhaps he, the composer, was to blame and that "the formless mush" he had written which now made him so "discontent" was responsible. Perhaps an entirely different style of writing was required. Strauss exclaimed, "To hell with the 'new world' into which a wicked fairy switched my birth. Long live *Tiefland, Trovatore, Tosca!*"[57] Strauss was struggling to reconcile the grace, simplicity, and directness of the Italian operatic tradition with his attachment to the compositional heritage that included Mozart and Wagner. He cited Eugen d'Albert's 1903 *Tiefland* (alongside Max von Schillings's 1915 *Mona Lisa*) as the most successful German appropriation of an Italian operatic aesthetic.

To Strauss, Puccini was both a rival and counterpart: the only truly successful composer of operas of his generation. Although Strauss seems never to have seriously disparaged Puccini's craft and facility—and he certainly admired Puccini's success—he was circumspect. He held the view that the fabric of opera needed to be less dependent on vocal virtuosity and simplified (or absurd) plots. The link between text and music needed to be close, requiring libretti that were not generic or superficial as they often were, in his view, in Italian opera. Like other German artists, writers, and composers, he envied the lightness, simplicity, and persuasive natural beauty of melody in the Italian tradition. He expressed this envy with a mix of flattery and irony by composing and inserting explicit and elegant Italian moments in *Der Rosenkavalier* and, at the end of his career, in *Capriccio*.[58]

Strauss's mix of envy and admiration had its limits, however. Strauss, who was fond of culinary analogies, compared "Puccini to a delicate white sausage that must be eaten at 10 am (2 hours after it was made), even though by 1 pm one already has an appetite for something more substantial." Then, referring to himself, "salami (more densely realized) lasts just a bit longer."[59] Strauss once commented to his collaborator and librettist Hugo von Hofmannsthal that as a composer he was a "cosmopolitan" figure midway between Puccini and Hans Pfitzner—that rather humorless and forbidding figure of German heaviness.[60]

Hofmannsthal's response provided a more revealing comparison. Puccini and his librettists were skillful (and therefore to be admired) for adaptations, "adoptions" of the work of others or of some vague "historical milieu," streamlining material and unintentionally stripping it of the very detail that once gave it power. Doing so with productions of Belasco was perhaps simpler than attempting it for works by Murger or Sardou. Although there has been some scholarly revisionism about the merit of Belasco's plays, Belasco was celebrated for his theatrical showmanship and his reliance on stagecraft, visual tricks, and dramatic conventions, rather than the subtlety of his language.[61] For Hofmannsthal, a proper text for music had to be an integrated, free-standing work of literary merit, consistent within itself and explicit in its attempt to engage complexity and ambiguity—in short, a literary effort that transcended melodrama or autobiography.[62]

Hofmannsthal's response aptly describes the most commercially successful of the Strauss-Hofmannsthal collaborations, *Der Rosenkavalier.* Hofmannsthal went so far as to publish it as a literary drama, even though it had been written explicitly with the intent of being sung. (Hofmannsthal would later make a distinction between this genre and a true libretto, a text more aware of its potential musical setting.) After *Salome* and *Elektra,* Strauss was looking to return to comedy, which he had last attempted in *Feuersnot,* his second opera. Although Wagner's *Meistersinger* remained a daunting model in the composer's mind, Strauss quickly embraced Hofmannsthal's idea of a comedy of manners set in the Vienna of Maria Theresa in the 1740s and based in part on source material from the life of her court. Strauss's lifelong veneration of Mozart gained the upper hand in his ambitions. In part spurred by the fin-de-siècle Biedermeier revival and the anti-Romantic, anti-monumental, and anti-historicist aesthetic of Jugendstil and avant-garde architecture and design, Strauss and Hofmannsthal turned to the mid-eighteenth century. Inspired by many sources—Casanova, the visual satire of William Hogarth, Molière, the canvases of Watteau, and the tradition of the comedy of manners—mid-eighteenth-century Vienna became a prism through which the two artists could explore the ironies, conceits, and contradictions of modern life.[63]

The complex three-act opera they produced rivaled Puccini's operas as a worldwide hit. Both Strauss and Hofmannsthal would later concede that the work had its dead spots and was probably too long, but neither felt strongly enough about that to shorten it. The opera is distinguished above all for its unrelenting attention to the precision and subtlety of words. The most famous example is the Marschallin's command of the complex tenses of "to be," which contrasts with the limited present tense employed exclusively by the ingénue Sophie.[64] "Language is the mother of thought," quipped Karl Kraus, and Strauss's opera depends more on characters as delineated by the virtuosic use of language than on its plot, which is painfully simple: an older woman's lover finds a partner his own age, one who has been engaged to an unsuitably older, boorish man. The plot possesses a layer of social critique, since the boorish man is a landed aristocrat from an old family and the potential young female victim the daughter of a rich man of business—a recently ennobled bourgeois—who seeks to escape his middle-class status via marriage and money. This tension between social status and social class, between aristocracy and wealth, had not diminished by 1910; it reappears in Strauss (in *Arabella*) just as it pervades the novels of Henry James and Edith Wharton. Puccini was also drawn to this issue. Oscar Wilde's *A Florentine Tragedy* (which Alexander Zemlinsky turned into a fine one-act opera in 1917) intrigued him as a possible subject. But it would be in *Gianni Schicchi* that Puccini ultimately addressed the conflict between class and status.

Strauss responded to the underlying social satire of the opera by using the waltz in an ahistorical manner, inserting a retrospective if not nostalgic musical language from the mid-nineteenth century (mixed in with references to the eighteenth), the Vienna of the Johann Strauss family. As for character, Strauss applied his skill at thematic transformation to the very opening motive—meant to represent the young lover—thus enabling the audience to follow Octavian's metamorphosis, and even his disguises.

With its many ear-catching melodies, duets, and trios, and its relative absence of the audible dissonances associated with *Elektra*, *Der Rosenkavalier* became both popular and controversial. The controversy arose because Strauss seemed to have turned his back on the modernist project of formulating a progressive musical language, taking refuge in a nostalgia that legitimated the score's Italianate grace, its emulation of Mozartian elegance, Schubertian eloquence, and crass Viennese ebullience. The opera's popularity stemmed from precisely these virtues that were so derided in some critical circles.

At *Der Rosenkavalier*'s core, however, lie the claims made on the music by language. The argument of the opera is about mortality and abandonment: the ephemeral character of intense love, the inevitability of aging, the erosion of innocence, the deception in courtship and seduction, the pain of loss, and the grace of forgiveness. They overwhelm the distance between spectator and stage, between the present and the historicist setting. These themes are sustained with subtlety, conveyed by three main female voices. Octavian's and the Marschallin's long ruminations in Act 1 give the opera an evident philosophical cast. The moment of erotic passion—an operatic source for both Strauss and Puccini—is actually hidden from view. The ceremonial moment of the presentation of the rose, the hectic scene at the Inn in Act 3, and the comic and cameo episodes that include secondary characters, punctuate a poignant portrayal of the ways in which desire, love, and loss influence self-knowledge on the part of the four main characters (including the comic Baron Ochs).

The opera's main protagonist is the Marschallin, who picks up the thread first spun in opera by Mozart's Countess Almaviva in *The Marriage of Figaro*. She loses love, observes a younger rival, and achieves graceful resignation (even though she is really quite young); she witnesses the painful and temporary blindness of infatuation and, through music, anticipates its eventual exhaustion and betrayal. This weighty main subject matter is interwoven with farce, conspiracies, and disguises that exploit the "trouser role" potential of Octavian. Satire in music and text are directed against the nouveau riche (Faninal) and the boorish landed aristocracy (Baron Ochs). The triumph of wisdom and grace is achieved through the music of the Marschallin, who carries the audience with her to the end, offstage, as her servant collects her successful rival's dropped handkerchief—a harbinger of what the smitten bride will soon encounter—on a silent stage, illustrated by the orchestra alone.

Whatever shortcomings plague *Der Rosenkavalier*—length, moments of overwriting, wordiness, extravagance—the music provokes a differentiated, skeptical, and reflective account of human conduct unlike *Jenůfa* or any Puccini opera. There is a symbiosis between literary language and music. The music deftly uses tonality to structure the drama and lend the work coherence, mixing melodic simplicity, intensity, and elegance, and overtly appropriating the musical past. There is no "closure," only a painful reminder of facets of life shared by all. There is no reductive moralizing between the good and the bad. A bittersweet sadness and the perception of mortality and frailty dominate over the sentimental. *Der Rosenkavalier* marks a turn in Strauss's work away from myth and tragedy toward comedy, from the conceits of late Romanticism to the refined and disciplined intersection of structure and ornament characteristic of eighteenth-century painting and instrumental music. Even Strauss's later operas based on myth—*Helena* and *Danae*—invert the mythic by presenting gods and heroic characters as plainly human, whether they be Jupiter and Menelaus or Helen and Danae.

Puccini's *Fanciulla*, which had its premiere a month before *Rosenkavalier*, was also regarded as a departure for its composer.[65] Although, like *Butterfly*, the libretto was adapted from a Belasco play, Puccini expanded and deepened the fundamental argument; he worked on the libretto himself, making decisive changes. Unlike *Butterfly* or any of Puccini's previous heroines, the main character is a woman who functions as more than a reflection of men's desires. Minnie is a powerful and fearless working equal in an all-male world, beloved not because she is beautiful or acts seductively, but because she is honest, moral, and shares aspirations, for not only money but also the experience of love. At the same time she hardly is innocent or naïve. Minnie is a Sunday School teacher and civilizing authority as well as a hard-drinking and card-playing female. In a rough and lawless mining town dominated by lonely homesick men, she shows both desire and heroism.[66]

The opera, like *Der Rosenkavalier*, is structured around the thoughts and actions of its lead female character, rather than the actions of men. The poker scene in which Minnie cheats and outwits Rance is the opera's dramatic high point. It comes after she gives her first kiss to Dick Johnson—her pledge of love. The end (love) justifies the means as she alternatively deceives and confronts Rance and thereby rescues Johnson, the man she has chosen. Minnie gives victory to empathy, hope, and forgiveness over revenge and envy. As later in *Turandot*, the symbolism of the first kiss takes on a pivotal function.

If the dramatic and musical characterization of Minnie is far more ambitious than in comparable female characters in Puccini's operas, so too are the two male leads, the "good" male figure, Dick Johnson, and his "sinister" rebuffed rival, Jack Rance. They may have direct parallels in *Tosca* (Cavaradossi and Scarpia) but Puccini approaches their characters with far more subtlety and ambition. Johnson assumes a complexity Puccini did not choose to assign to Des Grieux, Rodolfo, or Cavaradossi, and Rance invites empathy, even if some critics regard him as possibly less admirable than Scarpia—for whom Puccini permits no real sympathy.

Puccini does not resist the temptation of staged flourishes, such as the gallows scene at the end, but in *Fanciulla* he leaves more space for the music to insert meaning and complexity into the plot and characters. The reliance on unrelenting bursts of intense melodic expression is less pronounced, the music is constructed of longer episodes, and the harmonic and orchestral textures, evidently influenced by Debussy, allow for the expansion of time onstage, permitting differentiation in character development. Puccini's music functions more autonomously, and reaches beyond illustration and narrative meaning, both framing by contrast and matching the specificity of voice and action.[67] Puccini's expanded orchestra takes on a more independent role, often subordinating the voices. Most remarkably, Puccini takes on the hardest challenge, a happy ending—perhaps still melodramatic but considerably more nuanced than in any of Puccini's previous operas.

Nonetheless, *Fanciulla* encountered critical skepticism. Reviewers missed the riveting Puccini melodies they had been expecting, and the harmonic language seemed too sophisticated and complex to illustrate so simple a morality play. Some, perhaps rightly, saw in *Fanciulla* Puccini's turn to a Wagnerian model. Of all Wagner's works, Puccini admired *Parsifal* the most; its influence has been detected in *Le Villi* and in *Tosca*. But it is the theme of redemption that connects Puccini's *Fanciulla* to Wagner. Carner, on the other hand, suggested the influence of Strauss's *Salome* on the sonorities found in *Fanciulla*. Puccini did in fact admire the early Strauss. He was impressed with the extraordinary dramatic aspects of *Salome*, despite its "terrible" cacophony. But in *Elektra* he felt that Strauss had gone too far. It was a "horror." And Puccini would later dismiss *Die Frau ohne Schatten* as too intricate, too much like "logarithms."[68]

Ironically, just as Strauss was becoming more skeptical about moral absolutes and more confident in his atheism, Puccini in *Fanciulla* was offering a simplified representation of charity based on the Christian Bible.[69] Whatever the weakness of his original source, Puccini's reworking of Belasco's play shows a family resemblance to the highly popularized theology of Leo Tolstoy, whose fame was at its height in 1910, the year of Tolstoy's death. By the time of *Fanciulla*'s premiere, Tolstoy, through his utopian projects, his philosophical writings, and the 1899 novel *Resurrection*, had assumed the mantle of a living saint, the proponent of a Christian simplicity, egalitarianism, pacifism, and asceticism as a stark antidote to the materialism, inequality, and cruelty of modern life. In *Fanciulla* Puccini was taking on one of the central philosophical struggles of his time over meaning and value— comparable to the mystic celebration of community in *Parsifal*—by focusing on the redemptive action of a woman reborn through faith. In the opera, a simple but not innocent or saintly woman becomes the instrument of male redemption. Puccini, without a hint of poetic or philosophical pretense, offers an Italian appropriation, set in the American Wild West, of the closing lines of Goethe's *Faust, Part Two* about the power of the "eternal feminine." This theme also captivated the imagination of Gustav Mahler at the very same historical moment, as can be heard in the second part of his Eighth Symphony.

But in Puccini music overwhelms language; there is nothing autonomously poetic or philosophical in the language as is the case in *Rosenkavalier*.[70] Puccini's main provocation was his implicit theological challenge to the values of modern industrial urban life, augmented by thinly veiled aesthetic provocations in the form of what were then regarded, particularly in New York, as advanced harmonic usages. These made the opera less accessible.

Strauss, by appropriating the historically distancing frame of the eighteenth century, was not only giving himself the opportunity to redeem historical precedents, but to challenge a glib post-Wagnerian allegiance to the persistence of progressive change (as his modernist critics well understood). Puccini went in the opposite direction, becoming more adventuresome; his critique of the status quo in societal values (one can read a critique of the allure of wealth, for example, in *Fanciulla*) demanded a more recognizably resistant, modernist musical vocabulary.[71]

Although both operas were written before the "scandal concerts" of 1913 in Paris and Vienna and Futurism's first concert in Milan in April 1914, the tension aroused by stylistic novelty in the arts was already evident in *Fanciulla*'s muted reception in 1910 and *Der Rosenkavalier*'s triumph. The opera audience's allegiance to a late-Romantic vocabulary, albeit an expanded one, had the effect of circumscribing the extent to which the operatic form could be politicized. Strauss hid his critique in a seductive and ironic nostalgia. Puccini revealed it by refusing to repeat himself and by offering a more elusive and demanding musical experience.

Strauss's surface conservatism in *Rosenkavalier* was ironic. From the opening bars, the spectacular kaleidoscope of sonorities, harmonic colors, and tonal relationships represents a defense of the dynamic vitality and promise of tonality as the framing logic of musical time, and the priority of grace and transparency in melody and counterpoint over a dense, humorless Romanticism. Strauss and Hofmannsthal were taking aim at the clichés, rhetoric, and utilitarian moralism of the middle class, as well as the irresponsible delusions and inflated self-regard of a landed aristocracy whose political hegemony was clearly under siege. The ugliness of modernity was highlighted, and the oppressive weight of late nineteenth-century historicism was challenged by the reimagining of a refined humanism as represented by the eighteenth century and the opera's protagonist, the Marschallin.

As a work of social critique, *Fanciulla* can be seen as a covert commentary on the European fascination with America. Nearly two million Italians had moved to the United States by the end of 1910, and there was little prospect of this immigration slowing down. The lure of America—the land where streets were paved with gold—was based on economic need rather than political promise, despite widespread dissatisfactions with Italian politics.[72] But the immigrant reality, both urban and rural, was grim. Homesickness prevailed, and the cost of uprooting was socially corrosive. *Fanciulla* in Puccini's version (more than in Belasco's) suggests a form of redemption through the superiority of the European. The "authentic" American musical materials are submerged in and elevated by Puccini's score, so that cultural tradition triumphs over the frontier and "the new," as represented by the dangerous, violent, and spiritually impoverished daily life of the miners. Minnie's triumph, saving Johnson from being hanged by the miners, is a moral redemption, the triumph of Christian love and charity over ambition, violence, and greed—failings inevitably connected to the loss of the homeland. The genuine human community is located at home, the place where land and history secure the continuity of human bonds and cultural values.

The opera mirrors Puccini's attachment to his native Tuscany and the musical heritage exemplified by his own family. This loyalty suggests yet another link between Puccini and Strauss's operas. In both works the composers utilize a distant context, either historical (Strauss) or geographic (Puccini), to indicate their conservative resistance against the toll taken by the grim political and social realities of modern life. The most striking form that resistance takes is an unapologetic and insistent display of transparent melodic beauty in whose presence listeners are able to experience recognition, loss, and absence: key elements in the human search for love.

Sancta Susanna and Suor Angelica

Both of these one-act operas were composed as part of a triple bill (known in Puccini's case as *Il trittico*), but they were written three years apart. *Suor Angelica* had its premiere in 1918 and *Sancta Susanna*, completed in 1921, was first staged in 1922. Yet they shared the moment of a decisive historical break: World War I, which shattered the continuity between the nineteenth and twentieth centuries.

Puccini structured *Suor Angelica* along seven "stations" evocative of the Stations of the Cross.[73] The music evokes the insular stillness of the cloister. Only women's voices are heard, except for the use of a mixed chorus (albeit with boys' voices) at the end. The heroine is a model nun who has become the community's purveyor of herbal remedies. She is also from an aristocratic family. Her parents are dead. Her journey to membership in the convent was imposed and involuntary. The curtain rises seven years after she had a child out of wedlock and was punished. Yet she has embraced her fate and absorbed a deep faith, troubled only by worries about the fate of her child.

The pivotal dramatic moments are two. Angelica's heartless and domineering aunt arrives to get her to sign away her inheritance on account of her sister's impending marriage. In response to Angelica's entreaties to be able to see her child, the aunt brutally informs her of the child's death years earlier. Angelica vows to end her life, ingests a poison of her own making, then realizes her mortal sin and begs for forgiveness before a statue of the Virgin Mary. A miracle occurs: the Virgin Mary is seen in a blaze of light and in a manner Puccini must have realized is reminiscent of the end of *Lohengrin* (as well as many turn-of-the-century plays and pageants in which miraculous apparitions occur). The child appears to the dying Angelica, a sign of forgiveness and grace.

Puccini's music is intentionally static except for the scene with the aunt and the death scene. Time is elongated by the music so as to convey relentless duration and monotony, the temporal reality of the removal from life demanded by ascetic discipline.[74] This homogenous but eloquent fabric is broken by the aunt's visit and the heroine's transformation, her awakening to her old self—her recovery of the human capacity for despair and love. As she reclaims her emotional and sensual sense of life, the music departs from its restraint. Angelica's rebirth as a passionate mortal, the shedding of an enforced spiritual equanimity, is followed by the spectacular miracle. The miracle is granted in defiance of doctrinal orthodoxy, but gains approbation from Angelica's sisters in the closing chorus of praise to the Virgin Mary.

During the opera, Angelica's individuality is revealed gradually in three stages, each framed by musical and dramatic episodes. We first encounter her as kind and forgiving, beloved by her fellow nuns. She is clever and gifted. The description of the carriage carrying her aunt reveals that her spiritual distinctiveness also mirrors an exceptional inherited social status. In the second stage, the atmosphere and mood of the convent are broken by the visit. The third is the aftermath in which we witness, through the music, her abandonment to the suppressed sensuality and the breaking down of the enforced monastic acceptance of removal from the ordinary world audible at the start. The Virgin Mary rewards Angelica for embracing her true self, for giving voice to maternal love, the consequence of sexuality. Angelica is granted grace by an act that suggests human compassion despite the suicide, which is ultimately a sign of the loss of faith in the grace of God.

Suor Angelica, a work close to Puccini's heart perhaps on account of its relative lack of success—also the reason *Helena* and *Danae* would become so dear to Strauss—may have suffered because it appeared strikingly out of step with historical currents.[75] Most of Puccini's operas had focused on the realm of the intimate and erotic, even when political subtexts are apparent as in *Tosca* and *Butterfly*. *Butterfly* may indeed be a critique of

American and Western imperialism, but that impression remains peripheral to the affecting portrayal of love, betrayal, abandonment, and desire. Likewise, despite the role political history plays in *Tosca*, Cavaradossi is a martyr to love, not political principles.

Suor Angelica may contain a veiled critique of Church doctrine, and perhaps of the price paid by the otherworldly asceticism demanded for monks and nuns. Given the intense outpouring of emotion heard in Angelica's aria "Senza mamma," one could easily read the opera as a critique of Christianity's contempt for the body. But that would invest Puccini with a philosophical ambition he did not cultivate beyond the standard anti-clericalism he shared with his Italian contemporaries.[76] Even the portrayal of the aunt is personal, not political.

The closing miracle notwithstanding, the opera might inspire outrage for a girl unjustly banished to a convent and forced to abandon her child and forfeit her inheritance, all for having disgraced an aristocratic code of honor. But in *Suor Angelica* the musical treatment encourages sympathy with the heroine's emotional struggle and deflects political outrage. In 1918 both the subject and its musical treatment in *Suor Angelica* could easily have appeared to be oblivious to the need, in the realm of the aesthetic, to confront the consequences of the death and destruction that had overcome Europe.[77]

To apprehend the impact of 1918 one only has to compare Puccini's one-act opera set in a convent with Paul Hindemith's *Sancta Susanna*, written over the span of a few weeks in 1921. Hindemith's opera is a setting of August Stramm's Expressionist play. Like the music of *Suor Angelica*, the score of *Sancta Susanna* is tightly structured, not in seven sequential sections but through a set of five musical variations—of which the last is a double one.[78] Hindemith's nearly obsessive concern for the autonomous formal musical logic of the opera led him to create a two-part symmetrical structure in which the dividing point, which comes precisely halfway though the total number of measures, is also the moment when the key to the storyline of the opera is revealed. The second half of the opera then becomes a mirror-image reenactment of the past. Hindemith's obsession for form is plain: even the prelude has its own transparent inner structure of self-citation and recapitulation.

Sancta Susanna is electrifying and fast moving. In the tightly constructed musical drama the expectations of tonality frame the style, but the narrative rhetoric and rhythmic strategies are not exploited conventionally.[79] The music does not narrate the plot, but implies and enacts it. At the outset the audience encounters a young nun, Susanna, who is physically weakened and ill. An older nun, Klementia, watches over her. Susanna is anxious, rattled by the noise of wind and by a spider. She senses something uncanny. As the drama unfolds she hears her maid scream. The maid was making love with a peasant, who monosyllabically expresses his desire for the maid to Susanna in one line spoken in dialect—the only male voice heard in the work. Susanna is strangely curious and asks the maid about the erotic aspect of their interaction.

As the wind blows and the spider crawls, Klementia senses danger, a replay of an incident in the convent many years earlier, when a young nun, overcome with the intensity of her love for Jesus, tore off her habit and mounted the crucifix in the chapel, clasping Jesus's head, and masturbated. Klementia tells the story to Susanna, revealing that the young nun was punished by being walled in behind the chapel altar and buried alive; the defiled crucifix had been covered ever since. Hearing this, Susanna becomes ever more excited. She senses her body, revels in her beauty, enters the chapel, tears off the cloth covering the crucifix, and mounts it. Her fellow nuns watch in horror, proclaiming the presence of Satan. They pray for her and demand that she repent. Instead she stands before them triumphantly, challenging them to punish her as they did her predecessor, and refusing to repent. The curtain falls.

Hindemith in the 1920s took pride in writing music that did not "please" in the sense that Puccini's did. Music needed to strive to be "objective"—independent of illustration—and also down to earth, to be concrete (*sachlich*) and practical, if not useful (*Gebrauchsmusik*). His relationship to Expressionism was based on a rejection of the use of music to achieve a romanticized illusion of the real. Music was therefore to be held to its own logic.[80] The shocking narrative argument could only be communicated by a rigorous structural logic that subordinated the vocal line and integrated it into a unified, densely argued musical fabric.

Hindemith's musical vocabulary in this tight structure employs conventional dramatic strategies, including realist tone painting—depictions of wind, the scent of flowers, and a spider. Motives recur, and fragments imitative of liturgical music emerge toward the end. Hindemith's music is varied, with the sparse sinister tension established at the outset giving way to lush, nearly Wagnerian moments. At key dramatic points, the orchestra plays alone and the scenic action becomes pseudo-pantomime. The impression is one of opera as symphonic essay, economically organized around thematic development.

By contrast, Puccini's *Suor Angelica* is set in the open air, out of doors, albeit in a cloister garden, with music that underscores the placid visual stasis. Hindemith's drama is all indoors, and the music, through its self-referential independence and rigor, reinforces the visual enclosure. Hindemith's extremes in sonority, ranging from single instrumental lines to massively orchestrated textures—all placed inside the convent—suggest an oppressive, claustrophobic psychic space. Only windows and their shutters—and distant vocal sounds—suggest the idea of relief from incarceration and hint at the natural world.

Sancta Susanna makes evident Hindemith's affinity to literary Expressionism. The illusions of realism that emerge from narrative conventions of prose and poetry are set aside and replaced by a fragmented, non-ornamental use of language. Words, shorn of their decorative usage, open up the possibility for music to provide an ethical and aesthetic argument using music, for the most part, independently of language, illustration, and narration. The merger of formal musical autonomy with an economical and explicitly anti-dramatic use of language permits him to foreground human sexuality with disarming intensity and candor.[81] The spectator no longer is entertained, but becomes a voyeur. There is no sentimentalizing. Through the music, the confrontation between Klementia and the nuns and Susanna reaches well beyond the stylized character of Wagnerian eroticism; the ecstatic is rendered brutally through sound. Although the dramatic and melodic material is evocative in a familiar manner, Hindemith eschews the use of repetition as a means of reassurance. He intensifies the passage of musical time. *Sancta Susanna* delivers its riveting drama in less than half the duration of *Suor Angelica*.

These two works share not merely the dramatic locale with its distinctive inhabitants, but a common argument. Both Puccini and Hindemith challenge the psychological plausibility, if not ethical superiority, of a devotional love of God that demands the sacrifice of erotic desire and fulfillment. Through the image of her son and the memory of human love, Puccini's heroine breaks out of the self-imposed discipline of denying her body in service of the spiritual. She reclaims her ordinary humanity, with all its emotional range. Susanna, who has disciplined her body to the point of illness, is inspired by the nature external to herself—the wind and the spider—and by Klementia's storytelling. She breaks free to express her passionate love of God in a truly human way, with her body, erotically. Angelica dies but is forgiven and saved, redeemed and sent to heaven not as the bride and servant of Christ, absolved of sin, but as mortal mother of an innocent dead child. Susanna is still alive at the end of the opera, defiant but condemned, unrepentant and triumphant in her realization of human, physical love. Angelica is praised by her sisters.

Susanna inspires fury, envy, and condemnation. *Suor Angelica* sidesteps gracefully and with considerable lyrical sentiment any implicit political or social critique. On the contrary, humility and generosity within the religious community, including its hierarchy, are highlighted in Puccini's empathetic portrait. Hindemith unmasks the fear, resentment, repression, and cruelty that fester within a world founded on a sanctimonious ideology.

If *Suor Angelica* found little favor with Puccini's public, it was because of its slowness of pace and sentimental argument, not because of any subversive subtext or challenge to conventional moral reasoning. Angelica's dignified and cheerful acceptance of her fate inspires sympathy. The convent and the nuns are favorably juxtaposed to the cold, heartless aunt whose rigidity and inability to forgive and to love are placed in stark contrast to the warmth of Angelica's fellow nuns. Indeed, the evil aunt plays a role in the opera comparable to that of Pinkerton in *Butterfly*, and is a pale figure when placed against Janáček's stepmother in *Jenůfa*.

In Hindemith's opera Susanna has from the outset embraced monastic discipline with an erotic intensity Angelica suggests only at the end—to the near fatal detriment of her body. Like the Desert Saints—the ascetic Athanaël in Massenet's and Anatole France's *Thaïs*—Susanna transfers her erotic passion not to a human (as she observed her maid doing), but to the male figure of Jesus, thereby unmasking the hypocrisy and inhuman character of the demands for a purely spiritual love of God. Hindemith's condensation of the operatic medium was designed to shock and scandalize, and not merely through the story line. He compressed operatic time, stripped it of decoration, subjected it to an inexorable musical logic informed by classical procedure, and used late-Romantic sonorities with an expressionist radicalism. Language and music functioned as politics. Hindemith challenged the habits and conceits of conventional narrative and operatic drama, and in doing so he sought to rescue the aesthetics of opera against the complacency that had recently engulfed the world in a brutal war—one that had cost his father his life.

Rethinking Puccini

Scholars and critics intent on revealing Puccini's greatness and writing in the late twentieth century, after the decline of the prestige of modernism, have largely discredited the facile disparagement that Puccini once inspired. The melodic invention, the rhythmic vitality, the ingenuity with which he developed motivic material, the daring and idiosyncratic harmonic palette, and the consummate command of orchestral sonority are, after all, stunning. Inspired by an eclectic range of sources including Wagner and Debussy, Puccini succeeded in perpetuating Italian opera, adapting the strategies of turn-of-the-century modernism for operas that have survived endless repetition without any loss of enthusiasm among musicians or the public.

What accounts for Puccini's undiminished popularity? He clothed the innocuous and terrifying thoughts and feelings associated with the conduct of life in an almost lurid lyricism, economically structured and alluring in its harmonic colors. Puccini created a recognizable rhetoric of emotionalism through melodic gestures and outbursts that, when sung with beauty and conviction, never fail to stir the listener with disarming simplicity and unambiguous directness. These qualities turned the opera stage into a medium that could inspire a transaction of emotional and elevated engagement within a mass audience that ranged from the totally unsophisticated to the serious musician. The evident artificiality of the theater was simultaneously celebrated and cloaked by a mix of beauty and fantasy masquerading as realism. A musical fabric punctuated by soaring moments communicated a persuasive illusion of emotional realism.

Puccini's remarkable harmonic moves in a continuous fabric of musical narration allowed his operas to shed the markers that identified opera as a learned art. Puccini succeeded in supplanting through a richly textured music the specificity, complexity, and ambiguity of language. The banality of clichés that each of us easily resorts to when we seek to express our most intimate feelings found elevation through this musical mirror. Puccini's veil of beauty, intensity, and eloquence clothed the vulgar, ordinary, and predictable with an unforgettable lyric clarity so profoundly human that no one could fail to identify with and respond to it. Using music to suggest a seemingly natural stable human expressivity, Puccini rivaled Verdi's and Mozart's success in capturing the sympathy of the audience.

Puccini offered his audience a mesmerizing and accessible aesthetic transformation of the experience of desire, love, envy, and loss. He did this through a sophisticated condensation of the formal traditions of opera that made the representation of ordinary time onstage sound real, much the way the film and realist novel can, by hiding the presence of the writer and director within the evident artifice of theater. Words were no longer set to music. Rather, words became subordinate, permitting the composer to offer a continuous and varied musical narrative, whose meaning and import were dominated by music and not language. The primary lesson Puccini learned from Wagner was continuity.

But words in Wagner conveyed philosophical and moral arguments (however repugnant or absurd) and spun a web of mythic symbolism. Whether or not he did so successfully is open to question. But Wagner took his texts with shocking seriousness, giving readings and publishing them independent of any musical setting. Ideas and words spurred musical rhetoric. Difficult as it may be today to take seriously either the style or the claims of the Wagnerian texts, they are crucial to the music and in performance can help generate a sense of profundity. Wagner's weak suit was the visual, a dimension of opera for which Puccini possessed precise ideas and unerring instincts. In Puccini's work language was simplified, and the musical line and atmosphere carried the weight of the theatrical experience, assisted only by the non-linguistic visual spectacle. In Janáček and Strauss, however, language remained music's indispensable partner, dwarfing the significance of visual spectacle. Hindemith also subordinated the visual, using text to create dramatic tension by pairing the sparse linguistic narration with an autonomous musical structure.

Puccini's project was to reach the widest possible audience by adapting the traditions of opera. The most important characteristic of musical theater in the public realm was its power to entertain, to interrupt the consciousness of quotidian time. Puccini did so not by expanding it, as Wagner did, but by condensing it. His stroke of genius was to reduce the role of language in opera to the bare minimum required to tell a story through a synthesis of continuous melody and visual spectacle.

The focus on entertainment was a consequence of the era in which Puccini came of age. Operatic theater had experienced a radical de-politicization. The heroic, historical, and nationalist impulses that were once so central to opera in the age of Wagner and Verdi had been realized, albeit with compromises and disappointments. In *Parsifal*, Wagner advanced a spiritual philosophy whose underlying agenda was, however, ideological in that it suggested the transcendence of the political by the ideal of an exclusive spiritual community.

Although Verdi's engagement with the political within the operatic medium in his early career may have been exaggerated by critics in the decades immediately after Italy's unification, for Puccini's generation a connection between Verdi and politics was assumed. And even though a political subtext has been argued for *Falstaff*, Verdi at the end of his career took refuge in Shakespeare, taking on the setting of the most daunting poetic depiction of the subtleties, ambiguities, and complexities of the human condition in *Otello* and *Falstaff*.[82] After Wagner and Verdi, theater and opera, which had flourished as vehicles of political expression and symbolism linked to issues of national unification and identity, shifted focus in two directions—toward the creation of a new nationalist culture and toward an exploration of eroticism and violence among individuals, particularly the poor, in society. The *verismo* movement asserted a realism that was about human nature and, indirectly, psychology. Individual lives, and their emotions in the private sphere, in closely defined social settings, dominated. *Verismo*'s realism, through music, generated an aestheticized naturalism, but it was not about politics.[83]

Puccini's ambition was not to alter the world as he found it, but to succeed by telling stories of personal suffering (even *Tosca*, despite its surface, is not about politics but about love, jealousy, and desire), all (with the exception of *Il tabarro*) set in the past or faraway locations. Humperdinck and Catalani found an alternative in fairy tales to escape the daunting Wagnerian use of myth; likewise, Puccini's narratives of human love, defined as they were by transparent predicaments and resolutions, were pared down in a manner suggestive of the narrative simplicity of fairy tales.

The Italian public, shut out of participatory politics and decommissioned as soldiers of national unification after the 1870s, took refuge in entertainments that paralleled their own preoccupation with private fulfillment and personal ambition. *Verismo* and its aftermath, including the operas of Puccini, were public entertainments—national pastimes—whose function was to distract attention from the political and toward the personal. It is no accident that Puccini's innovative post-Wagnerian extension of formal Italian operatic traditions created compact, seamless musical dramas of love, suffering, death, and happiness that have lent themselves better than any other operas to commercial film adaptations. Puccini anticipated and fulfilled the requirements that still define popular success in the moving-image drama with sound, whether a Hollywood blockbuster or a TV mini-series. Through his use of music to convey economically a formulaic set of emotions, he subordinated the creative tension and symbiosis between musical form and linguistic narration that defines most great operas, from Mozart to Berg.

Puccini's success in his own time—the last achievement on that scale in the history of opera—exceeded that of Strauss, and his works continue to have mass appeal. Perhaps this success is understood best through the lens of Jean-Jacques Rousseau's critique of theater and the arts in so-called civilized society.[84] Indeed, twentieth-century criticism of Puccini, from Torrefranca to Adorno and Joseph Kerman, can be understood as an extension of Rousseau.[85] In Rousseau's view, theater exploited the limited human capacity for active empathy and compassion by exhausting it within the confines of the theater. For Rousseau, a successful aesthetic portrayal of suffering onstage retarded any chance for political action to relieve it through real change in the sources of that suffering. Rather, the self-congratulation of audiences regarding their high standard of aesthetic discernment, when combined with a sympathetic response to suffering onstage, would persuade theatergoers that just being moved to tears constituted a sufficient discharge of their responsibilities as citizens. In other words, the cathartic experience in the theater generated by an artistic representation of injustice or cruelty provided the educated classes with nothing but an illusion that they had advanced the cause of justice. Walking out of the theater, these spectators would allow a smug self-regard to substitute for any determination to change real circumstances.

For Rousseau, the musical theater was a matter of particular concern, because music augmented the power of language. Rousseau's notions of the origins of music bear a striking similarity to Janáček's theory of speech melody. The essence of music was melody, and that in turn derived from language. Harmony is for Rousseau not natural but an invention whose abuse can lead to the disfiguring of language by separating it from its natural source. Instrumental music was of little interest to him. The right kind of music was not "artificial," and shied away from harmonic and rhythmic elaboration. Rousseau harbored an ideological prejudice on behalf of the operatic traditions of the late sixteenth century, particularly those of the circle around Giovanni de' Bardi.[86]

Janáček's invocation of the "truthfulness" of his compositional procedure—of deriving melody from speech and evolving the harmonic vocabulary to support it— has its indirect roots in Rousseau, though he appears never to have read the Genevan philosopher. From the vantage point of a Rousseau-like critique, Puccini's virtuosity in the use of harmony exacerbates the seductive character of music by deepening its artificiality—its distance from language and reality, even though the subject matter remains overtly human. Suffering rendered musical heightened empathy, deepened the conceit of the listener, and depressed the moral conscience of the educated classes more severely than did the spoken theater. The more harmonically rich and ornamented the music became, the more it appealed to unnatural standards of beauty, breaking any possible link between the good and the beautiful.

The critique of music and the theater in relationship to politics and ethics has a long history predating Rousseau. But the appropriateness of that critique gained in force during the late nineteenth century when the audience for music and music literacy expanded, and opera took a major place in the public sphere of the arts. After the unification of both Germany and Italy, an art form that once sought to influence politics through culture found itself faced not with a radical revolutionary agenda but an affirmative one—the framing of a national cultural sensibility. (Janáček, working in a region in which the national question was unresolved, was the exception, his artistic credo being defined to the end by the struggle for Czech independence.) That a visible and significant form of public entertainment such as opera was tacitly supportive of a political status quo on the eve of World War I did not go unnoticed.

It is therefore not surprising that after 1918 a younger generation, brilliantly represented by Hindemith, looked with suspicion on both Puccini and Strauss as purveyors of a nearly addictive art form that could provide its listeners an ultimately false sense of cultural superiority and ethical complacency. This line of reproach against Puccini (and, in a somewhat more complicated manner, Strauss) helps locate the source of Puccini's unrivaled and lasting popularity. It bears a close resemblance to the charge of the manipulation of realism that was later applied to the moving image, particularly the sound film, opera's offspring and successor in the public imagination. The film's rise marks the decline of opera, as the audience shifted its attention and became enthralled with a new technology that could integrate language, the visual, and the musical within an illusion of realism.

Does it matter that Puccini's lasting popularity is the result of a brilliant variant on the commonplace and temporarily affecting experience of theatrical spectacle? There is no question that his operas offer an awe-inspiring encounter with musical imagination and skill, even if they fail to challenge the audience and its conceits. If Rousseau was right and even the more morally and philosophically ambitious triumphs of theater have in the end a negative impact on human conduct (as the barbarism of twentieth-century fascism, led by aficionados of Mozart, Wagner, Verdi, and Strauss attest), why deride his success as nothing more than refined entertainment? Can truly popular musical theater do more than entertain?[87]

Nevertheless, one may reject Rousseau yet hold on to some construct of higher purpose for the operatic form beyond connoisseurship of musical invention and craft. For all his greatness, Puccini may simply be too pat, too self-consciously beautiful, and too easy to listen to, with the result that his art ends up affirming passivity toward both injustice and vulgarity. Strauss, despite his cynicism, sought to achieve more, thinking as he did that Mozart, and to a lesser extent Wagner, had deepened man's capacity for critical self-recognition and aesthetic sensibilities. He therefore sought out texts with literary and philosophical ambitions. Janáček and Hindemith retained a faith in the ethical power of musical theater: Janáček for reasons of national pride, and Hindemith because of the need to come to terms with the Great War and its catastrophic consequences.

The distinguished Viennese-born, German theater and film director Arthur Maria Rabenalt (1905–1993), writing in the 1920s, sought to understand how one might rescue Puccini from misplaced snobbery and criticism. His primary interest was in the potential of new operas that experimented radically with the operatic tradition. In response to the question about whether it is possible to produce *Butterfly*, *Bohème*, or *Tosca* in a new way that lends them extra-musical theatrical significance, Rabenalt mused:

> The central purpose of modern opera production is to give shape to the contemporary conflicts that emerge from today's everyday life and human condition. Instead of merely limiting itself to simply portraying new locales, be they realistic or stylized, true to nature or abstract, achieving this has to be the fundamental mission. The purpose is to engage the debate regarding how a proper form can be given to the dramatic exploration of the human condition.
>
> To give an example: Let us disregard the specific exotic color of the music of *Butterfly*. If a modern milieu is mixed only superficially with the Far Eastern opera landscape and its mendacious flower magic, then it is of no consequence if the gunboat *Lincoln* arrives in the harbor of Nagasaki or a caravan of conquistadors is anchored at a harbor in the Indian Gulf, or if a B. F. Pinkerton abandons a Cio-Cio-san or a Vasco da Gama does the same to an African girl (who in actuality is Indian!)
>
> If this is done, then this tragic operetta becomes what, unfortunately, we are faced with every time: a kitsch picture-postcard melodrama. What would have to be shown in this "tragedy of a little Japanese woman" (the actual subtitle) is an unbridgeable inner difference between two worlds—even though on the surface they seem alike today. A hard and unrelenting contrast between two races, and the conflicts

and contradictions in culture and civilization in the life and mentality on two continents, would all have to be shown in a musical drama about two people.

Consider, by contrast, the modern setting of a marriage, as in Hindemith's opera *Neues vom Tage*. It offers the occasion to capture dramatically, with playful joviality, a comedy of errors, and to reveal the total confusion of today's mores about marriage and divorce. A setting in today's world of sports, for example, might also be useful for opera, not because of the visual and metaphorical novelties it would offer but because of the opportunity it gives to explore the crucial influence that sports prowess has in today's human society. In an erotic comedy a good backhand now plays a more important role than does, for example, the *jus primae noctis* of the Count or the sex appeal of Cherubino in *The Marriage of Figaro*.[88]

Rabenalt's challenge remains with us. Can—or should—anything be done to rescue *Butterfly* from being more than Rabenalt's "kitsch picture-postcard melodrama"? His skepticism can be gleaned from his characterization of the music and the difficulty in framing the exotic in a manner that realizes some deeper political and social critique in the opera. Not surprisingly, Rabenalt places his hopes on new operas, even though he indirectly implies that Mozart's *Marriage of Figaro*—like *Rosenkavalier* and *Jenůfa*—offered a social critique.[89] Dramaturgical modernization (Peter Sellars notwithstanding) may be a lost cause.

As an art form, opera has become far less significant than it was in the 1920s, despite the large number of new operas. And in the 1920s opera was already in decline, undermined by new technologies of entertainment. Puccini, Janáček, and Strauss were the last to provide successfully more than one opera for the stage, and Puccini has since certainly outstripped his competition. Given opera's political and cultural irrelevance, Puccini's popularity ought therefore to be a source of gratitude. Perhaps luxuriating in beauty is sufficient justification. Rabenalt was prescient about the failure of radical directorial shifts in the setting of the historical repertoire—the futility of staging and directing as a means of making *Butterfly* into something it may never have been intended to be.

Put on the stage as intended is *Butterfly* more than a "kitsch picture-postcard melodrama"? Puccini's subordination of language may condemn it to being just that. At the same time, by forcing the cast to inhabit

another culture visually and vocally, by only looking Japanese and singing in Italian using Italianate musical rhetoric to express their deepest
feelings, such a production might function today as a powerful critique
of contemporary identity politics and ideologies of ethnic essentialism—
a challenge to the charge of Orientalism. By remaining faithful to its theatrical artifice, *Butterfly* can make a much-needed political point as an
ironic inversion of the intent and impact of the opera when it appeared
in 1904.

Even if one rejects this suggestion, does the fact that *Butterfly* might
not be able to rise above kitsch and melodrama (hampered in part by its
unrelenting familiarity) in any way diminish it? The striking differences
in aspiration, subject, method, and purpose in Janáček, Strauss, Puccini,
and Hindemith matter only to a small minority. Instead, it is important
that Puccini's project be properly understood. He sought to become an
international success with new Italian opera. He construed his audience
as international (in contrast to the Janáček of 1904). By avoiding politics,
the literary and the philosophical Puccini propelled modern opera into
mass transnational popularity. His achievement has never been approxi-
mated and will never be matched. Puccini succeeded because he limited
the ambition and scope of his project.

Philosophical insight into the human condition and a subtle critical
sensibility may not be compatible with mass popularity. If true, this circumstance suggests humility and a profound recognition of reality on
Puccini's part, not a limitation and a shortcoming. The Puccini operatic
ideal, when integrated with the traditions of operetta—as Puccini himself
attempted—resulted in the twentieth- and twenty-first-century musical theater. But the challenge still remains: Can the mass popularity of
an opera be reconciled with an agenda that reaches beyond Puccini's?
Puccini created the most sophisticated works rooted in the traditions of
classical music to reach the public at large in a sustained manner. Puccini's
legacy ought to be regarded as exemplary. It stands as an inspiration to
the prospect that it may be possible to simultaneously fulfill the purely
aesthetic ambitions and traditions of opera and meet the demands of a
mass public over many generations without becoming tiresome, boring
or condescending.

NOTES

1. On Puccini's life and work, see for example Dieter Schickling, *Giacomo Puccini: Biografie* (Stuttgart: Carus, 2007); Julian Budden, *Puccini: His Life and Works* (New York: Oxford University Press, 2002); Mary Jane Phillips-Matz, *Puccini: A Biography* (Boston: Northeastern University Press, 2002); William Weaver and Simonetta Puccini, eds., *The Puccini Companion* (New York: W. W. Norton, 1994); Iris J. Arnesen, *The Romantic World of Puccini: A New Critical Appraisal of the Operas* (Jefferson, NC: McFarland & Co., 2009); Michael Klonovsky, *Der Schmerz der Schönheit: Über Giacomo Puccini* (Berlin: Berliner Taschenbuch Verlag, 2010); Sylvain Fort, *Puccini* (Paris: Actes Sud, 2010). I wish to thank Arman Schwartz, Emanuele Senici, Susan Gillespie, Christopher Gibbs, Irene Zedlacher, and Giselher Schubert for their invaluable assistance.

2. William Ashbrook, *The Operas of Puccini* (New York: Oxford University Press, 1968), xiii.

3. An excellent account of Puccini's innovative harmonic language and its reception is Giorgio Sanguinetti, "Puccini's Music in the Italian Theoretical Literature of Its Day," in *Tosca's Prism*, ed. Deborah Burton, Susan Vandiver Nicassio, and Agostino Ziino (Boston: Northeastern University Press, 2004), 221–48. See also Paolo Fabbri, "Metrical and Formal Organization," in *Opera in Theory and Practice: Image and Myth*, ed. Lorenzo Bianconi and Giorgio Pestelli (Chicago: University of Chicago Press, 1988), 151–220, on Puccini's text setting.

4. See Michele Girardi, *Puccini: His International Art*, trans. Laura Basini (Chicago: University of Chicago Press, 2000).

5. See Nicholas Baragwanath, *The Italian Traditions and Puccini: Compositional Theory and Practice in Nineteenth-Century Opera* (Bloomington: Indiana University Press, 2011).

6. See Alexandra Wilson, *The Puccini Problem: Opera, Nationalism, and Modernity* (Cambridge: Cambridge University Press, 2007). Wilson's book explores the issue of the critique of Puccini within Italy during the composer's lifetime. As an indication that an anti-Puccini bias still is perceived, see the witty book by William Berger, *Puccini Without Excuses* (New York: Vintage Books, 2005).

7. Quoted in Baraganwath, *The Italian Traditions and Puccini*, 38.

8. See Emanuele Senici's introduction to this volume.

9. Baraganwath, *The Italian Traditions and Puccini*, 310–11.

10. See William Ashbrook and Harold Powers, *Puccini's "Turandot": The End of the Great Tradition* (Princeton: Princeton University Press, 1991); and Andrew Davis, *"Il Trittico," "Turandot," and Puccini's Late Style* (Bloomington: Indiana University Press, 2010); see also Leonardo Pinzauti's "Giacomo Puccini's *Trittico* and the Twentieth Century," and Jürgen Maehder's "*Turandot* and the Theatrical Aesthetics of the Twentieth Century," in *The Puccini Companion*, 228–43 and 265–78, respectively.

11. On Toscanini's views, see Harvey Sachs, *Toscanini* (New York: Da Capo Press, 1978); also see Toscanini's 1935 letter from Salzburg expressing his pride that Arnold Rosé, the legendary and venerable concertmaster of the Vienna Philharmonic, stood up in front of the whole orchestra to praise his reading of *Fidelio*. Harvey Sachs, ed., *The Letters of Arturo Toscanini* (New York: Knopf, 2002), 191.

12. Ricordi was never quite so enthusiastic, for example, about *Butterfly* and encouraged Puccini to find libretti of literary subtlety. See Girardi, *Puccini*, 202; and Budden, *Puccini: His Life and Works*, 132.

13. See, for example, the letters Puccini wrote to Ricordi about possible libretti, including a potential collaboration with D'Annunzio, in *Letters of Giacomo Puccini*, ed. Giuseppe Adami (Philadelphia: Lippincott, 1931), 231–41.

14. Mosco Carner, *Puccini: A Critical Biography* (New York: Knopf, 1959), 229.

15. For a detailed discussion of Carner, see Arman Schwartz's chapter "Realism and Skepticism in Puccini's Early Operas" in this volume, especially the section "From Vienna to New Orleans, via Flanders."

16. See Mosco Carner, "In Defense of Puccini," in *Of Men and Music: Collected Essays and Articles*, 3rd ed. (London: Williams, n.d.), 28–31, quote at 29. The familiar question of how Puccini might be compared with Verdi is not discussed in this essay. However, the meaning of Carner's characterization is assumed to refer to Verdi's astonishing achievement in the use of musical means in opera—in terms of melodic invention and formal procedures—to realize complex character development and a dramatic experience that engages the human condition, including the political and the philosophical.

17. See George Knepler, *Geschichte als Weg zum Musikverständnis* (Leipzig: Reclam, 1977), 354–57.

18. See Girardi's discussion of this issue in *Puccini: His International Art*, 2–3.

19. See Jeremy Tambling, *Opera and the Culture of Fascism* (Oxford: Clarendon Press, 1996); Harvey Sachs, *Music in Fascist Italy* (New York: W. W. Norton, 1987); Alexandra Wilson, "Modernism and the Machine Woman in Puccini's *Turandot*," *Music & Letters* 86 (2005): 432–51, and the final chapter in her *The Puccini Problem*; Arman Schwartz, "Mechanism and Tradition in Puccini's *Turandot*," *Opera Quarterly* 25 (2010): 28–50; Michael P. Steinberg and Suzanne Stewart-Steinberg, "Fascism and the Operatic Unconscious," in *Opera and Society in Italy and France from Monteverdi to Bourdieu*, ed. Victoria Johnson, Jane F. Fulcher, and Thomas Ertman (Cambridge: Cambridge University Press, 2007), 267–88; and Ben Earle's contribution to this volume, "Puccini, Fascism, and the Case of *Turandot*."

20. Theodor W. Adorno, "Music in the Background" (ca. 1934), in *Essays on Music*, selected, with introduction, commentary, and notes by Richard Leppert (Berkeley and Los Angeles: University of California Press, 2002), 506–9, quote at 509.

21. Ibid. For Adorno on Schubert see the 1928 essay in Theodor W. Adorno, *Moments musicaux* (Frankfurt: Suhrkamp, 1964), 18–36. See also the parallel discussion in his *Introduction to the Sociology of Music* (New York: Seabury Press, 1976), 82–84. Central to Adorno's argument is history, and the altered context—the early twentieth century—in which Puccini was writing. In his view the content and form music assumed in Verdi— as was the case with Schubert—possessed a resistant and provocative authenticity and autonomy beneath the surface of lyricism—a fundamental arresting originality—that Puccini merely imitated in a reductive, accessible, and harmless albeit alluring manner.

22. See Georg Heym, *Ausgewählte Gedichte* (Berlin: Hofenberg 2014), 29.

23. See Karl Kraus on Offenbach, *Theater der Dichtung: Offenbach*, in *Schriften*, vol. 13., ed. Christian Wagenknecht (Frankfurt: Suhrkamp, 1994); and Siegfried Kracauer's *Jacques Offenbach and the Paris of His Time* (New York: Zone Books, 2003).

24. See William Ashbrook's essay on *Rondine* in Weaver and Puccini, eds., *The Puccini Companion*, 244–64. Micaela Baranello in her contribution to this volume, "The Swallow and the Lark: *La rondine* and Viennese Operetta," offers a more detailed discussion.

25. On this issue, see Alan Mallach, *The Autumn of Italian Opera: From Verismo to Modernism, 1890–1915* (Boston: Northeastern University Press, 2007); John Rosselli, *The Opera Industry in Italy from Cimarosa to Verdi: The Role of the Impresario* (Cambridge: Cambridge University Press, 1984); and Jay Nicolaisen, *Italian Opera in Transition, 1871–1893* (Ann Arbor: UMI Press, 1980).

26. See Alessandra Campana, *Opera and Modern Spectatorship in Late Nineteenth-Century Italy* (Cambridge: Cambridge University Press, 2015).

27. On Belasco, see the two-volume biography *The Life of David Belasco* by William Winter (New York: Moffat, Yard, and Co., 1920); Craig Timberlake, *The Bishop of Broadway*

David Belasco: His Life and Work (New York: Library Publishers, 1954); and Belasco's own *The Theatre Through Its Stage Door*, ed. Louis V. Defoe (New York: Blom, 1919, reissued 1969).

28. See Helen M. Greenwald "Realism on the Opera Stage: Belasco, Puccini, and the California Sunset," in *Opera in Context: Essays on Historical Staging from the Renaissance to the Time of Puccini*, ed. Mark A. Radice (Portland, OR: Amadeus Press, 1998), 279–96.

29. Jean Vermeil, *Conversations with Boulez: Thoughts on Conducting* (Portland, OR: Amadeus Press, 1996), 47; see also Klonovsky, *Der Schmerz der Schönheit*, 253.

30. See the excellent discussion, on which this section is based, in Ben Earle, *Luigi Dallapiccola and Musical Modernism in Fascist Italy* (Cambridge: Cambridge University Press, 2013), quote at 41.

31. See Henry-Louis de la Grange, *Gustav Mahler: Vienna: The Years of Challenge (1897–1904)* (Oxford: Oxford University Press, 1995), 601.

32. See Andreas Láng and Oliver Láng, *Puccini an der Wiener Oper* (Vienna: Vienna State Opera, 2009).

33. Max Kalbeck, "Die Bohème" (1897), in *Opernabende: Beiträge zur Geschichte und Kritik der Oper* (Berlin: Harmonie Verlag, 1898), 90–95.

34. Ibid., 95.

35. Ibid.

36. An excellent discussion of *verismo* can be found in Nicolaisen, *Italian Opera in Transition*, 244–46. See also Egon Voss, "Verismo in der Oper," *Die Musikforschung* 31 (1978): 303–13; and more recently, Adriana Guarneri Corazzol, "Opera and Verismo: Regressive Points of View and the Artifice of Alienation," *Cambridge Opera Journal* 5/1 (1993): 39–53; Andreas Giger, "Verismo: Origin, Corruption, and Redemption of an Operatic Term," *Journal of the American Musicological Society* 60/2 (2007): 271–315; and Arman Schwartz, "Rough Music: *Tosca* and *Verismo* Reconsidered," *19th-Century Music* 31/3 (2008): 228–44.

37. Girardi, *Puccini*, 191.

38. For this reason I have not chosen comparisons from within the impressive array of works by Italian contemporaries (Mascagni, Leoncavallo, Franchetti) and younger colleagues (Wolf-Ferrari, Pizzetti, Zandonai). For more on the intra-Italian situation, see for example Helmut Krausser, *Zwei ungleiche Rivalen: Puccini und Franchetti* (Munich: Edition Elke Heidenreich, 2010). The comparison and contrasts with Mascagni, once Puccini's roommate, have been extensively discussed, expecially given the links between the operas *Iris* and *Madama Butterfly*. See Alan Mallach, *Pietro Mascagni and His Operas* (Boston: Northeastern University Press, 2002); and David Stivender on Mascagni in *Mascagni: An Autobiography Compiled, Edited, and Translated from Original Sources* (White Plains, NY: Pro/Am Music Resources, 1988).

39. See Andres Briner, Dieter Rexroth, and Giselher Schubert, *Paul Hindemith: Leben und Werk in Bild und Text* (Zurich and Mainz: Atlantis and Musikverlag B. Schott's Söhne, 1988), 50–59.

40. See Giselher Schubert, *Paul Hindemith* (Reinbek: Rowohlt, 1981), 128. *Bohème* was the last opera Hindemith saw. Personal communication with Professor Schubert.

41. In Meinhard Saremba's *Leoš Janáček: Zeit, Leben, Werk, Wirkung* (Kassel: Bärenreiter, 2001), the connection between *Butterfly* and *Jenůfa* is slightly blurred in an otherwise excellent discussion by the use of the 1919 quote with regard to *Jenůfa* (170–72). The other Janáček opera with a potential link to Puccini is the *Makropulos Affair* whose heroine, Emilia Marty, is a singer, like Floria Tosca. See also Jennifer Sheppard, "Janáček's *Makropulos* and the Case of the Silent Diva," *Opera Quarterly* 25/1–2 (2010): 51–72.

42. Jan Smaczny, "Janáček and Czech Realism," in *Leoš Janáček: Jenůfa / Katya Kabanova*, Opera Guide 33 (London: Overture, 2011), 39.

43. See John Tyrrell, *Janáček: Years of a Life,* 2 vols. (London: Faber and Faber, 2006–7), 1:571.

44. See John Tyrell, *Janáček's Operas: A Documentary Account* (Princeton: Princeton University Press, 1992), 41–107.

45. Arnold Whittall makes this point brilliantly in his essay "The Challenge from Within: Janáček's Musico-dramatic Mastery," in *Leoš Janáček: Jenůfa/Katya Kabanova,* 21–30.

46. See Emanuele Senici's comments in his introduction to this volume and also Jann Pasler, "Political Anxiety and Musical Reception: Japonisme and the Problem of Assimilation," in *Madama Butterfly: L'orientalismo di fine secolo, l'approccio pucciniano, la ricezione,* ed. Arthur Groos and Virgilio Bernardoni (Florence, IT: Leo S. Olschki, 2008), 17–53.

47. See the essays in Groos and Bernardoni, *Madama Butterfly*; Groos, "Madame Butterfly: The Story," *Cambridge Opera Journal* 3/2 (1991): 125–58; also W. Anthony Sheppard, "Puccini and the Music Boxes," *Journal of the Royal Musical Association* 140/1 (2015): 41–92.

48. One might compare Pinkerton to Verdi's Duke of Mantua in *Rigoletto.* The Duke is a familiar version of aristocratic callousness, whereas Pinkerton, despite his American arrogance, plays the part of a romantic lead, manipulating the rhetoric of love and the institution of marriage.

49. See Mosco Carner, "The First Version of 'Madam Butterfly,'" in *Of Men and Music,* 32–35: and Jan van Rij, *Madame Butterfly: Japonisme, Puccini and the Search for the Real Cho-Cho-San* (Berkeley: Stone Bridge Press, 2000).

50. This is a contested opinion, as is evident from Groos's essay in this volume.

51. *A Working Friendship: The Correspondence between Richard Strauss and Hugo von Hofmannsthal* (New York: Vienna House, 1974), 331.

52. See Pasler, "Political Anxiety and Musical Reception."

53. Quoted in Tyrell, *Janáček's Operas,* 55.

54. Tyrrell, *Janáček: Years of a Life,* 1:660.

55. See "Max Brod on Leoš Janáček's *Jenůfa,*" in Leon Botstein, "The Cultural Politics of Language and Music: Max Brod and Leoš Janáček," in *Janáček and His World,* ed. Michael Beckerman (Princeton: Princeton University Press, 2003), 37–43 (Appendix A).

56. Richard Strauss and Karl Böhm: *Briefwechsel, 1921–1949,* ed. and with comments by Martina Steiger (Mainz: Schott, 1999), 42.

57. Richard Strauss and Clemens Krauss, *Briefwechsel,* ed. and with comments by Götz Klaus Kende and Willi Schuh (Munich: Beck, 1963), 234.

58. See Reinhard Schlötterer, "Ironic Allusions to Italian Opera in the Musical Comedies of Richard Strauss," in *Richard Strauss: New Perspectives on the Composer and His Work,* ed. Bryan Gilliam (Durham, NC: Duke University Press, 1992), 77–91.

59. Strauss and Krauss, *Briefwechsel,* 40.

60. Strauss and Hofmannsthal, *A Working Friendship,* 436.

61. See Marc Robinson, *The American Play, 1787–2000* (New Haven: Yale University Press, 2010); see as well Ellen Lockhart's essay on *Fanciulla* in this volume and "Photo Opera: *La fanciulla del West* and the Staging Souvenir," *Cambridge Opera Journal* 23/3 (2012): 145–66.

62. Strauss and Hofmannsthal, *A Working Friendship,* 437. It is for this reason that both Strauss and Hofmannsthal in their collaboration signaled, in passing, respect and admiration for Verdi, particularly for the last collaborations on Shakespeare with Arrigo Boito, whose libretti were more ambitious in literary terms than Piave's or those by Verdi's other earlier collaborators. From the start, Verdi's subjects and source commanded Hofmannsthal's respect.

63. See Bryan Gilliam, *Rounding Wagner's Mountain: Richard Strauss and Modern German Opera* (Cambridge: Cambridge University Press, 2014); Norman Del Mar, "Synopsis and Analysis" (21–78); and Alan Jefferson's analyses in Jefferson's *Richard Strauss: Der Rosenkavalier* (Cambridge: Cambridge University Press, 1985). See also *Richard Strauss: Der Rosenkavalier*, Opera Guide 8 (London: Overture, 2011).

64. See the discussion in Gilliam, *Rounding Wagner's Mountain*, 106–26.

65. On *Fanciulla* and *Rosenkavalier*, see Emanuele Senici, *Landscape and Gender in Italian Opera: The Alpine Virgin from Bellini to Puccini* (Cambridge: Cambridge University Press, 2005), 228–62, with reference to *Rosenkavalier* on 259; see also Annie J. Randall and Rosalind Gray Davis, *Puccini and the Girl: History and Reception of The Girl of the Golden West* (Chicago: University of Chicago Press, 2007).

66. See the comparative discussion of the subject of the opera in Beth E. Levy, *Frontier Figures: American Music and the Mythology of the American West* (Berkeley and Los Angeles: University of California Press, 2012), 130–32.

67. Ellen Lockhart's essay in this volume offers a different viewpoint.

68. Quoted in Carner, *Puccini: A Critical Biography*, 173; see also the discussion of *Fanciulla* in Girardi, *Puccini: His International Art*, 283–327.

69. See David Rosen, "'Pigri ed obesi dei': Religion in the Operas of Puccini," in Groos and Bernardoni, *Madama Butterfly*, 257–98.

70. See the discussion of Puccini and Italian literature vis-à-vis the choice of libretti in Marzio Pieri, "Opera and Italian Literature," in *Opera in Theory and Practice*, esp. 278–86.

71. See Senici, *Landscape and Gender*, for a different view on *Fanciulla* and modernity.

72. See ibid., 255–60; and Laura Basini, "*Manon Lescaut* and the Myth of America," *Opera Quarterly* 24/1–2 (2009): 62–81.

73. See the discussion of the opera in Davis, *Puccini's Late Style*, 108–37; Girardi, *Puccini: His International Art*, 396–414; and Ashbrook, *The Operas of Puccini*, esp. 179–80.

74. See also the discussion in James Hepokoski, "Structure, Implication and the End of *Suor Angelica*," *Studi pucciniani* 3 (2004): 241–64.

75. See Arman Schwartz, "Puccini in the Distance," *Cambridge Opera Journal* 23/3 (2011): 167–89.

76. See Rosen, "'Pigri ed obesi dei': Religion in the Operas of Puccini."

77. Recent scholarship has sought to counter this view. See Arman Schwartz, *Puccini's Soundscapes: Realism and Modernity in Italian Opera* (Florence, IT: Leo S. Olschki, 2016), for a discussion of *Gianni Schicchi* and *Suor Angelica* in the context of World War I.

78. This account relies on the outstanding monograph by Annegrit Laubenthal, *Paul Hindemiths Einakter-Triptychon* (Tutzing: Hans Schneider, 1986). See also the program notes for recent American performances by the American Symphony Orchestra in 2004 and at the Bard Music Festival of 2010, "Berg and His World."

79. On *Sancta Susanna*, see Rudolf Stephan, "Zur Musik der Zwanzigerjahre," and Manfred Wagner, "Zum Expressionismus des Komponisten Paul Hindemith," in *Erprobungen und Erfahrungen: Zu Paul Hindemiths Schaffen in den Zwanziger Jahren*, ed. Dieter Rexroth (Frankfurt: Schott, 1978), 9–14 and 15–26. See also Siegfried Mauser, "Expressionismus und Neue Sachlichkeit in den zwanziger Jahren," and Wolfgang Rathert, "Hindemiths Bühnenwerke der zwanziger Jahre und die 'Verhaltenslehren der Kälte,'" in *Hindemith Interpretionen: Hindemith und die Zwanziger Jahre*, ed. Dominik Sackmann (Berne: Peter Lang, 2007), 11–14 and 51–83, respectively.

80. See Wolfgang Lessing, *Die Hindemith Rezeption Theodor W. Adornos* (Mainz: Schott, 1999), 68.

81. Ibid., 66–67.

82. See the chapters on *Nabucco* and *Falstaff* in Roger Parker, *Leonora's Last Act: Essays in Verdian Discourse* (Princeton: Princeton University Press, 1997), 20–41 and 100–125, respectively.

83. See Schwartz, "Rough Music: *Tosca* and *Verismo* Reconsidered"; and Guarnieri Corazzol, "Opera and Verismo."

84. See Jean-Jacques Rousseau, "Lettre à M. d'Alembert sur les spectacles" (1758) and "Discours sur les sciences et les arts" (1750), in *Oeuvres complètes*, vol. 3 (Paris: Bibliothèque de La Pleiáde, 1964), 5–107.

85. See Joseph Kerman, *Opera as Drama* (Berkeley and Los Angeles: University of California Press, 1988).

86. See Jean-Jacques Rousseau, *Essay on the Origin of Languages*, trans. John H. Moran (Chicago: University of Chicago Press, 1966).

87. In response to Adorno's critique, one could argue that Puccini far exceeded the possibilities presented by his historical moment with respect to the potential of opera as a medium, and injected into popular culture music of unexpected autonomy and resistance.

88. Arthur Maria Rabenalt, *Schriften zum Musiktheater der 20er und 30er Jahre: Opernregie 1* (Hildesheim: Olms, 1999), 116–17.

89. On Hindemith's *Neues vom Tage*, see Briner, Rexroth, and Schubert, *Paul Hindemith: Bild und Werk*, 124–27.

PART 2

DOCUMENTS

Puccini on His Interpreters

INTRODUCTION, TRANSLATION, AND COMMENTARY
BY EMANUELE SENICI

"As a matter of fact Puccini was a peculiarly inexorable, and not always a very amiable judge of his conductors and singers, and his exaggerated demands and unmitigated candor often made the rehearsals an ordeal dreaded by everybody." Thus wrote Austrian critic Richard Specht after reporting a conversation with the composer from the early 1920s, in which Puccini had commented on Maria Jeritza's interpretation of *Tosca* at the Vienna State Opera, praising it enthusiastically but not refraining from a few words of criticism for her rather free way with the melody in "Vissi d'arte."[1] According to Specht, the composer's attitude toward the interpreters of his operas was remarkably uncompromising. However, if we place this statement in the context of Specht's general assessment of Puccini in his influential monograph of 1931, in which the sentence appears, it becomes clear that its function was to contribute to an interpretation of the composer's personality as "somewhat capricious," "thoroughly primitive," "contradictory," and characterized by "over-acute sensibilities."[2] What kind of attitude toward singers and conductors emerges if we turn instead to Puccini's own words as preserved in his letters?

Puccini's enormous correspondence contains hundreds of references to singers and conductors, but most of them amount to only a few words. Here is an early example (1884): "The orchestra is really good, ditto the chorus, but the singers a bit weak, especially the tenor."[3] And this is a late one (1923): "Last night *Butterfly* with Kurz, Act 3 a real disaster, the other acts less so, bad orchestra and dodgy tempos, an awful tenor, it was a painful evening."[4] Some of the letters reproduced below, though not particularly extended, count among the longest statements by Puccini about or to his interpreters that I have been able to find; of the other letters, only short excerpts dealing with singers or conductors are offered here, since references to them are usually mixed with other topics in a single missive. There are several reasons for the general brevity and lack of specificity of his critical comments, which are worth discussing here.

The composer's work-related correspondence seems mostly intended for communicating facts and thoughts in a direct, economical, speedy way—understandably, given how many such letters he had to write, often several in a single day; therefore, saying that singers were "a bit weak" or summing up the performance of Act 3 of *Madama Butterfly* as "a real disaster" was clear enough, without the need or desire to explain why in any detail. What is more, Puccini traveled extensively to many different cities in Italy and the rest of Europe, and made two journeys to the United States, specifically in order to supervise the performances that he and his publishers considered particularly important for the overall success of his operas—especially premieres. Therefore, the most important things he had to say to singers and conductors were conveyed to them *viva voce* during rehearsals and other meetings in person.

A further, historically broader and more complex reason for the nature of Puccini's discourse on his interpreters is connected to crucial changes in the position and status of singers and conductors in the opera world between the late nineteenth and the early twentieth century. Up through the early nineteenth century, singers had enjoyed considerable influence on the compositional process of operas: in most cases, composers waited to know who had been engaged for the initial run of performances before starting to put pen to paper, and often even before choosing a subject, since the vocal, dramatic, physical, and even psychological characteristics of a given singer would influence the kind of role assigned to them—an imperious queen rather than a demure young girl, say—as well as the number and type of their pieces (arias, duets, etc.), not to mention the vocal writing. Moreover, singers had a certain amount of freedom to improvise during performances, ornamenting the vocal line in order to show off their virtuosity and to vary repetitions of the same melodies.

Over the course of the nineteenth century, however, this kind of influence was subjected to a slow but steady process of erosion, caused primarily by the progressive establishment of a repertory of works constantly repeated rather than new ones performed each season, and the related idea of an aesthetic canon of "great" operas, so great and rich as to repay, and in fact demand, repeated hearings. Operatic works aspiring to enter both the repertory and the canon became ever more complex, requiring several years to compose, as the case of Puccini unmistakably proves. Therefore, the practice of composing "for" a specific singer disappeared almost completely. To begin with, it would have been impossible to engage a singer so far in advance of the premiere. At the same time, the complexity of the music left very little room for improvisation, at least in terms of singing notes different from the ones notated. Finally, an aspiration toward ever-increasing specificity and "realism" (for lack of a better word) in staging meant that the visual and more specifically gestural components of a singer's performance became ever more regulated by those in charge of the mise-en-scène—who, in the case of Puccini, often included the composer himself.[5]

This set of historical circumstances also directly contributed to the corresponding rise of the conductor, whose coordinating presence on the podium was made necessary by the increase in the musical complexity of new operas. At the same time, this very complexity—perhaps paradoxically—left room for interpretative interventions on the part of conductors, and even invited them. For example, in a Puccini score tempo changes are much more frequent than was the case in Italian opera until the 1870s; hence whoever is in charge of setting the tempo has more chances to make an impact on the overall flow and shape of the music.

Even if singers' influence on the composition of new operas and their freedom to ornament and improvise during performances were significantly reduced during the second half of the nineteenth century, their overall importance in the world of opera was not diminished. Interpretatively speaking, there was still a lot over which to exercise their artistic choice, both vocally and gesturally, and thus their contribution was still crucial to the overall outcome of a performance. Moreover, thanks to such epoch-making social and technological transformations as the significantly increased dissemination and influence of the periodical press, the spread of photography and later sound recording, as well as the exceptional improvement in the conditions and times of travel by train and ship, the media presence of singers, and therefore the potential reach of their fame, was dramatically enhanced over the course of Puccini's life. Singers could now become international and indeed intercontinental stars to a degree previously unthinkable, their voices heard live from Milan to London, from Paris to New York, and from Vienna to Buenos Aires, and—from the turn of the twentieth century—on records in many bourgeois households all over the industrialized world and its colonies.[6]

Tenor Enrico Caruso, the original Dick Johnson in *La fanciulla del West* and an interpreter usually (but not always) highly praised by Puccini in his other operas, is the first name, and certainly the most famous that comes to mind in this list of international divas and divos of the time, but many others could be added. Keeping to singers who participated in

Figure 1. Soprano Geraldine Farrar as Suor Angelica with contralto
Flora Perini as Zia Principessa at the Metropolitan Opera, 1918.

Puccini world premieres, the list includes: soprano Cesira Ferrani (Manon
Lescaut; also Mimì in *La bohème*), soprano Hariclea Darclée (Tosca),
soprano Rosina Storchio (Butterfly), tenor Giovanni Zenatello (Pinkerton
in *Butterfly*), soprano Emmy Destinn (Minnie in *Fanciulla*), soprano Gilda
Dalla Rizza (Magda in *La rondine*), tenor Tito Schipa (Ruggero in *La ron-
dine*), soprano Claudia Muzio (Giorgetta in *Il tabarro*), soprano Geraldine
Farrar (Suor Angelica), soprano Florence Easton (Lauretta in *Gianni
Schicchi*), baritone Giuseppe De Luca (Gianni Schicchi), soprano Rosa
Raisa (Turandot), and tenor Miguel Fleta (Calaf in *Turandot*).

Figure 2. The young Arturo Toscanini in the 1890s.

As for conductors, Arturo Toscanini towers well above all the others, both in terms of worldwide fame and power, and for his close relationship with Puccini's operas. The first that he conducted was *Le Villi* (Brescia, 1890); he would go on to lead the world premieres of *La bohème* (Turin, 1896), *Fanciulla* (New York, 1910), *Turandot* (Milan, 1926), and countless performances of the composer's works, especially in the most prominent Italian theaters—Milan's La Scala first among them—and at New York's Metropolitan Opera. The composer had the highest esteem for Toscanini's art, which he expressed many times both in private and in public; for example, after hearing him conduct *Manon Lescaut* at La Scala in 1922, Puccini wrote to a friend: "Toscanini is truly the best conductor in the world now, because he has everything: soul, poetry, delicacy, order, thrust, finesse, drama; in sum, a real miracle."[7] A few negative outbursts did not alter this generally enthusiastic opinion, since they were a knee-jerk response to Toscanini's very difficult and unpredictable personal character, which both maddened and frightened Puccini. No other conductor came close to Toscanini in the composer's regard, although Puccini did have words of praise for Franco Faccio, who conducted the premiere of *Edgar* in 1889 and was the most prominent Italian conductor active in the 1870s and 1880s; Cleofonte Campanini, who was in charge of *Butterfly* both at the Scala premiere and in Brescia in a revised version three months later; and Gino Marinuzzi, who led the first *Rondine*, among others. The case of Leopoldo Mugnone is a special and particularly interesting one, and therefore I have decided to devote specific attention to it below.

Puccini was well aware of the consequence and power of these and many other singers and conductors, and therefore spent a considerable amount of his energy trying to influence their selection for the premieres and other important performances of his operas on the part of impresarios (aided in this endeavor by his publisher Ricordi, which had considerable clout over casting). He was quick to vent his frustration if he considered interpreters unequal to their task, but equally ready to praise them if their work pleased him, as the letters reproduced below abundantly show. Moreover, there is some evidence that, in a few cases, the specific characteristics of a certain singer contributed to Puccini's conception of a particular role—which is not the same as saying that this role was composed "for" that singer; witness a couple of remarks he sent to Gilda Dalla Rizza in connection with Liù in *Turandot*, reproduced below. In other instances, it is very difficult to separate a specific singer's impact on a character's vocal profile from the impact due to the character's dramatic traits.

The most intriguing case in this sense is probably that of Caruso as Dick Johnson. On the one hand, Johnson's tessitura is generally lower than that of Puccini's previous leading tenor parts, and the role requires a heftier, more baritonal sound, especially in the middle range; at the same time top notes must be secure and with plenty of *squillo*; and these are precisely some of the main characteristics of Caruso's voice, well known to Puccini by the time he composed *Fanciulla*. On the other hand, Johnson is a different kind of man from the male leads in *Manon Lescaut*, *Bohème*, and *Butterfly* (and, in part, *Tosca*): more mature, more heroic, and more secure in his masculinity. Moreover, it was not at all certain that

Figure 3. Tenor Enrico Caruso as Dick Johnson in
La fanciulla del West at the Metropolitan Opera, 1910.

Caruso would be the first Johnson until the summer of 1910, when the opera was almost finished. Is Johnson's particular vocality more a result of Puccini's hope that Caruso would sing at the premiere, or rather of the character's specific psychological and narrative attributes? The best we can do is to take note of the convergence of a singer's vocal profile and a character's dramatic features in shaping the musical language of one of Puccini's most compelling tenor parts.

The letters reproduced below aim to offer a distinct point of view from which to consider Puccini's thoughts and feelings on the subject of the interpreters of his operas. I have grouped them in three sections. The first consists of a few missives to tenor Francesco Tamagno, which show the composer's insistent attempts to seduce a star tenor into performing his second (but first full-length) opera, *Edgar*. The second comprises letters to or about a few prominent sopranos, chosen because they date from different times of Puccini's career, exhibit different and at times opposite attitudes toward these singers, and display starkly divergent tones, from the adulatory and seductive to the whining and borderline obsessive. The third section, about Leopoldo Mugnone, concerns the intriguing case of a conductor who went from being one of Puccini's most trusted to one who elicited strings of insults from the composer. An additional criterion for my choice of interpreters has been their coverage in the previous literature on Puccini and the accessibility of letters to or about them in English-language publications: hence the exclusion of the more famous and therefore more widely discussed Caruso and Toscanini in favor of Tamagno and Mugnone.[8] Finally, when having to choose between two or more similar letters for reasons of space, I have opted for those still unpublished even in their original Italian, if available, or that have appeared in old, obscure, or hard-to-get publications.[9]

Francesco Tamagno

Tenor Francesco Tamagno (1850–1905) is especially famous for having sung the title role at the premiere of Verdi's Otello *in 1887. Thus, when Puccini contacted him the following year in order to try and persuade him to take part in the first performance of* Edgar, *he was at the height of his fame. No agreement was reached then, but Puccini tried again on the occasion of the Spanish premiere of the opera at Madrid's Teatro Real in 1892; he even went to visit Tamagno at his villa near Varese—admittedly not a long train journey from Milan, where Puccini was living at the time. He was successful, and the opera enjoyed a positive reception in the Spanish capital, undoubtedly thanks to Tamagno's interpretation as well as his renown.[10]*

Figure 4. Tenor Francesco Tamagno as Verdi's Otello at La Scala, 1887.

1. To Francesco Tamagno

Milan
31 December 1888

Dear Tamagno,

As I am about to have the parts of my opera copied, and in order to have no regrets later, I take the liberty of turning to you and asking whether you could let me know if I really have to give up the privilege of hearing you as Edgar.

You have been so kind to me that you are indeed a little bit to blame that I haven't given up hope. I have no peace after having heard you sing my music! . . . If you want, you can make my work duly appreciated: I would be so grateful to you!!

Looking forward to hearing from you, I wish you all the very best, also from Fontana.

Greetings from your
G Puccini[11]

2. To Francesco Tamagno

Milan
21 February 1889

Dear Tamagno,

As you will have heard, *Otello* here didn't go very well. Oxilia, after singing "Esultate" in a strained manner, collapsed vocally, and continued and finished the opera croaking: one felt sorry for him! Shortly it will be my turn, and may God be with me!

I still hope to have you! If you don't go to Florence, you would be free . . . Living in hope is already something, if anything it's better than a certainty that smells of mediocrity.

The life of every human being has a decisive moment, and for me the moment is the success of *Edgar*! Therefore, like a castaway who climbs onto the only plank left, I hold on to the one who can save me: my plank is you!!

I won't repeat my words of thanks and eternal gratitude etc. I will write again.

Warm and affectionate greetings from your

G Puccini[12]

3. To Francesco Tamagno

Milan
11 January 1892

Dearest Tamagno,

I have heard that you are about to leave for Madrid and, plucking up my courage, I dare say a prayer and ask you the greatest favor: should you respond to them, my career would be immensely improved.

Edgar should have already been performed at the Teatro Real last year, but it didn't happen for reasons of programming and timing. I was then formally promised by the management and specifically by the Count of Michelena that my work was going to be performed as part of the current season, and indeed rehearsals were already at an advanced stage. We were close to opening night when I heard that Durot had bolted! And therefore my poor *Edgar* was left with no protagonist and no hope of being performed!

Signore Tetrazzini and Pasqua were to be the other main interpreters. This for me is a tragedy, a terrible disaster, because I was counting a lot on this production of *Edgar* in order to give this opera a very helpful and necessary push, both morally and materially.

So the proposal-petition [*proposta-preghiera*] that I boldly put forward is that you create the crucial role of the Protagonist! . . . It takes courage and nerve, doesn't it? Yet, knowing your heart of gold, I dare suggest it. Shall my wish be fulfilled? I confess to you that I hope so.

The opera has been reduced to three acts. You already saw and studied it two years ago, and therefore it's not new to you and you could learn it with little effort. If you consent to sing a few performances, you can rest assured that my gratitude will be steadfast and boundless. If only I could have this chance after so many adversities!

I am writing to you as my heart dictates, I put words down in jolts . . . such is my emotion in thinking that perhaps . . . who knows? . . . you will sing my stuff!! . . . Should you accept, please send me a line.

It's up to you, dear friend, to make happy your most affectionate

G Puccini[13]

4. To Francesco Tamagno

Milan
13 January 1892

Dearest Tamagno,

Thank you for your letter.

I believe that, once you read the score, you will see that it won't be very hard for you, first on account of your phenomenal ability to learn quickly, and then because Edgar's part is not difficult. In Madrid everything is ready for the performance: I believe that with two or three rehearsals at most you would be ready to go on.

Since the opera is being reprinted because I have changed a few bits, I have asked Ricordi to prepare Edgar's part, which I'll get tomorrow. I will immediately send it to you, but if you want I could come to see you pronto (even tomorrow), and make you see firsthand that the role is effective without being difficult; and I will also have the pleasure of meeting Maestro Gnaga, something to which I attach great importance. If you approve of this plan please send me a wire and I'll leave immediately.

Meanwhile I send you cordial greetings and, hoping that this dream of mine becomes true, I remain your affectionate

G Puccini[14]

5. To Francesco Tamagno

Milan
15 January 1892

Dearest Tamagno,

Earlier today I arranged for a copy of the libretto to be sent to you, so you'll be able to get a precise idea of the story. I will also send a copy of the trio because its beginning is a little different from the version you have.

I have always in my ear the echo of your divine voice and think of the extraordinary, unhoped-for interpreter I will have! The finale of the opera sung by you becomes irresistible!

I won't go on thanking you . . . you can rest assured of my eternal gratitude.

Please give my best to the Storti family and to your daughter. To you a million greetings from your affectionate

G Puccini[15]

6. To Francesco Tamagno

Paris
24 March 1892

Dear Tamagno,

I didn't have the time to say a proper goodbye, so I do it now in writing, and I thank you most warmly for your outstanding interpretation of *Edgar*. I hope we'll see each other soon in Milan, where I will repeat in person all my gratitude to you.

Meanwhile I send you warm greetings and remain your affectionate

G Puccini[16]

A Soprano Miscellany

The first two letters translated in this section are addressed to Cesira Ferrani (1863–1943), whose main claim to fame is to have been the first Manon Lescaut and the first Mimì; both letters refer to the former role. In the second, Puccini congratulates her on the success of the first South American performance of Manon Lescaut, *which took place in Buenos Aires in June 1893.*

7. To Cesira Ferrani

Milan
15 July 1892

Dear Signorina,

I know from Signor Ricordi that you are in the countryside and have given up the idea of performing during the coming autumn season. I am very happy that you have come to this decision, because you can now rest and prepare yourself for my terrible battle!

I have you in my mind always, and keep telling myself that I was really lucky to meet you . . . You will be an ideal Manon, thanks to your figure, your talent, and your voice. I have agreed with Signor Ricordi that the vocal score will be sent to you immediately as soon as it is ready and copied.

All best wishes for your holidays[17]

Figure 5a. Soprano Cesira Ferrani as Manon Lescaut.

8. To Cesira Ferrani

Milan
5 July 1893

Dear Signorina,

I must give voice to my gratitude and my pleasure for the new success you have obtained: I read with the utmost interest the praises you have received, and how much your exceptional artistic merits have been admired! When I declared you the ideal Manon, the insuperable

Figure 5b. Soprano Cesira Ferrani in Act 3 of *La bohème* at Turin's Teatro Regio, 1896. Left to right: Baritone Tieste Wilmant (Marcello), Ferrani (Mimì), tenor Evan Gorga (Rodolfo), soprano Camilla Pasini (Musetta).

interpreter of my work, it was not a temporary expression in the heat of success: it was a true, heartfelt, indelible impression! May Heaven always grant me a person like yours to interpret my poor notes!

I send you my heartfelt greetings, then; consider me your foremost admirer, and may my enthusiasm for such a sublime artist as yourself never be extinguished.[18]

The next set of letters concerns Puccini's increasingly agitated reactions to soprano Marguerite Carré (1880–1947) during the lengthy rehearsals of Madama Butterfly *at Paris's Opéra-Comique in the fall of 1906. As explained in Michele Girardi's introduction to Albert Carré's staging manual for the opera (published elsewhere in the present volume), Marguerite was the wife of Albert, the theater's impresario, and therefore Puccini had no say in her choice for the title role. Hence, surely, his mounting frustration at her perceived shortcomings, which clearly emerges from several letters to his English friend and confidante Sybil Seligman (nos. 9–12), as well as from one to another friend, Tuscan aristocrat Giuseppe della Gherardesca, whom he calls "Beppino" (no. 13). In these and other letters in which Puccini discusses Carré, his tone becomes ever more self-pitying and melodramatic. In the end, though, the performances were a great success, and, as Girardi clarifies, Puccini considered this the definitive staging of the opera.*

9. To Sybil Seligman

Paris
24 October 1906

Dear Sybil,

[. . .] They are cutting the opera too much. Madame Carré will do fairly well, but she wants too many cuts, because she surely feels that the effort is too much for her strength. And there is no other way out because, if Madame Carré doesn't sing, the opera will be set aside and no longer mentioned. This is another reason for my low spirits. [. . .][19]

10. To Sybil Seligman

Paris
25 October 1906

Dear Sybil,

Worries upon worries! Here things go from bad to worse: steps backward, ridiculous demands, all because of Madame Carré, who in my opinion has a part that is too strong for her. I fear we won't perform, either never or very late—I say never because I expect that at the last moment, when the opera is performed in its entirety, she won't withstand it and will declare that she can't do it. Oh I expect exactly this . . . May I not be a prophet . . . It would be a fine mess for me wasting so much time, and the opera would be ruined in front of the entire world, because I am bound not to say the whole truth, which would mean ruining *Bohème* at the Opéra Comique as well! Imagine, then, how I feel! and I feel so wretched! [. . .][20]

11. To Sybil Seligman

Paris
31 October 1906

Dear Sybil,

[. . .] We haven't been rehearsing for two or three days; perhaps this is why I feel better! Let's hope for the best. But I fear for Madame Carré, she is weak and not very intelligent, but I must keep her if I want *Butterfly* to be performed, she can't be changed; in fact, I must make immense efforts to pay her compliments in order to see whether I can get something good out of her and encourage her. [. . .][21]

12. To Sybil Seligman

Paris
19 November 1906

Dearest Sybil,

Monday 6 p.m. I am just back from rehearsals. I am very worried about Madame Carré. I fear she won't have the strength to get to the end of the opera. Enough, we'll see, but I am really worried. And I am so tired of being here in Paris! I am leading a dull and wearisome life. [. . .][22]

13. To Giuseppe della Gherardesca

Paris
8 December 1906

Dear Beppino,

Friday night. I can't sleep tonight, and I just got up while everybody in Paris is asleep (it's 4:30 a.m.). The cause of my insomnia is *Butterfly*. I assure you that my days are really quite sad: the performance is no good. The protagonist is *not good enough*. [. . .]

The big and serious question is that of the protagonist! She is not good enough, she just barely makes it to the end; she never seems sincere, and she is never convincing: it's an interpretation wholly made of mannerisms instead of being the living, true exposition of a most painful drama. [. . .][23]

The third and final group of letters in this section is about—and mostly addressed to—Gilda Dalla Rizza (1892–1975), the first Magda in La rondine *and a very frequent interpreter of other works by Puccini, especially* Tosca, Madama Butterfly, La fanciulla del West, Suor Angelica, *and* Gianni Schicchi. *Puccini was impressed with her from the beginning, as the first letter testifies*

Figure 6. Soprano Marguerite Carré in costume for an unidentified stage role.

(no. 14), but soon his feelings grew into admiration and perhaps even infatuation. The composer had a high opinion not only of her artistic qualities, but also of her assessment of other singers and of operatic matters in general; for example, in 1923 he wrote to his trusted friend Riccardo Schnabl: "[Impresario Walter] Mocchi and Gilda disagreeing about [tenor Miguel] Fleta! I like it when Gilda argues with Walter: she has better judgment than he, she doesn't show it but it is so."²⁴ He might address her with the endearing diminutive "Gildina," but always used the formal lei *in his letters to her—as he did with Ferrani; with Seligman it was the less formal* voi, *while Schnabl and Ricordi's manager Carlo Clausetti received the familiar* tu *(as did della Gherardesca).²⁵*

14. To Riccardo Schnabl

Torre del Lago
2 March 1917

Dear Riccardo,
[. . .] Dalla Rizza? Let them talk. The only questionable things are elegant dressing and bearing, but she'll get there, and we'll dress her nicely. And anyway, whom to take otherwise? Raisa is staying in America and she is right to do it. [. . .]²⁶

15. To Gilda Dalla Rizza

[Rome]
11 January 1918

Dear Gilda,
Let the papers say what they want to say of my opera, but they won't speak other than well, supremely well, of you, dear Gilda! I am ever more convinced of your absolute priority over any other artist who might sing *Rondine.*

I am deeply grateful to you for your constant goodwill at rehearsals and for your skills as an exquisite interpreter.

Have a good day. Warm greetings from

G Puccini²⁷

16. To Carlo Clausetti

[n.p.]
8 April 1918

Dear Claudio,

[. . .] For *Schicchi* we need a candid little woman with a small figure and a fresh voice, without drama etc. Dalla Rizza, who wouldn't be ideal for *Suor Angelica*, could do Lauretta in *Schicchi* perfectly. I say that she wouldn't be ideal because for Angelica I had dreamed of a woman with an altogether different allure, but fine, let's have Dalla Rizza, who would do well in the end. [. . .][28]

17. To Gilda Dalla Rizza

Torre del Lago
20 May 1919

Dear Gilda,

A while ago I sent you a little letter full of sweetly admiring and grateful words. Poor letter, emanating straight from my heart on an evening full of infinite sadness and nostalgia, you were lost heaven knows where! I say this because, knowing how sensitive and gentle Gilda is, she would have replied immediately; not seeing a single line from you, I thought that the letter was lost and decided to write again. I do this gladly, because also this evening, as often happens, I feel very nostalgic for your sweet and dear voice, and my eyes and ears hear you and look for you, remembering the unforgettable notes of *Suor Angelica* that from your soul have reached both me and the public, that public that has heard you, loved you, admired you! Is it true that *Trittico* will be revived? I advise against that ugly cut to the flowers.

Warm greetings,
Yours
G Puccini[29]

Figure 7. Soprano Gilda Dalla Rizza as Suor Angelica.

18. To Gilda Dalla Rizza

Torre del Lago
31 August 1919

Dear Gildina,

Thank you for your postcards. I hope this letter reaches you in Buenos Aires. How did the season in Rio go? Surely well. And the anti-Puccinians? Did they enjoy the modern French tedium?

I can't wait to see you again. In London Beecham and Cunard went bankrupt—just as well.

I would like to do *Rondine* in Rome, but with great care . . . Crabbé would do very well for the new Prunier. And the tenor? You know the right kind. If only *we could have Schipa*! *You*, Schipa, Crabbé, the ideal trio. I am sorry this opera lies around lifeless. The music is good, perhaps some of the best I have written spontaneously. I would like to see *Rondine* performed in London as well, where you'll surely return. See you again in Rome. I will go to Maremma in mid-November. I'll wait for a visit from you. Greetings to the old friends in the company.

Very warm greetings
G Puccini[30]

19. To Gilda Dalla Rizza

Torre del Lago
20 May 1921

Thank you, dear Gildina, for your portraits. I was keen to have them because they remind me of your sweet and brave Minnie in Monte Carlo. Are you still amid the murky notes of the Revolution?

I am working on *Turandot* with faithful ardor. I think that little Liù will be a role for you; don't believe it's secondary, quite the contrary. Turandot might suit Gilda, but for the moment she is still in the wings.

It seems to me that Liù is coming along charmingly.

In sum, either Liù or Turandot, I am thinking of my dear Gildina.

Yours affectionately
G Puccini[31]

20. To Gilda Dalla Rizza

Viareggio
25 February 1924

Dear Gildina,

[. . .] How did it go in Monte Carlo this year? What will you sing at La Scala? And how many performances of *Manon*? Few, because Toscanini did not conduct. How did his substitute do? I am ever wilder here. I work from morning till night; I have made a lot of headway, almost to the end. And I am also quite happy with my work. We'll see how the cruel princess will be greeted once she appears at the big window; but I think little of this evil. I am well and rejoice in this.

I don't know whether Turandot might be for you, but surely Liù (the slave), a front-ranking role just like the other one, would be born for Gilda.

Many warm greetings, and please give me your news.

Yours
G Puccini[32]

Leopoldo Mugnone

The first known letter from Puccini to conductor Leopoldo Mugnone (1858–1941), dated 14 August 1895, shows that the two were already on friendly terms, addressing each other with the familiar tu. *The composer asked his opinions about singers and tried to enlist his help in convincing some of them to sing in his still-unfinished* Bohème. *At this time Mugnone was already a well-known and well-respected conductor—in 1890 he had led the premiere of Mascagni's* Cavalleria rusticana. *The first letter reproduced below (no. 21), addressed to Giulio Ricordi (the head of his family's publishing house), attests to the very high esteem in which Puccini already held Mugnone. The production of* Bohème *in Palermo mentioned did in fact take place; the composer, who attended one performance, wrote to a friend: "What a performance! Mugnone the absolute top." He also sent a note to the conductor thanking him "for the artistic care you took of* Bohème; *it will be difficult or rather impossible for me to find an artist as excellent and full of heart such as you."[33] A few months later Puccini referred to Mugnone's interpretive art in the following, revelatory terms: "Mugnone ne fa una vera creazione della mia musica," which literally means "He makes a true creation out of my music," or "He truly creates my music."[34] The implication is that the conductor's interpretation made the music sound new even to the composer, thus elevating him to the level of co-creator; hence Puccini's insistence on calling the conductor an "artist," a term that obviously implied something higher than simply "conductor" or even "musician." In the following years Puccini wrote to Mugnone frequently, addressing him with the diminutives "Popoldo" and "Popi"; he tried to secure him for as many performances of his operas as he could, and solicited his opinion about singers, impresarios, and financial matters. The collaboration became particularly close in the months preceding the premiere of* Tosca *(1900), which was conducted by Mugnone, to Puccini's complete satisfaction.*

Over the course of the following decade, however, the composer's opinion of the conductor began to change. Commenting on a Butterfly *at Rome's Teatro Costanzi in 1908, Puccini wrote to a friend: "Butterfly very good as to the voices, and a superb, unique mise-en-scène. Orchestra good, but Mugnone keeps it loud and quickens the tempos and forces a* Butterfly *that otherwise would have been ideal (entre nous)."[35] Three years later, a* Fanciulla *in Naples seems to have acted as the tipping point for Puccini's assessment of the conductor. He even took the trouble of writing to Mugnone (who had gone back to being "Leopoldo") with specific performance indications (no. 22)—a rare occurrence for the composer; and, once back home, he vented his anger to Clausetti, then Ricordi's representative in Naples, calling the conductor (a physically imposing man) "beast" and "colossus" (nos. 23–24). His mention of metronome marks in the second of these letters might even be understood as an attempt at preventing what he perceived as Mugnone's wrong-headed tempo choices. In 1917 Puccini managed to whip himself into a frenzy over Mugnone's perceived mishandling of the Italian premiere of* La rondine, *which took place at Milan's Teatro Dal Verme on 7 October with soprano Maria Farneti as the protagonist and tenor Gennaro Barra as Ruggero. I have chosen two letters (nos. 25–26) out of the several in which the composer lashed out at the conductor (and the soprano) with insulting epithets. A remark made to Sybil Seligman two years later (no. 27) makes it clear that Mugnone was now anathema to Puccini.*

It is very difficult to reconstruct from this evidence the reasons for Puccini's about-face with Mugnone. From the general drift of his performance indications to the conductor in letter no. 22, it might be surmised that Mugnone's interpretations had remained steeped in a late nineteenth-century aesthetic, while what Puccini wanted, especially for Fanciulla, *was something more modern, and perhaps even modernist—the kind of approach exemplified by Toscanini, with his emphasis on clarity, order, tightness of ensemble, and a more consistent approach to tempos. In the absence of Puccini recordings by Mugnone, however, this hypothesis remains highly speculative.*

21. To Giulio Ricordi

Pescia
15 September 1895

Dearest Signor Giulio,

[. . .] *Please think about the singers.* I hear that the first performance will take place in Turin. I am none too happy about this, because: 1) that theater's acoustics are bad; 2) *non bis in idem*; 3) the conductor is a difficult man; 4) it's too close to those Milanese dogs who will surely *screw me.* The premiere must happen in Naples or Rome. *Mugnone* has written to me that he is being sounded out for the production in Palermo. Please try to have him under contract wherever *Bohème* is performed, because he is the truest *artist* of them all; he might be a scoundrel but he *has soul*, something that *all the others* lack, including all those useless *Vanzos. I am really not happy about the premiere happening in Turin, not at all!* [. . .][36]

Figure 8. Puccini, his wife, Elvira, and conductor Leopoldo Mugnone, ca. 1903–4.

22. To Leopoldo Mugnone

Naples
12 December 1911

Dear Leopoldo,

Yesterday De Sanna told me that today there was no performance, so I arranged for my departure: I leave today at 1:45.

I want to thank you once again for the intelligent care you took of my *Fanciulla*. Let me emphasize the need to maintain the *vigor* and *color* [*colorito*] that are needed for performing this opera of mine. Let me remind you: a little more poetry and intimacy in the "nostalgia" scene. Minnie's entrance in Act 1 needs to be more effective onstage in terms of movement and merriment, and always vigorous orchestrally. I wish the section beginning with the 3/8 were more *mosso* and more lively in its rhythms and movements. The scene with the woman near the barrel a bit more *agitato*; and at the end of Act 1, after the violins' tremolo, both *crescendo* and faster; at the words "Un viso d'angelo" please pay attention to the *blast* where the French horns start the melody with the high D.

In Act 2, in the scene with the blood the baritone must always sing *sostenuto* and incisively; the peroration at the end of the act should be less slow, because otherwise it gets tiring for the singer, and an action that needs to end fast is held up instead. But the *allargando* at the bar with the A-natural, at the words "È mio," is necessary.

As for Act 3, remember that the chorus calling for death at the arrival of the tenor on horseback must be *sostenuto*, shouted by the choristers and with the trombones really sonorous and noisy. At the end of the act, mind the fermata before the beginning of "Addio mia dolce terra" (tenor and soprano together); then a little slower than what was done, up until the end, getting softer and softer, like a thing that drifts away and ends, with a lot of poetry both in the music and in the gestures onstage.

And with this I end, and you'll tell me it was about time, and you are right. But you know me by now, and besides I cannot control my impulses as the author, a tedious one perhaps, but always deferential, friendly and grateful for your efforts and your effective collaboration. So please don't send me packing and aim for a vigorous and lively performance.

Affectionate greetings
from your
Puccini[37]

23. To Carlo Clausetti

Torre del Lago
14 December 1911

Dear Carlo,

[. . .] The beast is champing at the bit? Good, but we need a whip to wake him up. Please keep me informed should he commit other crimes, and should he further misunderstand, or, better (that is to say, worse), weaken, flag, apocalypse. [. . .][38]

24. To Carlo Clausetti

Milan
25 December 1911

Dear Claudio,

Thank you for your informative letter. I am always interested to hear of the hysterical *colossus* with his slackenings and his rushings with neither fiber nor life. Send me immediately the new metronome markings that were put together because I want to include them in a new version. [. . .][39]

25. To Giovacchino Forzano

Milan
8 October 1917

Dear Forzano,

[. . .] The newspapers say all sorts of things about *Rondine*. I haven't read them. Only the *Corriere* is good. But I don't care about all this, nor does it sadden me. What gives me pain is instead seeing my opera so badly interpreted! That Mugnone is truly deleterious: no *finesse*, no nuance, no *souplesse*, things so necessary for *Rondine*. Act 1 heavy; Act 2 confused, unbalanced and faded; Act 3 heavy at the beginning and the rest vulgarly emphatic. In sum, between the *woman* (and I wasn't mistaken in my judgment of her), the square and imprecise tenor, with no shade of bel canto, and *Him*, I was massacred. The audience was too kind, given the performance. Renzo was not to be seen. Had he come, I would have explained to him that *Rondine* must not be treated like this. It will always be an ongoing sorrow if we don't provide for interpretations suited to the opera. [. . .][40]

26. To Giuseppe Adami

[Viareggio
10–19 October 1917]

Dear Adami,

Redaelli also wrote to me with more details, since he had the patience to sit through the whole of the second performance: he tells me that

Mugnone was truly heinous in conducting this poor opera of mine! How is it possible that we cannot prevent such a ruin? Do we have to take it all in silence? And that old Farneti, with her tired voice, who brutalizes a part made of subtleties, gentleness, and caresses? The conductor is an elephant and the woman a sow! I hope that Poli has also realized the fine meal he has served me. He was in Monte Carlo, he heard; now he is here and he must hear, otherwise he is truly a . . . moron. And what does Sonzogno say? It's a real sorrow for me! Dammit when I said yes! If you see Poli tell him my opinion, and then let him live and let me produce more works . . . but I swear to God and to his Saints that I will never give him an opera of mine, and if I could I would not allow him to re-stage my old works! Oh I would be happy to stigmatize Mugnone and the other one [Farneti] in a newspaper! I beg you to find a way, from Sonzogno or from hell, to put an end to the scandal and ruin of my *Rondine in Milan*! Mugnone Farneti Barra: three criminals, three assassins, three scoundrels! Tell Sonzogno to take action for Genoa, Turin, Verona, Padua, and Naples, otherwise he can put this *difficult* opera into the tombs of his ancestors! Best wishes, and let's calm down, otherwise we compromise our health.

Yours

G. Puccini[41]

27. To Sybil Seligman

Torre del Lago

15 April 1919

Dear Sybil,

[. . .] I certainly won't give it [*Trittico*] with Mugnone, it would mean ruining everything, I have proofs of this, *Rondine* in Milan and *Fanciulla* in Naples, and I swore I would no longer have him for important performances. They made a mistake to engage him, they should have taken Panizza who would have done very well because he has developed into a first-class conductor; but they didn't want him. [. . .][42]

NOTES

1. Richard Specht, *Giacomo Puccini: The Man, His Life, His Works* (New York: Knopf, 1933; original German ed., 1931), 13.

2. Ibid., 15, 18, 14.

3. Puccini to Tomaide Puccini, 18 December 1884, in Giacomo Puccini, *Epistolario*, vol. 1: *1877–1896*, ed. Gabriella Biagi Ravenni and Dieter Schickling (Florence: Olschki, 2015), 61.

4. Puccini to Riccardo Schnabl, 20 May 1923, in Giacomo Puccini, *Lettere a Riccardo Schnabl*, ed. Simonetta Puccini (Milan: Emme, 1981), 218. "Kurz" is soprano Selma Kurz, who sang the title role in *Madama Butterfly* at the State Opera.

5. For more on this aspect, see "Albert Carré's Staging Manual for *Madama Butterfly* (Paris 1906)" in the present volume.

6. See Karen Henson, *Opera Acts: Singers and Performance in the Late Nineteenth Century* (Cambridge: Cambridge University Press, 2015).

7. Puccini to Riccardo Schnabl, ca. late December 1922, in Puccini, *Lettere a Riccardo Schnabl*, 211.

8. For Toscanini, see Harvey Sachs, *Toscanini* (Philadelphia: Lippincott, 1978); and *The Letters of Arturo Toscanini*, ed. Harvey Sachs (New York: Knopf, 2002). For Caruso, see Howard Greenfeld, *Caruso* (New York: Putnam, 1983).

9. I would like to express my heartfelt thanks to the Centro Studi Giacomo Puccini, Lucca, and especially Dieter Schickling, for granting me access to their database of the composer's correspondence. My most enduring gratitude is to Gabriella Biagi Ravenni, director of the Centro, who put at my full disposal her unparalleled knowledge of this correspondence, of the composer's at times almost illegible handwriting, and of all things Puccinian. My annotations to the letters recently published by Biagi Ravenni and Schickling in the first volume of the critical edition of Puccini's *Epistolario* are heavily indebted to theirs. All translations are my own except when indicated otherwise. When translating previously unpublished letters, I have italicized words underlined in the original.

10. A major study has recently been devoted to Tamagno: Ugo Piovano, *Otello fu: La vera vita di Francesco Tamagno, il "tenore cannone"* (Milan: Rugginenti, 2005).

11. Puccini, *Epistolario*, 98. It is not known when Puccini might have heard Tamagno sing his music. Ferdinando Fontana was the librettist of *Edgar*.

12. Ibid., 99. Tenor Giuseppe Oxilia had indeed had serious trouble as Verdi's Otello at La Scala. "A certainty that smells of mediocrity" translates "una certezza che puzza di canile," literally "a certainty that smells of kennel," which refers to a common epithet for bad singers, *cani* (dogs).

13. Ibid., 178–79. French tenor Eugène Durot was enjoying a successful career at the time, but the reasons for his abrupt termination of the contract for the Madrid *Edgar* are unknown. Eva Tetrazzini sang the soprano part of Fidelia and Giuseppina Pasqua the mezzo one of Tigrana. We do not know exactly when and why Tamagno had studied *Edgar*, but perhaps it happened in connection with Puccini's attempt to secure the tenor for the Italian premiere. Giulio Ricordi supported Puccini's second attempt with three telegrams to Tamagno, flattering the tenor that "only you can secure [the composer's] future," and that "by accepting, with your talent and your kindness you can give life to a truly worthy young man" (179).

14. Ibid., 181. At the time Andrea Gnaga was composing the opera *Gualtiero Swarten*, which Tamagno premiered the following November in Rome.

15. Ibid., 182.

16. Ibid., 190.

17. Ibid., 200. The source is *Carteggi pucciniani*, ed. Eugenio Gara (Milan: Ricordi, 1958), 74, which unfortunately often omits salutations and signatures. Puccini addresses Ferrani as "gentilissima Signorina," which literally means "most gentle Miss," a very formal way of address. In the following letter she is just "gentle," which is only a little less formal.

18. Puccini, *Epistolario*, 242, from *Carteggi pucciniani*, 204.

19. Vincent Seligman, *Puccini Among Friends* (New York: Macmillan,1938), 93–94. All translations by Seligman have been checked against copies of the Italian originals held at the Centro Studi Giacomo Puccini and partially modified.

20. Previously unpublished. The original is owned by the heirs of Sybil Seligman; I have transcribed the text from a copy held at the Centro Studi Giacomo Puccini.

21. Seligman, *Puccini Among Friends*, 94–95.

22. Ibid., 96.

23. Michele Girardi, "Le droghe della scena parigina," in *"Madama Butterfly," mise en scène di Albert Carré*, ed. Michele Girardi, Disposizioni sceniche e Livrets de mise en scène, vol. 4, Edizione nazionale delle opere di Giacomo Puccini 3. (Turin: EDT, 2012), 10.

24. Puccini to Riccardo Schnabl, 5 July 1923, in Puccini, *Lettere a Riccardo Schnabl*, 228.

25. An interview with Dalla Rizza, including interesting remarks on her contacts with Puccini and her interpretation of his operas, can be found in Lanfranco Rasponi, *The Last Prima Donnas* (New York: Knopf, 1982), 121–29.

26. Ibid., 55. Soprano Rosa Raisa would be the first Turandot in 1926.

27. F. G. Rizzi, *Gilda Dalla Rizza: Verismo e Bel Canto* (Venice: TC, 1964), 28.

28. *Carteggi pucciniani*, 460. Puccini often addressed Carlo Clausetti as "Claudio," some sort of pun on his last name.

29. Ibid., 481–82; and Rizzi, *Dalla Rizza*, 36, both incomplete, but in different ways, so that it is possible to reconstruct the complete text. Puccini refers to a possible revival of *Trittico* in Rome, where Dalla Rizza was staying at the time, advising her against a common cut to the "aria dei fiori" (flowers aria) in *Suor Angelica*.

30. Rizzi, *Dalla Rizza*, 32. "Modern French tedium" (*le noie francesi moderne*) is clearly a reference to a contemporary French opera performed in Rio de Janeiro while Dalla Rizza was there, although the precise work is unknown. "Beecham and Cunard" are conductor Sir Thomas Beecham and his lover Lady Maud Cunard, but I could find no reference to them going bankrupt: the allusion might be to him as impresario of Covent Garden—unless Puccini is hinting metaphorically at the end of their relationship, which, however, continued for decades. The composer was thinking of Belgian baritone Armand Crabbé for the part of Prunier, which he had turned from tenor to baritone in the second version of *La rondine*.

31. *Carteggi pucciniani*, 505; and Rizzi, *Dalla Rizza*, 50, both incomplete, as described above. Dalla Rizza was singing Maddalena in Umberto Giordano's *Andrea Chenier*, set during the French Revolution.

32. *Carteggi pucciniani*, 549; and Rizzi, *Dalla Rizza*, 65, both incomplete, as described above.

33. Puccini to Alfredo Caselli, 1 May 1896, and to Mugnone, 20 May 1896, in Puccini, *Epistolario*, 523 and 526–27.

34. Puccini to Giulio Ricordi, 3 July 1896, ibid., 542.

35. Puccini to Luigi Pieri, 30 March 1908, in *Carteggi pucciniani*, 367.

36. Puccini, *Epistolario*, 451. *Non bis in idem* (not twice in the same place) refers to the fact that the premiere of *Manon Lescaut* had also taken place at Turin's Teatro Regio. "The conductor" is Toscanini, recently nominated principal conductor at this theater,

and who did in fact lead the premiere of *Bohème*. "All those useless Vanzos" translates "i Vanzi dei miei costanzi;" which contains an untranslatable reference to Rome's Teatro Costanzi, evoked probably because it both rhymes with the plural of the last name of conductor Vittorio Maria Vanzo, and hints at another, vulgar word commonly used in this expression, *coglioni* (balls), which Puccini is both suggesting and avoiding—he could not be quite so vulgar when writing to the venerable Giulio Ricordi. Vanzo had been mentioned in connection with the premiere of *Bohème*, but clearly the composer was less than enthusiastic about him.

37. Annalisa Bini, "Il fondo Mugnone nella Bibliomediateca dell'Accademia di Santa Cecilia: Una prima ricognizione," in *Musica come pensiero e come azione: Studi in onore di Guido Salvetti*, ed. Marina Vaccarini, Maria Grazia Sità, and Andrea Estero (Lucca: LIM, 2015), 623–44, quote at 644.

38. Previously unpublished. The present location of this letter is unknown; I have transcribed the text from a copy held at the Centro Studi Giacomo Puccini. The original of "weaken, flag, apocalypse" is "indebolisse, affievolisse, apocalisse"; Puccini, notoriously creative with language and particularly sensitive to its sound, adds *apocalisse* because it rhymes with the two preceding words, even if it makes no literal sense—although it somehow conveys his frustration and anger at Mugnone's perceived mistreatment of his music.

39. Previously unpublished. The present location of this letter is unknown; I have transcribed the text from a copy held at the Centro Studi Giacomo Puccini.

40. *Puccini com'era*, ed. Arnaldo Marchetti (Milan: Curci, 1973), 443–44. "Renzo" is Renzo Sonzogno, publisher of *La rondine*.

41. Previously unpublished. The original is owned by the heirs of Giuseppe Adami, one of the two librettists of *Turandot*; I have transcribed the text from a copy held at the Centro Studi Giacomo Puccini. The letter, not dated, was written between 10 and 19 October. Riccardo Redaelli was a Milanese friend of Puccini, and Oreste Poli was the impresario of the Teatro Dal Verme. "The tombs of his ancestors" translates "tombe degli avi suoi," which is a reference to "Tombe degli avi miei," the incipit of Edgardo's final scene in Donizetti's *Lucia di Lammermoor*.

42. Seligman, *Puccini Among Friends*, 300. Argentinian conductor Ettore (Héctor) Panizza would become Toscanini's assistant at La Scala between 1921 and 1931 and then go on to a very successful international career, with frequent engagements at New York's Metropolitan Opera, among other theaters.

The *Verismo* Debate

INTRODUCTION, TRANSLATION, AND
COMMENTARY BY ARMAN SCHWARTZ

Verismo—"realism" or, more literally, "truth-ism"—must surely rank among
the most vexed terms in the historiography of Italian opera. Should it
refer to all the stage works produced by the so-called *giovane scuola* (Pietro
Mascagni, Ruggero Leoncavallo, Umberto Giordano, Francesco Cilèa) or
only those with lower-class subjects? Was Puccini a realist in some, perhaps all, of his operas, or is there an essential difference between his style
and that of his contemporaries? Can an opera's music be realistic, or only
its setting, characters, and language? And does a meaningful connection
exist between Italian *verismo* and a host of seemingly related works—from
Sergei Rachmaninoff's *Aleko* (1892) and Jules Massenet's *La Navarraise*
(1894) to Eugen d'Albert's *Tiefland* (1903) and Leoš Janáček's *Jenůfa*
(1904)—produced in other countries?

As far as we know, the word *verismo* entered Italian discourse in 1867,
where it was used to refer to paintings with contemporary subject matter;
other early uses suggest an array of different connotations.[1] Soon, however, the term came to be associated with a literary movement that took
shape in the 1870s and '80s, spearheaded by the novelists Giovanni Verga
and Luigi Capuana. These writers are best known for their depictions of
the lives of impoverished characters in rural Sicily—a terrain that would
have seemed distinctly exotic to the majority of educated, middle-class
readers who consumed their works. Although Verga and Capuana were
influenced by the French novelist Emile Zola, their fiction exhibits little of his concern with social criticism. Instead, they were fascinated by
the "naturalist" aspiration to literary objectivity. In the most famous of
several manifesto-like statements on what he called "the science of the
human heart," Verga proposed an aesthetic in which "the work of art will
seem to have created itself, to have grown spontaneously and come to
fruition as though it were a part of nature, without preserving any point
of contact with its author." A perfect novel "will preserve no imprint of

the mind that brought it to life, no shadow of the imagination that first conceived it."[2]

Such pronouncements may seem incompatible with the most basic aims of opera. Nonetheless, the novelty and popularity of *verismo* literature clearly struck a nerve. On 9 April 1890, Stanislao Gastaldon's *Mala Pasqua!*, an adaptation of Verga's iconic short story "Cavalleria rusticana," debuted at Rome's Teatro Costanzi. Mascagni's *Cavalleria rusticana*, based on the same tale, premiered at the Costanzi some six weeks later. (Both operas drew heavily on Verga's own, enormously popular dramatization of his tale, which had its stage debut in 1884.) Although Gastaldon's work was soon forgotten, Mascagni's would prove to be the most influential Italian opera of at least the coming decade. Two obvious imitations premiered in 1892: Leoncavallo's *Pagliacci* and Giordano's *Mala vita*. Like *Cavalleria rusticana*, these operas are short, featuring lower-class, southern Italian characters and cruel denouements. A prototype had been cast and, in one estimation, some eighty operas based on Mascagni's model would debut in Italy between 1890 and 1933.[3]

Given this efflorescence, it is no surprise that Italian music critics felt compelled to comment. Like contemporary scholars, they asked what, if anything, could make an opera realistic. Unlike more recent writers, they felt the answer to this question offered vital information about the future of opera itself. (It should be noted that *verismo* was also a matter of considerable concern outside of Italy. As will be described in the next section of this volume, German critics discussed Mascagni's and Leoncavallo's newest operas in the loftiest of terms.) Although it would be impossible to do justice to the sheer number and variety of essays on the topic published in journals and newspapers throughout the 1890s, the three texts reproduced below may offer a glimpse of the specific issues that animated critics, as well as a sense of how the discourse on operatic *verismo* developed in the course of the decade in which it first emerged. One thing that did not change, however, was a widespread suspicion of the very notion of *verismo* opera. For critics enmeshed in the terms of Romantic idealism, realist opera could only seem (as they frequently remarked) an oxymoron. Their outrage may now seem antiquated, but their sense that the traditions of opera would not adapt easily to the aesthetics of modernity lives on in debates about "updated" stagings and about whether singers should also act well and resemble physically the characters they portray.

Verismo? . . .
Vito Fedeli

The Gazzetta musicale di Milano, *Italy's leading music weekly, published its first article devoted to the subject of* verismo *on 6 March 1892; its author was Vito Fedeli, a composer and frequent contributor to the journal. Fedeli's essay was inspired by the premiere in Rome of* Mala vita, *whose unsentimental depiction of prostitutes and other lowlifes in one of Naples's poorest districts had seemed to set a new standard for depravity. Fedeli may not have seen the work himself, but his sense of moral outrage—and his belief in the integrity, if not autonomy, of operatic music—was typical of responses to Giordano's first opera, and one shared by many early writers on* verismo.

Never, perhaps, has our art found itself in a state of uncertainty and bewilderment equal to that in which it finds itself today. The old system is overworked and exhausted; the only hope left is for modern operatic composers to search out a new path, a new cycle of transformation. This operation will have to be undertaken quickly, in order to ensure art's necessary evolution.

It cannot be denied that in Italy, even though they are completely neglected by the Government, opera composers study hard and often (perhaps too often) put themselves in the eyes of the public, showing the very best inclinations and the most steadfast resolutions. Up until today, however, even their most successful and commendable attempts have revealed nothing new, or have only hinted at the innovations so frequently invoked.

The works of the young, modern composers all resemble one another. Almost all of them have that uniformity of confused melodic-instrumental polyphony, that chaos of disconnected modulations, that infinite variety of little melodic ideas, badly developed if at all, which, taken together, betray the extent of a composer's uncertainty. He seems caught between old traditions—the binding aesthetic values with which he was raised—and the feverish desire to improve art itself by discovering the new path toward which recent progress and the needs of the public must point.

It is pointless to demonstrate here how such operatic innovations must primarily be based on music alone, concerning the libretto only to the extent to which it involves the arrangement of scenes, poetic lines, and anything else that could prove useful to the musical form. In an opera, as we Italians understand it, music must always dominate and reign over all the other representational arts. Moreover, we do not believe that to write new music it is indispensable to turn to new dramatic subjects. Neither did Rossini, when he embarked on *The Barber of Seville*, which had already been set with such success by Paisiello.[4] Rossini was an innovator, and for that reason the extraordinary success of his comic masterpiece must be attributed solely to the music.

Today, however, some composers would like to start from the opposite principle.

In the previous issue, our diligent Roman correspondent informed readers of a new opera by a young Neapolitan composer,[5] which was performed for three evenings in the Teatro Argentina.[6]

I will not discuss the music in any detail.

It is said that the author wanted to write a *realistic* opera [*un'opera verista*], bringing to the stage all that is most debased and lurid in the everyday lives of the very poorest people of Naples.

Without adopting the role of the defenders of morality and decency, we can ask: does the new school, in order to express itself, truly need to resort to such a type of *verismo*, to dramatic subjects of a realism that knocks against every aesthetic principle and every healthy aim of art? The mission of music is certainly not to call attention to that which in our society we should at least hide, and of which, as the civilized people we pride ourselves on being, we should be ashamed.

The art of music, more than any of the other arts, is capable of elevating minds, civilizing hearts, and improving social mores; it can and must ennoble souls even when it draws on elements outside of itself. But it must not be prostituted vilely in order to put on display nauseating pictures: insipid, deprived of concrete, logical, plausible intentions, and in complete disharmony with the traditions of Italian theater.

It would be preferable, in such a case, to invite onto the stages of our principal theaters Offenbachian troupes and others like them . . . and to declare that lyric opera is already dead and buried.

Art cannot ennoble all that is debased and lurid; and the artist who attempts to do so, even if he is unaware of the error of his ways, would risk being called depravity's pimp.

Our art must never be contaminated by such a type of *verismo*. It will flourish again on its own, by its own virtue, but never by procuring impossible, impenetrable, and shameful dramatic subjects.

Whatever form the operatic school of the future will assume, it will have to be essentially musical, and the divine art will have to predominate over all the other representational arts. We believe that the Italian school will be able to renew itself and prosper again only by following this principle.

All other artificial and secondary means are only capable of obtaining ephemeral successes, and will only demonstrate with even greater clarity the musical insufficiency of those who adopt them. For he who has a gentle heart and the feeling of an artist, *verismo* will be able to arouse one emotion only: disgust.

Contemporary Dress in Opera
Il Mondo Artistico

Discussions of verismo *grew in intensity throughout the 1890s, as new works premiered with increasing frequency, and as foreign audiences began to take notice of the trend. The years 1895 and 1896 might be described as something of a watershed in this discursive history. On 13 August 1896, a writer for the* Gazzetta musicale di Milano *asserted that "I would be happy to hear even once, instead of idle chatter, a good definition of this* verismo.*" Six Italian writers soon authored responses to his call.[7] But the* Gazzetta *was not the only venue where the question was debated; indeed, some of the most interesting writing on the subject appeared in the smaller Milanese weekly* Il mondo artistico. *Starting in March 1895,* Il mondo artistico *published a series of essays devoted to specific aspects of* verismo opera. *They summarized their arguments in an essay of 31 January 1896, titled "Il costume borghese nel melodramma" (Contemporary dress in opera).[8] With its acute sense of opera's fundamental "absurdity," this text anticipates many later modernist writings on the subject. Meanwhile, its consideration of the (at that point hypothetical) problems posed by staging Wagner's operas in modern dress may bring to mind some of the controversies that continue to swirl around the practices of contemporary stage directors.[9]*

A curious and, at the same time, interesting question is currently being discussed in the Parisian press, and the public has joined in as well, contributing letters that express opinions and judgments of every sort.

The question originated in the opinion expressed by the director of a lyric theater, to the effect that only the costumes of previous centuries are admissible in opera. This director thus indirectly condemned certain tendencies on display here and there, which aim to present contemporary, civilian costumes—and not just those of previous eras—on the lyric stage.

We have already had occasion to combat this tendency, indirectly, in two of our articles from last year: "Dangerous Tendencies" (21 March, nos. 14–15) and "The Decline of Opera" (10 May, no. 21).

In the first article we discussed the tendency to set prose libretti to music; in the second we returned to the same argument, debating the editor of the *Gazzetta provinciale* of Bergamo, Parmenio Bettoli. And we feel we placed the question so clearly in its proper light that our previous arguments might also speak to the question at hand, that of modern dress on the operatic stage.

We said that in Paris the public is very interested in the discussion. Unfortunately, this has not happened to the same extent in Italy.

Le Figaro provides excerpts from letters received by readers, but it does not seem that anyone has approached the question with precision and specificity.

One, for example, calls that theater director who expressed the unfortunate opinion against contemporary civilian dress "a guardian of routine and dead convention."

Another makes subtle but ultimately objectionable distinctions about the possibility of "lyricizing" [*lirificare*], for example, the soldiers of *La fille du régiment* versus those of Madagascar. But, naively, he doesn't understand that soldiers—whether Donizetti's, those in *Faust*, or those in Madagascar—do not wear civilian clothing.[10]

A third, smarter reader is of the opinion that we should try. Certainly—he says cautiously—the public would initially resist this novelty; but then they would get used to it, and find it extremely natural, as they do in spoken theater.

This person does not realize that lyric theater is an entirely different thing from prose theater, and that the conventionality of one has nothing to do with the conventionality of the other.

We have uttered the terrible word: *conventionality*. This is the key to everything. No one has been a greater enemy than us of the old conventions, against which art, in whatever field it unfolds, now tends to rebel ever more. But here it is necessary to be clear, since there is a danger that a desire to destroy the old conventions will lead only to the creation of new ones—combatting absurdities with other absurdities.

In one of our aforementioned articles from last year, we said: "If it is absurd to want to sever every last convention from an art form that has its origins and its *raison d'être* in a conventional union between the sung word and music, it is also just and logical that today, with changing tastes, one tries to bring new life to the old art, rejuvenating and modernizing it by rendering it more human in its content and more true in its form."

And in the other article, on the topic of prose libretti, we expressed the following opinion: "It is one thing to correct those aspects of lyric drama—'melodrama,' as they used to say—that are antiquated, thus rendering the whole more human in its content and more true in its form; but it is another thing to do away with those aspects altogether. Thus will prose libretti lead directly to the end of opera."

That which we claimed both for the subjects for lyric drama and for prose libretti we can only repeat today, because the question of mufti is only an aspect of this same question or, better still, an inevitable consequence of it.

What is an opera in itself? What is it as a form of art?

No one can deny that opera is one of the most inspired and at the same time one of the greatest aberrations of human intelligence. The history of opera, from 1600 to our present day, is nothing but the history of this aberration. Even Wagner, with all of his audacities—more apparent, perhaps, than real; the product of fantasy more than reflection and reasoning—was not able to free himself from this error.

Opera, if we consider its dramatic pretensions, is an error, because it represents an art form that expresses itself in a way that is contrary to truth and to human nature, and thus is false and grotesque.

Now, it is a law of nature that an error cannot be conquered until we have exhausted all the possibilities of its existence; this exhaustion, luckily, is far from being verified in the case of opera.

If attempts to discover new paths for art are more than praiseworthy—indeed, to be encouraged—it is both natural and evident, however, that the more we push aside the ancient forms the more we enter into the contemporary environment, into topical subject matter; the more, in short, we grant opera the form and appearance of prose theater, the more clearly we demonstrate the error that is the foundation of this form of musical art.

Wagner—let's be honest—skirted the issue by putting on stage fantastical characters, gods, giants, more or less enchanted knights, etc., etc., and, when he wanted to pay homage to human reality, as in *Die Meistersinger*, he chose a subject from centuries past, which had a fundamentally romantic basis and lent itself well to the musical stage.[11] But if he had wanted to bring to the stage a completely contemporary subject, he probably would have found himself too embarrassed to do the job well. Is it possible to imagine an opera of Wagner's with characters in top hats and tails, a Parsifal or a Tannhäuser or another romantic, knightly character with a blazer, an extremely high collar, rolled-up trousers, and a cane held by the tip?[12]

Many say that it is not logical that people speak, act, and in every way demonstrate their own passions and follow their impulses while singing.

This is true: but this illogicality would be even more evident, even more irritating, if these characters, instead of singing in the costumes of past epochs, sang in our own, everyday fashions. In this case, opera would be made a laughingstock, because the scenic representation of contemporary, quotidian life would be even less logical and more absurd with musical accompaniment.

Given a form of art that is inevitably conventional, one must accept it, and suffer it in all of its consequences.

Modernizing the form of opera does not therefore mean highlighting its incurable conventionality even further. Now, mufti in lyric drama would render this conventionality not only grotesque but almost intolerable, especially because the ordinary clothing we see each day on the streets of the city can only be used with an ordinary plot taken from the common, everyday, vulgar life we have under our own eyes and that we all lead.

Thus the question of costume is intimately linked to that of subject matter, which we have discussed previously.

We do not believe we have exhausted the question and exposed all of the artistic and aesthetic reasons against the introduction of contemporary, civilian costumes onto the lyric stage; there are many others and of a different order.

But so as not to go on too long, we will address them in another article.

Realism in Opera
Giuseppe Samoggia

Neither of the preceding essays go into much detail about what, to many, might seem to be the central question: What do verismo *operas sound like? For one important answer, we might turn to "Realismo nel melodramma," an essay by Giuseppe Samoggia published in the ambitious Neapolitan journal* Gazzetta teatrale italiana *on 16 January 1901. Samoggia identifies, with considerable alarm, a stylistic trait shared by many Italian realist operas: they rely, to an unprecedented degree, on sounds—whether bells and drum rolls or diegetic musical performances—that are located within the fictional space of the stage world. What is more, he claims that "it is not rare to find entire scenes, of capital importance for the action, in which song is lacking and the orchestra fills the space." Taken together, these features might be understood as a musical response to Verga's call for an art that will seem "to have grown spontaneously and come to fruition as though it were a part of nature." By naturalizing operatic sound, and by avoiding what* Il mondo artistico *had called the "absurdity" of sung speech,* verismo *composers might be described as attempting to put their art on a more objective footing.*

Throughout history artists in general, and musicians in particular, have always taken up valuable time theorizing to infinity: how well and how frequently do they profess the most extravagant of maxims! Luckily, the damage done by this is much less severe than it might at first seem. In practice, talented artists are graced with an infallible instinct that would lead them to ignore any theory in the world if it meant producing something ugly. As for the others, ultimately they will leave no trace, and therefore art is not terribly concerned with their defenseless efforts.

In any case, everything passes, and first of all the fashions of any given moment; the best advice is to let time do its work, resigning oneself to endure the phenomenon that Leibniz wittily called "human parroting."[13]

There was a time in which realism was in fashion: all art had to be realistic, and by extension even music. And so it was that, for the first time, they uncovered musical realism, two words that, combined, constitute an oxymoron.

It would be easy to demonstrate this, but the subject is unsuited to an article. What is more, it would not be worth the effort, since, thanks to the absurdity of the concept, there has never been a phrase used and abused in more different meanings.

Naturally the current of realism came from spoken theater, and the rules of the new aesthetic applied themselves most readily to theatrical music. But even when limited only to the cases in which music has a special function of describing facts of real life and of commenting on words and feelings, the new doctrine has given rise to the strangest and most exaggerated misunderstandings.

According to some, when Wagner extends the field of lyric drama, taking for his theme the depiction of characters, placing on the stage the movement and agitation of a multiple and divided crowd; when he breaks the old forms, the orchestra becoming in his hands the most nimble and flexible instrument for expressing, freely and precisely, the infinite gamut of human expressions and emotions; when from his advanced and perfected orchestral palette he draws forth new colors and more suggestive sonorities, Wagner is being a realist. When he puts forth the principle that musical language is only suitable for legendary characters, and explores how to render the contrast between song and human truth less strident, he would seem to be announcing a realistic gospel. And so they want to be realists: Mascagni, with his sketches of peasant life; Giordano with his characters in evening dress; Puccini, with his *parlati* and bells; even though all of this stands at the furthest possible remove from what the German school has always professed.[14]

In reality, the search for subjects more appropriate to the conventions of the sung word, the refinement and perfection of the means of expression, as well as of the old forms—all with the aim of attaining a greater correspondence and a more intimate union between the word and its musical signification—would lead to a *verismo* stronger in its effects, but would not alter the essence and the proper means of musical creation in the service of a self-proclaimed imitation of real life. On the contrary, the interest of the attempt, of the study, resides in reconciling the terms of the problem, which is to say, respecting the laws of verisimilitude without breaking the oath sworn to the requirements, to the fundamental principles that support a given artistic form, which in this case is musical composition.

The whole modern German school follows Wagner on this path, with Humperdinck and Strauss his most noteworthy disciples. They remain always and above all musicians, never enslaving, but rather attempting ingeniously to reconcile music to dramatic truth.

In France, however, we witness a development that responds to a completely opposite tradition and a quality of temperament that could accurately be described as an evolution in the meaning of realism. Just as in Italy, where comic opera had once provided the spark that allowed modern opera to develop out of *opera seria*, so too in France has comic opera been called on once again to renew opera and initiate a new phase in the history of the art. Bizet with *Carmen*, Massenet with *Manon* and then with *Werther* and later *Sapho*, and on and on up to Bruneau and Charpentier, represent the renewal of the old comic opera by way of a more elevated and more vivid sense of dramatic contrast, with all the resources of German instrumental music, and with certain procedures that imitate Wagnerian reforms.[15]

Except that, little by little, the question of realism threatens to become a minor question of mise-en-scène.

Whoever has seen Zola's or Daudet's novel set to music, perhaps on a prose libretto, and with characters in blouses or in top hats, will perhaps not retain an overly fond memory of these particularities, suggested above all by a craving to stand out, and by that inevitable search for the "new" that is the inferior and vulgar form of the aspiration to artistic perfection.[16]

So far is all of this from the aim of forging a truly new direction for art that the banner of realism, adopted as a marketing ploy, does not prevent anyone from resorting to the most outmoded means when another round of applause is at stake. It reconciles itself perfectly to the practical, merchant-like opportunism that prevails today, offering up a deafening grand finale or a straightforward, sentimental, and mannered romance.

The Italians, needless to say, have thrown themselves enthusiastically on this path, with the happy gifts of brilliance and spontaneity that are congenital to the race, but not always with taste, with the measure and the precise elegance of style that distinguishes the Parisian article, even in the field of music.

The fad will soon go out of fashion, and would not even be worth discussing were it not for a grave fact, a truly alarming symptom: for some time now, the music in new works has tended to eliminate itself, to slip away more and more. In the culminating points of the action music abdicates, it abstains, in order to cede its place to *parlati* and then to the explosions of an orchestral artillery that intervenes to resolve dramatic situations of every genre in the same way. It is not rare to find entire scenes, of capital importance for the action, in which song is lacking and the orchestra fills the space, accompanying out of habit—a convention, that is to say, even worse than that it intends to abolish. In modern works the musical component often enters as if by stealth, in most cases with a pretext, or as an episode, as dance used to do in operas from the past: hence the large number of inserted passages that are extraneous to the action—serenades, madrigals, *stornelli*, pastoral songs, private cantatas or piano or violin sonatas, drum rolls, fanfares, concerts of bells.[17] Remove all this—remove the orchestra's little descriptive pieces, and the romances inserted to show off a soloist—and of dramatic music, of that which in short constitutes the substance of melodrama, you will see how little remains. They have even found eloquent silences, expressive pauses, movements in which music reduces itself to a bare minimum, to the most disheartening harmonic and melodic nakedness.

All this is of an enormous gravity, and I believe this is the moment to sound the alarm. With the excuse of realism, the true musical substance becomes leaner and duller by the day: it is time to turn back.

If it is true that operatic realism means, above all, the precise, faithful, and clear notation of the movements of the soul expressed through words, no one has ever been more ardently and ingeniously realist than the great masters of the past, like Mozart, like Pergolesi, like Cimarosa, to whom sooner or later it is inevitable that one will have to return, to cleanse the palate, restoring melodic inspiration to its origins, and to its purest forms.

NOTES

1. See Andreas Giger, "Verismo: Origin, Corruption, and Redemption of an Operatic Term," *Journal of the American Musicological Society* 60 (2007): 271–315.

2. Giovanni Verga, "Gramigna's Mistress," in *Cavalleria Rusticana and Other Stories*, trans. G. H. McWilliam (London: Penguin, 1999), 94.

3. See Sefano Scardovi, *L'opera dei bassifondi: Il melodramma "plebeo" nel verismo musicale italiano* (Lucca: Libreria Musicale Italiana, 1994).

4. Giovanni Paisiello's version of Beaumarchais's comedy debuted in St. Petersburg in 1782; Gioachino Rossini's in Rome in 1816.

5. Giordano in fact hails from the city of Foggia in Puglia, although he moved to Naples for his musical studies at the age of fourteen.

6. See Ippolito Valetta, "Corrispondenze: Roma, 24 Febbraio," *Gazzetta musicale di Milano*, 28 February 1892.

7. These essays are compiled in Sergio Viglino, *La fortuna italiana della "Carmen" di Bizet (1879–1900)* (Turin: De Sono, 2003).

8. Throughout this essay, the author uses the adjective *borghese* to modify words like "dress" or "costume." In Italian, *borghese* can mean "bourgeois" or "middle class," but it can also, when applied to clothing, mean "mufti" or "civilian"—a *poliziotto in borghese* is a plainclothes police officer. In my translation, I have tried to use a variety of synonyms to reflect this range of meanings.

9. Although this essay is signed "Il Mondo Artistico," its author is almost certainly Carlo Arner. An essay published under his name in the *Gazzetta musicale di Milano* one month prior, "La morte dell'opera in musica," 12 December 1895, contains several passages written in almost identical language.

10. Gaetano Donizetti's opéra-comique *La fille du régiment* premiered in Paris in 1840; it was set, somewhat unusually, in the early nineteenth century. Charles Gounod's *Faust* premiered in Paris in 1859.

11. *Die Meistersinger von Nürnberg*, set in sixteenth-century Nuremberg, premiered in Munich in 1868.

12. *Parsifal* premiered in Bayreuth in 1882; *Tannhäuser* in Dresden in 1845.

13. Gottfried Leibniz discusses the concept of parroting, or psittacism, in Books 2 and 3 of his *New Essays on Human Understanding* (1704, published 1765).

14. By "characters in evening dress," Samoggia is presumably referring to Giordano's *Fedora* (1898), whose first two acts involve elegant parties in St. Petersburg and Paris. "Parlati," moments in which sung vocal lines are meant to approximate the characteristics of ordinary (if heightened) speech, are a common feature of *verismo* operas. The extensive use of bells in Puccini's *Tosca* (1900) alarmed many of its early critics.

15. Georges Bizet's *Carmen* premiered in Paris in 1875; Jules Massenet's *Manon* premiered there in 1884, followed by *Werther* in 1893 and *Sapho* in 1897. Alfred Bruneau, who wrote several operas in collaboration with Zola, and Gustave Charpentier, whose famously gritty *Louise* had debuted in 1900, were then the leading representatives of realist opera in France.

16. Alphonse Daudet's novel *Sapho* was the inspiration for Massenet's opera.

17. Many of the elements that Samoggia describes—improvised folksongs (or *stornelli*), private cantatas, drum rolls, bells—can be heard in *Tosca*. A madrigal is performed in the second act of Puccini's *Manon Lescaut* (1893). The first act of Giordano's *Andrea Chénier* (1896) contains an elaborate pastoral; the second act of his *Fedora* features a recital by an onstage pianist. An extended violin solo is performed onstage in the first act of Mascagni's *L'amico Fritz* (1891).

Leoncavallo's *Pagliacci*
and Modern-Realistic Opera
by Hans Merian

INTRODUCTION BY WALTER FRISCH
TRANSLATION AND NOTES BY ELAINE FITZ GIBBON

The arrival in German opera houses of Mascagni's *Cavalleria rusticana* and Leoncavallo's *Pagliacci* (usually called *Der Bajazzo* in Germany) in the early 1890s struck like a thunderbolt and unleashed extensive discussion in the pages of cultural journals associated with naturalism. German naturalism arose in the 1880s as a movement calling for art to reflect the qualities of everyday life in a newly industrialized and militarized nation, including the grit of urban existence and the plight of laborers. Strongly influenced by Zola in France, German naturalism was embodied by the plays of Gerhart Hauptmann, the poetry of figures like Arno Holz, and the graphic art of Käthe Kollwitz.

There was debate about how German opera, still dominated by Wagner's works and aesthetics, might relate to naturalism or become more naturalistic. Some critics praised Wagner as a naturalist *avant la lettre* for the psychological realism of his characters and their dramatic situations. Others felt German opera needed urgently to get beyond Wagner if it were to reflect contemporary cultural and artistic values. These debates, which unfolded in two of the leading naturalist periodicals, *Die Gesellschaft* (Society) and *Freie Bühne* (Free Stage), became especially intense with the advent of Italian verismo.

Hans Merian (1857–1902), a critic, editor, and author of several books on music history, was one of the broadest-minded writers on music for *Die Gesellschaft*. Although a devoted Wagnerian, Merian welcomed *Cavalleria rusticana* in 1891 as "the first real modern-realistic opera" because "everything lives and breathes truth." Two years later Merian wrote a longer article, translated here, now in praise of Leoncavallo's

Pagliacci, but also comprising what is likely the first full consideration in German of naturalistic opera.[1] He wonders aloud whether opera can be naturalistic—or his preferred term, "modern-realistic"—in the manner of Ibsen or Hauptmann, because aesthetic principles cannot simply be transferred from one medium to another. "The composer requires an entire aria to express what the poet says in one short sentence," Merian observes. And yet he argues that opera should not be excluded from the domain of realism.

Merian praises Wagner as a pioneer of modern-realistic opera because of his dismantling of the traditional number structure and the use of leitmotifs. But Wagner's impulses led to a "neo-Romantic" opera, not a truly realistic one. Today, Merian argues, opera must abandon gods and heroes and seek modern subjects. Merian sees much Wagnerian influence in Leoncavallo's use of leitmotifs, rich harmonies, and a polyphonic orchestral style. But he admires how *Pagliacci* shakes off Wagner in important ways, among them: (1) starting without prelude or overture, but directly with the Prologue; (2) powerful harmonic gestures that "paint" the characters' emotions; (3) a declamatory style of vocal delivery; (4) fluid but articulated musical phrases—no "endless melody"—defined by bold modulations and changes of instrumentation; and (5) the commedia dell'arte play-within-a-play (or opera-within-an-opera), whose dramatic and musical frame is shattered by Canio's murder of Nedda and Silvio and the final line, declaimed by Tonio, in the original version heard by Merian, "La commedia è finita."

For all their freshness and obvious appeal to German critics weary of Wagner, neither *Cavalleria* nor *Pagliacci* corresponds closely to the core principles of naturalism as manifested in contemporary literature and the visual arts. One would need to look to France, to a work like Charpentier's *Louise* of 1900, for a more plausibly naturalist opera. It would take another decade or so before German opera attained a starker naturalism, in musical and vocal style if not in subject matter, in Richard Strauss's *Salome* and *Elektra*. These compact, intense one-act operas demonstrated how aspects of Italian verismo could be grafted onto a Wagnerian inheritance—with epoch-making results for German opera.

Leoncavallo's *Pagliacci* and Modern-Realistic Opera
Hans Merian

. . . . Nicht die Märchen allein sind der Zweck der Kunst — —
Auch was er wirkich sieht, schild're der Dichter. . . .

. . . . Fairy tales alone are not the object of art — —
The poet should also depict that which he sees with his own eyes. . . .

A modern-realistic opera! — — Is there not already a contradiction inherent in this term? Can an opera even be realistic? These questions will present themselves to some in quiet moments, and it will not be quite clear whether they should be affirmed or rejected. If one speaks of a "modern-realistic" opera, the imagination conjures up such things as a sung Ibsen or orchestrated Gerhart Hauptmann play, and it is only natural that such an experiment would arouse every sort of doubt.

And yet, why should realism, which has until now been in a position to conquer all forms of art, be barred precisely from the domain of opera?

It is indeed quite simple, I already hear a wise "modern" aesthetician say: realism should depict real life, and in real life people are not at all wont to sing, or at least only in exceptional circumstances. In everyday life people speak, but in opera one must sing. How does this fit together?

This objection, however simple and evident it might seem at first glance, is indeed not cogent in any way and does not address the actual question at all. Art—including modern-realistic art—does not seek to, and in fact cannot, depict reality as such; with its own means of expression it can and should offer only a mirror image, a symbol of reality. In contrast to earlier so-called idealist art, modern-realistic art strives only to keep the mirror surface of its expressive means as smooth and pure as possible, so that the picture of reality does not suffer any displacements or distortions, as was so often the case in the manifoldly contorted and outlandishly twisted mirror surfaces of the idealist movements. That is the extent of the difference. Orchestral music and song, in addition to the mimetic and scenic arts, are the means of operatic expression, just as the spoken word is the means of dramatic expression. And in spoken drama, does one speak exactly as one speaks in real life? Not at all, even when the modern dramatist endeavors to bring the dialogue ever closer to reality. In reality, we speak like neither Schiller nor Ibsen in their dramas, and though in comparison the latter's dialogue seems to approach reality more than the former's, this means only that Ibsen sought to adapt characteristic turns of phrase and manners of speaking directly from reality. These naturalisms approach realist artistic development; they are analogous to those imitations of natural sounds that the older and newer composers—the old, outdated Haydn as well as the modern Richard Wagner—loved to add to their scores, which likewise have nothing to do with the question of realism as such. Song can thus be as equally effective a means of expression of realism in opera as speech is in spoken drama.

But now a second, more important question arises, namely: *Is all material just as well suited to operatic as it is to dramatic treatment?* This question must naturally be answered in the negative—it is here that a different circumstance enters into consideration: the boundaries of the expressive means of the respective art forms.

The expressive means of each art form are limited, and these limits in no way align in the case of closely related arts. In the fine arts, the limits of painting are different than those of sculpture; in the theatrical arts, opera with its means cannot express everything that drama can express and vice versa. At first glance it could then seem as if opera, possessing all the expressive means of drama as well as the powerful medium of music, and being thereby richer than spoken drama in direct expressive means, would rule over a larger domain than the latter and must consequently be superior. This, however, is not the case. What opera wins in the deeper and more powerful construction of individual moments through music it then forfeits, precisely as a consequence, to the flexibility and rich dramatic life of spoken drama. Music drama naturally gravitates toward the side of sentiment, spoken drama toward the side of reason. Music, as an art of sentiment or feeling, must linger longer over a given situation, simply because it requires a greater expanse of time to unfold its motives than the word requires to express an idea. The composer requires an entire aria to express what the poet says in one short sentence. Thus, music drama will not be in a position to follow the countless ideas and constantly changing sentiments of a dramatically active plot. And when this is nevertheless attempted by the composer, there occur those endless and unpleasant passages that we find throughout the works of Richard Wagner, and which even in the case of such an exceedingly gifted musician (which the Bayreuth Master certainly was) can disturb the full enjoyment of a work. In the case of a less able artist they can be downright distressing. Music cannot follow fast-moving dialog without delivering the listener into a state of turmoil and confusion through constant modulation and a rapid stampede of implied but not fully developed motives. Similarly, all narrative sections of the drama find themselves quite helpless in comparison. Thus, early (German) opera came upon the solution of musically shaping in closed forms such as arias, duets, trios, etc. only the drama's lyrical moments of repose, while all the remaining sections—the actual dramatic sections—were spoken. This mixed form had to gradually weaken the deference to a higher stylistic unity. Simpler dialogues and narrating sections were treated as so-called recitatives and wavered as such in their more declamatory garb between song and spoken discourse, particularly as they also lacked a richer orchestral accompaniment. Then the dramatic climaxes, which in comparison to the lighter, lyrical passages could not do without emphatic musical support, were unified in larger ensemble numbers, particularly at the conclusion of acts, the so-called finales. Here one sought to bring dramatic escalation to the fore and to follow it more quickly through interruptions of the strict lyric forms and the stringing together of short passages of a moving plot, and with the utilization of choruses and brilliant instrumentation. Yet even in these finales the text had to be subordinate to the music insofar as overly swift and overly substantive chains of thought had to be avoided, for even the shortest musical phrases require a certain amount of time to unfold. But this opera, a composite form of closed movements, recitatives, and finales, was not yet an organic whole, even when all spoken dialogue had been completely effaced from it. Only once Richard Wagner so ingeniously took the final step upon this path, completely dissolved the closed forms and thus brought into use the thus thoroughly realized "leitmotif" as the principle of formal unity, did a real music drama develop out of the early Singspiel and former opera.

But even this unified music drama, structured wholly analogously to the spoken drama of acts and scenes alone (no longer by individual "numbers"), still does not match spoken drama in its expressive means. The limits of modern opera are still more constricted, in terms of the shaping of the actual dramatic plot, than those of modern drama. Richard Wagner believed for a period of time that with his music drama he had, through the incorporation of music, created a richer drama, yes, even a *Gesamtkunstwerk*, comprising all other arts, a work that would have to surpass all other genres of art, for the limits of its expressive means were more ambitiously extended than those of all other genres. But it was exactly this conclusion that proved to be flawed, and even in the case of the Bayreuth Master an interesting, regressive thought process introduced itself. The efforts of Wagner, like those of his predecessors, were oriented toward bringing opera closer to nature, or, as it was then also formulated: to free the music drama from its heretofore inherent artificiality. "The most supreme illusion conceivable" was thus the catch-phrase of these reform efforts. The most cunning decorative effects, the most ingenious machinery were contrived. What Wagner and his imitators accomplished in these matters is too well known to require further discussion here. Strangely, it was precisely these "naturalistic" efforts that led not to an actual realistic opera, but instead to the neo-Romantic Wagnerian opera. It seemed to the Master that historical or even modern figures appearing on stage singing in the so cunningly structured music drama no longer seemed compatible with the supreme illusion toward which he strove. The limits of the all-art-work [*Allkunstwerk*], drawn so broadly at first, were then constricted so tightly that only the realm of the saga remained, a realm from which the material for music dramas, according to Wagner, should be exclusively obtained. Wagner's claims, which can be read in his ingenious book *Opera and Drama* (incidentally, a work that cannot be recommended enough), contain much truth. But the conclusions, which dispute the possibility and validity of a modern-realistic music drama whose material is obtained from the present or from history, rest upon the flawed "naturalistic" viewpoint that supreme illusion is the chief purpose of art, even above the dramatic. But this is not so, for this supreme illusion could only then be wholly attained if the artist himself were able to create nature from scratch. The artist—and with this we return to our point of departure—cannot and should not recreate nature, but should fashion its likeness, its symbol in his works, and he creates this symbol precisely with the means of expression handed to him by his art form.

Following these observations, three things should be more intelligible to us:

1. That an opera can be a realistic work of art just as well as any other artistic creation.

2. That, even if all materials are not equally suited for musico-dramatic treatment, modern material cannot by any means be excluded on principle; and furthermore, how a drama must be constituted if it is to be suitable for the modern-realistic form.

3. Why we in Germany, being upon the path that Wagner pursued, cannot move beyond the Master's grandiose creations, and why young German composers schooled in Wagner's ideas, cannot be led toward the actual modern-realistic opera.

The first of the three points does not require further elucidation; if one doesn't confuse or mix up the terms "realistic" and "naturalistic," the matter is self-evident. A naturalistic opera would be an impossibility and an absurdity, even if individual naturalistic features, decorative details, etc., can appear in realistic and in idealistic operas (for example, the Wolf's Glen music in *Freischütz*, the Magic Fire scene in *Walküre*, the Forest Murmurs in *Siegfried*). But there have always been and will always be realistic operas—one thinks of Mozart's *Don Giovanni* (despite the stone guest!) and of Beethoven's *Fidelio*.

Which material is best suited for treatment in the modern-realistic music drama stems from the idiosyncrasies of the musical expressive means. Music is predominantly an art of feeling; thus, the emotional element must also come before the rational in the musico-dramatic plot material. Complex psychological problems are therefore excluded *a priori*. The underlying facts of the piece should be of the simplest nature possible and thus render unnecessary the multiple explanations and long narrations at which even the most exquisite composer can futilely labor. The characters would be highly developed and well defined. Those complex figures and compound temperaments that seem so interesting, precisely in modern drama, can appear only dull and lifeless in music drama. But above all, the modern music-dramatist portrays great passions. If he does not wish to place the entire power of his work in question, he can never allow himself to give in to a philistine quality (which can be so powerful in spoken drama), for nothing seems more impossible, half-strange, and half-boring than a sung triviality. This is a rock upon which a composer risking the treatment of modern material is more easily stranded than he who takes for his material the historic or even the romantic saga. A great deal of modern or historical dramatic material would be unbearable in musical treatment not because, as Wagner says, we cannot imagine a hero from the present or authentic history to be "singing" (when we attend the opera, we absolutely never imagine the hero to be singing, but to be acting) and because only in the haze of Romanticism would the "stage marvel" become reality—but rather because the "singing" is all the less jarring the further one reaches into the past, for the simple reason that all petty commonplaces and banalities vanish in the broad perspective of ancient histories and myths and only the strong and essential persists, for the dramatic material is by nature arranged in such a way that we can use it solely for potent musico-dramatic treatment. — Given the above, it thus follows that *Otello, Cavalleria rusticana,* and *Pagliacci*, to name a few examples, provide eminent modern operatic materials, in comparison with the worst conceivable: *Hamlet, Kabale und Liebe, Hedda Gabler,* and *L'amico Fritz*.[2]

Romantic material—and in this, Wagner is incontestably correct—is above all best suited for musico-dramatic treatment, and especially treatment in the leitmotivic style introduced by Wagner himself. But how should this leitmotivic style cope with modern material when, as at present, opera hungers for nothing other than such modern material; when, after the long and resplendent period of romantic dreams conjured up by Wagner, it thirsts for "open air"?[3] It desires to free itself from the domain of fantastical gods and heroes, from the realm of singing dragons and of mystical grail cups. But German music was not capable of breaking this spell, it could no longer find the path out of the magic garden into which the great magician of Bayreuth had lured it. And unfortunately, the students of the Master were not themselves magicians—they did not know the words that would have made them into the rulers of this realm; thus, they simply remained under his spell. And those that Wagner had lured into his magic realm, they were the best and most able masters of our nation, the only ones from whom an advancement of German opera was even to be expected, for the others—those "who did not let themselves be lured in,"[4] or who in ludicrous dwarfishness had made a stand against the great Wagnerian artistic project because they were not able to grasp the grandeur and opulence of this universal spirit—they do not at all come into consideration in regard to our question. Courting the philistine masses, they continued to write their little operas [*Öperchen*] in the popular singing-club style, or worked as homeopathic diluters of the so-called Classical School, in which they of course felt themselves to be nothing less than second Mozarts and Beethovens, while they were and could be nothing other than apes of those great masters, whom they caricatured with their weak little works [*Werkchen*]. Thus, German art did not emerge from under the colossus Wagner because, according to its being and its natural development, German art had nowhere else from which to draw, for it had to pass beyond the colossus, it had to overcome him. Such an "overcoming" was of course never to be expected from the dwarfs who scuttled around him, searching to tinker with something here or there, for this required stronger composers with a congenial relationship to the Bayreuth Master—those whose developmental path did not by nature pass through the tremendous obstacle of Wagner and who could stride by, thoroughly admiring his grandiosity and letting the power of his artistic being influence them, without being captured by it. These new masters arose in a different land, in the land of cantos and of song, in Italy. They achieved the "overcoming of Wagner" here, from out of this new soil and in the tracks of a separate, richly unfolded and highly distinctive national artistic development. I need not say that the two young masters are Pietro Mascagni and Ruggero Leoncavallo. They found the magic word and broke the spell.

Could not a German—one will thus object—have been just as able, could we not also have drawn upon the Italians or something else and thus have struck out upon a new path? No, and once again, no because—I cannot repeat it enough—the development of art is not something contrived that allows itself to be calculated, worked out, and fabricated at its own leisure, but something that comes into being naturally and that eternally evolves, something that, like all cultural developments, rests upon incontrovertible natural laws. Art is also something that grows and thrives entirely upon national soil, the exact opposite of all that is international; and when a German artist wishes to create Italian works—or an Italian, German—what is produced therefrom is in the best case simply frail imitation, never fully valid and fully ripened artworks, artworks that flourish so amply and beautifully with strong roots that cling to the mother soil of nationality, so that all nations can gather under their broad peaks and refresh themselves in their splendor.

Thus, it is in Italy where the operatic artwork of the future, fertilized by German (Wagnerian) influences, begins to germinate today. And this is not a coincidence but, as we have seen, a natural consequence of artistic development. It is interesting to observe how since the time of the Renaissance, Germany and Italy have, in the matter of musical hegemony, continually superseded each other in alternation, whereas France always took a middling, mediating position between the two dominant music nations. This reciprocal supersession is also no coincidence and is closely correlated with the overall development of art, in that a distribution of work and roles based on national dispositions occurs simultaneously. In this distribution of roles, the shaping of melody falls to the Italians, that of harmony to the Germans, and an amalgamation of both to the French, with percussive and sometimes also screaming and shrieking effects, especially those of a theatrical nature. This is not the place to further elaborate upon this subject and to provide examples from the history of opera. It would lead us too far afield, but so much is clear without the need for further clarification: that following the laws of the pendulum's swing, every period of one-sided melodic development must, as a natural reaction, be followed by a period of rich, unfolding harmony, and vice versa. That melody lies predominantly in the natural temperament of the Italians, and harmony predominantly in that of the Germans thus makes self-evident the constant swaying to and fro of musical development between Italian and German influences.

Wagnerian art had endowed music drama with a heretofore unprecedented opulence of harmony. All contrapuntal arts were applied with staggering and exceedingly brilliant instrumentation, with new and surprising modulations, and in the last works of Wagner in particular the voice-leading is so convoluted that sometimes the phrases seem even pedantic or brooding. For this reason, the melodic reaction could not fail to materialize and could only naturally come again from the Italians, and here of course only from the masters of the new, not from the adherents of the old, the conventional. Similarly, the new developments of opera could no longer sail in the old idealistic, palliative fairways, but had to turn toward the generally prevailing artistic movement of realism, today the only modern aesthetic trend.

For a long time already, Italy has had in Giuseppe Verdi a real master of realistic art, the first true revolutionary of Italian operatic music. The Italians already recognized the revolutionary character of this master in his *Trovatore*. This must seem more than strange to us Germans, for we glimpse in this opera—ground from every street organ—the oldest, most hackneyed, most fictitious opera, in short, the very prototype of the old opera that was dismissed once and for all by Richard Wagner. And yet the fact cannot be denied: Verdi is the first Italian operatic realist. But his realism—even in *Trovatore*—lies someplace other than where we usually care to search for it. It lies, namely, in the melody. Verdi's operatic melodies, as they appeared for the first time in *Trovatore*, were something completely new in Italy, and if we did not then notice it right away, this is simply because we do not possess the delicate ear for melody that the Italians do. In his melodies, Verdi sought to go beyond simple mood-painting and to develop his characters in an entirely realistic fashion. Thus, in his melody, he strove for the same thing that Wagner had in his harmonically and contrapuntally so richly endowed orchestral accompaniment. Thus, in the early works of Verdi we must also search in the melody alone—yes, even the sung melody—for the naturalisms that approach realistic art, those that Wagner, for example, had relocated to his richly endowed orchestration. One example among many: both composers wish to depict a conflagration. In this case, Verdi—as in the aria "Di quella pira" (*Trovatore*)—will seek to depict the restless flickering and sparkling of the flames in the sung melody, while Wagner—as in the "Magic Fire Music" (*Die Walküre*, *Siegfried*)—surrounds the actual, serene melody with sparkling, restless flickering instrumental figurations. That the Wagnerian expressive means are in this case endlessly more beautiful and effective than those employed by Verdi is obvious, and in this lies indeed an aspect of the progress effected by Wagnerian art. But Verdi, by nature, could not himself have thought of such methods, because, as an Italian, he always thinks first of the melody. But entirely in contrast to many of his German colleagues who pursued Wagner and what he represented solely with scorn and derision, the eternally young Italian Master fully recognized the preeminence of the Wagnerian expressive means and, even more significantly, sought to make them his own as much as he could. We therefore experience a strange and beautiful drama: the Italian Old Master steadily grows under the fruitful influence of the great German Master and preserves in his age a youthful freshness that many young artists might envy. Thus, Verdi wrote his *Aida*, in which Wagner's influence is asserted even more in outer appearances; thus, Verdi later wrote his *Otello*, in which he consciously employed the principles of the Wagnerian art, not as gaunt imitator and epigone, but as an independent artist who learns well from his comrade, but does not plagiarize him and least of all renounces his national and individual nature in the imitation of the foreign. And thus, the nearly octogenarian Italian Old Master, with recent trust in this seemingly inexhaustible friendship, had risked the creation of a *Falstaff*, about which I unfortunately cannot report based on personal experience, but which, according to everything one hears about the work, must be a credit to its creator.

Thus, the Old Master Verdi himself leads toward the new restructuring of Italian opera.

Of course, this restructuring requires above all young talent, and Italy possesses this young talent. It sounds strange, almost a little fanciful, how the two entirely unknown young people suddenly appeared and, in a flash, conquered all opera stages on both sides of the Alps. An Italian music publisher issued a prize competition for the best opera; a certain Pietro Mascagni received the first prize with his *Cavalleria rusticana*. And the strangest thing is, and what most astonished the world: the opera really had something; and though usually nothing intelligent comes out of prize competitions, this time the adjudicators not only hit upon a strong talent, but a truly modern composer as well. But there is more strangeness to come. In the same competition there was a second work that, in its inspired conception, is superior even to *Cavalleria*: Leoncavallo's *Pagliacci*.[5] It is then indeed the same old story, some might thus think, the distinguished adjudicators have this time, as always, missed the mark again and crowned, if not the unworthy, still, the less talented! But no, such a reproach would in this case be entirely unjust; on the contrary, the adjudicators, in crowning the musically "richer" of two works moving upon similar paths, solved their task in the way that best behooved them. But now, as the works of both artists appear on stage, the idea that the public and critics, who reckon by completely different factors than a musical jury, are bound to recognize Leoncavallo as the stronger talent is a fact that—I think one may risk the prophecy—will be confirmed by the future works of both composers.

We have already spoken of Mascagni many different times in *Die Gesellschaft*; we therefore do not need to repeat what has already been said.[6] Mascagni is the younger of the two, but his successes are older than those of Leoncavallo. He has an advantage over the other insofar as he has already brought three operas to the stage, while we only know Leoncavallo's debut work. We can thus already observe a kind of development in Mascagni, and it thus becomes clear that the young master walks upon the pathways of an honest and beautiful talent, that he constantly endeavors to eliminate more and more the *Sturm und Drang*–like qualities from his scores in order to cut through to the most beautiful and most noble phrase possible. But in doing so, he has essentially prepared his all too fervid admirers for disappointment. The shortest, most passionate accents were awaited from him, something daring, but instead he only offered his overworked scores. Additionally, he had decidedly bad luck with his libretti. This then suited Leoncavallo with his *Pagliacci* quite well. The daring quality, the strong accents that had been sought for in vain in the works of Mascagni were found here. And perhaps it was exactly for this reason that the opera had such phenomenally rapid success.

The dramatic content of *Pagliacci*, or *Bajazzo* (Clown), the title under which the opera is performed upon German stages, is extremely simple. An Italian second-class stage comedian suffocates his wife in a bout of jealousy during a theatrical performance before the assembled public.[7] But what does Leoncavallo do with this material? He forms it into a work that one follows from beginning to end with steadily rising suspense.

To state it without further ado: Leoncavallo is his own librettist. This is always an immense advantage when the composer also has a gift for theatrical routines. We observed this in the case of Richard Wagner and see the opposite in that of Mascagni, who, after the superb success of "Rustic Chivalry,"[8] from then on had to labor over and exsanguinate from unwieldy, maladroit libretti.

Not that one might then think that the "poet" Leoncavallo puffs out his cheeks in order to create something unprecedented, never before seen. No, he approaches the work as simply as possible, highlighting only the most important moments of the plot and filling the holes that might develop with operatic trappings, just as the old opera loved to do, entirely unconcerned about any questions of "style"—indeed, with a certain naïveté.

He ostentatiously calls his work a "drama" and prefaces it not with an overture, but with a "prologue," and at that, a prologue that is actually sung. This Prologue is interesting in two ways. First, because it truly exemplifies an innovation, and second, because to a certain degree it contains a "program" of the artist and his conception. In this program, the artist freely and openly confesses his dedication to realistic art, and it made a peculiar impression upon me when Tonio, in a clown's costume, steps out from behind the parted curtain and, from the stage, which is otherwise wholly scorned by modern realism, sings the words:

Ihr seht die heitern Masken wohl mit Staunen im ernsten Spiele,	With astonishment, you see the gay masks in solemn play,
Und da will es der Brauch, daß ich des Dichters Ziele	And thus, according to custom, I will name and quickly explain to you
Euch nenne und kurz erkläre.	The poet's goals.
Denn nicht wie sonst gilt heut' der Satz:	For unlike before, today the saying no longer holds true:
Die Thräne der Bühne sind falsch, sind Lug,	The tears of the stage are false, are lies,
Falsch alle Seufzer auch, und die Schmerzen Betrug;	All sighs are false as well, and all pain deception;
Nehmt drum die Bühne nicht ernst.	Thus, do not take the stage seriously.
Nein!—Heut' schöpfet der Dichter Kühn aus dem wirklichen Leben schaurige Wahrheit.	No!—Today the poet boldly Creates gruesome truth out of daily life.
Ach, nicht die Märchen allein sind der Zweck der Kunst——	Alas! Fairy tales alone are not the object of art——
Auch was er wirklich sieht, schild're der Dichter,	The poet should also depict that which he sees with his own eyes,
Dann erringt er der Menschen Gunst.	For then he wins mankind's favor.

That is a large enough excerpt, especially as the Prologue goes on to announce that the actions upon the stage stem from the memory of an event experienced by the author himself.

Musically, this Prologue is structured quite skillfully and creates for the performer a highly effective number. As early as the first few measures, one knows what the composer is after, and one hears immediately that he has under his control all the expressive means of his art and, unlike so many other novices, he will not let himself be controlled by instrumentation, voice-leading, modulation, etc.

The composition begins with a short, strongly rhythmicized and utterly characteristic motive that plunges immediately into the dominant seventh of the subdominant, which finds its semi-resolution in a short, laughing run of the flute. All of this covers only four bars and could be called the "comedian motive," as it portrays the forced gaiety of the professional jester with exceeding jubilance. Out of the first characteristic measure of the motive, the composer creates an eight-bar passage, whose upper voice somersaults downward from its heights into the complete comedian-motive, this time lying a half step lower; the motive is then directly repeated without any sort of transition, and therefore with a harmonic leap, in order to sound again at its original pitch. This harmonic leap is highly characteristic and is sometimes used by the composer when he wishes to depict the discordant exclamations of the comedians, their screaming advertisement of the coming delights with which they seek to entice the curiosity of the public, and thus also when he desires to create a kind of cacophony; but simultaneously, this harmonic leap should characterize the torn inner being of the clown, that contradiction between being and seeming that forms the actual tragic motive of his drama. Another somersaulting cadence of twelve measures (actually fourteen, with the fermata-like final note, held for two further measures), formed similarly to the first, appears again, is extended, *pianissimo*, in the basses for eight (or rather ten, including the fermata) measures and finally, at a sustained *piano*, dies away in a delightful play of contrary motion, during which the laughing flute run is also repeated three times in different registers and by different wind instruments. Then the horns bring forth a new motive that in the opera, in the so-called Clown Song,[9] characterizes the culmination of Canio-Pagliacco's despair and in that moment is set to the words: "Lache, Bajazzo, schneid' die tollsten Grimassen" (Laugh, clown, make the most fantastic faces);[10] but here, in the Prologue, the closing phrase is repeated over the course of six measures (with the transition, seven). Directly thereafter appears the wonderfully tender and yet passionately emphatic, so southerly warm-blooded love motive, which later in the drama creates the basis of the magnificent love duet between Nedda-Colombina and Silvio, sounding with exceptional gentleness, while being simultaneously communicative of the reason for despair. This motive continues for twelve measures, dying gradually away (*cantabile sostenuto assai*). Then an interplay of the strongly rhythmicized figure and the flute run (twenty-four measures) begins again in the original tempo (*Vivace*), created from the comedian motive and bursting out laughing tremendously, tumbling over itself, and in its final eight measures it falls with a frantic run into the original comedian motive, at which point the entire first section of the composition, the exposition as it were, is repeated in the original key (C major), before being suddenly cut off by a diminished seventh chord after the second, somersaulting cadence. Two full measures of rest follow and then a laughing run (the second half of the comedian motive) appears, this time in B major, then again two measures of rest, again the same run in G major; then the curtain is parted and Tonio, in the mask of a clown, sticks his head through the curtain and walks up to the forestage to sing the Prologue. The vocal part is wholly declamatory. The orchestra at first accompanies quite discreetly, but, especially during the introductory words, with a certain gravitas. At the words, "Denn nicht wie sonst gilt heut' der Satz: Die Thränen der Bühne sind Lug" (For unlike before, today the saying no longer holds true: The tears of the stage are lies) etc.,[11] the comedian motive must hand over its material to the accompaniment. "Heut schöpfet der Dichter" (Today the poet boldly creates)[12] etc. is supported by individual chords in the manner of a recitative, whereas at the passage that directly follows, "Jüngst taucht in des Autors Seele jäh die Erinn'rung auf an ein Ereignis, das tief ihn dereinst erschüttert" (Recently, the memory of an event that had once deeply unsettled him suddenly arose in the author's soul)[13] etc., a wonderfully plaintive melody with dragging, syncopated accompaniment is heard, its construction somewhat reminiscent of the love motive. Thereafter, the love motive itself, with charming voice-leading, appears at the words, "Laßt euch im Stücke rühren der Liebenden Schicksal, das eurem oft gleichet" (Let yourself be stirred by the fate of the lovers in the drama, whose fate often resembles your own),[14] while the passionate jealousy motive appears at the words, "Den Haß selbst sehet wüten, den Neid sehet nagen" (See hate itself raging, see jealousy festering) etc.,[15] as it is heard in Canio's beautiful arioso, set to the words, "Anders wäre's im Leben, fänd ich Nedda jemals treulos" (It would be different in real life were I to ever find Nedda unfaithful).[16] The jealousy motive rises to a *fortissimo* until a passionate cadence, broken by syncopation, leads to a new lyrical passage (*Andante cantabile*) that, with a magnificent, serene, and stately melody, introduces a kind of fundamental moral of the drama:

O glaubt mir:	O, believe me:
Wie euch, schlägt voll Lust und Leid auch in des Gauklers Brust ein Herz,—	Like you, a heart full of passion and suffering also beats in the traveling artist's breast,—
Grad wie euch quillt lindernd ihm die Thräne,	Just like you, he is soothed by welling tears
Wenn ihn bedrückt ein Schmerz.	When suffering afflicts him.
Wir alle auf Erden wandeln im gleichen Licht;	All of us walk the earth under the same sun
Bis dem Reichsten wie dem Ärmsten einst das Auge bricht.	Until the day that both the richest and the poorest find their eternal rest[17]

A few concluding words in recitative from the withdrawing Tonio (four measures) and a coda of sixteen measures, formed from the comedian motive and reminiscent of the opening, close the composition.

This analysis of the Prologue, purposely somewhat drawn out, has allowed us a variety of insights into Leoncavallo's artistic character. At first glance, we recognize the audacious go-getter who carelessly forges his own path past old rules and conventions. In his Prologue, he does not rely upon any heretofore extant form, and yet the composition is, as we have seen, nowhere near formless. Indeed, if we compare the numbers of measures mentioned above, we see that there is a certain harmony and symmetry that rules over the individual sections, a certain uniformity and rigor of the structure that, for example, cannot be found in the later works of Wagner, where the waves of sound surge boundlessly forth. (That a "higher" symmetry of course also prevails in Wagner's creations is noted here to obviate any misunderstandings and for the benefit of certain people who, because they never wish to learn anything, cry "Aha!" or "You see!" and look to capitalize upon misunderstood remarks made against the great Bayreuth Master; wherein the particulars of such symmetry lie cannot, of course, be thoroughly discussed here). Furthermore, the continual return of section lengths divisible by four and eight in Leoncavallo's phrases teaches us that the young Italian does not wantonly allow his leitmotifs to disintegrate as Wagner so often loves to do, true to his principle of the so-called "unending melody"; instead, he seeks to develop them into closed phraselets or phrases. Conversely, this means that Leoncavallo, in further contrast to Wagner, does not look down upon full and half cadences, but gladly utilizes these moments of rest and separation. Indeed, with the help of the instrumentation, he allows the organization of his phrases to stand out even more clearly in that he readily lets the alternation of instrumental timbre coincide with the conclusion of a period. But in this way, he emancipates himself as much as possible from the old rules of modulation. He modulates frequently, rapidly, boldly, and sometimes also through leaps; he does not shy away from enharmonic transitions and, as we have just seen, also utilizes even the most daring harmonic leaps sensibly, highly idiomatically, and with careful deliberation. What distinguishes Leoncavallo—and the young Italians generally—from the older masters of his nation, and where the powerful influence of the great German music-dramatist shows itself, is in the abandonment of older homophony and the wholly polyphonic phrase. The beautiful vocal melody has not been abandoned—it hovers triumphantly over the phrase, particularly in dramatically and musically significant moments—but conversely, the orchestral part is also much more fully developed than was the case in earlier Italian opera. The orchestra no longer simply serves as it did before, when throughout entire numbers it had only to support the voice with individual, rhythmic chords and, when it rose to the surface, appeared only as an autonomous introduction or interlude before falling back again to its serving role as soon as the voice returned to its rightful position. As we all know, this oompah-pah accompaniment lent the Italian opera melody something of a waltz- or polka-like character that to our German sensibility is in no way commensurate with the grandeur of music drama, and which too easily lures superficial composers to banality. With the young Italians, the orchestra, in self-contradiction, approaches song; it executes individual leitmotifs independently, alongside those of the voice and simultaneously with them, just as in the works of Richard Wagner; occasionally, and at those places that seem appropriate to the composer, it even takes control and lets the vocal melody that moves with less important motives or in simple repetition of pitch recede into the background. Precisely with these means, the composer attains quite beautiful effects; through the alternating dominance of the voice and the orchestra, the entire passage gains in the process a rich and beautiful diversity. And if one considers that in music drama the voice represents and symbolizes the sphere of thought or rationality and the orchestra the sphere of emotion, the sphere of passions, it is thereby easy to recognize what fine expressive means are made available to the composer through this particular interplay. When, for example, in those passages where Canio's jealous desperation is depicted—with the orchestra fervently seething upward, its passionate waves of sound flooding the vocal melody—the music-dramatist creates therewith the most beautiful, realistic image conceivable of the passion that seethes from the innermost being of man, that passion that clouds and stifles his powers of reason, while the victoriously, again upward-floating melody of the charging orchestra magnificently characterizes the victory over passion, consolation, and resignation. We are thus given a genuinely dramatic image of the eternal struggle that man must face—sometimes in victory, sometimes in defeat.

[...]

Leoncavallo deserves the extraordinary success that his work has received everywhere. He is a modern composer whose first work already shows that he possesses the tools that lead toward the finest progress. He not only commands a strong ability for characterization and sharp, striking accents, but also a rich trove of melodies and a versatile, splendidly honed formal talent. —His work is just as true as it is beautiful.

NOTES

1. This essay appeared originally as Hans Merian, "Leoncavallo's *Pagliacci*, und die modern-realistische Oper," *Die Gesellschaft* 9/2 (June 1893): 734–55.

2. An adaptation of Shakespeare's *Hamlet* was set by Ambroise Thomas in 1868; *Kabale und Liebe (Intrigue and Love)* is the title of Schiller's 1784 bourgeois tragedy (*bürgerliches Trauerspiel*), set by Verdi in 1849 under the name *Luisa Miller*. *Hedda Gabler* is the title of Henrik Ibsen's 1890 drama—it had not at the time been set in operatic form. *L'amico Fritz* is Mascagni's 1891 opera, a setting of the 1864 French novel *L'ami Fritz* by Émile Erckmann and Pierre Alexandre-Chatrian.

3. A reference to the practice of operatic (and theatrical) productions in open-air theaters, known as *Frelichttheatern* or *Freilichtbühnen*.

4. Merian is here assumed to be caricaturing the self-descriptions of such anti-Wagnerians.

5. Merian is wrong on this point. *Pagliacci* was not among the works submitted to the Sonzogno competition, and Leoncavallo only began to conceive his opera in the wake of Mascagni's success.

6. See in particular the article by Hans Merian, "*Cavalleria rusticana*," published two years earlier in *Die Gesellschaft* 7 (1891): 1451–52.

7. Merian uses the verb *ersticken* (to suffocate); however, in the opera, Canio murders his wife, Nedda, by stabbing her with a knife.

8. Merian uses the German translation of *Cavalleria rusticana*, "Bauernehre," to refer to the opera.

9. Merian refers here to the aria "Vesti la giubba." In all quotations below from the libretto of *Pagliacci*, Merian cites a German text that strongly resembles Ludwig Hartmann's singing translation of 1893, *Der Bajazzo* (Berlin: Adolph Fürstner Verlag), which is versified and written in a poeticized German. However, Merian's quotations occasionally deviate from Hartmann's text. It is not known which translation Merian owned. Because of its significant discrepancies in both style and meaning to Leoncavallo's Italian libretto, Merian's German text is reproduced here. All English translations are my own; page numbers are given according to Hartmann's translation to allow for orientation within the libretto. For the passage cited in the epigraph to this essay, see pages 5–6. In Hartmann's translation of the libretto, "Vesti la giubba" is prefaced with the title, "Bajazzo's Lied" (29).

10. Ibid., 29. Merian deviates here from Hartmann's text, which reads: "Lach' doch, Bajazzo, schneid' tolle Grimassen."

11. Ibid., 5.

12. Ibid.

13. Ibid., 6. Hartmann uses the word *Erlebnis*, rather than *Ereignis*.

14. Ibid.

15. Ibid.

16. Ibid., 12, Act 1, scene 1. Hartmann's translation reads: "Anders jedoch wär's im Leben! / Fänd' ich Nedda je treulos, wär's ihr Ende."

17. Ibid., 6. See Hartmann's text for differences in punctuation, versification, and word choice, particularly in the final two lines quoted here, which in Hartmann's translation read: "Wir Alle auf Erden / Wandeln im gleichen Licht, / Bis am Ziele dem Reichen wie dem Aermsten / Einst das Auge bricht . . . "

Albert Carré's Staging Manual for
Madama Butterfly (1906)

INTRODUCTION BY MICHELE GIRARDI
TRANSLATION BY DELIA CASADEI
STAGING MANUAL TRANSLATION BY STEVEN HUEBNER

The French premiere of *Madama Butterfly*, which took place at the Parisian Opéra-Comique on 28 December 1906, occupies a particularly prominent position in the opera's history. It was on this occasion that Puccini, who was present at rehearsals, elaborated what is commonly considered the final version of a work that he had repeatedly, almost obsessively altered ever since its first, unsuccessful performance in Milan in February 1904.[1] This version emerged from the close collaboration between the composer and the director of the Opéra-Comique, Albert Carré (1852–1938), who had been involved with the stage all his life, first as an actor, then as a librettist, impresario, and director. In 1898 he had taken over the management of the Opéra-Comique where, before *Butterfly*, he had staged, among other works, *Carmen* and *Tosca*, and the premieres of Charpentier's *Louise* (1900) and Debussy's *Pelléas et Mélisande* (1902). In this theater he also acted as *régisseur*, assuming direct and complete responsibility for the mise-en-scène of the operas performed on its stage.

As had been customary in France since the early nineteenth century, operatic stagings considered of particular importance—usually premieres, and almost always from Parisian theaters—were textualized in the form of so-called *livrets de mise en scène*, translated as "staging manuals" or "production books," on which further performances should be based. This practice was later adopted in Italy, notably for operas published by the Milanese house of Ricordi, including several by Verdi as well as *Manon Lescaut*. Carré had already prepared staging manuals for *La bohème* and *Tosca*, which had been performed at the Opéra-Comique in 1898 and 1903, respectively, clearly considering his mise-en-scènes worth preserving, and hoping that the manuals might function as blueprints for subsequent performances and revivals, at least in France. Puccini had been present at rehearsals for these productions, as he later would be for *Butterfly*; the *livret* drawn up for the "Japanese tragedy," however, is unique insofar as it documents a production Puccini not only considered exceptional, but led him eventually to settle on a final version for this troubled opera, thus bringing to an end the convulsive revisions of the previous three years.

This *livret* was published in 2012 in a critical edition, and the excerpts printed here, in Steven Huebner's English translation, are the frontispiece; the introductory texts and drawings for Acts 1 and 2 (see Figure 1 for the original drawing); and the final portion of Act 3, beginning with Butterfly's entrance.[2] These excerpts have been chosen with two aims in mind. The first is to give a clear idea of the nature of these kinds of documents, which, in the words of Mercedes Viale Ferrero, contain "notes relative to the various aspects of a performance in its different stages: the exact placing of the ground plans of settings and anything needed to make them; [. . .] tools and props; stage directions, including movements for singers, chorus, and extras; the relationship between their gestures and voices and the orchestral score; and ways of expressing visibly a dramatic situation."[3] The second is to provide the reader with an opportunity to test my interpretation of the final scenes of the opera as staged by Carré, which I set forth below, against the text of the *livret*.

Puccini had already given ample evidence of his gift for conceiving stage action in relation to music, yet with *Madama Butterfly* he focused his efforts on aligning every detail with the nodal points of the drama. *Madama Butterfly*, both a psychological and costume drama, certainly lent itself to a visual and gestural interpretation of the musical and verbal texts, and for this reason Puccini worked unceasingly, together with conductor Arturo Toscanini among others, to make tiny yet constant adjustments to the score.[4] It was the encounter with a director of Carré's caliber, however, that drove Puccini to perfect the theatrical idea and musical form of *Madama Butterfly*, a process that led to some fundamental choices in the treatment of the opera's subject matter.[5] The dramaturgical sticking points encountered in previous versions were overcome in Paris: the contrast between East and West was placed on a symbolic plane more strongly connected with the protagonist's intense personal tragedy, making for a more gripping finale. The tragic conclusion was strengthened by Puccini's elimination from the Paris version of the brief, sarcastic *buffa* scenes in which the Japanese were either ridiculed or placed in a subordinate position. This in turn promoted

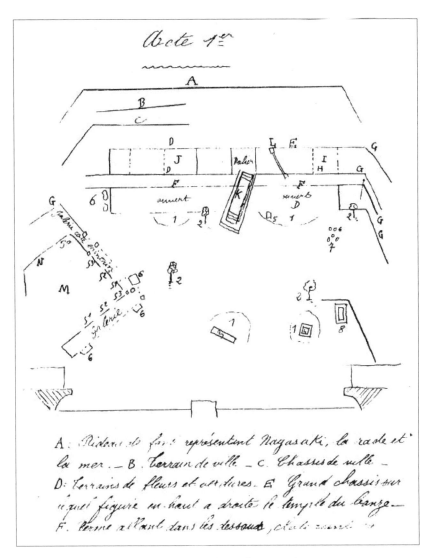

Figure 1. A page from Albert Carré's
livret de mise en scène for *Madama Butterfly*, Paris, 1906.

the dramatic premise of the opera—the clash between East and West—into
an active background for the individual tragedy.

The composer arrived in Paris on 23 October 1906, and was joined
there by librettist Luigi Illica on 7 December. Illica had been summoned to
Paris not only for moral support, but also to make alterations to *Butterfly*'s

Figure 2. A red bridge in the Japanese garden of
Edmond de Rothschild's family castle, Boulogne-Billancourt, Paris.

text in view of a new Italian-language edition of the score: a sign that
Puccini was already anticipating that *Butterfly* would reach its optimal version on the Parisian stage. In those years the French capital was swept
up by a vogue for all things Japanese, inspired by the two universal exhi-
bitions of 1867 and 1900 and evident in texts that ranged from Pierre
Loti's famous novel *Madame Chrysanthème* (1887) to operettas.[6] By 1906 the
press and the public's expectations for "the first Japanese costume opera
performed at the Opera-Comique" (at least according to Puccini) must
have run quite high. Faithfulness to an "original" Japanese setting was
one of Carré's objectives; to this end he researched the topic scrupulously,
especially with respect to the costumes, and had his wife, Marguerite, who
performed in the leading role, study with the famous actress Sada Yakko
in order to learn to move and handle the fan like a geisha.[7]

In his *Souvenirs* Carré recounted how he prepared for *Madama
Butterfly*. He was in the habit of visiting the places in which operas were
set, but this time he went no farther than Boulogne-Billancourt, in the
suburbs of Paris, where a peculiar character named Albert Kahn had

Figure 3. Marcel Jambon and Alexandre Bailly, sketch for Act 1
of *Madama Butterfly*, Paris, Opéra-Comique, 1906.

begun to reproduce—among other things—a Japanese village and garden in such vivid detail that the theater's scene painter, Alexandre Bailly,
was told merely to copy what he saw there.[8] By the time of the French
premiere of *Madama Butterfly*, Kahn had not yet built Japanese bridges on
his property, but banker Edmond de Rothschild had commissioned the
construction of a Japanese garden around the lake in front of his family's
castle, also located in Boulogne-Billancourt, that boasted no less than two
red bridges (see one of them in Figure 2). Carré and his scene painters
thus had a model for the bridge that features at the center of the stage in
Act 1 (Figure 3).[9]

Carré took great care to emphasize blocking and the stage's setting for
dramatic effect. In the scene for the first act in the Milan version (Figure
4), the characters enter from a path that disappears into the background,
whereas in Paris, after entering on the left and climbing a hill, they have
to cross a bridge that further separates Butterfly's garden from the world
outside (MES, 59–61). This will also be the setting for the Bonze's departure (although he enters on the right), an action that precipitates the

Figure 4. Vittorio Rota, sketch for Act 1 of
Madama Butterfly, Milan, Teatro alla Scala, 1904.

protagonist's traumatic detachment from her people. As he lingers on the bridge on his way out, the Bonze briefly dominates the crowd of relatives: stage directions instruct him to adopt a violent demeanor; he snarls his curse and then rushes toward his niece and shoves her (MES, 83). Such violence obliterates all matrimonial serenity, transforming the garden into a reject's refuge.

This setting pleased Puccini a great deal, and he relayed his enthusiasm to Giulio Ricordi in a letter of 25 November 1906, to which we will return below. The Bonze's devastating behavior is clearly motivated by Butterfly's conversion to Christianity; indeed, the priest screams "Elle a trahi nos Dieux" (She betrayed our Gods), instead of "Ci ha rinnegato tutti" (She disowned us all), as he had in the original Italian version. The issue of religion will also be emphasized by the director in two subsequent scenes. At the beginning of Act 2, the knife that Cio-Cio-san had produced from the sleeve of her kimono in the previous act appears again, this time hung next to the altar that holds the statue of Buddha, as if to establish an association between the instrument for the imminent tragic ritual and the image of the traditional divinity (MES, 96). On the shelves to the left of the altar we find two other important objects: a white veil that Butterfly will wrap around her neck once she has wounded herself and a portrait of Pinkerton that the tenor will behold with great emotion upon his return in the final scene. Before beginning the ceremony of suicide, Butterfly will go over to these shelves, pick up Pinkerton's image, and, after placing it next to the statue on the altar, kneel down to pray (MES, 150). The protagonist thus returns to her original religion and retrieves the dignity she lost after the devastating collapse of her ideals.

The most important changes concern the heroine's relationship to the world that surrounds her, suspended as she is between her traditional upbringing and the potentially disruptive new rules imposed by a Western man. Carré's contributions to the representation of Japan changed the relationship between the two civilizations in the opera, moving the center of gravity to the East. In Paris, the excision of the short *buffa* scenes gave back at least some dignity to the Japanese characters, which were now much more forcefully contrasted with the Western ones. This also afforded greater psychological coherence to the female protagonist, whose unwavering refusal to adapt to her society's custom of arranged marriages provides the scaffolding for the catastrophe.

The most obvious sign of Carré's desire to downplay the servile behavior of the Japanese characters is found, however, at the very beginning: Cio-Cio-san and her friends enter the scene with dignified composure and do not kneel down to the incarnation of the Western god in an officer's uniform, but instead bow gracefully in a courteous gesture consistent with their custom (MES, 61). This will also be the behavior of the relatives at the end of the post-wedding *concertato*, a scene in which they do not throng the refreshments table as they had done in Milan (MES, 80).

Pinkerton also comes across as less vulgar on the Paris stage. Yet, though he no longer openly mocks the servants as he had done at La Scala in 1904, he still walks away irritably from Suzuki and continues to talk and laugh with the Consul when the relatives arrive; what is more, besides drinking whiskey with his compatriot, he boldly lights up a cigarette before intoning the hymn to the "Yankee vagabondo" (MES, 55). He then proceeds to show off his wealth by paying for the imperial commissary and a musician, thus further humiliating his wife's impoverished family. Given the disappearance from the French version of nearly all of the clumsy behavior of the Japanese characters, including the uncle's annoying drunkenness, Pinkerton is left fully responsible for expressions such as "Faisons vite, la famille est bouffonne, que l'Hymen ici me donne!" (Let's hurry up, it is a ludicrous family that marriage gives me here), which betray his racist prejudices. Carré was certainly not kind with the standard bearer of crass Occidentalism.

Figure 5. Marcel Jambon and Alexandre Bailly, sketch for Act 2 of
Madama Butterfly, Paris, Opéra-Comique, 1906.

Goro, the ensign of cultural contamination who serves as the suture
between East and West, maintains his role in Paris, albeit with a few changes
to further assimilate his behavior to Western models. Carré has him pour
the beverages himself (MES, 54), thus pointing to his familiarity with
American customs. Always attentive to practical demands over the course
of the wedding ceremony, he claps his hands to signal the beginning of
the reception, and steals away behind relatives after the Bonze unleashes
his wrath upon the scene. In Act 2, his utilitarian behavior provokes a
much stronger reaction in the protagonist. When he smirks at Butterfly's
recounting of Pinkerton's unkept promises, she walks over toward him
threateningly and then strikes him (MES, 106). Later, after Suzuki drags
him back onstage, Butterfly throws herself upon him brandishing a knife:
she is furious to hear from her servant that he goes around saying that
nobody knows the identity of the father of her child (MES, 119).

In the original version Prince Yamadori was to take on an analogous
role to Goro, and was therefore "vestito all'Europea" (dressed in the

Figure 6. Carlo Songa, sketch for Act 2 of *Madama Butterfly*,
Milan, Teatro alla Scala, 1904.

European style). Yet the Yamadori episode takes on a unique role in
Carré's staging, as we learn from Puccini's enthusiastic description of a
key detail in the letter to Giulio Ricordi of 25 November:

> Yamadori does not enter the room but instead sits courte-
> ously on the stoop outside the garden: because you must
> know that the level of the room was raised forty centimeters
> above the stage and they specially built a small, lighted plat-
> form for it, and most of the thickness of the raised platform
> facing the audience is covered by flowers. The garden thus
> remains forty centimeters below.[10]

Carré simply writes "Prince Yamadori has moved toward the house, but
remains in the garden" (MES, 108), because the manual has already
indicated that the little house, shown from outdoors in Act 1 and as a
cross-section of the interior opening on the veranda in Act 2, is raised
forty centimeters above stage level (MES, 44–45 and 96; see Figure 5).
No such elevation appears in the scene for Act 2 in Milan (Figure 6).
This is not just a detail, but rather forms part of a strategy that coher-
ently outlines Cio-Cio-san's psychology as she relates to the world that
surrounds her. Carré steadily pursued his intent to separate Butterfly's
illusory microcosm from reality, thus increasing the importance of the

role of the Consul, the only character who can enter into the protagonist's "American" world.

Pinkerton's two wives meet in the opera's finale, an epilogue that took its shape thanks to a few textual modifications that radically changed the audience's perspective of the action on stage. Carré immediately showed the Western woman to the audience, thus confining her to the emblematic role she will maintain in the following scenes (MES, 137). After deciding— during the drafting stage of the libretto—to eliminate the scene set in the American consulate, where Cio-Cio-san was to meet her rival before the finale, Puccini had felt the need to tighten Kate's scene, and communicated this to Illica.[11] If up until the Paris version Kate and Suzuki had walked into the house from the garden, thus giving Butterfly the opportunity to address Kate directly, in Paris the heroine turns to Sharpless instead, in a moment of desperate realization: "Quella donna? Che vuol da me?" (That woman? What does she want from me?). Originally, Kate had been meant to gently approach the heroine, be rejected, and then sing the line "È triste cosa" (It's a sad thing), showing herself to be profoundly moved; nowadays we see the same scene unfold (with a modified text) between Butterfly and the Consul.[12] Despite Kate's compassionate demeanor, the line that now defines her character, delivered in the deafening silence that dominates this scene, is the cruel and inhumanely pragmatic question that she poses to Sharpless: "E il figlio lo darà?" (So, will she give up her son?). Although not meant to be heard by Butterfly, the protagonist nonetheless overhears it, and perceives it as a further, final blow.

In his review of the Paris premiere, critic Henri de Curzon described the finale of the opera with the following words: "In the denouement, Pinkerton's new wife turns out to be the person sent out to look for the child. [. . .] Mr. Carré has left the foreigner in the distance, in the garden, like a passing shadow." This passing shadow condenses the idea that governs both the staging and the drama at large: Pinkerton's wife is translated into a ghost. Puccini's letter to Ricordi of 25 November 1906 shows that he had no reservations about the finale of the new version:

> I have the score nearly ready, tomorrow it will be completed and as far as the mise-en-scène goes, shall I leave it as it is or have the important things changed? Carré has changed nearly everything, and has done it well. [. . .] Everything has been well rehearsed and I hope it will be a really good performance. Act 3 as Carré has done it (taking away much of Kate's part and having this woman stay outside in the

garden, which is at the same level as the stage and without the hedge, that is, without obstacles) pleases me very much.[13]

Although Puccini had had doubts about Kate's scene even before the Milan premiere, it was only in Paris that he settled on a solution he found entirely satisfactory, and explicitly credited Carré and his idea to keep Pinkerton's American wife "outside in the garden." Kate's modified role and the transferring of her lines to Cio-Cio-san and the Consul allow for a more coherent dramatic unfolding. The blocking for the character of the American wife takes on a key role: left outside the room, as had been the case with Yamadori, she becomes a ghostly projection of the protagonist's private obsessions, and will remain substantially foreign to her. Kate's complete lack of musical personality—she is given but a few notes in a musical world in which everything is intensely connotated—makes her character entirely functional: when Butterfly finds Kate standing before her, she will grasp in one moment all that she has refused to understand up until then.

A final staging detail works to lend symmetry to the narrative as it returns full circle, in perfect tandem with the musical conclusion on an unresolved first-inversion chord—the same chord that had closed Act 1. After gently pushing her child into the garden and before committing suicide, the heroine locks herself in (MES, 152–53), using the same locks she had referred to at the beginning of Act 2, when she had interpreted them positively, a sign of Pinkerton's jealousy and therefore love. Not only does the gesture color the ritual sacrifice with a touch of grim irony, but it also emphasizes Butterfly's final realization of her situation. She now understands that she has been locked into a cage ever since Pinkerton left, and now locks the room herself, so that nothing and no one may prevent her from dying.

Excerpts from
Albert Carré's Staging Manual for *Madama Butterfly*

Théâtre National de l'Opéra-Comique

Madame Butterfly

A Japanese Tragedy

In three acts,

by Msrs. L. Illica et Giacosa.

Translated by M. Paul Ferrier.

Music by Mr. Giacomo Puccini
Staging
by Mr. Albert Carré

And recorded by Mr. Carbonne

English translation by Steven Huebner

Cast of Characters

Pinkerton	M. M. Ed.[mond] Clément
Sharpless	" Jean Périer
Goro	" [Émile] Cazaneuve
The Bonze	" [Gustave] Huberdeau
Prince Yamadori	" [Fernand] Francell
Yakuside	" [Louis] Azéma
The Imperial Commissioner	" de Potter
The Registry Officer	" [André] Février
Madame Butterfly	Mes Marguerite Carré
Suzuki	" B[erthe] Lamare
Kate	" [Marguerite] Beriza
The Cousin	" R[achel] Launay
The Aunt	" Villette
The Child	La petite Planson

Act I

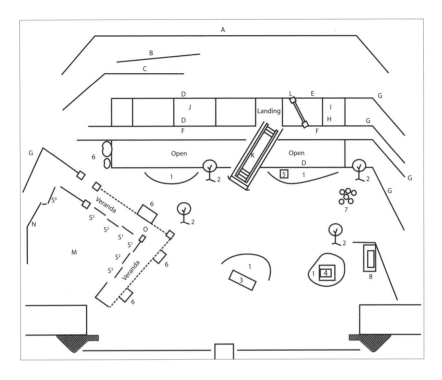

A: Backdrop showing Nagasaki, its harbor, and the sea. – B: City views. – C: Flat representing the city. – D: Flowers and greenery. – E: Large flat showing the Bonze's temple on the upper right. – F: Flat running above, delimiting the open area facing the audience. To the left of the bridge, flowers. To the right of the bridge, greenery and rocks. – G: Flat showing trees. – H: Small flat with greenery and rocks. – I: Elevated platform leading to the Bonze's temple. – J: Platform with broad stairs descending to the first lower level (Platforms I and J meet at a landing at the bridge). – K: Japanese arched bridge. – L: Decorative portico (Japanese *dori*). – M: Butterfly's house (on a platform). – N: Interior in the background (partial representation of the Act 2 interior). O: Veranda on the same level as the interior. – S: Numbered shoji screens on sliding tracks, S^0 shoji in the back, S^1 S^2 S^3 shojis foreground – S^1 S^2 S^3 shojis in the background.

1: Grassy mounds with rocks and flower pots. – 2: Natural-growth trees – willow, cherry trees, green bamboo, wisteria. – 3: Rustic bench. – 4: Large stone lantern. – 5: Small wood lantern on a tree trunk. – 6: Rocks. – 7: A group of tree trunks joined together, on which flower pots have been placed. – 8: Set of shelves for vases and plants – dwarf trees in various pots.

A garden designed in Japanese style with flower beds bordered by large rocks on which plants in porcelain pots have been placed. Toward the middle, a garden bench. To the right, a set of shelves holding plants, all in pots. Also to the right, a large stone lantern. To the left, at an oblique angle, the house raised by 40 centimeters. Access is gained by three large rocks that take the place of stairs. The house is surrounded by a narrow veranda. It is closed off by sliding shojis (screens made of paper tiles that slide on tracks). Wisteria travels along the roof and its flowering tendrils fall over the facade. Beyond the garden, a path rises from left to right. At center stage, a walkable bridge leads into the garden. To the right, a path leads underneath a "dori," a religious portico, to the Bonze's temple located high above in the wings, stage left.[1] In the background, the city, the port, and Nagasaki's harbor as seen from the top of the hill.

Props

In the house

A mat, trimmed in black, covering the entire floor of House M. – Four cushions on the mat. – *Kakemono* scroll hanging on the wall N, visible to the audience. – A small Japanese dressing table with mirror. – A square stool, made of bamboo and fairly high. This stool is moved to the middle of the room for the marriage; it is used as a table during the ceremony. The Imperial Commissioner places it in front of himself. The Official Registrar stands to one side and Butterfly kneels in front of it.

---

1. Carré's "left" and "right" are from the audience's point of view. However, when the locutions "stage left" and "stage right" appear, they are meant from the actors' point of view, as is customary in English (they translate "coté cour" and "coté jardin" respectively). Therefore, here, for example, the path "to the right" leads to the Bonze's temple, located "stage left." (This and all the following footnotes to the manual excerpts are mine. —E. S.)

In the wings, stage right

A full tray of European drinks on which are placed: a bottle of whiskey – two metal tumblers with drinking straws – two carafes filled with punch–glasses, one of which is filled with crushed ice; some spoons; two lemons. – Two small trays with little Japanese cups or bowls for the refreshments the servants carry onstage after the marriage and present to the guests. – Six electric lanterns on bamboo poles for six male relatives who will carry them for the marriage ceremony. – The same kind of electric lantern for Goro. – The same kind of electric lanterns for the three servants. – Ten electric lanterns without bamboo poles for the lighting on the house's facade. – Two lantern-lighters. – A Japanese musical instrument, which is brought into the room when the marriage ceremony takes place.

Stage left

Two electric lanterns for the carriers (two) who precede the Bonze.

For the artists

Butterfly: a parasol, a fan to put in her sleeve, paper tissues; an opium pipe; a belt; a small clip; a mirror; a fan; a small bottle of dye; a sabre or long Japanese knife; *ottokis* (small statuettes of the gods).
Pinkerton: a cigarette case; a box of matches.
Sharpless: A European umbrella (bright color).
Registry Officer: an inkpot, with pen and accessories. A role of parchment for the contract.
Geishas, Relatives, and Friends: 14 parasols; 22 fans.
Two Japanese children (Guests): For each a bamboo pole on which trinkets are fastened; small balloons; dolls; flags, etc. . . . a cardboard baby doll that a young Japanese girl carries on her back.

Act II

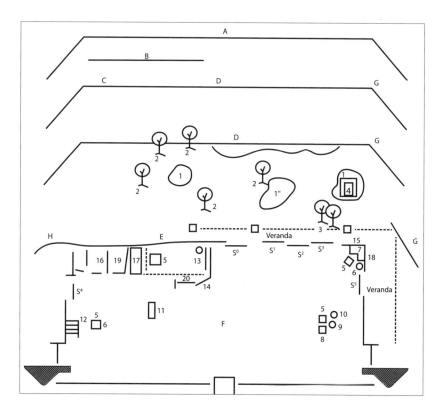

A: Backdrop showing Nagasaki, its harbor, and the sea. – B: City views. – C: Flat representing the city. – D: Low flower beds. – E: Alcove containing a family altar to Buddha. F: The interior of the house on a platform 40 centimeters high. – G: Flats with trees. – H: Back of the interior. $S^0 S^1 S^2 S^3$ shojis, sliding screens that open on the garden. – S^4 shoji opening into Butterfly's bedroom. – S^5 shoji on the right opening to the exterior.

1 and 1": Grassy mounds with rocks and pots of flowers. – 2: Natural-growth trees. – 3: A cherry tree with two spreading branches between which Butterfly sits. – 4: Large stone lantern. – 5. Small mats. – 6: Vases containing wilted flowers. – 7: Wooden shelves in a corner cupboard holding three vases containing slightly wilted flowers. 8: A Japanese makeup mirror on a stand to which a small hand mirror for Butterfly is attached with a string. – 9: Japanese vase shaped like a bamboo stalk containing flowers. – 10: Makeup kit containing a brush, rouge, a comb, and some

hairpins. – 11: Japanese headrest. – 12: A *hibachi*, a kind of brazier, to heat tea. – 13: Round Japanese stool, made of straw. – 14: Screen. – 15: Sailor's telescope attached to doorframe. – 16: A set of shelves with closed compartments, containing the following objects:[2] in the lowest compartment, closed by no. 8, the white veil and a Japanese money box; above: no. 1, a little Japanese wicker basket; no. 2, a Japanese box; no. 3, a smoker's supply box, containing an opium pipe, a box of matches, tobacco containers; no. 4, a bronze vase; no. 5, a picture of Pinkerton; no. 6, a smoker's supply box; no. 7, a carton of American cigarettes. – 17: An altar to Buddha with the following objects:[3] no. 1, two Japanese electric lanterns lit like nightlights; no. 2, two Japanese vases with flowers; no. 3, a small wooden bell with stick to call upon the gods; no. 4, Buddha; no. 5, short sabre. – 18: A small extravagant Japanese basket attached to the wall. – 19: *Kakemono* scroll attached to the wall above the Buddha. – 20: Butterfly's dress hung in the alcove behind the sliding screen. A Japanese mat bordered with black bands producing a frame around the middle covers the entire floor of the house.

Butterfly's House

The floor is raised about 40 centimeters over the stage. A room with little depth. To the rear left, taking up about half the width, a kind of alcove containing the family altar. In this recess, to the left, a statue of Buddha. On the altar, two Japanese lamps that can be switched on. Small wood bells to attract the gods' attention. Two flower vases. A short sabre suspended by a string on the left corner of the altar. On the rear wall of the alcove *kakemono* scrolls painted in very soft hues. To the right, set apart near the alcove, a sliding screen. To the left, built into a partition, a small set of shelves the lower part of which can be closed by panels on sliding tracks. Some Japanese boxes, and the white veil that Butterfly uses in Act 3, are kept inside, behind the panels. On the shelves, a smoker's supply box, the opium pipe, carton of cigarettes, matches. Little Japanese knickknacks, the framed picture of Pinkerton. On the right in the rear, sliding shojis open, acting as a large picture window onto the garden. – In the garden to the right, near the house, a large flowering cherry tree.

---

2. A small drawing of the set of shelves shows exactly where the objects must be placed; the numbers in the text refer to this drawing.
3. A small drawing of the altar shows exactly where the objects must be placed; the numbers in the text refer to this drawing.

In the background, a view of Nagasaki and the shore. – Shoji or sliding door on the left leading to the bedroom. – To the right a sliding door leading outside. To the left, in the foreground, on the ground against the partition, a small brazier to heat tea. – Downstage left, a Japanese headrest. To the right, a small Japanese makeup table with mirror. In the rear right corner, positioned at an angle, a set of shelves with vases and flowers. On the frame of the open doors to the rear, on the right, a sailor's telescope hangs from a nail. The floor is entirely covered with mats bordered in black. All shoji doors are on tracks. Wall decorations are very plain.

Props

In the wings

Two interior lamps, lit with matches. A kind of wood cube on a pedestal, open on the top with a fixed handle and paper tiles.[4] – A tray used for cups and tea service. – Three large sprays of flowers: one in the wings, stage left, another in the wings, stage right, and the third spread behind the flower pots placed on the grassy knoll 1" in the middle of the garden.

Stage left

Prince Yamadori's litter or sedan chair. A certain number of cut cherry blossoms that will be thrown at Butterfly when she sits on tree no. 3. These flowers are to appear as if they fall from the tree when it is shaken.

For the artists

For *Sharpless*, a letter; for *Butterfly's child*, a Japanese puppet (toy).

---

4. A small drawing of the wood cube shows exactly what is meant here.

Act III

"Suzuki! Where are you?"[5] [*Suzuki! Dove sei?*]

Sharpless motions to Kate to hide in the garden. Kate stays behind a stone lantern. Suzuki goes to the left, toward the bedroom.

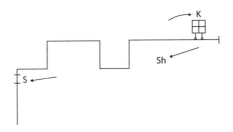

"I was praying and putting things back." [*Pregavo e rimettevo a posto.*]

At the orchestra measure that follows, Butterfly opens the shoji of the bedroom and appears at the door on the left. She wants to come in. Suzuki stops her and wants to prevent her from entering.

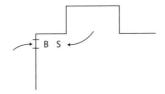

"He's here, he's here." [*È qui, è qui.*]

Butterfly pushes Suzuki aside and comes onstage.

"He's here, he's here." [*È qui, è qui.*]

Butterfly moves to the right upstage from Suzuki and finds herself face to face with Sharpless. She stops in her tracks, surprised. The Consul bows.

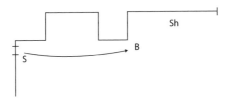

---

5. As explained in the introduction, we reproduce here the portion of Act 3 from Butterfly's entrance to the end of the opera.

"And where? where?" [*e dove? dove?*]

Uneasy, she goes to look behind the screen.

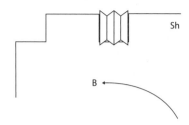

During the orchestra measures that follow

Butterfly goes to look out the door on the right. She opens the shoji, does not see anyone, and closes it again.

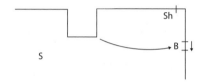

"He's not here!" [*Non c'è!*]

In the following orchestra measures, Butterfly returns to the left of the window, near the screen, opens shoji no. 0 that looks into the garden. She sees Kate.

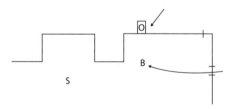

"That woman?" [*Quella donna?*]

Butterfly addresses Sharpless with concern. Suzuki at left, turning her back to Butterfly, weeps.

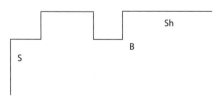

"What does she want from me?" [*Che vuol da me?*]

Kate reveals herself a bit in the garden. Butterfly steps back, anxious and surprised.

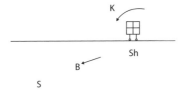

"No one speaks!" [*Niuno parla!*]

Butterfly looks at Sharpless and Suzuki who remain motionless. Butterfly goes over to Suzuki.

"Why are you crying?" [*Perché piangete?*]

Butterfly spins Suzuki around, pulling violently on her arm. Suzuki falls to her knees and weeps, holding her head in her hands. Sharpless advances toward Butterfly to speak to her. Butterfly turns around, and seeing Sharpless approach lets go of Suzuki and gestures to Sharpless to stop . . . she fears the truth and says:

"No! tell me nothing!" [*No: non ditemi nulla!*]

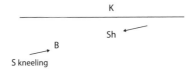

"You, Suzuki." [*Tu, Suzuki.*]

Butterfly goes toward Suzuki and kneels by her, affectionately takes her by the arms and questions her in a feverish manner.

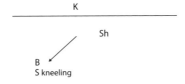

"He'll come no more. They have told you!" [*Ma non viene più. Te l'han detto!*]
  Suzuki turns her head away to the right, not daring to answer.
At measure 12, page 233[6]
  Butterfly lifts Suzuki's head, turns it toward her and tries to read the
  truth in her face. Suzuki turns away and lowers her head without
  answering.
"Wasp! I want you to reply!" [*Vespa! voglio che tu risponda!*]
  Butterfly, irritated by Suzuki's silence, lifts her head again with both
  hands and shakes it violently. In the garden, Kate has come forward
  to listen.
"He arrived yesterday? – Yes." [*Ma è giunto ieri? – Sì.*]
  Butterfly remains dumbfounded.
"Ah! That woman terrifies me!" page 234 [*Ah ! quella donna mi fa tanta
  paura!*]
  Butterfly gets up quickly, and runs in Kate's direction, crossing to
  the right, her back to the audience, looking toward the garden. Kate
  listens and watches the whole scene. Sharpless, seeing Butterfly's
  actions, approaches and takes her in his arms, stopping her.
  Butterfly, restrained by Sharpless, turns before him.

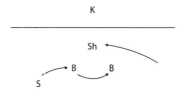

"Ah! she's his wife!" last line, page 234 [*Ah! è sua moglie!*]
  Extremely agitated, Butterfly addresses Sharpless and pushes him
  roughly and nervously to the left. He backs up somewhat. Then
  Butterfly stops cold.

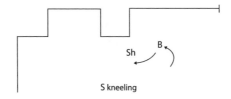

---

6. This page number refers to the piano-vocal score, as do the others below.

"Everything is over!" page 235 [*tutto è finito!*]
  Butterfly collapses, arms stretched forward, into Sharpless's arms,
  and he holds and supports her in a paternal manner. Suzuki rises and
  makes a movement toward Butterfly to help her.

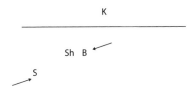

"To take everything from me! My child!" [*Prendermi tutto! il figlio mio!*]
  Butterfly anxiously questions Sharpless, who turns his head away and
  dares not answer. Suzuki runs to the door of the bedroom, to the left,
  closes the sliding screen, and crouches in front of it on her knees as if
  to bar entry.

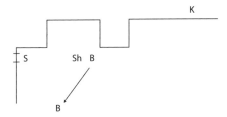

"Make this sacrifice for him." page 236, first line [Sharpless:[7] *Fatelo pel
suo bene il sacrifizio.*]
  Butterfly questions Sharpless with hopeless despair.
"Ah! Sad mother!" [*Ah! triste madre!*]
  Kate moves toward the house.

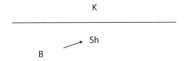

---

7. When it is not clear from the text of the staging manual we have added the name of
the character singing the line.

"Abandon my child!" [*Abbandonar mio figlio!*]
Butterfly weeps in Sharpless's arms.
"So be it! I must obey him!" [*E sia! a lui debbo obbedir!*]
Butterfly straightens herself, resigned, and with the greatest sorrow.
"Can you forgive me, Butterfly?" [Kate: *Potete perdonarmi, Butterfly?*]
Kate, in the garden, starts to move toward Butterfly.
"Beneath the great vault of the sky." [Butterfly: *Sotto il gran ponte del cielo.*]
Supported by Sharpless, Butterfly remains facing the audience, immobile, not looking at Kate.
"But I would like that he be told."[8]
Butterfly addresses Sharpless, beseeching him.
"Mercy! Not that!" last measure, page 237
Butterfly crosses left, passing in front of Sharpless with a pronounced gesture of refusal.

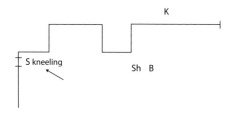

"Poor little one!" [Kate: *Povera piccina!*]
Sharpless returns to Kate upstage.

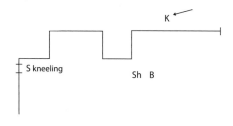

---

8. This line and the following one were cut from the final Italian version; the French text reads: "Mais je voudrais pourtant qu'on le lui dise"; "Par grâce! pas cela!"

"I will give him his son." [*A lui lo potrò dare.*]

Butterfly delivers this whole phrase facing the audience, looking neither at Kate nor Sharpless.

"If he comes to fetch him." [*se lo verrà a cercare.*]

Suzuki, in front of the bedroom door on the left, half rises.

At the last measure of page 238

Sharpless gestures to Kate to leave. Kate begins to return upstage in order to exit on the right. Suzuki rises completely to stand before the bedroom door and stretches her arms against the partition as if to prevent entry.

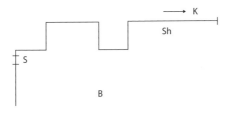

"Climb the hill in half an hour." [Butterfly: *Fra mezz'ora salite la collina.*]

Kate exits the garden to the right. Sharpless follows her. After having followed all of Butterfly's gestures, he leaves very concerned and resolved to take action with Pinkerton because he has guessed Butterfly's thoughts and intentions.

The 2/4 allegro that follows begins only after the departure of Kate and Sharpless

On the first chord, Butterfly, who remains still and restrained until then, suddenly collapses and falls outstretched, her face to the ground. Suzuki goes to help Butterfly and kneels to console her.

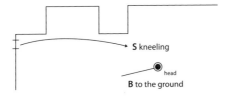

"Too much light shines outside." [Butterfly: *Troppa luce è di fuor.*]
Butterfly, recovering somewhat, raises herself.
"Close it!" [*Chiudi.*]

During the orchestra measures that follow, Suzuki rises to close the shojis at the rear right. She begins by pushing shojis nos. 1, 2, and 3 from right to left, and the little shoji no. 0 from left to right. The view is thus closed.

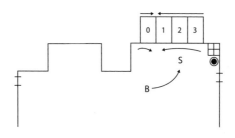

Suzuki then returns to Butterfly, still prostrate.

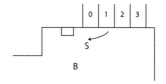

"He is playing . . . Shall I call him?" [*Giuoca ... lo chiamo?*]
Suzuki passes behind Butterfly, moving to the bedroom on the left.

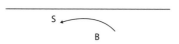

"Let him play . . . go and keep him company," [*Lascialo giuocar ... va a fargli compagnia.*]

Butterfly gets up quickly and goes to Suzuki, pushing her toward the bedroom.

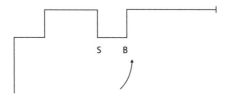

Suzuki, staring at Butterfly and understanding her intentions, stops and
  firmly decides not to leave. She falls to her knees at Butterfly's feet,
  implores, begs her to let her stay.
"Go, go. I order it." [*Va, va. Te lo comando.*]
  Butterfly goes to Suzuki, highly agitated, and forces her to go into
  the bedroom by pushing and shoving her. Violent skirmish. Suzuki
  drags herself on her knees behind Butterfly, who keeps pushing her
  away. Screams and tears, Suzuki's supplications.
Toward measure 10 on page 242
  Suzuki is pushed back into the bedroom. Butterfly closes the sliding
  door on her. We hear Suzuki weep and beg in the bedroom. The
  sobbing weakens little by little.

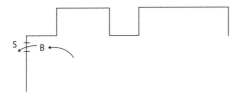

At measure 13 of the orchestral passage (*Meno*) on page 242
  Butterfly goes to the little piece of furniture to the left of Buddha
  and takes the white veil from a lower compartment, which is closed
  by panel no. 8.

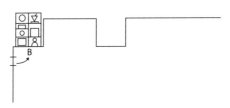

She takes from an open compartment of the same piece of furniture
  the portrait of Pinkerton, which she kisses. She then goes toward the altar.
First measure, page 243
  Butterfly kneels in the recess of the altar, places Pinkerton's portrait in
  front of her and prays.

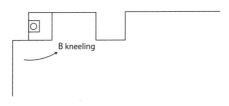

At measure 11, page 243

Butterfly seizes the Japanese knife suspended on the left corner of the Buddha altar.

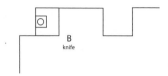

"He dies honorably" etc. [*Con onor muore*]

Butterfly on her knees, holding the knife handle in her right hand reads the words engraved on the blade in a religious manner.

"Survives with honor" [*serbar vita con onore*]

During the four orchestra measures that follow, Butterfly covers her hand holding the knife with the veil.

At the orchestra measures of the first line, page 244

The sliding door of the bedroom opens and on measure 6 (second line), the child, pushed by Suzuki, comes onstage and runs to Butterfly, arms outstretched. Suzuki's arm is seen passing through the door, pushing the child (c) toward his mother. Butterfly quickly hides the knife in the ground near the screen.

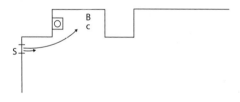

"You? You?" [*Tu? tu?*]

Butterfly takes her child in her arms and drags herself forward on her knees.

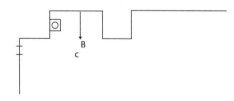

"You must never know it." [*Non saperlo mai.*]
  Butterfly, kneeling, holds the child in her arms. He stands before
  her, a little to the left and his back to the audience, facing his mother.
"Sent to me from the throne." [*O a me, sceso dal trono.*]
  Butterfly caresses the child.
"Look carefully! Farewell, beloved!" [*guarda ben! Amore addio!*]
  Butterfly takes the head of the child in her hands.
"Farewell, my little love!" [*addio! piccolo amor!*]
  Butterfly gives a long kiss to her child with all her soul.
"Go! Play! play!" [*Va. Gioca, gioca!*]
  Butterfly rises and guides the child toward the shoji screens at the
  rear right. She opens shoji no. 2 and gently pushes the child into the
  garden, and then closes it.

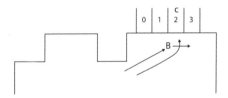

At measure 5, page 247
  Butterfly goes to the door on the right and positions a small peg with
  a chain to take the place of a bolt.

At measure 8, page 247
  Butterfly crosses the stage to the bedroom where she also positions a
  peg, and thereby locks the house.

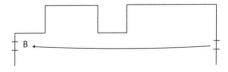

At measure 9

Butterfly goes to the altar and kneels near the screen.

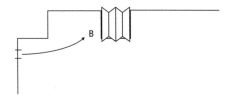

At measure 12

Butterfly takes the knife, covers it with the white veil and prepares to strike herself. She goes behind the screen.

At the beginning of the last measure, page 247

Butterfly strikes. The knife is heard falling from behind the screen.

After the first "Butterfly!"

Pinkerton calls from the wings, stage left. Butterfly, her neck enveloped in the veil to hide her wound, appears on her knees from behind the screen.

At the second "Butterfly!"

Butterfly comes onstage, dragging herself on the ground and holding her bandaged neck with her hand.

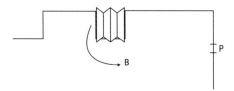

After the third "Butterfly!"

She crawls dragging herself on the ground and goes toward the door, stage left, to open it.

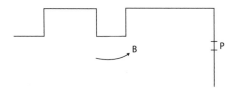

At the 3/4 measure, measure 15, page 248

Exhausted, Butterfly falls to the ground.

At the 4/4 measure, measure 16

She gets up and again starts towards the door, dragging herself.
Pinkerton knocks on the door.

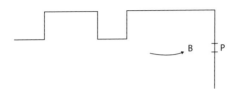

In the orchestra measures that follow

She continues to drag herself toward the door.

At measures 3 and 4 of the last line

Butterfly, still dragging herself, tries to get to the door. With super-
human effort she gets up, but then falls dead just before the last
measure.

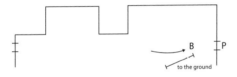

Curtain falls quickly.

The End

NOTES

1. For a thoroughly documented summary of the revisions of *Madama Butterfly*, see Dieter Schickling, *Giacomo Puccini: Catalogue of the Works* (Kassel: Bärenreiter, 2003), 283–87.

2. The opera was performed in three acts, as was always the case, except at the Milan premiere, which was in two acts. The present introduction is based on the much longer version, titled "Le droghe della scena parigina," in the critical edition of Carré's *Livret*: *"Madama Butterfly," mise en scène di Albert Carré*, ed. Michele Girardi, *Disposizioni sceniche e livrets de mise en scène*, vol. 4, Edizione nazionale delle opere di Giacomo Puccini 3 (Turin: EDT, 2012), 3–31; for details of the various documents on which the edition is based, see 35–38. References to the text of the staging manual (39–155) will be indicated as MES in text citations.

3. Mercedes Viale Ferrero, "Staging Rossini," in *The Cambridge Companion to Rossini*, ed. Emanuele Senici (Cambridge: Cambridge University Press, 2004), 212. Viale Ferrero's general description also includes costumes, but Carré's *livret* does not contain information on them.

4. For the Bologna performances of October 1905, Puccini instructed Toscanini regarding the opera's final scene, requesting "a violent ray of sunlight, strong, and a wide strip of light within which the final scene will take place." *Carteggi pucciniani*, ed. Eugenio Gara (Milan: Ricordi, 1958), 299.

5. See Arthur Groos, "Lieutenant F. B. Pinkerton: Problems in the Genesis and Performance of *Madama Butterfly*," in *The Puccini Companion*, ed. William Weaver and Simonetta Puccini (New York and London: W. W. Norton, 1994), 169–201.

6. In 1893 *Madame Chrysanthème* was adapted for the stage by Georges Hartmann and Alexandre André and set to music by a composer who was very close to Carré, André Messager.

7. Sada Yakko's fame had risen with the Kawakami Play Company's Paris *tournée*: she charmed the French public at the Universal Exposition of 1900 by interpreting the female lead in *La Ghèsha et le samouraï*.

8. On Albert Kahn (1860–1940), the utopian philantropist who went bankrupt in the 1929 financial crisis, see *Albert Kahn, réalités d'une utopie (1860–1940)*, ed. Jeanne Beausoleil and Pascal Ory (Boulogne-Billancourt: Musée Albert-Kahn, 1995).

9. It is, however, important to remember that the Japanese bridge was a recurrent object in *japoniste* French iconography at the time, and was even more generally featured in visual arts—see, for instance, Vincent van Gogh's *Pont sous la pluie (d'après Hiroshige)* (1887). My critical edition of Carré's staging manual contains many images that help contextualize the iconography of the scenes for the Opéra-Comique production, and chart their influence on later productions of *Madama Butterfly*.

10. Giacomo Puccini, *Epistolario*, ed. Giuseppe Adami, 2nd ed. (Milan: Mondadori, 1982), 101.

11. See Puccini's letter of 31 January 1903, in *Carteggi pucciniani*, 232. The draft of the consulate scene can be read both in Illica's and Giacosa's versions in Arthur Groos, "Luigi Illica's Libretto for *Madama Butterfly* (1901)," *Studi pucciniani* 2 (2000): 91–204.

12. See Girardi, "Le droghe della scena parigina," 28–29.

13. Adami, *Epistolario*, 101.

Selections from Fausto Torrefranca's
Giacomo Puccini and International Opera

INTRODUCTION BY ALEXANDRA WILSON
TRANSLATION BY DELIA CASADEI

Giacomo Puccini e l'opera internazionale (1912) is one of the most important Puccini reception documents of the composer's lifetime: an audacious 133-page diatribe by a twenty-nine-year-old critic and aspiring musicologist, Fausto Torrefranca.[1] Of noble Sicilian descent, the grandly named Fausto Acanfora Sansone dei duchi di Porta e dei duchi di Torrefranca graduated from the Turin Polytechnic in 1905, before changing direction and becoming a prolific writer about music. In 1912 Torrefranca, a musical autodidact, had already established a reputation as a critic and was about to embark upon a career as a music academic and librarian; eventually, in the 1940s, he would become the first holder of a music professorship in Italy. His Puccini book is structured in four sections. The first, "Psychology of Puccinian Opera," discusses the decadence of Italian opera and Puccini's personality; the second, "The Artistic Life of Puccini and His Background," is a caustic biographical profile and commentary on Puccini's operas up to 1910. The third, "Puccini, Man of the Theater," examines Puccini's attitudes toward dramatic structure and characterization, and the final section "Puccini the Musician?" is an assessment of the composer's musical style and influences.

Torrefranca's book was part of a wider movement by a small group of early twentieth-century Italian intellectuals to challenge national musical orthodoxies, particularly the long-standing obsession with opera. It was published by the Turin-based publishing house Fratelli Bocca, which also published *Rivista musicale italiana* (*RMI*), Italy's most serious-minded music journal, founded by Luigi Torchi in 1894, which was well known for its hostility toward contemporary Italian opera.[2] It was *RMI* that offered Torrefranca his first professional experience as a writer about music: from 1907 on he contributed historical articles and reviews of books such as Wagner's complete prose works.[3] For Torrefranca, Puccini was merely the most prominent embodiment of a wider artistic malaise. The young critic lamented a national musical culture that he characterized as mediocre, limited, cliché-ridden, and crassly commercial, and criticized the "cultural semi-illiteracy" of most of the Italian population.[4] Opera was, for Torrefranca, an ephemeral type of music that appealed to the cultural "working classes," and he depicted Italy as a nation that did not even know its own "real" musical history.[5] (A subsection of the book is emphatically titled "The History of Italian Music Is Not the History of Opera.")[6] The nineteenth century was, according to Torrefranca, an aberration in the context of Italian music history.[7] He and his circle were committed to the revival of early Italian instrumental music and to the promotion of contemporary Italian non-operatic music.[8] Torrefranca saw himself as spearheading a young generation of critics and musicians that was willing to raise its voice in protest against a prevailing culture in which the majority of music journals and composers were bound up in a commercial relationship with publishing houses.[9]

By the time Torrefranca's book was published, Puccini's status as Italy's most successful and popular composer and the successor to Verdi was confirmed: his operas *Manon Lescaut, La bohème, Tosca,* and *Madama Butterfly* were firmly established in the international repertory, even if the early reception of some of these works had been somewhat fraught.[10] Torrefranca's book stands in sharp contrast to the gushing, hyperbolic, and nationalistically inspired enthusiasm for Puccini that was disseminated widely by his publisher Ricordi and by other sectors of the press. However, the book appeared at a difficult moment for Puccini. Following *Madama Butterfly*, which had prompted a near riot in its first incarnation, there had been a hiatus of six years before Puccini's next opera, *La fanciulla del West*, which had, in turn, attracted considerable criticism at its New York premiere in 1910 and subsequent performances in Italy. As Puccini embarked upon a more modern course in his music—*Fanciulla* was widely considered to have ushered in a distinctive second stylistic phase in his career—it seemed that he could please nobody: the forward-looking techniques used in *Fanciulla*, influenced by foreign musical trends, were considered too modern by conservative commentators and not modern enough by the modernists.[11]

A concern about internationalism lies at the heart of Torrefranca's polemic, as the title of his book indicates: he calls Puccini "the international opera composer *par excellence*."[12] Although published in 1912, the book was written in 1910, just as the furor over *La fanciulla del West* was breaking. Torrefranca was profoundly unimpressed by Puccini's engagement with a range of foreign musical influences. The composer, he argued, picked at various different national styles and cobbled together their crudest features in ad hoc fashion to create a sort of musical patchwork quilt or mosaic. Puccini could pass himself off, to a limited extent, in these various musical "languages"—at least to the uninformed listener—but the musical result was deceitful and lacked any distinctive or original characteristics of its own. Ironically, Torrefranca's rhetoric was hardly original: his comments about Puccini are disturbingly reminiscent of comments Wagner had made about the linguistic and musical abilities of Jews in his essay *Das Judenthum in der Musik*, which had been translated into Italian and published in the *Rivista musicale italiana* in 1897.[13] Although Puccini was not Jewish, Torrefranca sought to depict him as an outsider as part of a broader strategy to undermine the received wisdom that lyric opera was the "indigenous" music of Italy. Even within the debased world of opera, as Torrefranca saw it, Puccini was a particularly offensive figure. To the outside world he seemed to represent musical Italy, yet in Torrefranca's summing up he was the best exemplar of the "progressive *de-nationalization* of the Italian lyric theater."[14] Anxiety about musical "internationalism" was a pan-European phenomenon in the early decades of the twentieth century; in the late 1920s a British journal reported that "as Ravel once remarked, the nationalists of all countries are friends, their enemy is international."[15]

Torrefranca also attempted to humiliate and undermine Puccini by associating him with a variety of other "weak" or "insignificant" figures within contemporary Italian society. Puccini was, Torrefranca argued, "the perfect womanly musician," and not only womanly but comparable to a lower-class, ignorant, and silly woman.[16] In the context of the Italy of the 1910s, this was an insult that functioned at many levels. Not only was Puccini, by Torrefranca's reckoning, not a real man—Torrefranca also associated Puccini with sexual "inverts"—he was also labeled incapable of any meaningful artistic endeavor. Torrefranca sought to reinforce his argument by reference to the fashionable theoretical writings of the day and by harking back to the clichés and neuroses of the fin de siècle. His comments about women lowering artistic and intellectual standards and, indeed, being "parasites" upon male creativity correspond closely to those employed by such contemporary figures as the anthropologist Paolo Mantegazza, who set out to prove women's supposed intellectual inferiority.[17]

Part of Puccini's appeal was widely acknowledged to be his ability to identify with his female characters and to use them as vessels for the audience's empathy. For Torrefranca, however, this, and the fact that Puccini's operas were particularly popular with women, was entirely a sign of weakness.[18] He subscribed to the view expressed by the German writer Otto Weininger in his *Sex and Character* (*Geschlecht und Charakter*) of 1903 that "those men who claim to understand women are themselves very nearly women."[19] Torrefranca's gendered critique of Puccini was influenced by Weininger's misogynist tract, in which he depicted women as an obstacle to men's achievement of moral spiritual and intellectual enlightenment. The book was published in Italian almost contemporaneously with Torrefranca's and by the same publishing house, and there was much discussion of Weininger's theories in Italian periodicals, including the Florentine journal *La voce*, to which Torrefranca was a contributor.[20]

If Puccini was "womanly" on the one hand, he was "childlike" on the other: Torrefranca claimed that "Puccini remained a baby, never reached manhood," or, to translate more literally from the original Italian, "did not attain virility."[21] The infantilism charge was a small step from Torrefranca's misogyny, for the woman-child association was deeply ingrained in turn-of-the-century culture. Women and children were often conflated as similarly ingenuous, irresponsible, and simple-minded. Mantegazza wrote that "in woman we find a character that is childlike and above all atavistic," and "woman was and is and always will be less intelligent than man; and her thoughts are generally infantile."[22]

Torrefranca also uttered pseudo-scientific-sounding claims about Italy's cultural preferences being indicative of the race's decline, positing opera as "a thing of obscene decadence" and the opera composer as a lesser species of musician: "a failed musician, an incomplete artist, a poor-quality physiological product of Italian culture."[23] Torrefranca's publisher, Fratelli Bocca, had carved out a particular niche in the emerging fields of psychology, sociology, criminology, and sexology, publishing the first Italian translations of Richard von Krafft-Ebing's *Psychopathia Sexualis* (1887) and Max Nordau's *Degeneration* (1896), and we see the influences of all of these disciplines in Torrefranca's text. Wearing his crypto-psychologist's hat, he was candid about looking for explanations of the composer's art in the composer's life.[24] Puccini, depicted as fit, sporting, and manly by his supporters, was portrayed by Torrefranca as unhealthy and neurotic; he was, variously, "a symptom of decadence," "anaemic and emaciated," and "a neurasthenic."[25] The characters in his operas, furthermore, were characterized by Torrefranca as embodying the same characteristics as their creator. Inspired by contemporary psychopathological terminology, Torrefranca posited Des Grieux, Marcello, Rodolfo, and Pinkerton as "invertebrate men," similar in type to "neurasthenic lovers" and "violent hypochondriacs."[26] These nervous conditions were, not coincidentally, primarily associated with women.

All of this has to be placed within the context of a new type of "manly" nationalism that Torrefranca and his circle espoused. Torrefranca was part of the generation born around 1880 whose members were too young to have lived through the Risorgimento, or the process of Italian unification. Craving a heroic cause for which to fight, they felt the mood of the current age was characterized by political and cultural apathy. The way forward, these idealistic young men believed, was to promote an aggressive, expansionist nationalism and a violent model of full-blooded manliness. These ideas were disseminated most vociferously by Filippo Tommaso Marinetti's Futurists and would ultimately find their extreme fulfillment in the rise of the Fascists. However, similar theories were widely espoused by prominent cultural publications such as *La voce*, whose founder Giovanni Papini would call for Italy to enter the First World War as a cure for the "emasculated" state of a country ruled by "the impotent," "those without backbone."[27] Such vocabulary seems strikingly similar to the words chosen by Torrefranca to describe Puccini, and the shared rhetoric is no coincidence, given Torrefranca's status as a regular contributor to *La voce*. Shortly after the publication of the Puccini book, he would also become music critic for Enrico Corradini's far-right nationalist newspaper *L'idea nazionale*. Authoritarianism and a profound hatred of the democratic process were further hallmarks of the nationalists' anti-populist credo and they loathed the rise to prominence of the "effeminate," acquisitive bourgeoisie: precisely the people who adored Puccini's operas. An elitist perspective colored Torrefranca's views on music as well as on politics.

Puccini and Ricordi ignored the book in public and there is only one reference to it in the Puccini correspondence, suggesting Torrefranca needed "a good cudgelling."[28] However, the intensity of Puccini's recorded responses to much milder cases of criticism would suggest that he must have been devastated. Torrefranca's book was not reviewed in the popular press but attracted attention from serious cultural periodicals published in Milan, Turin, Rome, Florence, and abroad. Some reviewers defended Puccini, but a significant number praised the book for being incisive and frank, and for voicing the thoughts many others (young people in particular) had been afraid to express. Torrefranca's comments about Puccini's "effeminacy" and his strategies to associate him with outsider groups went unchallenged. A contextualization of Torrefranca's theories quickly reveals that he was not some isolated extremist. Rather, his comments about Puccini can be connected to a broad range of contemporary discipline-crossing debates and widely shared neuroses not only about the future of music but about questions of identity: what it meant to be an Italian and what it meant to be a man. Torrefranca's obituarists may have played down the significance of the Puccini book within his oeuvre—some claiming that the author himself later dismissed it as a foolish error of youth[29]—but the book would have a legacy that would endure well beyond Puccini's lifetime, coloring the tone of numerous modernist critiques ideologically opposed to the composer's music.

Excerpts from *Giacomo Puccini and International Opera*
Fausto Torrefranca

Alongside the heroes who have molded the clay of the world with their own strong hands and great creative minds, there have been other heroes—all too often forgotten—who molded themselves in accordance with the world that surrounded them. Cagliostro's mesmerism is surely as important an indication of past times as Rousseau's naturism. After all, are not mesmerism and naturism but two facets of the same fetish for nature's secret primal forces, two ways of tracing these forces back to their point of origin? Scientific superstition and philosophical élan are perfectly complementary: they are light and shadow upon the same object, slopes descending from one crest of thought, which is itself but the gentle crease of history upon world spirit.

If our great ironist Thomas Carlyle were to speak of contemporary heroes nowadays and had to choose from among them a musician hero, he would be hesitating a long time between Richard Strauss and Giacomo Puccini. Yet he would certainly end up by choosing to study the Italian maestro, and this precisely by virtue of this composer's lesser importance in the realm of ideas.

If there's a musician fashionable in all five continents of the world, capable of gaining the approval of each and every theater audience, it is precisely Puccini. The interest he arouses is mostly an interest in gossip columns and changing social mores; this, in turn, is the sort of interest that the world of fashion holds for an art critic. What's more, Puccini has all the other external traits of a fashionable hero: first among them, that of being liked by a predominantly female public.

Let us now take a moment to consider the heroes who were swallowed up by history; we'd have to admit that they were all adored by womankind, and that in turn they were tailor-made to elicit such adoration. Figures like Marini, or Casanova, or Vogler, or even Oscar Wilde are no longer heroes all over the world today precisely because they were once the heroes of one half of the world, and often, even, of the demimonde. [. . .]

The Female of the Musician

That which interests me here is the fact that, among these feminine artists, among these heroes of demimonde culture, Puccini stands out nowadays as the typical composer hero. And if I now turn to Puccini it is because by studying him we can grasp a whole facet of modern culture, a facet that future generations will eventually cease to understand at all, just as we ourselves do not understand much of what was in vogue in our grand-parents' day. Puccini's artistic passivity, his indolent domestic character, his intellectual mediocrity are all most readily revealed to us when we consider this: he is not a true composer, but only a composer of operas. Now, the opera composer is the female of the musician for very different and better reasons than Boccherini is said to be the female of Haydn. The composer of operas is an artist who creates not so much out of an urge to create, but out of the urge to be possessed by any creative spirit. This in itself would not be a bad thing if the chosen male were not just anyone who is willing. And we all know that this someone usually turns out to be a fourth- or fifth-rate poet going by the title of "librettist."

The most pitiful symptom of the secret illness of our race, one which we might call *morbus melodramaticus*, is the sensuous frenzy with which the "true opera composer"—a product of the decadence of a stock that was once the most musically gifted on earth—breathlessly seeks a libretto for years and years. This libretto is, naturally, the one thing that will allow him to create the masterpiece he is unable to create by his own devices, a masterpiece which—for this very reason—he is sure never to create.

The Opera Composer's Poverty of Ideas

Indeed, it is only natural that the opera composer should fail: a composer who limits himself to writing only operas is implicitly admitting that he is incapable of producing music that can stand on its own without the aid of words or a stage. Therefore the opera composer is not an accomplished *artist* in his chosen medium—not in the loftier meaning of the word "art"—because he has confessed that he has no understanding of music in and of itself, that he cannot fully seize upon music's ideal value. He can only understand music that is propped up by poetry.

But an architect who is not able to build anything without propping up the scaffolding externally is no constructor; he is but an ordinary fellow ignorant of Vignola's most elementary ancient principles, or even of the modern science of construction.[30] And in the end, that is all the contemporary opera composer amounts to: a musician ignorant of his own trade's greatest resources, an artist who did not sufficiently tire his hand by working on the combination of musical lines. For this reason his spirit is deeply impoverished, lacking not so much musical grammar and syntax as inner experience; a spirit too limited to be able to achieve the complexity of ideas found in a symphony or even in the simplest of sonatas. It is not a coincidence that Mascagni prefers, in his orchestral conducting, Tchaikovsky's overwrought and theatrical *Pathétique*, and wisely avoids measuring himself against any one of Beethoven's symphonies.

These artists, and most of all Puccini, are not up to the task that newspaper music critics assign to them on behalf of the nation: the task of representing Italy's contemporary music. They are far too inferior to the educated and well-trained young talents emerging nowadays!

In these artists' music you will not find the ancient beauty of a bass line's fine motion and even finer harmonization, nor the tenderness of a "simple, pure, and unaccompanied" melody—all elements that would mark them as continuing practitioners of an ancient musical craft. Nor will you find the bold instrumentation or striking chord sequences that would qualify a composer as *modern*.

And in the work of our anemic, skinny Puccini you will not find the kind of flaws that one notices even in the music of the greatest composers: certain moments of exuberance that still carry the flavor of an amateurish exercise and yet, for that very reason, prepare the way for future masterpieces. Thus the self-conscious eclecticism of a *Rigoletto* or of a *Don Carlos* prepares the way for the rejuvenated Verdi of the later works. But in Puccini there is an absence of a genuine personal quest for the new: he merely applies rather than rediscovers, he works carefully with what's already been done, and assimilates the work of the French, Russians, Germans, and of other living Italian composers. And by merely applying what he knows, he never builds upon what he has learned from others but rather uses it as a kind of "commonplace" of modern music, consecrated by success and approved by fashion. [. . .]

In the end, the opera composer—particularly in our day—can only appear to us as a failed musician, an incomplete artist, a poor-quality physiological product of Italian culture. He is not an architect of harmonies but a mere laborer of sounds, unaware of the ideal meanings that are proper to sounds. He is tormented by the vague nostalgia for poetry that all humans experience when attempting to create anything, a nostalgia that is as strong as the creative effort is convulsed and spasmodic. He eventually seeks the aid of poetry and drama because they are the only external means of galvanizing into pretend life the dry anatomical samples populating his acoustic laboratory. [. . .]

Puccini Is Not a National Composer

Italian opera composers are, and have always been, ambitious songwriters, and such an ambitious songwriter is also, necessarily, Puccini. Yet because the tradition of great Italian music schools is extinguished, and our art never experienced the emergence of an instrumental music that was genuinely national, Puccini is the kind of songwriter who [. . .] gathers into his puny soul the most short-lived mannerisms in the history of Italian and foreign arts. These mannerisms range from the affected sensuality of Arcadia to a ceremonious elegance or musical *verbiage* of French origin; from ditties that lack all folkloric freshness to rhetorical emphasis, the last remnant of the feathered pomposity typical of imported Romanticism. Leitmotif and *chanson à boire*, sparkly instrumentation and impressionist harmonies all lend Puccini's music the "evolved and self-conscious" airs that befit a product aimed at international recognition. This is the sort of international appeal typical of assorted secondhand goods, and also the sort that is most commercially lucrative. Puccini therefore exemplifies, better than other composers, the progressive *de-nationalization* of the Italian lyric theater. And this is why he succeeded in being the international opera composer *par excellence* at a time in which—with exception of the brief episode of *Cavalleria rusticana* and the isolated instance of *Falstaff*—our national art did not have as much as a single word to say to the world that was truly its own, nothing that was truly characteristic or deeply expressive of its unique historical moment. Puccini, who in the eyes of foreigners is—inexplicably—the most typical and representative composer of modern Italy, actually bears only a slight trace of Italy in his work: the eighteenth century—indeed, a late eighteenth-century—

manner one easily recognizes in his maudlin sentimentality. Because this sentimentality is insincere, it is also precarious, and thus devolves into affected comedy one moment and into overemphatic tragedy the next. This eighteenth-century tradition, to which belong Guglielmi's *Pastorella nobile* and Paisiello's *Nina pazza per amore*, straddles idyll and pathos, and might be defined as the tradition of *mezzo carattere* opera: a compromise between lyricism and high drama, enacting well-worn sentiments at average intensity. What is genuinely Italian about all of this is in fact only a residue of past habits—which fortunately have a tendency to disappear—best summed up by the expression "Noli sollicitus esse in crastinum,"[31] from the Gospel according to Matthew, here naturally stripped of its biblical meaning but rich, nonetheless, in good pragmatic common sense.

Puccini as a Symptom of Decline

Because Puccini's is a *mezzo carattere*[32] kind of art, it not only fails to manifest the profound ideals that lend historical dignity to an artist or to a work of art, but it also cannot be deemed anything more than the most elementary kind of historical symptom. That is, it constitutes the sort of historical fact that might serve to retrieve or shed light upon many other historical facts, but is little more than a transient phenomenon in its own right. Puccini's art is the historical symptom of malaise rather than of well-being, and like all symptoms it is only a partial and approximate representation of the illness. The illness itself has been going on for nearly a century, and has been exacerbated by the ignorance, rhetoric, and commercial greed of famous impresarios first, and of great music publishers later. We call this illness decadence. [. . .]

Character Stereotypes of Puccini's Operas

Des Grieux and Marcello, Rodolfo and Pinkerton—all belong to the world of what we may call invertebrate men, which is also the world of neurasthenic lovers and raging hypochondriacs. They are the mollusks of literature, weightless diaphanous Medusas and Hydras that may take a graceful and attractive form when floating about the shallow waters of the little poetic pond that bred them. If we take them outside of their element, however—and artificial lakes sometimes dry up in seasonal droughts or are drained for sanitation purposes—they become little more than shapeless lumps of jelly.

To this same world of invertebrates belongs the female type favored in Puccini's operas, a type Puccini inherited from the Verdi of *La traviata*, and adapted by downplaying her human depth and sincerity: the type of the sentimental and unhappy courtesan.

Modern opera, relished as it is by the demimonde of culture, could not help but display an irresistible affinity for the heroes and heroines of the demimonde of love. In this respect, modern opera performs *verismo* in the most literal meaning of the word, true until the end to her impure tendencies, tendencies that therefore will not lead her anywhere but toward impure literature, impure feeling, and impure life. Opera favors the character of the cocotte because it is itself the cocotte of both literature and music at once. Yet in Puccini the cocotte-opera has become a grisette-melodrama. It has become plebeian and sentimental, bold and yet naïvely sensual, fun-loving and yet romantically melancholic, carefree but tearfully consumptive like Mimì or fragile like Manon: a student's fallen woman![33]

In the demimonde of both literature and life there was still something that preserved a touch of freshness and liveliness: the love between the student and the seamstress. Puccini sensed, to his merit, that last shred of instinctive poetry and had the vision necessary to exploit it in a theatrical setting. In this artistic choice Puccini displays once again the quality that raises him slightly above slovenliness varnished as refinement and rhetoric masked as spontaneity: a feminine sentimentality, slightly nervous, restless, and possibly genuinely corrupt, typical of a modern pretty young lady.

Puccini's Femininity

Puccini has a kind of sensuous softness that, if it is often no more than weakness, can at times also turn into intimacy and understanding of life's small joys and humble miseries, simply because easy sensuality tends to have temporary and genuine relapses into compassionate innocence. He brings to his operas a sense of proportion—a good legacy of his Tuscan heritage—and adds to it an economy of compositional means that, though it proves his scarce fecundity and is akin to the practical sense of a housewife pinching her melodic pennies, is not without its moments of bourgeois dignity. Nor does he lack a certain rudimentary flair for bringing out a theme or a melody with the heightened intensity that the narrowness of his artistic vision allows.

And if he sometimes exhausts himself by dint of simple repetition and halfhearted self-reference, it is also true that he sometimes succeeds in lending these melodic returns a small dose of poetry. In these rare moments he appears to us like a sensual, silly young mother who, because she cannot quite find any kind and good words to say to her baby, caresses and kisses it while endlessly repeating some silly nonsense. This nonsense, though meaningless, is moving in the way in which all words twisted with the effort to speak one's heart are moving and, like any meaningless word that ends with a kiss, is warm with instinctive poetry. The baby, however, faced with the monotony of such a lullaby of caresses and words, can only fall asleep.

For some naïve music lovers Puccini's operas are like one of those silly, shy little mothers we might fall in love with just because their instinctive and sensuous motherly love appears to us full of fine sentiment and poetry.

Like a woman who does not know how to express herself other than with kisses and caresses, Puccini's music is never so obtuse as to fail to know when to be silent, and let her gaze alone speak of the instinctive quivers coursing through her veins. And the man who is about to fall for this young-mother music believes he is seeing—hidden in those silent gazes, quiet smiles, and timid half replies—not spiritual shallowness, but profound intensity of thought; not sentimental vacuity, but exquisite agreement, assent, and mute insight into the soul. Of course—he will think—only an excess of refinement prevents her thoughts from translating into words; only shy dignity prevents her sentiment from blossoming into a gesture. And thus her silence will strike him as a "revelation."

The secret behind all this is very simple. The composer, by falling silent and withdrawing at the right moment, has let the words speak on his behalf; he has allowed others to suggest to his audience something he was unable to express with his own devices. And if the libretto is good enough to make a powerful impression, the deal is sealed. The spectator will be just like a man in love: he will see a whole world in a mere blossoming flowerbed, and will experience sublime love in what is only a whim, a flare of desire.

NOTES

1. I have analyzed Torrefranca's book in more detail in *The Puccini Problem: Opera, Nationalism, and Modernity* (Cambridge: Cambridge University Press, 2007); and in "Torrefranca vs. Puccini: Embodying a Decadent Italy," *Cambridge Opera Journal* 13/1 (2001): 29–53.

2. For further reading on the *Rivista musicale italiana*, see Caterina Criscione, *Luigi Torchi: Un musicologo italiano tra Otto e Novecento* (Imola: La Mandragora, 1997); and Alexandra Wilson, "Music, Letters, and National Identity: Reading the 1890s Italian Music Press," *19th-Century Music Review* 7/2 (2010): 99–116.

3. Torrefranca's published works are listed in *Fausto Torrefranca: L'uomo, il suo tempo, la sua opera. Atti del Convegno Internazionale di Studi, Vibo Valentia, 15–17 dicembre 1983*, ed. Giuseppe Ferraro and Annunziato Pugliese (Vibo Valentia: Istituto di Bibliografia Musicale Calabrese, 1993), 373–89.

4. Fausto Torrefranca, *Giacomo Puccini e l'opera internazionale* (Turin: Bocca, 1912), 8, viii.

5. Ibid., 12, ix.

6. Ibid., 19.

7. Ibid., 17.

8. Torrefranca was a particular advocate of the Italian quartet. See Klaus Fischer, "Osservazioni sull'avviamento alla storia del quartetto italiano di Fausto Torrefranca," in *Fausto Torrefranca*, 133–40.

9. Torrefranca, *Giacomo Puccini*, vii.

10. See Wilson, *The Puccini Problem*, chaps. 2–4.

11. See ibid., chap. 6.

12. Torrefranca, *Giacomo Puccini*, 24.

13. Richard Wagner, "Il Giudaismo nella musica," *Rivista musicale italiana* 4 (1897): 95–113.

14. Torrefranca, *Giacomo Puccini*, 24.

15. Edwin Evans, "The New Insularity," *The Dominant* 2 (1929): 9.

16. Torrefranca, *Giacomo Puccini*, 76.

17. Ibid., 4; Paolo Mantegazza, *Fisiologia della donna*, 3rd ed., 2 vols. (Milan and Rome: Treves, 1893).

18. Torrefranca, *Giacomo Puccini*, 2.

19. Otto Weininger, *Sex and Character* (London and New York: Heinemann and G. P. Putnam's Sons, 1906), 56.

20. Otto Weininger, *Sesso e carattere*, trans. G. Fenoglio (Turin: Bocca, 1912).

21. Torrefranca, *Giacomo Puccini*, 94.

22. Mantegazza, *Fisiologia della donna*, 1:292 and 2:207.

23. Torrefranca, *Giacomo Puccini*, 11, 10.

24. See the subsection "Il Puccini uomo chiarisce il Puccini artista" (Puccini the man explains Puccini the artist), in ibid., 36–38.

25. Ibid., 25, 8, 81, 10.

26. Ibid., 30.

27. Giovanni Papini, "Il nostro impegno," *Lacerba* (15 November 1914), repr. in *Fascism*, ed. Roger Griffin (Oxford and New York: Oxford University Press, 1995), 23–24.

28. Puccini to Alfredo Vandini, 11 February 1915, in *Carteggi pucciniani*, ed. Eugenio Gara (Milan: Ricordi, 1958), 432–33.

29. See, for example, Leonardo Pinzauti, "Memoria di Fausto Torrefranca," *L'approdo musicale* 21 (1966): 169.

30. Jacopo Barozzi da Vignola, usually called just "Vignola," was a sixteenth-century architect and architectural theorist. His *Regola delli cinque ordini d'architettura* (Canon of the five orders of architecture, 1562) was continuously reprinted and widely known.

31. In English: "Take no thought for the morrow."

32. Literally "half character," meaning neither tragic nor comic, but in between, and implying a lack of serious dramaturgical ideals.

33. Original: *traviata da studente*.

Index

Page numbers followed by "n" indicate chapter endnotes.
Page numbers in italics refer to figures and musical excerpts.

Contributors

Micaela Baranello is McPherson/Eveillard Postdoctoral Fellow in musicology at Smith College. Her research focuses on operetta and opera in twentieth-century Vienna. Recent publications include "*Arabella*, Operetta, and the Triumph of *Gemütlichkeit*" (*Opera Quarterly*, 2015), and "*Die lustige Witwe* and the Creation of the Silver Age of Viennese Operetta" (*Cambridge Opera Journal*, 2014). She received a PhD in musicology from Princeton University in 2014 and is also a contributor to *The New York Times*'s Arts & Leisure section.

Leon Botstein is president and Leon Levy Professor in the Arts of Bard College, author of several books, and editor of *The Compleat Brahms* (1999) and *The Musical Quarterly*. The music director of the American Symphony Orchestra and conductor laureate of the Jerusalem Symphony Orchestra, he has recorded works by, among others, Szymanowski, Hartmann, Bruch, Dukas, Foulds, Toch, Dohnányi, Bruckner, Chausson, Richard Strauss, Mendelssohn, Popov, Shostakovich, and Liszt.

Alessandra Campana is associate professor of music at Tufts University. Besides her work on opera, her research spans more broadly the interfaces of hearing and seeing in theater, film, and video. She is the author of *Opera and Modern Spectatorship in Late Nineteenth-Century Italy* (Cambridge University Press, 2015), and is now writing a book on sound-image synchronization in film entitled *Aural Anamorphosis and Sound Clues*.

Delia Casadei has recently obtained her PhD in musicology from the University of Pennsylvania with a dissertation titled *The Crowded Voice: Speech, Music, and Community in Milan, 1955–1974*, and is currently a postdoctoral fellow at the University of Cambridge. She has published in the *Cambridge Opera Journal* and *The Opera Quarterly*, and her most recent article is forthcoming with the *Journal of the Royal Musical Association*. She was a recipient of the Alvin H. Johnson AMS 50 Dissertation Fellowship for the academic year 2014–2015.

Ben Earle is lecturer in music at the University of Birmingham (UK). He is the author of numerous articles and book chapters on mid-twentieth-century British and Italian music, focusing primarily on issues of cultural politics and analytical methodology. In 2013 Cambridge University Press published his monograph *Luigi Dallapiccola and Musical Modernism in Fascist Italy*. A critical edition of the full score of Arthur Bliss's 1944 ballet *Miracle in the Gorbals* is forthcoming from Novello & Co.

Elaine Fitz Gibbon is a graduate student in the German department at Princeton University. She received a BA in German studies and musicology from the University of Pennsylvania, after which she spent a year at the University of Heidelberg pursuing research on György Kurtág, Friedrich Hölderlin, and Paul Celan. She is particularly interested in opera, vocal music, and Musiktheather of the twentieth and twenty-first centuries, in addition to aesthetic reflections on the Baroque and neo-Baroque in the latter half of the twentieth century.

Walter Frisch is H. Harold Gumm/Harry and Albert von Tilzer Professor of Music at Columbia University, where he has taught since 1982. He has written widely about music from the Austro-German sphere in the nineteenth and twentieth centuries. His book *German Modernism: Music and the Arts* (2005) investigates relationships between different artistic movements in the years around 1900. Frisch serves as general editor of a series of period music histories from W. W. Norton, Western Music in Context. His own volume in the series, *Music in the Nineteenth Century*, appeared in fall 2012.

Michele Girardi is associate professor of musicology at the University of Pavia, and has held visiting appointments at the Leoš Janáček Academy, Brno, and the University of Paris 8. He is the author of *Puccini: His International Art* (University of Chicago Press, 2000; original Italian edition 1995), for which he was awarded the Massimo Mila Prize in 1996, and of essays on Verdi, Boito, and Berg among other composers. He is the editor of the series of opera monographs, "La Fenice prima dell'opera," member of the scientific committee of the Centro Studi Giacomo Puccini, and co-editor of *Studi pucciniani*.

Arthur Groos is Avalon Foundation Professor in the Humanities at Cornell University. His interests range from medieval and early modern culture to German and Italian opera. Publications include *Giacomo Puccini: La bohème* (1986), *Romancing the Grail: Genre, Science, and Quest in Wolfram's Parzival* (1995), and *Madama Butterfly: Fonti e documenti* (2005), as well as nine edited volumes, including *Reading Opera* (1988) and *Richard Wagner: Tristan und Isolde* (2011). Founding co-editor of the *Cambridge Opera Journal*, he is also editor of *Cambridge Studies in Opera*. He is associate director of the Centro Studi Giacomo Puccini, and he also co-edits both *Studi pucciniani* and the center's monograph series.

Steven Huebner's research focuses on French and Italian music of the nineteenth and early twentieth centuries. His work covers a wide variety of methods and approaches, including music sociology and politics, opera analysis and criticism, and reception history. He is the author of three books: *The Operas of Charles Gounod* (Clarendon, 1990), *French Opera at the Fin de Siècle: Wagnerism, Nationalism, and Style* (Oxford University Press, 1999), and *Les Opéras de Verdi: Éléments d'un langage musico-dramatique* (forthcoming, Presses de l'Université de Montréal). Recent essay titles include "Ravel's Politics," "Édouard Dujardin, Wagner, and the Origins of Stream of Consciousness Writing," and "Francis Poulenc's *Dialogues des Carmélites*: Faith, Ideology, Love." Huebner currently teaches at McGill University.

Ellen Lockhart is assistant professor of musicology at the University of Toronto. Her monograph *Animation, Plasticity, and Music in Italy, 1770–1830* is forthcoming in 2017 from the University of California Press, and she has co-edited with James Davies a volume on music and science in London during the period 1798–1851 (University of Chicago Press, 2016). Her critical edition of Puccini's *La fanciulla del West* (Ricordi) had its premiere at La Scala in May 2016 under Riccardo Chailly; she is also co-editing (with David Rosen) a critical edition of the original *mise-en-scène*. She has recently become reviews editor for the *Cambridge Opera Journal*.

Christopher Morris is professor of music at the National University of Ireland Maynooth. He is is author of *Reading Opera Between the Lines: Orchestral Interludes and Cultural Meaning from Wagner to Berg* (Cambridge University Press, 2002) and *Modernism and the Cult of Mountains: Music, Opera, Cinema* (Ashgate, 2012). He has published widely on topics in opera, German modernism, and music and screen media, including "The Mute Stones Sing: *Rigoletto in Mantua*," *TDR: The Drama Review* (Winter 2015). He is an associate editor of *Opera Quarterly*.

Arman Schwartz is the author of *Puccini's Soundscapes: Realism and Modernity in Italian Opera* (Olschki, 2016) and editor of "Opera and the Avant-Garde," a special issue of *Opera Quarterly*, on whose editorial board he serves. He is currently a Birmingham Fellow in Music at the University of Birmingham (UK) and previously held postdoctoral fellowships at Columbia University and the University of Pennsylvania. Major awards and fellowships include a Rome Prize from the American Academy in Rome, the biennial Premio Rotary Giacomo Puccini, and the Royal Musical Association's Jerome Roche Prize. He is a member of the scientific committee of the Centro Studi Giacomo Puccini.

Emanuele Senici is professor of music history at the University of Rome La Sapienza. He is author of *"La clemenza di Tito" di Mozart: I primi trent'anni, 1791–1821* (Brepols, 1997) and *Landscape and Gender in Italian Opera: The Alpine Virgin from Bellini to Puccini* (Cambridge University Press, 2005), editor of the *Cambridge Companion to Rossini* (Cambridge University Press, 2004), and former co-editor of the *Cambridge Opera Journal*. Recent publications include "Genre" (*The Oxford Handbook of Opera*, 2014), and "Delirious Hopes: Napoleonic Milan and the Rise of Modern Italian Operatic Criticism" (*Cambridge Opera Journal*, 2015).

Alexandra Wilson is reader in music at Oxford Brookes University, where she co-directs the OBERTO opera research unit. She is author of *The Puccini Problem: Opera, Nationalism, and Modernity* (Cambridge University Press, 2007) and *Opera: A Beginner's Guide* (Oneworld, 2010), and has published in *Cambridge Opera Journal* and *Music & Letters*. Her research interests include opera and operatic culture of the late nineteenth and early twentieth centuries, reception studies, music's political and aesthetic contexts, and opera in film. She is currently working on a project about operatic culture in 1920s Britain and writing a book on *La bohème* for Oxford University Press.

OTHER PRINCETON UNIVERSITY PRESS
VOLUMES PUBLISHED IN CONJUNCTION WITH
THE BARD MUSIC FESTIVAL

Brahms and His World
edited by Walter Frisch (1990)

Mendelssohn and His World
edited by R. Larry Todd (1991)

Richard Strauss and His World
edited by Bryan Gilliam (1992)

Dvořák and His World
edited by Michael Beckerman (1993)

Schumann and His World
edited by R. Larry Todd (1994)

Bartók and His World
edited by Peter Laki (1995)

Charles Ives and His World
edited by J. Peter Burkholder (1996)

Haydn and His World
edited by Elaine R. Sisman (1997)

Tchaikovsky and His World
edited by Leslie Kearney (1998)

Schoenberg and His World
edited by Walter Frisch (1999)

Beethoven and His World
edited by Scott Burnham and Michael P. Steinberg (2000)

Debussy and His World
edited by Jane F. Fulcher (2001)

Mahler and His World
edited by Karen Painter (2002)